Multidimensional Poverty in America

Roger White

Multidimensional Poverty in America

The Incidence and Intensity of Deprivation, 2008–2018

palgrave
macmillan

Roger White
Department of Economics
Whittier College
Whittier, CA, USA

ISBN 978-3-030-45915-4 ISBN 978-3-030-45916-1 (eBook)
https://doi.org/10.1007/978-3-030-45916-1

This Palgrave Macmillan imprint is published by the registered company Springer Nature Switzerland AG.
The registered company address is: Gewerbestrasse 11, 6330 Cham, Switzerland

For my friends on Crosby, Bittman, and Rockwell Court. Thank you for everything.

Preface

The message of this book is simultaneously commonplace and necessary. We know that deprivation exists in contemporary America. We also know that it has existed to varying degrees throughout the nation's history. And it is true that deprivation need not exist in such a wealthy and advanced society. The resources and means required to eliminate deprivation in America are in place and, frankly, have been for quite some time. Unfortunately, even when adequate resources are available, the elimination of deprivation requires that several conditions are fulfilled, one or more of which may be lacking. First, it is necessary to identify the forms of deprivation that are to be countered. Second, accurate measurement of these deprivations in both incidence and severity is needed. Finally, and likely most essential, the public and the nation's policy makers must acknowledge that deprivation exists and consider its elimination an important goal.

My intention is to provide useful information that may contribute to the reduction or elimination of deprivation in America. We begin by introducing multidimensional poverty, discussing the associated literature, and detailing the process of measuring deprivation. This serves to provide a basic understanding for any readers who are not deeply familiar with the topic while also communicating the necessary details regarding our application of multidimensional analysis to those who are more familiar with the topic. Once our preliminaries are in place, we present a detailed accounting of America's multidimensionally poor. This is followed by three studies that serve as examples of how multidimensional poverty analysis can inform public policy and a counterfactual analysis of the deprivation-reducing effects of several public policies. We close with a general discussion of the associated public policy implications. Throughout our empirical treatments, we examine data from the 2008 through 2018 American Community Surveys. This large and detailed data set is well-suited for our purposes as, for our reference period of 2008–2018, it provides information for more than 34 million U.S. residents.

I hope that this work proves useful to policy makers, while also being of interest to students, faculty, researchers, and members of the general public. Because this work is intended to serve both as a record and as an examination of multidimensional poverty in the U.S., remaining objective and providing a largely descriptive portrait of deprivation is a key imperative. To that end, while every effort has been made to remain neutral and objective, there is some risk that neutrality has not been achieved or sustained throughout the work and, as a result, objectivity has suffered. To the extent that this has occurred, I take full responsibility. Likewise, I take complete responsibility for all errors of commission or of omission.

Whittier, CA Roger White

Acknowledgments

I wish to convey my gratitude to the administration of Whittier College for their continued funding of my research efforts. Accordingly, I acknowledge the generous research support provided by the Douglas W. Ferguson Chair in International Economics.

I am indebted to a number of individuals without whose contributions and support the completion of this book would not have been possible. First and foremost, I owe a debt of thanks to my friend, Feridoon Koohi-Kamali, for introducing me to the topic of multidimensional poverty. My work has also benefitted greatly from the efforts of three Whittier College students: Lindsey Macdonald '17, Kiara Pojoy '21, and Lindley Lee-Niegas '22. Each of these bright, hard-working, and creative individuals has provided outstanding research support during different stages of this project. Additionally, the work presented here benefitted considerably from prior research efforts. Namely, I wish to thank two additional Whittier College students, Stacy Yamasaki '17 and Thomas Bailleul '19, with whom I was fortunate to have co-authored works on the subject of multidimensional poverty. Stacy and I completed a chapter titled, "Multidimensional Poverty among the Native- and Foreign-born in the U.S.: Evidence from the 2010–2014 American Community Surveys" that was published as part of Palgrave Macmillan's *Measuring Multidimensional Poverty and Deprivation: Incidence and Determinants in Developed Countries.* Similarly, Thomas and I contributed a chapter named, "Multidimensional Poverty Across the Life Cycle: The United States as an Empirical Example" to the *Routledge International Handbook of Poverty.*

These specific works serve as the foundations for the examples of multidimensional poverty analysis that are presented as Chaps. 9 and 10.

I would be remiss if I did not also express my gratitude to Elizabeth Graber, commissioning editor, and to Sophia Siegler, editorial assistant, and to their colleagues at Palgrave Macmillan for their confidence in this project and for their feedback, continued support, and help during the completion of this book.

Lastly, very special thanks are in order for Michelle Espaldon for her tremendous friendship, continued patience, and much-appreciated loving support, and to Scout for continuing to be her usual, charming, goofy, and wonderful self.

Contents

Abbreviations

ACA	Affordable Care Act
ACS	American Community Survey
AF	Alkire-Foster
AIAN	American Indian and Alaska Native
ANES	American National Election Studies
BMI	Body Mass Index
CPS	Current Population Survey
DC	District of Columbia
DID	Difference-in-difference
ESL	English as a Second Language
EU	European Union
GED	General Equivalency Diploma
GSS	General Social Survey
MD Poor	Multidimensionally Poor
MPI	Multidimensional Poverty Index
NHIS	National Health Interview Survey
NHPI	Native Hawaiian and Pacific Islander
OECD	Organization for Economic Co-operation and Development
OLS	Ordinary Least Squares
OPHI	Oxford Poverty & Human Development Initiative
OPM	Official Poverty Measure
PCA	Principal Component Analysis
PUMA	Public Use Microdata Area
PUMS	Public Use Microdata Sample
SPM	Supplemental Poverty Measure
WIC	Women, Infants, and Children

List of Figures

List of Tables

PART I

Introducing Multidimensional Poverty

CHAPTER 1

Poverty and Deprivation in America

It is important to acknowledge at the outset that for nearly all of human existence extreme poverty has been the norm for the vast majority of the world's population. Bourguignon and Morrisson (2002), for example, estimate that as recently as 1820 more than 89 percent of the global population lived in extreme poverty and that this value remained above 50 percent through the 1960s before finally falling to 48 percent in 1970.[1] It is also important to remember, with select historical exceptions acknowledged, that broad public programs to assist the poor are somewhat recent inventions, even in developed economies, and that significant reductions in poverty have only been witnessed in recent decades. Specifically, while we have observed further decreases in extreme poverty incidence over the past half-century, it is only now, in the early decades of the twenty-first century, that the global extreme poverty rate has fallen below 20 percent (World Bank 2019).

Taking care to not conflate income poverty in the U.S. with the extreme poverty experienced in developing economies, as recently as 1949 an estimated 40.5 percent of the U.S. population was income poor (Ross et al.

[1] Extreme poverty is defined by Bourguignon and Morrisson (2002) as living on less than 1.9 international dollars per day. International dollars are adjusted for price differences between countries and for price changes over time.

R. White, *Multidimensional Poverty in America*,
https://doi.org/10.1007/978-3-030-45916-1_1

1987).[2] Although the U.S. income poverty rate had declined to 22.2 percent in 1960 (U.S. Census 2020), President Lyndon Johnson announced the War on Poverty in 1964 when, during his State of the Union address, he declared: "Our aim is not only to relieve the symptom of poverty, but to cure it and, above all, to prevent it." (Johnson 1968, p. 114). At that time, 36.1 million residents of the U.S. (i.e., 19 percent of the country's population) were income poor; that is, they lived on incomes that were less than the federal poverty threshold. By 1973, the U.S. income poverty rate (i.e., the nation's Official Poverty Measure) had decreased to 11.1 percent, representing a reduction of more than one-third in the number of U.S. residents who were income poor—a decrease equal to 13.1 million people (U.S. Census 2020).[3]

While the War on Poverty showed significant initial progress, it is unfortunate that subsequent successes were not realized and that President Johnson's stated aims have not been fully achieved.[4] To wit, during the 45 years from 1974 through 2018, the U.S. income poverty rate remained largely unchanged, fluctuating from a low of 11.2 percent in 1974 to a high of 15.2 percent in 1983. In fact, in 2018, at a time when U.S. output and its unemployment rate were at or near record high and low levels, respectively, nearly one in every eight American residents (i.e., 11.8 percent of the population) lived below the income poverty threshold. This value is only slightly higher than the rate that was observed nearly five decades earlier in 1973; however, due to population growth, the number of income poor Americans increased, rising from 23 million individuals in 1973 to 38.1 million in 2018. Worse still, it is noteworthy that more Americans were income poor in 2018 than at the onset of the War on Poverty in 1964 Fig. 1.1 illustrates.[5]

In the figure, we see pronounced initial decreases in both the income poverty rate and the number of income poor U.S. residents. Both series

[2] The poverty rate estimated by Ross et al. (1987) is based on all money income. Considering only earnings income, the authors estimate the U.S. poverty rate was equal to 68.1 percent in 1939 and 53.2 percent in 1949. An "all money income" rate is not provided for 1939.

[3] We use the terms "income poverty rate" and "Official Poverty Measure" (and the abbreviation "OPM") interchangeably, with equivalent meaning, throughout the text.

[4] Information presented in this paragraph is from the U.S. Census (2020).

[5] Other than the seven years from 1997 to 2003, in all years during the period from 1992 through 2018, the number of income poor Americans has exceeded the level that was observed in 1964.

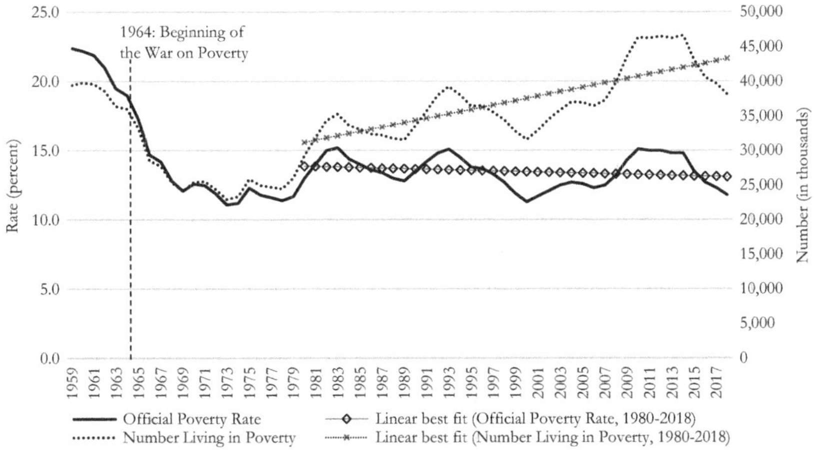

Fig. 1.1 Official poverty rate and number living in poverty, 1959–2018. (Note: Constructed using data from the U.S. Census 2020)

exhibit marked decreases between 1959 and 1973. In the early-1980s, however, although the time path of each series largely mirrors that of the other, we see the series diverge. Specifically, from 1980 to 2018, the income poverty rate generally remained between 12 percent and 15 percent. The quite stable time path of the income poverty rate since 1980 is illustrated by the nearly horizontal line of best fit. However, coupling the largely unchanged income poverty rate with a steadily increasing population has resulted in a general upward trend in the number of income poor individuals. This trend is indicated in the figure by the upward-sloping line of best fit.[6] In more stark and definitive terms, while the proportion of the U.S. population that were income poor largely remained unchanged during the past several decades, the number of individuals in the U.S. in 2018 who suffered income poverty was nearly 9 million individuals higher than it had been in 1980 (i.e., 38.1 million individuals as compared to 29.3 million). While this is a considerable increase, it is also notable that the number of income poor individuals peaked in 2014, at 46.7 million (14.8 percent of the population) during the recovery from the Great Recession.

[6] Also indicative of the initial similarity in the two series and their subsequent divergence is the difference in pairwise correlation coefficients: 0.9951 for the 1959–1979 period and 0.4799 for the 1980–2018 period.

1.1 The Poor and the Rich Are Different

To this point, we have identified poverty solely as a lack of income or means. Inadequate income or insufficient means certainly is a form of deprivation, and the persistence of income poverty in the U.S. remains, rightfully so, an important issue.[7] Limiting the scope of deprivation to a lack of income affords a certain convenience; income poverty is easily conceptualized and it can be tracked over time without much difficulty. There are valid criticisms of how income poverty is measured, however, and there are many additional forms of poverty that individuals may suffer, with each form being indicative of some type of deprivation—for example, lack of access to health care, an insufficient amount of food, inadequate education and so on. Much the same as a lack of income, these additional forms of deprivation present hardships and adverse consequences for those afflicted. While the effects of these additional deprivations—much like income poverty—are unknown to the majority of U.S. residents, significant portions of the population are affected by one or more of these deprivations and must grapple, on an ongoing basis, with the associated consequences.

Thinking more broadly and allowing that deprivation is not limited to income poverty, if we accept that other forms of deprivation can be significantly detrimental and, perhaps in some instances, more detrimental than a lack of income, then we also must acknowledge that any individual's experiences with poverty and deprivation are such that the effects are intensely personal. In other words, our perceptions and understandings of the corresponding consequences can vary greatly based on our experiences with and our understandings of deprivation. An anecdote about Ernest Hemmingway and F. Scott Fitzgerald that is recounted in Michael Harrington's *The Other America* illustrates:

> Fitzgerald is reported to have remarked to Hemingway, "The rich are different." And Hemingway replied, "Yes, they have money." Fitzgerald had much the better of the exchange. He understood that being rich was not a simple fact, like a large bank account, but a way of looking at reality, a series

[7] There are numerous definitions of the word "deprivation". Because we rely heavily on the term in this work, there is a considerable benefit to reducing any potential ambiguity at the outset. We consider deprivation to be a state of not having something that people need: the state of being deprived of something. It is the damaging lack of material benefits considered to be basic necessities in a society. It is a state of poverty.

> of attitudes, a special type of life. If this is true of the rich, it is ten times truer of the poor. Everything about them, from the condition of their teeth to the way in which they love, is suffused and permeated by the fact of their poverty. And this is sometimes a hard idea for a Hemingway-like middle-class America to comprehend. (Harrington 1962, p. 16)

Although Harrington's work was published more than a half-century ago, this passage may well provide a quite accurate contemporary depiction of the general relationship between America's rich and its poor. The poor do differ from the rich, and the two broad groups (which are, admittedly, overly generalized here) very much inhabit different worlds. U.S. residents who are racial minorities, Hispanic, female, and/or immigrants are more likely to be income poor as compared to residents who are white, non-Hispanic, male, and/or native-born (U.S. Census 2019). Other differences between rich and poor can be subtler and, thus, are not as easily identified. One quite interesting example is from Kraus et al. (2010) who find that individuals from higher socioeconomic groups perform poorly relative to their counterparts of lower socioeconomic status when they are shown photographs of human faces and asked to identify emotions. Likewise, when placed in real-life situations and asked to perceive emotional states, individuals of higher socioeconomic status are again found to be less accurate relative to their lower-status counterparts. This points to an inability to empathize, particularly among the rich. Kraus, et al. attribute these differences to higher-status people often thinking of themselves and others in terms of fixed traits while lower-status individuals are more likely to use contextual explanations for people's behavior. From this, it follows that the persistence of poverty in the U.S. may be partially attributable to the portion of the population that is not poor—and who comprise a majority of the population and, thus, are empowered both by means and by numbers—simply being unable to fully empathize with those who suffer deprivation and, accordingly, generally being less inclined to consider the elimination of poverty as a high priority.

Perhaps emblematic of an inability to empathize with the poor, Fig. 1.2 presents persistent differences in how individuals from different income classes view the poor. The series represent the average values provided by respondents to the 1972–2016 American National Election Studies (ANES) when they were asked to indicate their feelings toward poor people. The "group thermometer" question format asks survey respondents to indicate their feelings toward a particular group (i.e., "poor people" in

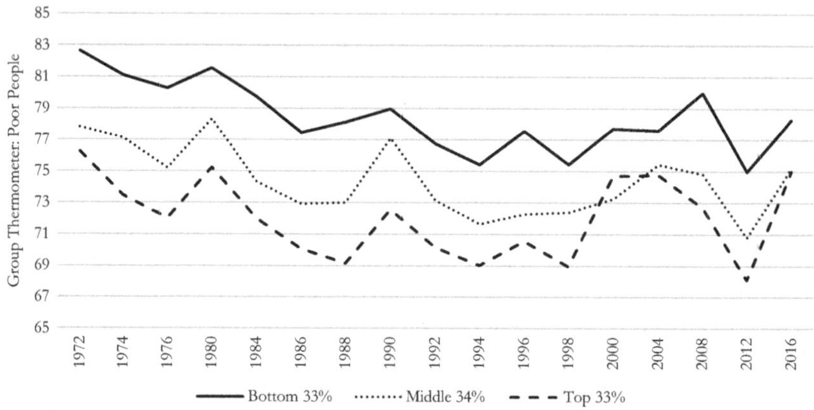

Fig. 1.2 Opinions of poor people by income class, 1972–2016. (Note: Constructed using data from the ANES 2019)

this instance) by providing a value ranging from 0 to 100.[8] Higher scores indicate warmer, or more positive, views toward the poor while lower values represent cooler, or more negative, views. As part of the ANES, survey respondents also provide information on family income. This allows each respondent to be classified as a member of the bottom, the middle, or the top third of the family income distribution. This categorization then allows for the comparison of views toward the poor across these three income cohorts.[9]

[8] To provide greater clarity, the introductory text for the "Group Thermometer" questions in the ANES reads as follows: "There are many groups in America that try to get the government or the American people to see things more their way. We would like to get your feelings towards some of these groups. I have here a card on which there is something that looks like a thermometer. We call it a 'feeling thermometer' because it measures your feelings towards groups. Here's how it works. If you don't know too much about a group or don't feel particularly warm or cold toward them, then you should place them in the middle, at the 50-degree mark. If you have a warm feeling toward a group or feel favorably toward it, you would give it a score somewhere between 50 degrees and 100 degrees, depending on how warm your feeling is toward the group. On the other hand, if you don't feel very favorably toward some of these groups—if there are some you don't care for too much—then you would place them somewhere between 0 degrees and 50 degrees."

[9] Table 1.2, in the appendix, provides the average group thermometer values for all ANES respondents and for each family income cohort.

It is interesting to see that universally, across all 17 ANES surveys, the individuals in the lowest-income cohort indicate, on average, more favorable feelings toward the poor than do those who fall within the middle or top thirds of the family income distribution. We also see, with the exceptions of 2000 and 2016, that the respondents who are in the top one-third of the family income distribution hold the coolest, least favorable views toward poor people. The pattern of relative mean values across time and family income cohorts, while not necessarily indicative of a causal relationship, is consistent with the findings reported by Kraus et al. (2010). Specifically, if higher-income individuals are at a disadvantage in terms of their ability to empathize with those in the bottom third of the family income distribution and are more likely to view lower-income individuals in terms of fixed traits, it then follows that they may report cooler feelings toward the poor (i.e., lower group thermometer values). Likewise, the warmer feelings expressed toward the poor by lower-income individuals may be attributable to a greater capacity to empathize and being more likely to view others contextually; that is, lower-income individuals may see the poor as being poor not because of who they are but because of what they have experienced.

Another set of survey results also identifies a cleavage across the income distribution in terms of how the poor are viewed. Figure 1.3 illustrates the responses to 22 surveys that were completed periodically between 1964 and 2018.[10] Each survey asked respondents to indicate if they thought the cause of poverty was more often the result of too little effort being made to avoid poverty or due to circumstances beyond the control of those who live in poverty.[11] Notably, based on the findings of Kraus et al. (2010), the view that the poor are poor because they exert too little effort—that is, that they are "lazy, unmotivated, undisciplined, and undeserving" (Massey 2007, p. 15)—corresponds with the fixed traits viewpoint often shared by individuals of higher socioeconomic status, and the view that the poor are poor due to circumstances outside of their control is a contextualized viewpoint that is associated with being of lower socioeconomic status.

In the figure, we see a striking consistency across the 55-year period. In 19 of the 22 surveys, between 30 and 40 percent of respondents indicated

[10] Table 1.3, in the appendix, summarizes the results across surveys.

[11] The specific wording of the survey question was "In your opinion, which is generally more often to blame if a person is poor? Lack of effort on his or her own part, or circumstances beyond his or her control?"

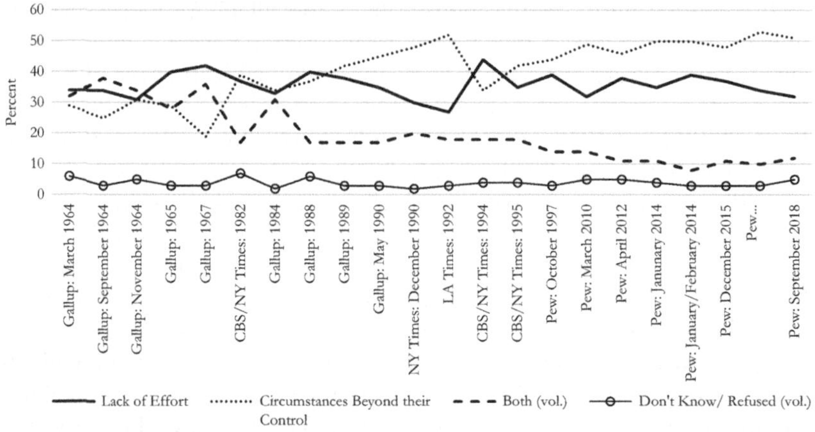

Fig. 1.3 Opinion survey results, "In your opinion, which is generally more often to blame if a person is poor? Lack of effort on his or her own part, or circumstances beyond his or her control?" (Various surveys, 1964–2018). (Source: Pew Research Center 2018)

that they believed the cause of poverty was "too little effort". We also see a general increase over time in the share of respondents who point to circumstances outside of the control of poor individuals as being more often the cause of poverty. This series ranges in value from about 20 percent to 30 percent throughout the 1960s before increasing to nearly 40 percent in 1982 and reaching a value of 53 percent in 2016. Corresponding with the relatively stable "lack of effort" and the rising "circumstances beyond their control" response shares is a pronounced and generally steady decline in the share of respondents who volunteered a view of both effort and circumstances being most often to blame if a person is poor.

Extending from the survey results that are summarized in Fig. 1.3, Table 1.1 summarizes responses from the most recent survey, which was conducted in September 2018, allows for the comparison of responses across three income classifications: individuals who have an annual household income below \$40,000 (i.e., relatively low-income), individuals with incomes of at least \$40,000 but less than \$100,000 (i.e., middle-income), and those with incomes of \$100,000 or above (i.e., high-income). The responses, taken collectively, generally correspond with the income-specific mean group thermometer values reported in Fig. 1.2. Specifically, we

Table 1.1 Opinion survey results, "In your opinion, which is generally more often to blame if a person is poor? Lack of effort on his or her own part, or circumstances beyond his or her control?"

Annual income	*Effort (%)*	*Circumstances (%)*	*Both (vol.) (%)*	*Don't know/refused (vol.) (%)*
Less than $40 K	27.8	56.4	9.8	6.0
$40 K–$99.999 K	33.5	48.4	13.0	5.1
$100 K and above	34.6	48.6	14.8	2.1
Total	31.8	51.2	12.5	4.5

Source: Pew Research Center (2018). $N = 763$

see a considerable difference between the frequency of responses for the low-income individuals relative to the middle- and high-income individuals. Only 27.8 percent of low-income respondents pointed to a lack of effort as the primary cause of poverty as compared to about 34 percent for their middle- and high-income counterparts. Similarly, while about 48.5 percent of the middle- and high-income respondents indicate that circumstances outside an individual's control is most often the cause of poverty, a much higher percentage of low-income respondents (i.e., 56.4 percent) are of the opinion that circumstances are the most frequent cause of poverty. This is consistent with the notion that individuals of lower socioeconomic status are more likely to contextualize the situations of those who live in poverty while individuals of higher socioeconomic status more frequently view being impoverished as the result of a fixed characteristic(s) of the deprived individual.

One conclusion to be drawn from these survey results is that, as the title of this section asserts, the poor and the rich are different. These differences extend from demographic characteristics to include differences in how income and wealth classes view the poor and what they see as the primary cause(s) of poverty. Obviously, the differences are not uniform and there is no strict delineation of the poor and the rich along these lines. What we see though is a general tendency, a set of differences between groups, that is identifiable at the aggregate level and which has persisted over a rather lengthy period of time.

1.2 Three Poverty Measures

As noted, income poverty is but one form of deprivation, and a large number of studies have argued that the U.S. income poverty rate imprecisely represents (i.e., understates) deprivation. Blank (2008), Cauthen and Fass (2008), and Smeeding (2006), for example, stress that the Official Poverty Measure (OPM) suffers from two major failings: (1) the OPM is based on outdated assumptions of household expenditures and (2) it fails to accurately measure all family resources. The OPM was developed in 1963–1964 by Mollie Orshansky of the Social Security Administration, and the initial poverty thresholds for families of three or more individuals were constructed as being equal to three times the amount of after-tax income that was spent on food (Fisher 1992).[12] It was assumed that an adequate diet would require expenditure equal to one-third of a family's income. This assumption was based on household expenditure patterns and data from the 1950s. Although the poverty thresholds do vary based on family size and composition and while the thresholds have been adjusted annually for inflation, they are otherwise largely unchanged from their initial construction.[13] To the extent that the initial thresholds were determined based on faulty assumptions and/or that consumption shares or consumption patterns have changed over the past two generations, the current thresholds are imprecise.[14]

Adding to the potential inaccuracy of current poverty thresholds and, hence, income poverty rates, Ouellette et al. (2004) note that the OPM is calculated using only current income and, thus, does not account for

[12] Orshansky (1963) focused on poverty in families with children. A modified process was employed to calculate thresholds for one-person and two-person households (Orshansky 1965).

[13] Changes have been minor and extremely infrequent. For example, prior to 1981 there were two poverty thresholds, one for farms and one for non-farm households (Kratzer 2018).

[14] It is quite noteworthy that Orshansky pointed to the need for periodic adjustments to the poverty measure she developed, writing "Drawing the poverty line is not yet a task in which it is possible to achieve consensus particularly when the line is above the level of mere subsistence as it is in the United States. The difficulties in setting the poverty line are increased when the definition is to be used to measure progress over a span of time. Statistical nicety will be better served if the criterion selected remains invariant. The realities of everyday living suggest it cannot be—at least not for very long. Though the change in consumption patterns from any one year to the next might be miniscule, over the long run the upgrading that goes with the developing United States economy will be too great to be ignored. Research in consumer economics is not yet at a stage precise enough to specify just how long the long run is." (Orshansky 1966, p. 22)

household wealth, debt, access to credit, or other ways by which goods and services can be obtained (e.g., gifts, barter, and/or charitable/public services). Additionally, the authors note that the OPM does not adjust for geographic differences in the cost of living nor does it account for in-kind benefits such as child care assistance, subsidized housing, and/or tax credits. There are at least two reasons for the methodology used to construct the OPM having largely remained unchanged over time. First, a large body of legislation stipulates that the OPM be used to determine the allocation of federal grants to state and local governments. Changes to the calculation of the OPM would alter grant allocations. Since legislators may wish to avoid the uncertainty related to changes in allocations, this is a political impediment to OPM revision. Second, and not entirely unrelated to the first impediment, replacing or revising the OPM would require identification of new, more accurate thresholds and, similar to the initial construction of the OPM, this would entail judgments to be made. This is also likely to be politically problematic. The consequence is simply that the benefits of accurately quantifying income poverty may well be outweighed by the costs (either real or perceived) that would be borne if the construction of the OPM were to be revisited.

As an alternative to revising or replacing the OPM, the U.S. Census Bureau acknowledged, at least tacitly, the shortcomings of the measure in 2011 when it released a complementary poverty metric known as the Supplemental Poverty Measure (SPM) (Renwick and Fox 2016; Chung et al. 2013; Hutto et al. 2011). The SPM largely mirrors the OPM in that it compares a measure of income to a threshold to determine if members of a household suffer poverty and, from this, the SPM derives a poverty rate.[15] Thus, the SPM serves as an alternative poverty metric that, while also income-based, is an extension/refinement of the OPM. The primary difference is that the SPM seeks to more accurately identify the resources available to an individual or to a family that can be used to purchase basic items (e.g., food, clothing, and shelter). These family resources are calculated as money income from all sources plus any additional resources and a variety of costs/expenses incurred. The list of additional resources includes benefits from the Supplemental Nutrition Assistance Program (SNAP) (which was formerly known as the Food Stamp Program), the Supplementary Nutritional Program for Women, Infants, and Children

[15]Table 1.4, in the appendix, details OPM and SPM rates and numbers living in poverty for select years.

(i.e., the WIC Program), the National School Lunch Program, the Low Income Home Energy Assistance Program, housing subsidies, and tax credits. The costs and expenses include taxes paid, work-related expenses, child care expenses, child support paid, and non-reimbursed medical expenses (Fox et al. 2014).

Figures 1.4 and 1.5 illustrate the time paths of annual OPM and Historical SPM rates and incidences, respectively.[16] In both figures, we see similar time paths for the two series with the SPM series consistently at a higher level than the OPM series. While the series follow similar paths, it is not simply a case where the SPM series accounts for OPM values plus some additional portion of the population. Both measures are income-based; however, given the differences in the construction of the series, it follows that although some who live in poverty according to the OPM are included in the SPM there is not complete overlap. Focusing on Fig. 1.4, we see that the OPM series has remained nearly flat since 1967. In that year, the OPM rate was equal to 14.2 percent. Although there is some variation observed during the intervening decades, more than 50 years later, in 2018, the OPM rate had only decreased to 11.8 percent. Similarly, the SPM value in 1967 was 17.2 percent. A half-century later, in 2017, it had declined only to 13.9 percent. The decreases in the SPM rate has corresponded with similar proportional increases in the size of the U.S. population. As a result, in Fig. 1.5 we see that the number of U.S. residents who lived in poverty, based on the SPM, typically ranged between 40 and 50 million throughout the 1967–2017 period. This stands in contrast to the OPM series which indicates an increase in the number of people living in poverty during this period.

The practical implications of income poverty are illustrated by the links between a lack of income and other commonly accepted measures of well-being. Reeves et al. (2016, p. 2) speak to this connection, somewhat

[16] Meyer and Sullivan (2012, 2017, 2018) argue in favor of consumption-based poverty measures, citing the shortcomings of the OPM and difficulties in accurately measuring pre-tax money income when calculating the SPM. The measurement of poverty is an issue that we address in greater detail in Chap. 3 where we detail the construction of the Multidimensional Poverty Index.

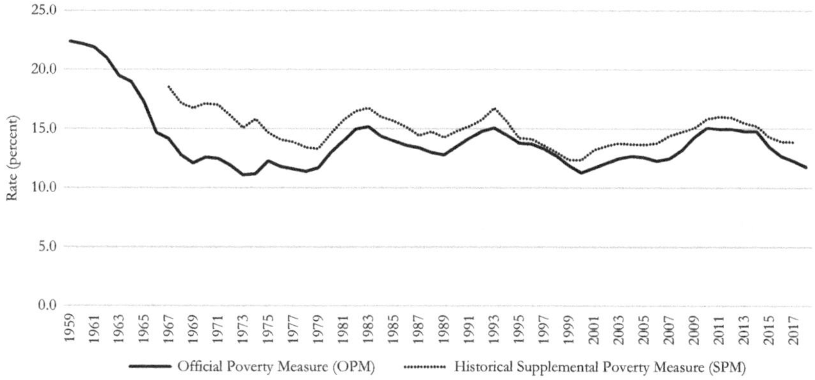

Fig. 1.4 Official poverty measure (1959–2018) and historical supplemental poverty measure (1967–2017). (Note: Constructed using data for the Official Poverty Measure that are from the U.S. Census (2020) and data for the Historical Supplemental Poverty Measure that are from the Center for Poverty & Social Policy (2020))

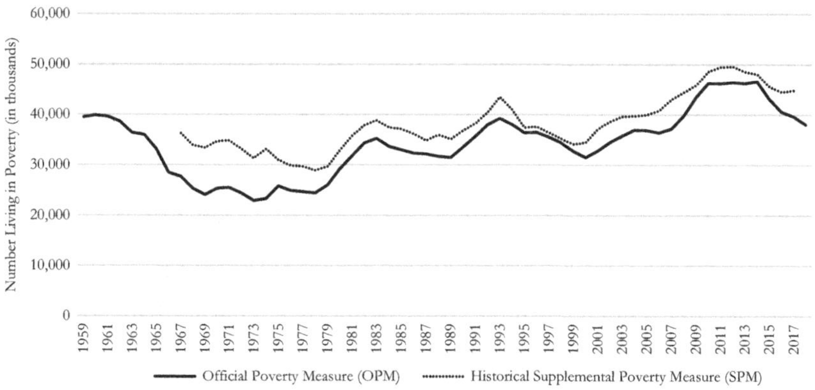

Fig. 1.5 Official poverty measure (1959–2018) and historical supplemental poverty measure (1967–2017) incidence. (Note: Constructed using data for the Official Poverty Measure that are from the U.S. Census (2020) and data for the Historical Supplemental Poverty Measure that are from the Center for Poverty & Social Policy (2020))

generally, as part of a very informative discussion of William Beveridge's "Five Giant Evils" and the need for their elimination[17]:

> Of course poverty is about a lack of money. But it is not *only* about that. This is one reason many other labels are used: disadvantaged, vulnerable, at-risk, low-skilled, economically insecure, socially excluded, and so on. Poverty as a lived experience is often characterized not just by low income, but by ill health, insecurity, discomfort, isolation, and lack of agency. In practice, of course, the various dimensions of poverty often go together. A lack of paid work almost always means low income, which can induce stress that leads to health problems, make accessing health care more difficult, and so on.

Extending from Beveridge's eloquence, some specific examples of the connection between income poverty and other forms of deprivation include a correspondence between a lack of money and food insecurity and, as a result, nutrition-deficient diets (Bhattacharya et al. 2004). Income poverty also contributes to a reduced likelihood of receiving preventive medical care and/or dental care relative to higher-income individuals (MacDougall 2016; Choi 2011). This can contribute to a higher incidence of chronic health problems for lower-income individuals. The poor often experience a more frequent incidence of stress, anxiety, and clinical depression as compared to higher-income individuals (Heflin and Iceland 2009). Income poverty can also hinder physical development, including that of the brain and, thus, adversely affect cognitive functioning (Johnson et al. 2016; Hair et al. 2015; Mani et al. 2013). For example, a scarcity of financial resources can limit parents' abilities to plan and provide for their families' material needs. This may contribute to housing instability and lead to fewer books and other educational resources in the household and/or reduced involvement in extra-curricular educational activities that enrich learning. Perhaps most striking is that individuals with higher incomes may live significantly longer lives, on average, relative to lower-income individuals. Chetty et al. (2016) estimate gaps in the life expectancies between the richest one percent and the poorest one percent of the income distribution equal to 14.6 years for men and 10.1 years for women.

[17] The broad goals/solutions that were offered by Beveridge, with each "evil" noted parenthetically, are identified by Reeves et al. (2016, p. 2) as "improved housing (squalor), universal secondary education (ignorance), income transfers to the poor (want), full employment (idleness), and a national health service (disease)".

It is the extensive connections between poverty, broadly defined to encompass a lack of income as well as other deprivations, and individual well-being that underscore the importance of accurate poverty/deprivation measurement. Similarly, the relationship between deprivation (income or otherwise) and well-being emphasizes the need for comprehensive deprivation measurement to avoid a scenario in which poverty and/or deprivation are viewed as being reduced or eliminated based on narrow, and perhaps misleading, measures (e.g., income at/above a given level).[18] This is essentially the rationale for the application of multidimensional poverty analysis to data that represent the U.S. population. Emphasizing the alleviation of income—or consumption-based poverty is insufficient since doing so would fail to fully address other forms of deprivation and, thus, would not ensure the targeted/desired levels of individual and societal well-being. This is where the breadth and flexibility of multidimensional poverty measurement is most helpful. In addition to providing a general measure of deprivation, multidimensional poverty measurement is able to both identify and track multiple forms of deprivation, including income poverty, over time and across population cohorts. Stated in basic terms, if a societal goal is to eliminate the suffering of those within our population who experience deprivation, then a reasonable and necessary first step is to accurately identify the incidence and intensity of the deprivations suffered by members of the society.

As noted, the Multidimensional Poverty Index (MPI) includes income poverty as one form of deprivation. It also includes a large number of non-income deprivations. The Atkinson Commission Report on Global Poverty (World Bank 2017) asserts that poverty measures should include non-monetary indicators as well as monetary indicators to adequately reflect quality of life. In Chap. 3, we detail the construction of the MPI; however, we introduce the measure here to provide a brief comparison to the OPM and the SPM. An additional strength of the MPI is its flexibility, and any number of variations have been employed depending on the society being examined, the forms of deprivation being considered, and the methods of construction researchers have employed. In the chapters that follow, as we focus on the U.S., we categorize deprivations into four

[18] The concept of deprivation extending beyond merely a lack of income or wealth has been emphasized in several recent studies including Stiglitz et al. (2009), Beja (2013), and Madonia et al. (2013).

dimensions (i.e., Economic Security, Education, Health, and Housing). These four dimensions are comprised of a total of nine binary indicators.

Looking to the indicators within each of the four dimensions provides a more detailed illustration of the MPI. The Economic Security dimension, for example, is comprised of two indicators. The first identifies individuals who are unemployed, while the second identifies those individuals for whom household income is below the corresponding federal poverty line.[19] Similarly, the Education dimension and the Health dimension also contain two indicators. The indicators for the Education dimension identify individuals who lack a high school diploma or equivalent credential[20] and those who are linguistically isolated (i.e., those who live in a household where no one 14 years of age or older speaks only English at home or if speaking another language at home does not speak English "very well"). The Health dimension includes indicators that identify individuals who are disabled and/or who lack health insurance. By contrast, the Housing dimension includes three indicators that identify whether an individual lives in a crowded house (i.e., there are more household residents than there are rooms in the housing unit), whether the unit has incomplete kitchen or bathroom facilities, and/or if the household costs (i.e., the rent or the owner-related costs) are equal to or greater than one-half of household income.

While we utilize four dimensions and nine indicators, other researchers employ different calculation methods. Alkire and Foster (2011), for example, consider three dimensions: Education, Health, and Standard of Living. Each of these dimensions is comprised of related indicators to represent whether individuals suffer deprivation. For instance, within the related literature, the Health dimension often identifies individuals who are disabled and those who do not receive proper nutrition as being deprived. Similarly, individuals are considered deprived in terms of education if they lack a basic education or have a limited ability to speak the common language of the society in which they live. Note that while these dimensions and indicators are not directly related to income or consumption, their incidence would render an individual significantly deprived

[19] Note that while the MPI includes income poverty as an indicator, it is only one of nine indicators (i.e., deprivations) that are considered.

[20] For individuals less than six years of age, the indicator that identifies having a level of educational attainment less than a high school diploma is set equal to zero. Likewise, the indicator is set equal to zero for individuals six years of age or older who lack a high school diploma or equivalent but report being currently enrolled in school.

(i.e., poor in terms of that dimension or indicator). One example would be a person who earns a salary above the income poverty threshold but who is linguistically isolated and lacks access to health care. A traditional income-based approach would not consider this individual to be poor or deprived despite the apparent deprivations. A contrary example would be an individual whose income is slightly below the income poverty line but who has access to most, or all, other amenities. This individual would be considered income poor and could even become the recipient of social welfare benefits such as nutrition support and education waivers. Ultimately, because a unidimensional approach to poverty analysis relies entirely on one factor—typically, income—to infer deprivation across all other dimensions of life, reliance on such measures carries significant risk in the form of an inefficient allocation of public assistance to the poor members of society.

As we have noted, a detailed discussion of MPI calculation is provided in Chap. 3. Here, we have only sought to provide a brief depiction of the measure, to compare and contrast it with the OPM and the SPM, and to provide a foundation for a discussion of the related literature in the following chapter. With this in mind, the remainder of this chapter offers a road map to inform readers of the scope and aims of the book and to refocus attention before beginning our much more detailed discussion of multidimensional poverty measurement.

1.3 A Road Map

Beginning with a broad view before delving into specifics, this book aims to achieve four objectives. First, we introduce multidimensional poverty measurement to readers who are unfamiliar with the topic and we communicate the necessary details regarding our application of multidimensional analysis to readers who are familiar with the topic. Second, we provide a detailed portrait of multidimensional poverty in America during the period from 2008 through 2018. Third, we present the findings of three studies that utilize the multidimensional approach to the identification and measurement of deprivation. These studies serve as examples of multidimensional poverty analysis while also accomplishing our fourth objective—namely, providing important information that can be used to craft public policies that are aimed toward the enhancement of societal well-being through the reduction or elimination of deprivation.

This book is comprised of 12 chapters that are organized into four parts. The first part consists of three chapters that discuss poverty and deprivation, generally, and that provide an accompanying introduction to multidimensional poverty, a review of the related literature, and a detailed discussion of how multidimensional poverty is measured.

We follow, in the second part, with four chapters that offer a detailed accounting of the incidence and intensity of multidimensional poverty in the United States. This entails an initial focus at the aggregate (i.e., national) level of detail before we turn our attention to multidimensional poverty within smaller geographic units (i.e., regions, divisions, states, and Public Use Microdata Areas (PUMAs)) and a number of socio-demographic cohorts (e.g., gender, age, race/ethnicity, educational attainment and so on). We close the second part of the book with an econometric analysis that identifies the determinants of multidimensional poverty incidence. The information in this section provides a foundation for the empirical studies presented in our third section.

The third part of this book includes three studies of multidimensional poverty. With each presented as a separate chapter, the studies illustrate the public policy relevance of multidimensional poverty analysis. We begin by considering the potential influence of Medicaid expansion under the Affordable Care Act on multidimensional poverty incidence and intensity. This is followed by an examination of the extent to which multidimensional poverty may vary between native- and foreign-born U.S. residents and across immigrants based on their home countries. We close this portion of the book with a study of the potential variation in the path of multidimensional poverty incidence over the life cycle.

The remaining two chapters comprise the final part of the book. In Chap. 11, we present the results of several counterfactual exercises in which, using data for 2018, we consider the extent to which multidimensional poverty would be decreased if U.S. policy makers (1) implemented a universal health care system, (2) adopted a universal basic income, (3) incentivized the completion of high school through the provision of free/discounted college, or (4) expanded English as a Second Language program and/or sought improvements in program effectiveness to eliminate linguistic isolation. Our final chapter provides a summary of our work, discusses related public policy implications and opportunities, and offers a concluding discussion.

Appendix

Table 1.2 Opinion of poor people by income class, 1972–2016

		Income class		
	All respondents	*Bottom 33%*	*Middle 34%*	*Top 33%*
Year	*(a)*	*(b)*	*(c)*	*(d)*
1972	78.9734 (18.4085) *N* = 2705	82.67*** (17.9623) *N* = 902	77.85* (18.1723) *N* = 971	76.28*** (18.5408) *N* = 832
1974	77.4851 (17.3345) *N* = 1575	81.13*** (17.4192) *N* = 545	77.1421 (16.3527) *N* = 584	73.48*** (17.5793) *N* = 446
1976	76.0529 (18.9084) *N* = 2248	80.29*** (18.835) *N* = 847	75.2200 (18.4475) *N* = 641	72.03*** (18.4192) *N* = 760
1980	78.8228 (18.455) *N* = 1614	81.57*** (18.6405) *N* = 660	78.3488 (18.2097) *N* = 516	75.24*** (17.8291) *N* = 438
1984	75.9039 (19.6596) *N* = 2257	79.76*** (20.3566) *N* = 922	74.35* (18.749) *N* = 706	72.00*** (18.6096) *N* = 629
1986	73.8575 (19.0057) *N* = 2176	77.47*** (19.4364) *N* = 838	72.9354 (18.4605) *N* = 712	70.08*** (18.1846) *N* = 626
1988	73.8412 (20.4259) *N* = 2040	78.14*** (20.493) *N* = 780	73.0212 (19.8865) *N* = 660	69.16*** (19.8053) *N* = 600
1990	76.4217 (18.991) *N* = 1980	78.97*** (19.2119) *N* = 799	77.1214 (18.2772) *N* = 552	72.57*** (18.7302) *N* = 629
1992	73.5706 (18.6832) *N* = 2485	76.76*** (19.1477) *N* = 967	73.1643 (17.6096) *N* = 694	70.17*** (18.3954) *N* = 824
1994	72.3287 (18.8073) *N* = 1795	75.43*** (18.8485) *N* = 688	71.6748 (18.8571) *N* = 572	69.04*** (18.0932) *N* = 535
1996	73.8547 (18.7134) *N* = 1714	77.57*** (18.9497) *N* = 663	72.29* (18.3462) *N* = 573	70.58*** (17.9654) *N* = 478
1998	72.4700 (19.4663) *N* = 1281	75.44*** (20.8289) *N* = 475	72.4146 (19.12) *N* = 410	68.96*** (17.4873) *N* = 396

(*continued*)

Table 1.2 (continued)

		Income class		
	All respondents	*Bottom 33%*	*Middle 34%*	*Top 33%*
Year	*(a)*	*(b)*	*(c)*	*(d)*
2000	75.8572 (20.7103) $N = 1807$	77.73** (20.4504) $N = 896$	73.26** (21.7728) $N = 438$	74.7200 (19.8746) $N = 473$
2004	76.2154 (19.0755) $N = 1212$	77.6200 (19.3373) $N = 535$	75.4495 (17.8512) $N = 327$	74.7800 (19.6764) $N = 350$
2008	76.6731 (19.4074) $N = 2322$	80.00*** (19.267) $N = 1021$	74.84** (19.2463) $N = 821$	72.73*** (18.8542) $N = 480$
2012	71.6659 (20.8225) $N = 5914$	74.99*** (21.4768) $N = 2267$	70.8135 (20.1084) $N = 2011$	68.10*** (20.0685) $N = 1636$
2016	76.2122 (19.9507) $N = 4270$	78.31*** (20.7114) $N = 1459$	75.2363 (19.2923) $N = 1261$	75.03** (19.5984) $N = 1550$

Source: Author's calculations based on data from the ANES (2019)

Standard deviations in parentheses. ***, **, and * indicate statistical significance from the corresponding "All Respondents" mean value at the 1%, 5%, and 10% levels, respectively

Table 1.3 Opinion survey results, "In your opinion, which is generally more often to blame if a person is poor? Lack of effort on his or her own part, or circumstances beyond his or her control?"

Survey: Date	*Lack of effort*	*Circumstances beyond their control*	*Both (vol.)*	*Don't know/ refused (vol.)*
Gallup: March 1964	34	29	32	6
Gallup: September 1964	34	25	38	3
Gallup: November 1964	31	31	34	5
Gallup: 1965	40	29	28	3
Gallup: 1967	42	19	36	3
CBS/NY times: 1982	37	39	17	7
Gallup: 1984	33	34	31	2
Gallup: 1988	40	37	17	6
Gallup: 1989	38	42	17	3

(continued)

Table 1.3 (continued)

Survey: Date	*Lack of effort*	*Circumstances beyond their control*	*Both (vol.)*	*Don't know/ refused (vol.)*
Gallup: May 1990	35	45	17	3
NY Times: December 1990	30	48	20	2
LA Times: 1992	27	52	18	3
CBS/NY Times: 1994	44	34	18	4
CBS/NY Times: 1995	35	42	18	4
Pew: October 1997	39	44	14	3
Pew: March 2010	32	49	14	5
Pew: April 2012	38	46	11	5
Pew: January 2014	35	50	11	4
Pew: January/February 2014	39	50	8	3
Pew: December 2015	37	48	11	3
Pew: November/ December 2016	34	53	10	3
Pew: September 2018	32	51	12	5

Source: Pew Research Center (2018)

Table 1.4 OPM and historical SPM rates and incidence, select years

		Official poverty measure (OPM)		*Historical supplemental poverty measure (SPM)*	
		Below poverty		*Below poverty*	
Year	*Population*	*Rate*	*N living in poverty*	*Rate*	*N living in poverty*
1959	176,557	22.4	39,490	.	.
1960	179,503	22.2	39,851	.	.
1961	181,277	21.9	39,628	.	.
1962	184,276	21.0	38,625	.	.
1963	187,258	19.5	36,436	.	.
1964	189,710	19.0	36,055	.	.
1965	191,413	17.3	33,185	.	.
1966	193,388	14.7	28,510	.	.
1967	195,672	14.2	27,769	18.6	36,320
1968	197,628	12.8	25,389	17.2	33,984
1969	199,517	12.1	24,147	16.8	33,488
1970	202,183	12.6	25,420	17.2	34,727
1971	204,554	12.5	25,559	17.1	34,886

(continued)

Table 1.4 (continued)

		Official poverty measure (OPM)		*Historical supplemental poverty measure (SPM)*	
		Below poverty		*Below poverty*	
Year	*Population*	*Rate*	*N living in poverty*	*Rate*	*N living in poverty*
1972	206,004	11.9	24,460	16.1	33,200
1973	207,621	11.1	22,973	15.1	31,409
...	...	...	...	.	.
1978	215,656	11.4	24,497	13.4	28,965
...	...	...	...	.	.
1983	231,700	15.2	35,303	16.8	38,891
...	...	...	...	.	.
1988	243,530	13.0	31,745	14.8	36,057
...	...	...	...	.	.
1993	259,278	15.1	39,265	16.8	43,530
...	...	...	...	.	.
1998	271,059	12.7	34,476	13.0	35,298
...	...	...	...	.	.
2003	287,699	12.5	35,861	13.8	39,690
...	...	...	...	.	.
2008	301,041	13.2	39,829	14.8	44,476
2009	303,820	14.3	43,569	15.1	45,913
2010	306,130	15.1	46,343	15.9	48,694
2011	308,456	15.0	46,247	16.1	49,573
2012	310,648	15.0	46,496	16.0	49,676
2013	313,096	14.8	46,269	15.5	48,653
2014	315,804	14.8	46,657	15.3	48,175
2015	318,454	13.5	43,123	14.3	45,629
2016	319,911	12.7	40,616	13.9	44,608
2017	322,549	12.3	39,698	13.9	44,858
2018	323,847	11.8	38,146	.	.

Source: Data for the Official Poverty Measure are from the U.S. Census (2020) and data for the Historical Supplemental Poverty Measure are from the Center for Poverty & Social Policy (2020)

Note: Population and N Living in Poverty values are in thousands

References

Alkire, Sabina, and James Foster. 2011. Counting and Multidimensional Poverty Measurement. *Journal of Public Economics* 95 (7–8): 476–487.

American National Election Studies (ANES). 2019. Time Series Cumulative Data File (1948–2016). https://electionstudies.org/data-center/.

Beja, Edsel. 2013. Subjective Well-being Approach to the Valuation of International Development: Evidence for the Millennium Development Goals. *Social Indicators Research* 111 (1): 141–159.

Bhattacharya, Jayanta, Janet Currie, and Steven Haider. 2004. Poverty, Food Insecurity, and Nutritional Outcomes in Children and Adults. *Journal of Health Economics* 23 (4): 839–862.

Blank, Rebecca M. 2008. How to Improve Poverty Measurement in the United States. *Journal of Policy Analysis and Management* 27 (2): 233–254.

Bourguignon, François, and Christian Morrisson. 2002. Inequality Among World Citizens: 1820–1992. *American Economic Review* 92 (4): 727–748.

Cauthen, Nancy K., and Sarah Fass. 2008. *Measuring Poverty in the United States.* National Center for Children in Poverty, Columbia University Mailman School of Public Health Fact Sheet.

Center on Poverty & Social Policy at Columbia University. 2020. *Anchored Poverty Rates 1967 to 2017.* Columbia Population Research Center. https://www.povertycenter.columbia.edu/s/Anchored-and-Historical-Poverty-Rates-1967-to-present.xlsx.

Chetty, Raj, Michael Stepner, Sarah Abraham, Shelby Lin, Benjamin Scuderi, Nicholas Turner, Augustin Bergeron, and David Cutler. 2016. The Association Between Income and Life Expectancy in the United States, 2001–2014. *JAMA* 315 (16): 1750–1766.

Choi, Moonkyung K. 2011. The Impact of Medicaid Insurance Coverage on Dental Service Use. *Journal of Health Economics* 30 (5): 1020–1031.

Chung, Yiyoon, Julia Isaacs, and Timothy Smeeding. 2013. Advancing Poverty Measurement and Policy: Evidence from Wisconsin during the Great Recession. *Social Science Review* 87 (3): 525–555.

Fisher, Gordon M. 1992. The Development and History of the Poverty Thresholds. *Washington, DC: Social Security Administration; Social Security Bulletin* 55 (4): 3–14.

Fox, Liana, Irwin Garfinkel, Neeraj Kaushal, Jane Waldfogel, and Christopher Wimer 2014. *Waging War on Poverty: Historical Trends in Poverty Using the Supplemental Poverty Measure.* NBER Working Paper No. 19789.

Hair, Nicole L., Jamie L. Hanson, and Barbara L. Wolfe. 2015. Association of Child Poverty, Brain Development, and Academic Achievement. *JAMA Pediatrics* 169 (9): 822–829.

Harrington, Michael. 1962. *The Other America: Poverty in the United States.* New York: Macmillan.

Heflin, Colleen M., and John Iceland. 2009. Poverty, Material Hardship, and Depression. *Social Science Quarterly* 90 (5): 1051–1071.

Hutto, Nathan, Jane Waldfogel, Neeraj Kaushal, and Irwin Garfinkel. 2011. Improving the Measurement of Poverty. *Social Science Review* 85 (1): 39–74.

Johnson, Lyndon B. 1968. *Public Papers of the Presidents of the United States: Lyndon B. Johnson, Containing the Public Messages, Speeches, and Statements of the President, 1967.* Washington, DC: U.S. Government Printing Office.

Johnson, Sara B., Jenna L. Riis, and Kimberly G. Noble. 2016. State of the Art Review: Poverty and the Developing Brain. *Pediatrics* 137 (4): e20153075.

Kratzer, Nate. 2018. *A Multidimensional Poverty Index for the United States.* Theses and Dissertations—Public Policy and Administration. https://uknowledge.uky.edu/msppa_etds/24.

Kraus, Michael W., Stéphane Côté, and Dacher Keltner. 2010. Social Class, Contextualism, and Empathic Accuracy. *Psychological Science* 21 (11): 1716–1723.

MacDougall, Hannah. 2016. Dental Disparities among Low-Income American Adults: A Social Work Perspective. *Health & Social Work* 41 (3): 208–210.

Madonia, Giuseppina, Maria F. Cracolici, and Miranda Cuffaro (2013) "Exploring Wider Well-being in the EU-15 Countries: An Empirical Application of the Stiglitz Report", Social Indicators Research 111(1): 117–140.

Mani, Anandi, Sendhil Mullainathan, Eldar Shafir, and Jiaying Zhao. 2013. Poverty Impedes Cognitive Function. *Science* 341 (6149): 976–980.

Massey, Douglas S. 2007. *Categorically Unequal: The American Stratification System.* New York: Russell Sage Foundation.

Meyer, Bruce D., and James X. Sullivan. 2012. Identifying the Disadvantaged: Official Poverty, Consumption Poverty, and the New Supplemental Poverty Measure. *Journal of Economic Perspectives* 26 (3): 111–136.

———. 2017. *Annual Report on U.S. Consumption Poverty: 2016.* Washington, DC: American Enterprise Institute.

———. 2018. *Annual Report on U.S. Consumption Poverty: 2017.* Washington, DC: American Enterprise Institute.

Orshansky, Mollie. 1963. Children of the Poor. *Social Security Bulletin* 26 (7): 3–13.

———. 1965. Counting the Poor: Another Look at the Poverty Profile. *Social Security Bulletin* 28 (1): 3–29.

———. 1966. Recounting the Poor: A Five-Year Review. *Social Security Bulletin* 29 (4): 20–27.

Ouellette, Tammy, Nancy Burstein, David Long, and Erik Beecroft. 2004. *Measuring Material Hardship.* Final Report, Office of the Assistant Secretary for Planning and Evaluation, U.S. Department of Health and Human Services, Washington, DC.

Pew Research Center. 2018. September 2018 Political Survey, Final Topline, September 18–24, 2018. https://www.people-press.org/wp-content/uploads/sites/4/2018/10/topline-for-release1.pdf.

Reeves, Richard V., Edward Rodrigue, and Elizabeth Kneebone. 2016. *Five Evils: Multidimensional Poverty and Race in America.* The Bookings Institution.

Renwick, Trudi, and Liana Fox. 2016. *The Supplemental Poverty Measure: 2015.* Current Population Reports P60-258 (RV).

Ross, Christine, Shelden Danziger, and Eugene Smolensky. 1987. The Level and Trend of Poverty in the United States, 1939–1979. *Demography* 24 (4): 587–600.

Smeeding, Timothy. 2006. Poor People in Rich Nations: The United States in Comparative Perspective. *Journal of Economic Perspectives* 20 (1): 69–90.

Stiglitz, Joseph E., Amartya K. Sen, and Jean-Paul Fitoussi. 2009. *Report by the Commission on the Measurement of Economic Performance and Social Progress.* Paris: Commission on the Measurement of Economic Performance and Social Progress.

U.S. Bureau of the Census, Current Population Survey, Annual Social and Economic Supplements (US Census). 2020. Table 2. Poverty Status of People by Family Relationship, Race, and Hispanic Origin. https://www2.census.gov/programs-surveys/cps/tables/time-series/historical-poverty-people/hstpov2.xls.

U.S. Bureau of the Census/American Factfinder (US Census). 2019. *American Community Survey (Annual Data, 2008–2018).* U.S. Census Bureau's American Community Survey Office. http://factfinder.census.gov.

World Bank. 2017. *Monitoring Global Poverty: Report of the Commission on Global Poverty.* Washington, DC: World Bank.

World Bank. 2019. *PovcalNet: An Online Analysis Tool for Global Poverty Monitoring.* http://iresearch.worldbank.org/PovcalNet/#.

CHAPTER 2

A Survey of the Literature on Multidimensional Poverty

To facilitate a more complete understanding of the relationship between poverty and deprivation, a considerable portion of the initial chapter is devoted to the relationships between income poverty and non-monetary forms of deprivation. This entailed considerable discussion of income-based poverty measures, which led to a more limited discussion of multidimensional deprivation and to the introduction of the Multidimensional Poverty Index (MPI). We now extend our understanding of these topics through a review of the related literature. The survey presented in this chapter serves to expand our understanding of multidimensional poverty while simultaneously demonstrating the flexibility and usefulness of the multidimensional approach to poverty measurement. Our goal is to develop a more complete understanding of multidimensional poverty which, in turn, fosters the more comprehensive discussions of the MPI, its dimensions and indicators, and the associated measures that we present in the following chapters.

It seems that a reasonable starting point is to note that the literature on multidimensional poverty is quite vast. To date, several hundred articles on the topic have appeared in peer-reviewed journals, and a significant number of books and chapters in edited volumes have examined the topic.[1] Among this literature are works that focus on the bases for

[1] Bibi (2005), Zeumo et al. (2011), and Aaberge and Brandolini (2015) provide quite informative surveys of the related literature.

R. White, *Multidimensional Poverty in America*,
https://doi.org/10.1007/978-3-030-45916-1_2

multidimensional poverty measurement and on the corresponding mechanics.[2] However, the majority of published works involve application of the multidimensional poverty framework, doing so for far more than 100 countries. Among these studies are those that focus on country groups (e.g., global regions and/or sub-regions), on individual countries, or that consider multidimensional poverty at the sub-national level. A large majority of these works examine developing countries. Thus, by comparison, a relatively small number of studies examine multidimensional poverty in developed countries and, of course, a still smaller number are focused on the U.S. Specifically, an exhaustive search of the academic literature in early 2020 identifies only 16 studies of multidimensional poverty in the U.S.

Given the voluminous literature relating to multidimensional poverty, the survey provided in this chapter is admittedly incomplete. A complete review of the literature is unmanageable given its size. A review of the entire literature is also unwarranted since multidimensional poverty in the U.S. is the focus of this book. As an alternative, we provide a brief, selective review of studies that are unrelated to the U.S. coupled with a complete and detailed review of those studies that examine multidimensional poverty in the U.S.

We begin our review with a sampling of the studies that examine multidimensional poverty in countries other than the U.S. We then turn our attention to a detailed review of works that have examined multidimensional deprivation in the U.S. By structuring our literature survey in this manner, we are able to highlight some of the depth and breadth of the literature while also emphasizing the studies that examine the U.S. The result is a survey that enhances the understanding of our topic while simultaneously functioning as a bridge from the more general discussion of poverty and deprivation that is provided in our initial chapter to the more technical material that is specific to the U.S. and that is presented in subsequent chapters.

[2] See, for example, Seth and Santos (2019) for a review of the most prominent multidimensional poverty measure. Similarly, Pattanaik and Xu (2018) provide a general discussion of the measurement of multidimensional poverty and suggest an alternative to the methodology adopted by Alkire et al. (2015).

2.1 A Sampling of the Depth and Breadth of Non-U.S. Studies

As noted, a large majority of the studies of multidimensional poverty are focused on developing countries. A smaller number of works have examined developed economies, often involving European nations but not entirely limited to this region. A considerable number of works have examined groups of countries as well. Some examples include Alkire and Housseini (2014) which offers an overview of trends in multidimensional poverty among 37 countries located in sub-Saharan Africa. Similarly, Milliano and Plavgo (2018) examine multidimensional poverty among children in sub-Saharan Africa.[3] Nozaki and Oshio (2016) compare and contrast multidimensional poverty in China, Japan, and South Korea, while Bérenger (2016) examines Cambodia, Indonesia, and the Philippines to compare the index-based approach of Alkire and Foster (2011) to measures that are sensitive to the distribution of deprivation counts across individuals (Chakravarty and D'Ambrosio 2006; Rippin 2010; and Aaberge and Peluso 2012). A final example, Pinilla-Roncancio (2018), considers the relationship between multidimensional poverty and disability status in Brazil, Chile, Colombia, Costa Rica, and Mexico.[4]

While the number of countries for which studies have been undertaken is striking, perhaps equally impressive is the range of applications that have involved multidimensional poverty measurement. Trani et al. (2016), for example, provide a detailed accounting of multidimensionalpoverty in Afghanistan in 2005, finding among many other interesting results that almost all adult Afghans suffer deprivation in one or more dimensions and that those who live in rural locales, who are female, elderly, disabled, or are from minority ethnic groups are typically the most deprived. Another example is Guie et al. (2019) who apply Principal Component Analysis (PCA) to county-level data from the 2000 and 2010 China censuses to produce an integrated MPI that is used for the geographical identification of poverty-stricken counties. The authors emphasize the relevance of their

[3] Batana (2008) and Alkire et al. (2017) are two additional examples of works that focus on sub-Saharan Africa.

[4] Similar works by Brucker et al. (2015) and Terraneo (2017) examine the relationship between disabled status and deprivation in the United States and in 14 European countries, respectively. Additional studies of multidimensional poverty that examine groups of countries in Latin America include Nájera Catalán and Gordon (2019), Santos and Villatoro (2018), Santos et al. (2010), and Gasparini et al. (2008).

measure for public policy, reporting that the counties with higher index values tend to be concentrated and conjointly distributed in southwest China. Yet another example is the work of Kasri and Ahmed (2015) which illustrates how Maqāṣid al-Sharīʿah principles can be implemented in the assessment of socioeconomic policies in Muslim societies. The authors develop a simple, linear, and decomposable multidimensional Maqāṣid al-Sharīʿah-based poverty index that encompasses five dimensions of well-being/poverty that are consistent with the maqāṣid perspective. Lastly, Bucheli et al. (2018) incorporate multidimensional poverty measurement with infrastructure project assessment by employing a difference-in-differences approach to document a positive impact of rural road construction on multidimensional deprivation in Nepal. These studies represent a small number of the inventive applications that researchers have made involving multidimensional poverty measurement.

A set of similar examples that focus on developed countries other than the U.S. include Callander and Schofield (2015, 2017), Martinez and Perales (2017), and Saunders and Naidoo (2018), who examine various facets of multidimensional poverty in Australia. More specifically, Callander and Schofield (2015) show that multidimensional poverty can predict chronic income poverty, and Callander and Schofield (2017) examine individuals age 65 and older and show that being multidimensionally poor for three or four years corresponds with a statistically significant reduction in self-efficacy scores. Martinez and Perales (2017) document a general decrease in multidimensional poverty in Australia during the 2001–2013 period; however, the general decrease masks increases in deprivation for some dimensions (i.e., education, health, material resources, and social health) that were offset by decreases in other dimensions (i.e., community participation, employment, and safety perceptions). Somewhat similarly, Kim et al. (2015) study the health impacts of multidimensional poverty on children in South Korea, finding that consistent poverty and food insufficiency were statistically significant predictors of physical health and mental health problems. Sanchez-Garcia et al. (2019) introduce a multidimensional adjusted poverty index to measure educational poverty in Organization for Economic Co-operation and Development (OECD) member countries.

While the study of multidimensional poverty in developed countries has extended beyond the U.S. and Europe, it remains true that a large number of the studies that involve developed societies are focused on European countries. Several studies have examined the members of the European Union (EU), while others focus more narrowly on individual countries or at the sub-national level of detail.[5,6] For example, Chzhen et al. (2016) examine the overlap in child deprivation between monetary poverty and multidimensional deprivation across EU members. Similarly, using the multidimensional framework, Leturcq and Panico (2019) and Dickerson and Popli (2018) examine various facets of child poverty in the U.K. Botti et al. (2012), on the other hand, analyze the gendered nature of multidimensional poverty with respect to the EU policy framework, while Vizard and Yang (2017) explore potential relationships among EU members between income inequality and several measures of material deprivation and multidimensional poverty.[7] D'Ambrosio et al. (2011) examine data for Belgium, France, Germany, Italy, and Spain to determine the extent to which three different multidimensional approaches to poverty measurement identify the same households as poor. Rippin (2015) and Suppa (2016) also compare income-based and multidimensional measures of poverty, examining data for Germany, while Ulman and Šoltés (2015) pursue a similar analysis for Poland and Slovakia and Coromaldi and Drago (2017) overlap monetary and non-monetary measures of poverty in Italy to produce a more comprehensive poverty measure. Again, among these works we see examples of the significant diversity that exists with respect to the range of applications.

As indicated at the outset of this section, given the volume of literature on multidimensional poverty, at best, we can only briefly discuss a sample of the existing works. We hope that doing adequately demonstrates the depth and the breadth of the literature. As we now turn attention to the studies that focus on the U.S., we also begin a more thorough and detailed discussion of our topic.

[5] Two examples of research at the sub-national level are Arcagni et al. (2019), which employ a multidimensional fuzzy analysis of poverty and social fragility among migrants in the Lombardy region of Italy, and Ulman et al. (2018), which discuss rural material deprivation in the Northeast region of Romania.

[6] A number of studies examine multidimensional poverty at the sub-national level in non-European locales. Examples include Singh and Sarkar (2014), which measure multidimensional deprivation in Andhra Pradesh, India; Das (2019), which examines credit access and income on multidimensional poverty in rural Assam, India; Bijaya et al. (2015), which focus on the Bajhang District of Nepal; Afzal et al. (2015), which assess the Multidimensional Poverty Index in the Punjab Province of Pakistan; Mulyasari et al. (2019), which examine the Bengkulu Province of Indonesia; and Amao et al. (2017) and Loaiza et al. (2018) who study rural Nigeria and Antioquia, Colombia, respectively.

[7] Additional studies that focus on multiple EU member states include Betti et al. (2015), Guimarães et al. (2015), Ribeiro et al. (2015), and Whelan et al. (2014).

2.2 A Review of U.S.-Centered Studies

As we have noted, a relatively small number of studies have examined multidimensional poverty in the U.S. A summary of these works is provided as Table 2.1. In the table, we see that Dhongde and Haveman (2015) was the first study to examine multidimensional poverty in the U.S. using American Community Survey (ACS) data. In the years since, with the exceptions of Brucker et al. (2015) and Mitra and Brucker (2019) that examine data from the U.S. Current Population Survey (CPS) and Mitra and Brucker (2017) that utilize both ACS and CPS data, the ACS has become something of an "industry standard" data set for examination of multidimensional poverty in America. The table also notes the reference period of each study. We see that the early works, whether using ACS data or another source, more often were focused on single years; however, as more data have become available, it is increasingly common for reference periods to span periods of up to a decade.[8]

Comparing indicators and/or dimensions across the studies listed in Table 2.1, we often see both considerable variation and strong similarities. The indicators and dimensions used in prior studies are loosely grouped into five categories, four of which correspond with the dimensions that we employ when measuring multidimensional poverty in this book. Within each of the categories, we see several indicators are included in a majority of the listed studies. For example, within the Economic Security category, 12 of the 17 studies include a measure of income poverty as a form of deprivation and 11 of the studies include a measure of employment status. With respect to the Education category, all studies include a measure of educational attainment and for 15 of these studies the chosen measure is the completion of a high school diploma or equivalent credential. The one study that deviates from this measure is Dhongde (2017) which, being focused on multidimensional poverty among U.S. seniors, opts for the completion of grade 8 rather than the completion of high school. Turning to the Health category, we see that 13 studies include a measure of health insurance coverage. Two of the remaining studies (i.e., Wagle 2014, 2008) instead use a measure of individual subjective health status, while Dhongde

[8] On this subject, it is also seen that all studies which evaluate ACS data, with the exception of Koohi-Kamali and Liu (2017), begin their analysis in 2008 or later. The reason for this seems to be that the ACS did not include a question regarding health insurance until 2008. Koohi-Kamali and Liu opted to not include health insurance coverage as an indicator or dimension of deprivation and, thus, were able to include data for the years 2006 and 2007.

Table 2.1 Studies of multidimensional poverty in the United States

Indicators	*Dhongde and Haveman (2019)*	*Dhongde et al. (2019)*	*Mitra and Brucker (2019)*	*White and Bailleul (2019)*	*Dhongde (2017)*	*Dhongde and Haveman (2017)*	*Glassman (2017)*	*Koohi-Kamali and Liu (2017)*	*Mitra and Brucker (2017)*	*White and Yamasaki (2017)*	*Reeves et al. (2016)*	*Brucker et al. (2015)*	*Dhongde and Haveman (2015)*	*Wagle (2014)*	*Alkire and Foster (2011)*	*Wagle (2008)*
Economic security																
Employment status		✓	✓	✓			✓	✓	✓	✓	✓	✓	✓			✓
Family income														✓		✓
Food security				✓				✓		✓		✓				
Income-poverty ratio		✓	✓	✓	✓		✓	✓	✓	✓	✓	✓	✓		✓	
Industry																✓
Occupational prestige														✓		✓
Receipt of public assistance income								✓								
Receipt of supplementary security income								✓								
Respondent's income																✓
Satisfaction with financial situation																✓
Self-employment indicator																✓
Treated with respect at work																✓
Weeks at work																✓
Work status																✓
Education																
Educational attainment < high school diploma	✓	✓	✓	✓		✓	✓	✓	✓	✓	✓	✓	✓	✓	✓	✓

(*continued*)

Table 2.1 (continued)

Indicators	*Dhongde and Haveman (2019)*	*Dhongde et al. (2019)*	*Mitra and Brucker (2019)*	*White and Bailleul (2019)*	*Dhongde (2017)*	*Dhongde and Haveman (2017)*	*Glassman (2017)*	*Koohi-Kamali and Liu (2017)*	*Mitra and Brucker (2017)*	*White and Yamasaki (2017)*	*Reeves et al. (2016)*	*Brucker et al. (2015)*	*Dhongde and Haveman (2015)*	*Wagle (2014)*	*Alkire and Foster (2011)*	*Wagle (2008)*
Educational attainment < grade 8					✓											
Lives in a limited English-speaking household	✓	✓		✓		✓				✓			✓			
Health																
Has one or more disabilities	✓			✓						✓			✓			
Has two or more disabilities	✓	✓			✓	✓	✓									
Individual reports fair or poor health			✓						✓					✓	✓	✓
Lacks health insurance coverage	✓	✓	✓	✓		✓	✓		✓	✓	✓	✓	✓		✓	
Housing																
Crowded house (n persons > n rooms in HH)	✓	✓		✓		✓	✓	✓		✓			✓			
Does not own a housing unit								✓								
Housing (continued)																
Has housing costs ≥ 50% of household income	✓	✓		✓	✓	✓				✓			✓			
Incomplete kitchen and/or plumbing facilities		✓		✓			✓			✓						
Neighborhood quality							✓				✓					

Social inclusion, miscellaneous																
Associational memberships														✓		✓
Electoral participation														✓		✓
Group membership																✓
Political activism														✓		✓
Lacks private vehicle for transportation				✓				✓		✓						
Social contacts														✓		✓
Data source(s)	ACS	ACS	CPS	ACS	ACS	ACS	ACS	ACS	CPS/ACS	ACS	ACS	CPS	ACS	GSS	NHIS	GSS
Time period	2008–2017	2008–2015	2013–2017	2008–2017	2013	2008–2013	2008–2016	2006–2010	2013/2012	2010–2014	2014	2010–2011	2011	2004	2004	2004

Note: NHIS = National Health Interview Survey; GSS = General Social Survey; CPS = Current Population Survey; ACS = American Community Survey

(2017) bases health status on whether the individual suffers two or more disabilities. Within the Housing category, we see that nine studies include a measure of crowded housing. This measure is generally defined such that a household is considered to be crowded if the number of household members is greater than the number of rooms in the dwelling. The fifth category, which does not correspond with the dimensions used to measure multidimensional poverty in the present work, includes a measure of social inclusion and other miscellaneous measures. Other than three studies of ACS data that include a lack of access to private transportation as a form of deprivation, Wagle (2014, 2008) provides the only other studies represented in this category. In both cases, a number of measures are included to proxy for social inclusion, the logic being that a lack of inclusion is a form of deprivation.

While there is a certain lack of uniformity across studies in terms of the chosen indicators and/or dimensions, the corresponding advantage is that this strand of the literature, although quite small, employs a variety of deprivation measures. In a sense, the literature has evolved to be characterized by greater uniformity but this evolution has entailed the exploration of potential alternative deprivation measures. In other words, if common sets of indicators and dimensions were utilized in every study, we would not know if any given alternative measure might be a better option.

In the remainder of this section, we review the studies that have examined multidimensional poverty in the U.S. The primary purpose of the review is to inform readers of the efforts, methodologies, and findings of this particular strand of the literature. A secondary goal is the identification of commonalities and differences across studies. Without yet delving into details, simply from the information that is presented in Table 2.1 and that is discussed in the preceding paragraph, even with a limited number of studies having been completed on our topic it is evident that there are several similarities (and some differences) across studies. In the discussion that follows, we hope to identify additional connections and, to the extent possible, develop a narrative on the progression of these works. We proceed by discussing the works within groupings that are loosely based on a chronology of publication as this may allow for the illustration of connections across studies and for a better depiction of the evolution of the related literature.

Although not focused on deprivation in the U.S., Wagle (2002) offers a comprehensive foundation for the application of multidimensional analysis to the subject of well-being. Providing cogent, well-reasoned arguments for the multidimensionality of poverty, Wagle argues for the development of more integrative approaches to poverty measurement, thus serving as a basis for a subsequent work, Wagle (2008), which applies a dimensional approach to the measurement of poverty in the U.S. Moreover, Wagle (2008) uses PCA to divide 18 indicators into three dimensions (i.e., Economic Well-being, Capability, and Social Inclusion), with the scores from the analysis being averaged across the three dimensions to produce an overall poverty rating.

Examining the initial studies of multidimensional poverty in the U.S. results in several interesting findings. Using a dimensional approach, Wagle (2008) examines data from the 2004 U.S. General Social Survey (GSS) and finds considerable variation in multidimensional poverty across demographic groupings. Specifically, in terms of races and ethnicities, Wagle reports that whites and Asians have the lowest levels of multidimensional poverty, with values near/below the national average, while blacks, native Americans, and Hispanics have levels that are considerably higher than the national average. Similarly, when considering variation according to marital status, Wagle reports that individuals who are single and those who are widowed have higher incidences of multidimensional poverty as compared to those who are married, divorced, or separated. Somewhat surprisingly, Wagle finds very little difference in multidimensional poverty incidence between women and men and between the native-born and immigrant cohorts. Likewise, Wagle finds only minor variation in poverty incidence across household sizes and according to the number of children who reside in a household.

As part of a broader study that is largely focused on multidimensional poverty measurement and which proposes what has become known as the Alkire-Foster (AF) method, Alkire and Foster (2011) provide illustrative examples of multidimensional poverty measurement involving Indonesia and the U.S. Examining data from the 2004 U.S. National Health Interview Survey (NHIS) and limiting their analysis to survey participants 19 years of age and older, the authors utilize four variables to represent forms of deprivation. They categorized individuals as deprived (1) if their household income was less than the corresponding official poverty threshold, (2) if they reported their health as either "fair" or "poor", (3) if they lacked health insurance, and (4) if they had not earned their high school diploma. The authors used a cut-off of deprivation in at least two of these variables to identify individuals as being multidimensionally poor.

Alkire and Foster report that a majority of the U.S. population (59.8 percent) was not deprived in any of the four dimensions considered and that another 23.82 percent of the population was deprived in only one dimension; thus, 16.38 percent of the population was deprived in two or more dimensions (i.e., were multidimensionally poor). The authors also reported that deprivation was more common for the Health Insurance dimension (18.3 percent of the U.S. population) and the Educational Attainment dimension (18.5 percent) as compared to the remaining two dimensions. Comparing across races and ethnicity, however, Alkire and Foster reported that individuals who self-identified as black or as Hispanic accounted for greater shares of the multidimensionally poor than they did of the total population. This finding is similar to that obtained by Wagle (2008) when evaluating the 2004 GSS data.

While not seeking to diminish the findings reported in Alkire and Foster (2011), it is difficult to argue that the larger contribution of their 2011 paper is not the introduction of the AF method. Perhaps somewhat illustrative of the magnitude of this contribution, Wagle (2014) revisited the 2004 U.S. GSS data examined in Wagle (2008) to assess the AF method relative to the dimensional approach. The two approaches differ in that the latter uses dimensional indices (i.e., poverty status, intensity, and gap indices) while the former uses the indicators of the dimensions to recognize poverty and aggregate deprivations. In other words, to be considered multidimensionally poor, the dimensional approach requires an individual to be deprived in a certain number of dimensions while the AF method requires an individual to be deprived in a specified number of indicators.

Wagle (2014) contends that a dimensional approach that employs a two-step process provides greater insights into poverty and can better help analyze related issues and inform public policy. Relative to the AF approach, Wagle finds that the headcount ratio is more than 20 percent lower under the dimensional approach.[9] Similarly, variation is observed across the two approaches in terms of the contributions of each dimension to deprivation. For example, relational resources appear to be the biggest contributor to multidimensional poverty under the dimensional approach; however, under the AF approach, economic resources are found to be the largest factor. Even so, regardless of the approach employed, variation is reported in terms of the MPI values across race and ethnicity cohorts.

[9] Wagle argues that the AF method overstates the magnitude of poverty since it employs a single cut-off rather than the two-step process of the dimensional approach.

While delineation is neither clean nor clear, a second grouping of studies of multidimensional poverty in the U.S. can be defined as those works that examine data for a single year, thus providing snapshots in time. There are five studies in this group and, collectively, they examine the period from 2011 through 2014. In these works, we see a transition from the early studies to the more recent examinations of multiple years and a coalescing around the ACS as the primary data source for research into multidimensional poverty in the U.S.[10] This is important because data availability often dictates the set of indicators that researchers choose as being representative of the dimensions of deprivation being studied. Certainly, it is not unreasonable for researchers to do the best they can with the available information; however, the use of a common data source limits the available information and, thus, likely has implications for how we define deprivation and, correspondingly, for the construction of the MPI.

Examining ACS data for 2011, Dhongde and Haveman (2015) emphasize the insufficiency of income-based poverty measurements and contend that we must also consider other elements of well-being if we wish to accurately depict deprivation. The authors identify eight indicators of deprivation that are grouped, in pairs, within four dimensions. These dimensions are Education, Health, Housing, and Standard of Living. The corresponding indicators (with the associated dimensions noted in parentheses) identify individuals as deprived (1) if grade 12 was not completed or (2) they live in a household with limited English fluency (Education dimension); (3) if the individual lacks health insurance or (4) the individual has one or more disabilities (Health dimension); (5) if their housing costs are equal to or greater than one-half of household income or (6) if the individual lives in a household where there are more occupants than rooms (Housing dimension); or (7) if the individual's family income is below the federal poverty line or (8) the individual is unemployed (Standard of Living dimension). The authors adopt a threshold of deprivation in two or more of the eight indicators to identify individuals as multidimensionally poor.

Dhongde and Haveman estimate the MPI and related measures both at the national level and across Census Bureau-defined geographic regions.

[10] Unlike the initial set of works that examined the GSS and the NHIS, three of the five studies gathered into this second set of studies employ the ACS, another examines the CPS, and one work examines both ACS and CPS data.

They also estimate these same measures for age, gender, nativity, and race/ethnicity cohorts. The authors find that 20.1 percent of the adults residing in the U.S. in 2011 were multidimensionally poor and that the corresponding MPI value was equal to 6.6. By comparison, 42 percent of individuals were deprived in at least one indicator and 8.4 percent were deprived in three or more indicators. Furthermore, the dimension with the highest contribution to multidimensional poverty was standard of living (28.3 percent),[11] and the two indicators found to influence deprivation the most captured a lack of health insurance and having a severe housing burden.

Echoing the findings reported in Wagle (2014), Dhongde and Haveman identify variation in the incidence of multidimensional poverty across race, ethnicity, nativity, gender, and age cohorts. Asians, blacks, and Hispanics were found to be disproportionately poor, in a multidimensional sense, relative to their respective population shares. Asians had higher than average deprivation incidence in the crowded house and English fluency indicators, while Hispanics had higher than average deprivation frequencies for the health insurance, high school completion, English fluency, and crowded house indicators.[12] With respect to regions, Dhongde and Haveman found that the incidence of multidimensional deprivation in the West (24.0 percent) and South (21.9 percent) regions were greater than that reported for the nation (and, of course, for the remaining two regions: the Midwest and the Northeast). The authors also reported that individuals aged 18 to 64 years had a higher incidence of multidimensional poverty (21.2 percent) as compared to older individuals (16.4 percent). Lastly, a much higher percentage of the foreign-born population (42 percent) were identified as multidimensionally poor as compared to the native-born population (16.7 percent).

Differing somewhat from the approach of Dhongde and Haveman (2015), Reeves et al. (2016) employ five dimensions of deprivation, each of which corresponds to a single indicator. The authors examine data from the 2014 ACS. The dimensions they employ are (1) Low household income (for which an individual is defined as deprived if their household income is below 150 percent of the federal poverty level), (2) Limited

[11] The dimension with the lowest contribution to multidimensional poverty was reported to be education (21.5 percent).

[12] Specifics regarding deprivation incidence for the black cohort is not provided in the paper.

education (with deprivation identified as not having earned a high school diploma), (3) No health insurance (deprived if individual lacks coverage), (4) Unemployment (deprived if no one in the household, ages 25 to 61 years, is employed), and (5) Low-income area. Deprivation in the form of this final dimension is defined as living within a Public Use Microdata Area where the income poverty rate is greater than 20 percent. The rationale for the inclusion of the Low-income area dimension is that living in an area with a high poverty rate may disadvantage an individual beyond that of their own household income poverty status. For example, disadvantages experienced by those who live in a high poverty area may include a higher incidence of crime, less social capital, poor quality of schools, and limited job connections.

Largely consistent with earlier studies, Reeves et al. (2016) report that multidimensional poverty is much more common among blacks and Hispanics as compared to Asians and whites. With respect to the incidence of multidimensional deprivation, the authors do not specify a particular threshold; however, if we apply a threshold of being deprived in two or more two dimensions/indicators to identify multidimensional deprivation, then approximately 34 percent of their sample is identified as multidimensionally poor. This appears unusually high. Dhongde and Haveman (2015), using a lower threshold (i.e., two or more of eight indicators), report that 20.1 percent of the U.S. population between the ages of 18 and 64 years in 2011 were multidimensionally poor. Given that Reeves, et al. examine data for individuals of a similar age range (i.e., 25–61 years) in 2014, when more time had passed since the end of the 2007–2009 recession, it would lead one to expect a value below that reported by Dhongde and Haveman (2015).[13]

Seeking to measure multiple overlapping deprivations, Mitra and Brucker (2017) examine data from both the March 2013 U.S. Current Population Survey and the 2012 American Community Survey. The use of CPS data is noteworthy as Mitra and Brucker are the only researchers who employ the data to study multidimensional deprivation in the U.S.[14] While the authors reference the eight dimensions that Stiglitz et al. (2009) sug-

[13]The authors restrict their analysis to the 25–61 age range to exclude individuals who may still be completing their education and, thus, have a tenuous attachment to the labor force and those individuals who are eligible for Social Security benefits.

[14]In two subsequent works (i.e., Brucker et al. 2015; Mitra and Brucker 2019), the authors again examine CPS data.

gest should be represented, similarly due to limited data availability, only five of these eight dimensions are employed.[15] Specifically, deprivation in material well-being is considered to have occurred if an individual's income is below the official poverty threshold. Also, individuals are considered to be deprived in terms of the Health dimension if they report being either in poor or fair health. With respect to the Education dimension, an individual is considered to be deprived if they have less than a high school education. An individual is also considered to be deprived in terms of the Personal Activity dimension if they are unemployed.[16] Finally, if an individual lacks health insurance coverage, they are categorized as deprived in the Insecurity dimension.

Equal weights are assigned to the dimensions, and the authors set a cutoff of being deprived in at least two dimensions to be considered multidimensionally poor. Mitra and Brucker find that 15 percent of Americans experienced multiple deprivations, with Hispanics, immigrants, and individuals with disabilities being more likely to suffer multiple deprivations. Comparing their findings to the income poverty measure, the authors conclude that because 5.5 percent of the multidimensionally deprived (i.e., more than one-third of those who were multidimensionally poor) were not also income poor, the income poverty measure is a poor proxy for multiple deprivations.

As noted, one advantage of diversity in data sources is the opportunity to consider different cohorts of indicators and/or dimensions when examining multidimensional poverty. Perhaps more so than any other study of multidimensional deprivation in the U.S., Brucker et al. (2015) exploit this opportunity. The authors examine data from the March 2013 U.S. Current Population Survey and their two constructed measures are described as an economic measure and as a socioecopolitical measure. In both instances, there are five dimensions and each dimension corresponds to a single indicator. Likewise, regardless of the measure examined, the authors set the threshold for categorization as multidimensionally deprived as deprivation in two or more of the five dimensions/indicators.

[15] The eight dimensions that Stiglitz et al. (2009) recommend for inclusion are (1) material well-being (income, consumption, and wealth), (2) health, (3) education, (4) personal activities, including work, (5) political voice and governance, (6) social connections and relationships, (7) environment (present and future), and (8) insecurity of an economic or physical nature.

[16] For those under 17 years of age, the individual is considered deprived if the household head lacks a high school education and/or is unemployed.

The two measures are examined in conjunction with the Official Poverty Measure (OPM) and the Supplemental Poverty Measure (SPM) to determine whether being disabled is positively correlated with being poor and the extent to which differences in poverty incidence vary across poverty measures and disabled status.

The dimensions and indicators for the economic measure include (1) Educational Attainment (with an individual considered deprived if they did not complete high school), (2) Employment Status (deprived if the individual has been unemployed during the past year), (3) Health Insurance Status (deprived if one or more family members lack health insurance), (4) Income (deprived if household income is below the official income poverty threshold), and (5) Food Security (deprived if the household had low to very low food security for the past 12 months). The dimensions for the socioecopolitical measure also include (1) Educational Attainment and (2) Employment Status, but the remaining three dimensions of the economic measure are replaced by (3) Social Connectedness (deprived if the individual scores five or lower on a social connectedness scale), (4) Computer/Internet Access (deprived if the household does not own a computer or, if a computer is owned, lacks Internet access), and (5) Political Participation (deprived if the individual did not vote in the recent election). In some aspects, the socioecopolitical measure is similar to a number of indicators utilized by Wagle (2008, 2014) to represent social isolation. Wagle, however, examined data from the 2004 U.S. General Social Survey; thus, the specific measures differ.

Limiting their analysis to the working-age population (i.e., those aged 25 to 61 years), Brucker et al. report that, regardless of which poverty measure is examined, disabled individuals have a greater likelihood of being multidimensionally poor than do non-disabled individuals. The authors also find that, when the multidimensional measures are considered, the gap in poverty rates between disabled and non-disabled cohorts is greater than the difference that is calculated when using either the OPM or the SPM. Specifically, based on the economic measure of multidimensional poverty, 48.8 percent of those who were disabled were also multidimensionally poor, while the socioecopolitical measure identified 62.6 percent of the disabled as multidimensionally poor. These values far exceed the multidimensional poverty incidence values of 16.9 percent and 27 percent that were reported for non-disabled individuals when using the economic and socioecopolitical measures, respectively.

Considering differences across cohorts of native- and foreign-born individuals, Brucker et al. find that among those who are not disabled, 14 percent of the native-born suffer economic multidimensional poverty as compared to 32.8 percent of the foreign-born. When using the socioeco-political measure, the difference is less pronounced: 24.4 percent for the native-born as compared to 39 percent for their foreign-born counterparts. Among those who are disabled, the multidimensional poverty rates are less divergent: 48.3 percent for the native-born and 55.1 percent for the foreign-born (economic measure) and 62.5 percent for the native-born and 63.6 percent for the foreign-born (socioecopolitical measure). As a result, the authors assert that neither the OPM nor the SPM truly represent the deprivations experienced by those with disabilities.

The final study among the five works that examine data for individual years, Dhongde (2017) examines deprivation among the elderly population of the U.S. using ACS data for 2013. The author employs four dimensions of deprivation: Health, Standard of Living, Education, and Economic Security. Each dimension corresponds to a single indicator. The respective indicators are suffering two or more disabilities (Health), having a household income that is less than the federal poverty level (Standard of Living), having not completed grade 8 (Education),[17] and having housing costs equal to or greater than 50 percent of their income (Economic Security). The threshold employed for classification as multidimensionally poor is deprivation in two or more indicators/dimensions. Dhongde estimates the headcount ratio for this cohort as equal to 12.27 percent. The average intensity of deprivation among those who are identified as multidimensionally poor is 0.57. As a result, the MPI for this cohort is 6.94. Additionally, Dhongde notes high deprivation incidence among Asians and blacks with the Hispanic community having a particularly high rate and that older Hispanic adults suffered frequent deprived in the education and standard of living dimensions, while blacks faced deprivation in terms of the standard of living and housing dimensions.

The final group of works that examine multidimensional poverty in the U.S. are marked by greater commonality than is observed among earlier works. To an extent, this is expected since the reference periods of the studies all fall within the 2006–2018 period, examine a period at least five

[17] Because Dhongde focuses on the elderly population and high school completion was less common when the current elderly population were in high school, a lower threshold is set for the education indicator relative to studies that focus more broadly on the population.

years in length (and, thus, often overlap), and in all cases but one the studies examine ACS data. Evaluating similar data during similar time periods hinders the uniqueness of the individual works. Even so, the studies do vary significantly, whether in the dimensions and indicators that are used to identify deprivations or in the topics to which multidimensional poverty measurement is applied.

Dhongde and Haveman (2017) produce annual estimates for the period from 2008 through 2013 to examine trends in multidimensional poverty among the adult, working-age population (i.e., those who are 18 to 64 years of age). While the authors rely on the guidance provided by Stiglitz et al. (2009) regarding their choice of dimensions, they do not include two of the recommended dimensions (i.e., Personal Activities and Political Voice and Governance). As a result, six dimensions are used with one indicator included for each dimension. Specifically, Dhongde and Haveman consider an individual to be deprived if they lack health insurance, suffer two or more forms of disability, have not earned their high school diploma, or live in a household characterized by limited English fluency, where housing costs are equal to or greater than 50 percent of income, or where there are more occupants than rooms. The threshold for being categorized as multidimensionally poor is being deprived in two of more of the six indicators/dimensions. In addition to aggregate measurement, the authors also examine race/ethnicity and gender cohorts, finding that low rates of high school completion and health insurance coverage contribute to relatively higher incidence of multidimensional poverty among Hispanic individuals.

Mitra and Brucker (2019) examine data from the U.S. Current Population Survey that captures activity during the period from 2013 through 2017. Similar to Dhongde et al. (2019), Mitra and Brucker consider trends in multidimensional poverty during their reference period. The rationale for considering trends in multidimensional poverty is that declines have been observed in both income poverty and consumption-based poverty measures during the years following the Great Recession (Fontenot et al. 2018; Meyer and Sullivan 2018). To the extent that multidimensional poverty corresponds with measures of income poverty and consumption-based poverty measures, which is an admittedly imperfect correlation, we expect multidimensional poverty to also decrease.

Each of the five dimensions corresponds with a single indicator. The dimensions are (1) Material Well-being, (2) Health, (3) Education, (4) Personal Activities, and (5) Insecurity. Deprivation in the respective indicators is determined as follows. An individual is considered to be deprived in the Material Well-being dimension if they are in a family whose income during the past year falls below the official poverty line. With respect to the Health dimension, an individual is considered to be deprived if their self-assessed health status indicates that they are in poor or fair health. If the individual has less than a high school education, the individual is considered to be deprived with respect to the Education dimension.[18] In terms of Personal Activities, an individual is considered to be deprived if they were unemployed during the past week. And in terms of Insecurity, if an individual lacks health insurance coverage for the entire calendar year they are considered to be deprived.

The authors find that the percentage of the total population experiencing multidimensional deprivation decreased significantly on an annual basis. The authors also note that an increase in deprivation related to health insurance coverage contributed to a more modest decline in multidimensional poverty from 2016 to 2017. Looking to the changes in multidimensional poverty incidence for various demographic cohorts across the 2013 to 2017 period, we see decreases for all cohorts with the largest absolute decreases being observed for Hispanic individuals (i.e., a decrease of 9.36 percentage points), the foreign-born (i.e., 9.05 percentage points), and those individuals with disabilities (i.e., 7.71 percentage points). When considering proportional decreases in incidence rates, we again see the foreign-born (i.e., a decrease of 33.81 percent) and Hispanic individuals (i.e., a decrease equal to 32.91 percent) as well as Asians (i.e., a decrease of 32.38 percent) were the most affected.

Examining a somewhat lengthier period, 2008 through 2016, Glassman (2017) constructs a measure of multidimensional deprivation that also follows the recommendations of Stiglitz et al. (2009). The dimensions used by Glassman, with the corresponding category from Stiglitz et al. noted parenthetically, include: (1) Health (health); (2) Education (education); (3) Standard of Living (material well-being); (4) Consumption (material well-being)[19]; (5) Economic Security (personal activities); (6) Housing Quality (environment); and (7) Neighborhood Quality (insecurity of

[18] For individuals under the age of 18, the high school educational attainment of the head of household is considered for this indicator.

[19] Glassman (2017) deviates from Stiglitz et al. (2009) in that two dimensions, Standard of Living and Consumption, are used separately to represent material well-being.

economic or physical nature).[20] With respect to the Health dimension, an individual is considered by Glassman to be deprived if they suffer two or more disabilities. An individual is deprived in terms of the Education dimension if they are at least 19 years of age yet have not completed a high school diploma.[21] If an individual lives in a household for which family income is less than the corresponding federal poverty level, they are considered deprived in the Standard of Living dimension. If one lacks health insurance and/or lives in a household that does not have complete kitchen or plumbing facilities, they are considered deprived in the Consumption dimension. Regarding the Personal Activities dimension, an individual is considered deprived if no one in the family is employed.[22] If the household has more members than the dwelling has rooms, then the individual is said to be deprived according to the Housing Quality dimension. Finally, similar to Reeves et al. (2016) and corresponding with the Environment dimension, Glassman identifies individuals are deprived if they live in a census tract that has an income poverty rate of 20 percent of higher.

If an individual is deprived in two or more of the seven dimensions employed by Glassman, they are identified as multidimensionally deprived. Glassman thoroughly considers variation in multidimensional deprivation across race and ethnicity categories, by age, nativity, household structure, etc., and provides several interesting results. For example, as in prior studies, individuals who are Hispanic, black, American Indian or Alaskan Native, or of some other race(s) (other than white or Asian) are found more likely to suffer multidimensional poverty. And, again, we see considerably higher incidence of multidimensional poverty among immigrants relative to native-born individuals. Likewise, those who are at least 65 years of age are less likely to be categorized as multidimensionally poor relative to younger individuals, and married households have a lower likelihood of multidimensional poverty as compared to single-parent households and non-family households.

Unlike most earlier studies of multidimensional poverty in America, Glassman (2017) employs regression analysis to estimate, separately, the determinants of income poverty and of multidimensional poverty in the

[20] The two dimensions suggested by Stiglitz et al. (2009) that are not included are Political Voice and Governance and Social Connections and Relationships.

[21] If younger than 19 years of age, the educational attainment of the head of the household in which they live is used to determine the individual's deprivation status.

[22] The author makes exceptions for retirees and students.

U.S. The regression model employs a dichotomous dependent variable series that is equal to one if the individual is classified as multidimensionally poor and is otherwise equal to zero. The set of explanatory variables includes individual-specific measures such as race/ethnicity categories, nativity, age category, household structure, home ownership status, rural/urban location, and migration status. The estimation results are consistent with the findings of the descriptive analysis that are reported in the prior paragraph.

Dhongde et al. (2019) also examine a lengthy time period. In this case, the period from 2008 through 2015. The measure of multidimensional deprivation that is employed is constructed based on seven dimensions and nine indicators, with multidimensional deprivation being defined as deficiencies in four or more indicators. The authors examine variation in multidimensional poverty across demographic cohorts, placing an emphasis on social well-being during the Great Recession and in the years of recovery that followed. The seven dimensions the authors consider are Standard of Living, Health, Education, Personal Activities (including work), Economic Security, Social Connections and Relationships, and Environment. As with many of the studies discussed in this section, the choice of dimensions is based on the recommendations set forth by Stiglitz et al. (2009). For all dimensions except Standard of Living and Environment, for which there are two associated indicators, a single indicator corresponds with each dimension.

Unique relative to earlier studies, with the exceptions of Mitra and Brucker (2019) and Dhongde and Haveman (2017), the authors emphasize the change in multidimensional poverty across demographic cohorts. They find, for example, that while the white population typically has lower rates of deprivation relative to the remaining race-based cohorts, it was the white population that experienced the greatest increase in deprivation during the Great Recession. This same cohort experienced the smallest decrease in deprivation during the subsequent recovery. To the contrary, black individuals experienced the largest decrease in deprivation during the recovery.

Similar to Reeves et al. (2016), Dhongde and Haveman (2019) place an emphasis on those 18 to 65 years of age. Examining data for the years 2008 through 2017, the authors employ six dimensions and six corresponding indicators to measure multidimensional deprivation. The dimensions include Health (i.e., deprived if experiencing two or more forms of disability), Education (i.e., deprived if not having completed high school),

Standard of Living (i.e., housing costs are equal to or greater than 50 percent of household income), Economic Security (i.e., deprived if lacking health insurance), Social Connections (i.e., deprived if living in a limited English fluency household), and Housing Quality (i.e., deprived if there are more occupants in the household than rooms in the housing unit). Individuals are identified as multidimensionally deprived if they suffer deprived in two or more dimensions. The lengthy time period examined allows the authors to measure annual changes in deprivation levels at the aggregate level, across geographic areas (i.e., states and regions), and demographic groupings (i.e., age, gender, income, nativity, race, and ethnicity (Hispanic)). They find that 13.5 percent of individuals deprived in at least two dimensions. Ranged during the period from a high of 15.5 percent in 2010 to a low of 10.5 percent in 2017.

Interestingly, the authors do not include income as an indicator. The rationale is that they wish to identify the multidimensionally deprived and then compare that cohort to those who are income poor. In all likelihood, this understates the extent of multidimensional poverty. Inclusion of income poverty would increase the incidence and intensity of deprivation, thus increasing the MPI. It is particularly odd when the alternative was available to compare those who were income poor but not multidimensionally poor to those who were both income poor and multidimensionally poor to those who were multidimensionally poor but not income poor.

Demonstrating the usefulness of multidimensional poverty measurement to policy makers, White and Bailleul (2019) examine annual ACS data from 2008 through 2017, placing emphasis on quantifying variation in multidimensional poverty and in forms of deprivation (at the dimension and indicator levels) across the life cycle. The authors quantify multidimensional poverty in the U.S. while emphasizing the usefulness of decomposition to the dimension and indicator levels to inform public policy of targeted interventions. The choice of dimensions and indicators, along with the threshold for classification as multidimensionally poor is identical to White and Yamasaki (2017). To illustrate the usefulness of aggregate measurement and decomposition, the authors include two counterfactuals. The first counterfactual assumes that all U.S. residents had health insurance during 2017. All else equal, this difference alone would have reduced the number of multidimensionally poor in the U.S. by about 3.95 million individuals. The second counterfactual extends from the first such that, in addition to universal health insurance, all 2017 household incomes were assumed to equal at least 130 percent of the federal poverty level.

The estimated decrease in multidimensional poverty, again all else held constant, was estimated to equal 13.55 million individuals. This represented a 58.7 percent decrease in multidimensional poverty incidence.

Also examining ACS data, Koohi-Kamali and Liu (2017) examine multidimensional poverty at the sub-national level, focusing on the State of Pennsylvania. The authors consider the intersection of race, gender, and motherhood during the five-year period from 2006 through 2010. Four dimensions and a total of nine indicators are employed, with the dimensions equally weighted at 25 percent and the indicators equally weighted within the corresponding dimension. The specific dimensions and indicators (in parentheses) are Educational Attainment (i.e., deprived if the household head lacks a high school diploma), Employment Status (i.e., deprived if neither the household head nor their spouse, if present, works full-time), Supportive Income (i.e., deprived if in receipt of food stamp/SNAP benefits, public assistance income, or supplemental security income or of household income is below the federal poverty level), and Living Standard (i.e., deprived if the number of household members is more than two times the number of bedrooms in the dwelling; if they do not have access to a vehicle for private transportation; or if they do not own real estate). Deprivation in three or more indicators is the threshold for categorization as multidimensionally poor. The authors report high incidence of deprivation among African-American and Hispanic households, with female-headed Hispanic households with children being the most deprived and female-headed African-American households with children being the second most deprived.

White and Yamasaki (2017) examine ACS data for the years 2010 through 2014. The primary contributions of this work are the documentation of multidimensional poverty among the foreign-born population in the U.S. by home country cohorts and the presentation of results from an econometric analysis of the determinants of multidimensional poverty and the examination of variation in the determinants across both native- and foreign-born cohorts and across several groups of immigrants' home countries. The authors categorize deprivation according to 11 indicators that are grouped into four dimensions. Dimensions are equally weighted at 25 percent and indicators are equally weighted within each dimension to sum to 25 percent. The dimensions are Education, Health, Housing Costs, and Standard of Living. The corresponding indicators (with dimensions noted in parentheses) are (1) individual's educational attainment is below the level of a high school diploma; (2) individual lives in a household where English is not the primary language and no one within the household age 14 or older who speaks English well (Education dimension); (3) individual has at least one disability; (4) individual lacks health insurance coverage; (5) the individual's household receives benefits from the Supplemental Nutrition Assistance Program (Health dimension); (6) individual lives in a household for which there are more occupants than rooms; (7) housing costs are equal to or greater than one-half of income (Housing dimension); (8) individual lives in a housing unit that has incomplete kitchen or plumbing facilities; (9) household income is less than the federal poverty threshold; (10) the individual lacks a private vehicle for transportation; and (11) the individual is unemployed (Standard of Living dimension).

The sum of the weights assigned to the indicators in which the individual is deprived is equal to the deprivation score. Individuals are categorized as being multidimensionally poor if their deprivation score is equal to or greater than one-third. Based on this cut-off, the authors find that 9.48 percent of U.S. residents during this period were multidimensionally poor, that the average deprivation intensity (i.e., the average deprivation score among those categorized as multidimensionally poor) was equal to 0.4164, and the MPI was equal to 3.95. Further, among these individuals 7.99 percent were found to have experienced moderate multidimensional poverty (i.e., a deprivation score of at least 0.33 but less than 0.5), while 1.49 percent suffered severe multidimensional poverty (i.e., a deprivation score of 0.5 or higher). The 90.52 percent of U.S. residents who were not identified as multidimensionally poor consisted of 75.8 percent of the population that was neither multidimensionally poor nor vulnerable to multidimensional deprivation and 14.72 percent who were categorized as being vulnerable to multidimensional poverty. Looking at variation in multidimensional poverty across native- and foreign-born cohorts of the U.S. population, White and Yamasaki (2017) report significant variation across the two groups and across groupings of foreign-born residents based on their home countries.

From our brief review of studies that are not focused on the U.S., we see impressive applications of multidimensional poverty analysis. We have presented some evidence of just how common is the measurement of multidimensional poverty outside of the U.S.. Our discussion of these works is intended to hint at the tremendous depth and the breadth of studies that have examined this topic. Our more detailed discussion of studies that have examined multidimensional poverty in the U.S. is more centered on the specifics of measurement (i.e., indicators and dimensions), data sources, reference periods, and thresholds for classification as multidimensionally poor. Collectively, the works provide a large body of information related to multidimensional poverty in the U.S., and we can see the progression of the literature from the early works of Wagle and of Alkire and Foster to the more recent offerings of Dhongde and Haveman and of Mitra and Brucker. Having provided this review, we now wish to delve deeper by continuing our introduction to multidimensional poverty with details related to its measurement.

References

Aaberge, Rolf, and Andrea Brandolini. 2015. Multidimensional Poverty and Inequality. In *Handbook of Income Distribution, Volume 2A*, 141–216. Amsterdam and Boston: Elsevier, North-Holland.

Aaberge, Rolf, and Eugenio Peluso. 2012. *A Counting Approach for Measuring Multidimensional Deprivation*. Discussion Paper No. 700, Research Department, Statistics Norway.

Afzal, Muhammad, Shamim Rafique, and Farhan Hameed. 2015. Measurement of Living Standards Deprivation in Punjab Using AF Method (Periodical Comparison Approach). *The Pakistan Development Review* 54 (4I–II): 739–763.

Alkire, Sabina, and James Foster. 2011. Counting and Multidimensional Poverty Measurement. *Journal of Public Economics* 95 (7–8): 476–487.

Alkire, Sabina, and Bouba Housseini. 2014. *Multidimensional Poverty in Sub-Saharan Africa: Levels and Trends*. OPHI Working Paper 81. Oxford, United Kingdom: Oxford Poverty & Human Development Initiative.

Alkire, Sabina, James Foster, Suman Seth, Maria Emma Santos, José Manuel Roche, and Paola Ballon. 2015. *Multidimensional Poverty Measurement and Analysis*. Oxford, United Kingdom: Oxford University Press.

Alkire, Sabina, Christopher Jindra, Gisela Robles Aguilar, and Ana Vaz. 2017. Multidimensional Poverty Reduction Among Countries in Sub-Saharan Africa. *Forum for Social Economics* 46 (2): 178–191.

Amao O. Joshua, Ayantoye Kayode, and E. Fanifosi Gbenga. 2017. An Analysis of Multidimensional Poverty and its Determinants in Rural Nigeria. *Journal of Development and Agricultural Economics* 9 (11): 303–311.

Arcagni, Alberto, Elisa Barbiano di Belgiojoso, Marco Fattore, and Stefania M.L. Rimoldi. 2019. Multidimensional Analysis of Deprivation and Fragility Patterns of Migrants in Lombardy, Using Partially Ordered Sets and Self-Organizing Maps. *Social Indicators Research* 141 (2): 551–579.

Batana, Yélé Maweki. 2008. Multidimensional Measurement of Poverty Among Women in Sub-Saharan Africa. *Social Indicators Research* 112 (2): 337–362.

Bérenger, Valérie. 2016. *Measuring Multidimensional Poverty in Three Southeast Asian Countries using Ordinal Variables*. ADBI Working Paper, No. 618, Asian Development Bank Institute (ADBI), Tokyo.

Betti, Gianni, Francesca Gagliardi, Achille Lemmi, and Vijay Verma. 2015. Comparative Measures of Multidimensional Deprivation in the European Union. *Empirical Economics* 49 (3): 1071–1100.

Bibi, Sami. 2005. *Measuring Poverty in a Multidimensional Perspective: A Review of Literature*. PMMA Working Paper No. 2005-07.

Bijaya, G.C.D., Cheng, S.K., Bhandari, J., Liu, X. J., and Xu, Z.R. 2015. Multidimensional Poverty in Bajhang District of Nepal. *Pakistan Journal of Agricultural Sciences* 52: 1131–1137.

Botti, Fabrizio, Marcella Corsi, and Carlo D'Ippoliti. 2012. *The Gendered Nature of Multidimensional Poverty in the European Union*. Working Papers CEB 12-026, ULB—Universite Libre de Bruxelles.

Brucker, Debra L., Sophie Mitra, Navena Chaitoo, and Joseph Mauro. 2015. More Likely to Be Poor Whatever the Measure: Working-Age Persons with Disabilities in the United States. *Social Science Quarterly* 96 (1): 273–296.

Bucheli, José R., Alok K. Bohara, and Kira Villa. 2018. Paths to Development? Rural Roads and Multidimensional Poverty in the Hills and Plains of Nepal. *Journal of International Development* 30 (3): 430–456.

Callander, Emily J., and Deborah J. Schofield. 2015. Multidimensional Poverty and Health Status as a Predictor of Chronic Income Poverty. *Health Economics* 24 (12): 1638–1643.

———. 2017. Impact of Multidimensional Poverty on the Self-efficacy of Older People: Results from an Australian Longitudinal Study. *Geriatrics Gerontology International* 17 (2): 308–314.

Chakravarty, Satya R., and Conchita D'Ambrosio. 2006. The Measurement of Social Exclusion. *The Review of Income and Wealth* 52 (3): 377–398.

Chzhen, Yekaterina, Chris De Neubourg, Ilze Plavgo, and Marlous de Milliano. 2016. Child Poverty in the European Union: The Multiple Overlapping Deprivation Analysis Approach (EU-MODA). *Child Indicators Research* 9 (2): 335–356.

Coromaldi, Manuela, and Carlo Drago. 2017. An Analysis of Multidimensional Poverty: Evidence from Italy. In *Measuring Multidimensional Poverty and Deprivation: Incidence and Determinants in Developed Countries*, ed. Roger White. New York, NY: Palgrave Macmillan.

D'Ambrosio, Conchita, Joseph Deutsch, and Jacques Silber. 2011. Multidimensional Approaches to Poverty Measurement: An Empirical Analysis of Poverty in Belgium, France, Germany, Italy and Spain, Based on the European Panel. *Applied Economics* 43 (8): 951–961.

Das, Tiken. 2019. Does Credit Access Lead to Expansion of Income and Multidimensional Poverty? A Study of Rural Assam. *International Journal of Social Economics* 46: 252–270.

Dhongde, Shatakshee. 2017. Assessing Multidimensional Deprivation Among the Elderly in the USA. In *Measuring Multidimensional Poverty and Deprivation: Incidence and Determinants in Developed Countries*, ed. Roger White. New York, NY: Palgrave Macmillan.

———. 2019. *A Comparison of Income Poverty and Multidimensional Deprivation: Lessons Learned from the United States.* Paper prepared for the IARIW-World Bank Conference, Washington, DC, November 7–8, 2019.

Dhongde, Shatakshee, and Robert Haveman. 2015. *Multi-Dimensional Poverty Index: An Application to the United States.* Institute for Research on Poverty Discussion Paper No. 1427-15.

———. 2017. Multi-Dimensional Deprivation in the U.S. *Social Indicators Research* 133 (2): 477–500.

———. 2019. *A Decade-Long View of Multidimensional Deprivation in the United States.* Institute for Research on Poverty Discussion Paper No. 1440-19.

Dhongde, Shatakshee, Prasanta K. Pattanaik, and Xu Yongsheng. 2019. Well-being, Deprivation, and the Great Recession in the U.S.: A Study in a Multidimensional Framework. *The Review of Income and Wealth* 65 (S1): S281–S306.

Dickerson, Andrew, and Gurleen Popli. 2018. The Many Dimensions of Child Poverty: Evidence from the UK Millennium Cohort Study. *Fiscal Studies* 39 (2): 265–298.

Fontenot, Kayla, Jessica Semega, and Melissa Kollar. 2018. *Income and Poverty in the United States: 2017.* Washington, DC: U.S. Census Bureau.

Gasparini, Leonardo, Walter Sosa-Escudero, Mariana Marchionni, and Sergio Olivieri. 2008. Multidimensional Poverty in Latin America and the Caribbean: New Evidence from the Gallup World Poll. *The Journal of Economic Inequality* 11 (2): 195–214.

Glassman, Brian. 2017. *A Multidimensional Poverty Measure Using the American Community Survey.* U.S. Census Bureau, Poverty and Statistics Branch, SEHSD Working Paper Number 2017-47.

Guie, Li, Zhongliang Cai, Ji Liu, Xiaojian Liu, Shiliang Su, Xinran Huang, and Bozhao Li. 2019. Multidimensional Poverty in Rural China: Indicators, Spatiotemporal Patterns and Applications. *Social Indicators Research* 144 (3): 1099–1134.

Guimarães, Duarte, Ana Paula Ribeiro, and Sandra Tavares Silva. 2015. Macroeconomic Fundamentals of Poverty and Deprivation: An Empirical Study for Developed Countries. *The European Journal of Development Research* 27 (1): 37–66.

Kasri, Rahmatina, and Habib Ahmed. 2015. Assessing Socio-economic Development Based on Maqasid al-Shari'ah Principles: Normative Frameworks,

Methods and Implementation in Indonesia. *Islamic Economic Studies* 23 (1): 73–100.

Kim, Jung-Eun, Won-Hong Min, Bong Joo Lee, and In Hoe Ku. 2015. A Panel Study to Examine the Impact of Multidimensional Poverty on Korean Adolescents' Health. *Asia Pacific Journal of Social Work and Development* 25 (3): 145–156.

Koohi-Kamali, Feridoon, and Ran Liu. 2017. US Multidimensional Poverty by Race, Ethnicity and Motherhood: Evidence from Pennsylvania Census Data. In *Measuring Multidimensional Poverty and Deprivation: Incidence and Determinants in Developed Countries*, ed. Roger White. New York, NY: Palgrave Macmillan.

Leturcq, Marion, and Lidia Panico. 2019. The Long-Term Effects of Parental Separation on Childhood Multidimensional Deprivation: A Lifecourse Approach. *Social Indicators Research* 144 (2): 921–954.

Loaiza Quintero, Osmar Leandro, Guberney Muñetón Santa, and Juan Gabriel Vanegas. 2018. Forced Displacement and Multidimensional Poverty in Antioquia, Colombia: An Assessment by Means of a Seemingly Unrelated Regression. *Investigaciones Regionales* 167–90.

Martinez, Arturo, Jr., and Francisco Perales. 2017. The Dynamics of Multidimensional Poverty in Contemporary Australia. *Social Indicators Research* 130 (2): 479–496.

Meyer, Bruce D., and James X. Sullivan. 2018. *Annual Report on US Consumption Poverty: 2017*. Chicago: University of Chicago.

Milliano, Marlous de, and Ilze Plavgo. 2018. Analysing Multidimensional Child Poverty in Sub-Saharan Africa: Findings Using an International Comparative Approach. *Child Indicators Research* 11 (3): 805–833.

Mitra, Sophie, and Debra L. Brucker. 2017. Income Poverty and Multiple Deprivations in the High-Income Country: The Case of the United States. *Social Science Quarterly* 98 (1): 37–56.

Mitra, Sophie, and Debra Brucker. 2019. Monitoring Multidimensional Poverty in the United States. *Economics Bulletin* 39 (2): 1272–1293.

Mulyasari, Gita, Irham, Lestari Rahayu Waluyati, and Any Suryantini. 2019. The Importance of Combining Various Methods in Assessing Poverty Level: The Case of Marine Capture Fishermen in Bengkulu Province, Indonesia. *Journal of International Studies* 12: 241–57.

Nájera Catalán, Héctor E., and David Gordon. 2019. The Importance of Reliability and Construct Validity in Multidimensional Poverty Measurement: An Illustration Using the Multidimensional Poverty Index for Latin America (MPI-LA). *The Journal of Development Studies* 56 (9): 1763–1783.

Nozaki, Kayo, and Takashi Oshio. 2016. Multidimensional Poverty and Perceived Happiness: Evidence from China, Japan and Korea. *Asian Economic Journal* 30 (3): 275–293.

Pattanaik, Prasanta K., and Yongsheng Xu. 2018. On Measuring Multidimensional Deprivation. *Journal of Economic Literature* 56 (2): 657–672.

Pinilla-Roncancio, Mónica. 2018. The Reality of Disability: Multidimensional Poverty of People with Disability and their Families in Latin America. *Disability and Health Journal* 11 (3): 398–404.

Reeves, Richard, Edward Rodrigue, and Elizabeth Kneebone. 2016. *Five Evils: Multidimensional Poverty and Race in America*. Washington, DC: Brookings Institution.

Ribeiro, Ana Paula, Sandra Tavares Silva, and Duarte Guimaraes. 2015. Macroeconomic Fundamentals of Poverty and Deprivation: An Empirical Study for Developed Countries. *European Journal of Development Research* 27: 37–66.

Rippin, Nicole. 2010. *Poverty Severity in a Multidimensional Framework: The Issue of Inequality between Dimensions*. Courant Research Center, Discussion Paper No. 47, University of Göttingen.

———. 2015. Multidimensional Poverty in Germany: A Capability Approach. *Forum for Social Economics* 45 (2–3): 230–255.

Sanchez-Garcia, Juan-Francisco, Maria-del-Carmen Sanchez-Anton, Rosa Badillo-Amador, Maria-del-Carmen Marco-Gil, Juan-Vicente LLinares-Ciscar, and Susana Alvarez-Diez. 2019. A New Extension of Bourguignon and Chakravarty Index to Measure Educational Poverty and Its Application to the OECD Countries. *Social Indicators Research* 145 (2): 479–501.

Santos, Maria Emma, and Pablo Villatoro. 2018. A Multidimensional Poverty Index for Latin America. *The Review of Income and Wealth* 64 (1): 52–82.

Santos, Maria Emma, María Ana Lugo, Luis Felipe López-Calva, Guillermo Cruces, and Diego Battiston. 2010. Refining the Basic Needs Approach: A Multidimensional Analysis of Poverty in Latin America. In *Research on Economic Inequality*, ed. John Bishop. Melbourne, Australia: Emerald Group Publishing Limited.

Saunders, Peter, and Yuvisthi Naidoo. 2018. Mapping the Australian Poverty Profile: A Multidimensional Deprivation Approach. *Australian Economic Review* 51 (3): 336–350.

Seth, Suman, and Maria Emma Santos. 2019. On the Interaction between Focus and Distributional Properties in Multidimensional Poverty Measurement. *Social Indicators Research* 145 (2): 503–521.

Singh, Renu, and Sudipa Sarkar. 2014. *The Relationship of Household Monetary Poverty and Multidimensional Child Deprivation: A Longitudinal Study of Children Growing Up in India*. Young Lives Working Paper No. 121.

Stiglitz, Joseph E., Amartya K. Sen, and Jean Paul Fitoussi. 2009. *Report by the Commission on the Measurement of Economic Performance and Social Progress*. Paris: Commission on the Measurement of Economic Performance and Social Progress.

Suppa, Nicolai. 2016. *Comparing Monetary and Multidimensional Poverty in Germany*. OPHI Working Paper 103. Oxford, United Kingdom: Oxford Poverty & Human Development Initiative.

Terraneo, Marco. 2017. Material Deprivation, Health and Well-Being in Older Age: A Comparative Analysis of 14 European Countries. In *Measuring Multidimensional Poverty and Deprivation: Incidence and Determinants in Developed Countries*, ed. Roger White. New York, NY: Palgrave Macmillan.

Trani, Jean-Francois, Jill Kuhlberg, Timothy Cannings, and Dilbal Chakkal. 2016. Multidimensional Poverty in Afghanistan: Who Are the Poorest of the Poor? *Oxford Development Studies* 44 (2): 220–245.

Ulman, Paweł, and Erik Šoltés. 2015. The Monetary and Non-Monetary Aspects of Poverty in Poland and Slovakia. *Entrepreneurial Business and Economics Review* 3 (1): 61–73. Centre for Strategic and International Entrepreneurship at the Cracow University of Economics.

Ulman, Simona-Roxana, Vasile Isan, Costica Mihai, and Mihaela Ifrim. 2018. The Responsiveness of the Rural Area to the Related-Decreasing Poverty Measures of the Sustainable Development Policy: The Case of North-East Region of Romania. *Transformations in Business and Economics* 17: 780–805.

Vizard, Polly, and Lin Yang. 2017. *Multidimensional Poverty and Income Inequality in the EU*. CASE Papers /207, Centre for Analysis of Social Exclusion, LSE.

Wagle, Udaya. 2002. Rethinking Poverty: Definition and Measurement. *International Social Science Journal* 54 (171): 155–165.

———. 2008. Multidimensional Poverty: An Alternative Measurement Approach for the United States? *Social Science Research* 37 (2): 559–580.

———. 2014. The Counting-Based Measurement of Multidimensional Poverty: The Focus on Economic Resources, Inner Capabilities, and Relational Resources in the United States. *Social Indicators Research* 115 (1): 223–240.

Whelan, Christopher T., Brian Nolan, and Bertrand Maitre. 2014. Multidimensional Poverty Measurement in Europe: An Application of the Adjusted Headcount Approach. *Journal of European Social Policy* 24 (2): 183–197.

White, Roger, and Thomas Bailleul. 2019. Multidimensional Poverty Across the Life Cycle: The United States as an Empirical Example. In *Routledge International Handbook of Poverty*, ed. Bent Greve. Oxfordshire, UK: Routledge.

White, Roger, and Stacy Yamasaki. 2017. Multidimensional Poverty among the Native- and Foreign-born in the United States: Evidence from the 2010–2014 American Community Surveys. In *Measuring Multidimensional Poverty and Deprivation: Incidence and Determinants in Developed Countries*, ed. Roger White. New York, NY: Palgrave Macmillan.

Zeumo, Vivien Kana, Blaise Some, and Alexis Tsoukias. 2011. *A Survey on Multidimensional Poverty Measurement: A Decision Aiding Perspective*. Working Papers hal-00875525, HAL.

CHAPTER 3

Measuring Multidimensional Poverty

If it is a goal of policy makers to enhance social welfare through the reduction or elimination of deprivation in our society, then the first step toward the realization of this goal is identifying the specific forms of deprivation that policies will target. The second step is accurately measuring the extent to which deprivation exists, as such measurement is necessary for assessing the effectiveness of policy efforts. In this chapter, we propose a set of indicators, each of which corresponds to one of four dimensions that represent a variety of potential deprivations. Using these indicators, we illustrate multidimensional poverty measurement by providing a detailed discussion of the calculation of the Multidimensional Poverty Index (MPI) for the U.S. This advances our understanding of our topic while simultaneously setting the stage for the analyses and related discussions that are provided in subsequent chapters.

3.1 Construction of the Multidimensional Poverty Index

We measure multidimensional poverty in the U.S. following the methodology proposed by Alkire and Foster (2011). This technique, commonly referred to as the AF method, is an extension of the Foster-Greer-Thorbecke (Foster et al. 1984) family of poverty metrics. The AF method utilizes a dual cut-off approach to identify who is (and who is not)

R. White, *Multidimensional Poverty in America*,
https://doi.org/10.1007/978-3-030-45916-1_3

multidimensionally poor. Specifically, the first cut-off involves the selection of the dimensions and the indicators to be considered and the corresponding deprivation criteria. The second cut-off involves the choice of the cross-dimensional threshold for the classification of individuals (or households, depending on the unit of analysis) as suffering multidimensional poverty. The AF method is so widely accepted that it is used by the United Nations in the calculation of the Global Multidimensional Poverty Index, which is largely focused on developing nations and is discussed in some detail in Sect. 3.2. Similarly, the AF method has been used to measure deprivation in a number of European countries (Whelan et al. 2014; Weziak-Bialowolska and Dijkstra 2014).

A rather simple interpretation of the MPI is that it is equal to the product of two values which is then scaled by 100. The first of these values is the headcount ratio (H). This is a measure of the frequency, or incidence, of multidimensional poverty. The headcount ratio indicates the percentage of the population that is categorized as multidimensionally poor. The second value is the average deprivation intensity (A). This value is equal to the mean deprivation score among those who are categorized as being multidimensionally poor. Using slightly more technical terms, the average deprivation intensity is the censored deprivation score. Thus, as the product of the measures of incidence and intensity, the MPI captures both the breadth and the depth of deprivation. Equation (3.1) illustrates,

$$MPI_{jt} = H_{jt} \times A_{jt} \times 100 \tag{3.1}$$

The subscripts j and t represent the geographic locale (e.g., country) and time period (e.g., year), respectively, for which the MPI is being calculated.

When the headcount ratio value is equal to zero, the average deprivation intensity value is also equal to zero. Thus, when no individuals are categorized as suffering multidimensional poverty the MPI is equal to its minimum value of zero. Note that in such an instance there still can be (and likely is) deprivation. It is merely that the incidence of deprivation is sufficiently infrequent and/or diffuse among the population as to result in no individual being sufficiently deprived to be identified as suffering multidimensional poverty. The maximum value of the MPI is 100. This is the value that would be realized if all members of a population were to simultaneously experience the maximum possible level of deprivation (i.e., if all members of the population were to be deprived in all indicators). Such circumstances would correspond with a headcount ratio value of 100 percent and an average deprivation intensity value of one.

To further illustrate our calculation of the MPI, eqs. (3.2) and (3.3) indicate the construction of the headcount ratio, H, and the average intensity of deprivation, A.

$$H_{jt} = \frac{q_{jt}}{p_{jt}} \tag{3.2}$$

In eq. (3.2), q represents the number of individuals in the population who are categorized as being multidimensionally poor and p is the total population. As noted, the headcount ratio measures the incidence, or the frequency, of multidimensional poverty.

$$A_{jt} = \frac{m_{jt}}{q_{jt}} \tag{3.3}$$

In eq. (3.3), the numerator, m, is the total deprivation (i.e., the sum of individual deprivation scores) experienced among the portion of the population that is categorized as multidimensionally poor. As in eq. (3.2), q is the number of individuals in the population that are identified as multidimensionally poor. Stated differently, A is the average deprivation intensity value among those who suffer multidimensional poverty. As noted, this is also referred to as the censored deprivation score due to the inclusion of only those individuals who have been identified as multidimensionally poor.

To provide a more complete depiction of the construction of our MPI values, we can look a bit deeper to the components of the measures H and A—that is, to q, p, and m—which are given by eqs. (3.4) through (3.6), respectively.

$$q_{jt} = \sum_{i=1}^{n} w_{it} \mid d_{it} \geq X \tag{3.4}$$

$$p_{jt} = \sum_{i=1}^{n} w_{it} \tag{3.5}$$

$$m_{jt} = \sum_{i=1}^{n} d_{it} \mid d_{it} \geq X \tag{3.6}$$

The subscript i represents observations (i.e., survey respondents, or individuals, given our data source), w is the population weight assigned to each observation, d is the deprivation score that corresponds to each observation. The deprivation score for any individual observation is calculated as $d_{it} = \sum_{v=1}^{n} (z_v \times I_{vit})$, where v identifies each indicator, I, that represents a form of deprivation, and z is the weight assigned to a given indicator. X is the second cut-off associated with the AF method.[1] This second cut-off is the threshold value that must be met or exceeded for an observation to be categorized as multidimensionally poor. It is the cross-dimensional threshold for the classification of an individual (or household) as suffering from multidimensional poverty.

Inserting eqs. (3.2) and (3.3) into eq. (3.1) and then substituting eqs. (3.4) and (3.5) for H and eqs. (3.6) and (3.4) for A results in eq. (3.7).

$$MPI_{jt} = \left(\frac{\sum_{i=1}^{n} w_i \mid d_i \geq X}{\sum_{i=1}^{n} w_i} \right)_{jt} \times \left(\frac{\sum_{i=1}^{n} d_i \mid d_i \geq X}{\sum_{i=1}^{n} w_i \mid d_i \geq X} \right)_{jt} \times 100 \tag{3.7}$$

Equation (3.7) is simply a restatement of eq. (3.1); however, the more detailed depictions of H and A illustrate that, because the numerator in the H term is identical to the denominator in the A term, eq. (3.7) can be simplified as eq. (3.8).

$$MPI_{jt} = \left(\frac{\sum_{i=1}^{n} d_i \mid d_i \geq X}{\sum_{i=1}^{n} w_i} \right)_{jt} \times 100 \tag{3.8}$$

From eq. (3.8), we can see that the MPI is equal to the mean value, across the entire population, of the censored deprivation scores scaled by 100. That is, the MPI is equal to the average deprivation of those who are multidimensionally poor (i.e., the total deprivation experienced by those

[1] The value of the population weight, w, is equal to one in a case where population weighting is either not necessary or not possible.

within the population who are categorized as multidimensionally poor) divided by the total population. Yet another interpretation of the MPI is that it represents the share of weighted deprivations that are experienced by those who are identified as multidimensionally poor divided by the maximum possible deprivations that could be experienced if all people were identified as multidimensionally poor and suffered deprivation in all indicators. Finally, revisiting our starting point of eq. (3.1), we can again note that the MPI is equal to the product of the headcount ratio, H, and the average deprivation intensity value among the multidimensionally poor, A. While understanding the different interpretations of the MPI is of value for a more complete understanding of the measure, in subsequent chapters we generally focus our discussions on this final interpretation. Doing so allows an emphasis to be placed on the incidence of multidimensional poverty which, as we shall see, is quite relevant for public policy formulation.

3.2 The 2019 Global MPI

With the goals of further illustrating the MPI and of fostering a more informed perspective of deprivation in developing countries relative to the developed world, generally speaking, we now consider the measure in the context of developing nations. Specifically, Table 3.1 provides details regarding the dimensions and indicators that are utilized in the construction of the Global Multidimensional Poverty Index. A key difference between the measure of multidimensional poverty we construct for the U.S. and the construction of the Global MPI is that only five of the nine indicators that we employ are household-related, with the remaining four indicators being related to the individual, while all ten indicators in the Global MPI are related to household characteristics. Additionally, a review of the dimensions and indicators that are employed to construct the Global MPI and comparison to the dimensions and indicators employed when constructing the MPI for the U.S. highlights the relativity of deprivation across societies at different stages of economic, human, and social development while also illustrating the flexibility of the multidimensional approach.

We see there are three dimensions included in the Global MPI: Education, Health, and Living Standards. As with our construction of the MPI for the U.S., each dimension is weighted as an equal portion of the index value. Similarly, within each dimension, the corresponding

Table 3.1 Dimensions and Indicators of the Global MPI

Dimensions	*Indicators*	*Deprived if living in the household where…*	*Weight*
Education	School attendance	Any school-aged child is not attending school up to the age at which he/she would complete class 8.	1/6
	Years of schooling	No household member aged ten years or older has completed six years of schooling.	1/6
Health	Child mortality	Any child has died in the family in the five-year period preceding the survey.	1/6
	Nutrition	An adult under 70 years of age or a child is undernourished.	1/6
Living standards	Assets	The household does not own more than one of these assets: radio, TV, telephone, computer, animal cart, bicycle, motorbike or refrigerator, and does not own a car or truck.	1/18
	Cooking fuel	The household cooks with dung, wood, charcoal, or coal.	1/18
	Drinking water	The household does not have access to improved drinking water (according to Sustainable Development Goals (SDG) guidelines) or safe drinking water is at least a 30-minute walk from home, round trip.	1/18
	Electricity	The household has no electricity.	1/18
	Housing	Housing materials for at least one of roof, walls and floor are inadequate: the floor is of natural materials and/or the roof and/or walls are of natural or rudimentary materials.	1/18
	Sanitation	The household's sanitation facility is not improved (according to SDG guidelines) or it is improved but shared with other households.	1/18

Source: Alkire and Jahan (2018)

indicators are equally weighted so that their sum is equal to the dimension weight. Since the AF method is employed to construct the Global MPI, the dual cut-off approach is followed. The first cut-off involves the selection of indicators and indicator thresholds above which deprivation is identified. All indicators are dichotomous variables; thus, a value of one identifies deprivation and a value of zero corresponds with a lack of deprivation. The second cut-off involves the choice of the deprivation score threshold that is used to categorize observations as multidimensionally poor. The Global MPI utilizes 0.3333 as the threshold. As noted earlier, we employ this same threshold value and, likewise, all of our indicators are dichotomous, so the differences between the measure we calculate and that of the Global MPI involve the choice of indicators employed to represent deprivation and whether the indicators identify individual or household characteristics.

The construction of our measure for the U.S. largely mirrors the construction of the Global MPI. This is intentional as we wish to limit the differences, to the extent possible, to the forms of deprivation that are potentially experienced. Looking at the dimensions in the Global MPI, we see that within the Education dimension there are two indicators: school attendance and years of schooling, each of which carries a weight of 0.1667. An individual is considered to be deprived in terms of the school attendance indicator if any school-aged child within the household is not attending school until the age at which they would complete class 8.[2] The years of schooling indicator is equal to one if no member of the individual's household who is ten years of age or older has completed six or more years of schooling.

The Health dimension is also comprised of two indicators: child mortality and nutrition. Again, as there are two indicators within the dimension, each indicator is assigned a weight of 0.1667. An individual is considered to be deprived in terms of the child mortality indicator if any child in the household has died during the five-year period immediately prior to the survey. The nutrition indicator reflects malnourishment of anyone under age 70 in the household. Individuals 20 years of age and older are considered to be malnourished if their Body Mass Index (BMI) value is less than 18.5 kg/m^2 (i.e., if their BMI value is such that they are considered to be "underweight"). Those who fall within the age range of 15 to 19 years are categorized as malnourished based on the World Health Organization's age-specific BMI cut-off values. Children are categorized as malnourished if the z-score for either height-for-age (stunting) or weight-for-age (underweight) values is two or more standard deviations below the corresponding median value of the reference population.

The Living Standards dimension consists of six indicators: assets, cooking fuel, drinking water, electricity, housing, and sanitation. Since each indicator is equally weighted within the dimension, each indicator is assigned a weight of 0.0556. Regarding assets, individuals are identified as deprived if their household lacks at least one basic asset (e.g., a radio,

[2] Since the official school entrance age varies across countries, so too does the age at which a child is expected to complete class 8.

television, bicycle and so on). An individual is considered deprived in terms of the cooking fuel indicator if the household uses dung, wood, charcoal, or coal as a heat source when cooking. Individuals are also considered deprived if they lack access to clean drinking water (i.e., water sourced from piped water, a public tap, a borehole or pump, a protected well, protected spring or rainwater, and the water source is located within a 30-minute walk (round trip) from the household).[3] Likewise, if a household lacks electricity then the individuals who reside in the household are considered to be deprived. In terms of housing, an individual is deprived if the floor and/or roof or walls of their household is made of natural materials. Specifically, a household is categorized as deprived if the floor is made of mud, clay, earth, sand, or dung or if the household lacks a roof or walls or if one (or either) has been constructed using "cane, palm/trunks, sod/mud, dirt, grass/reeds, thatch, bamboo, sticks or rudimentary materials such as carton, plastic/polythene sheeting, bamboo with mud/stone with mud, loosely packed stones, uncovered adobe, raw/reused wood, plywood, cardboard, unburnt brick or canvas/tent" (Alkire and Jahan 2018, p. 10). For the sanitation indicator, a household is considered to be deprived if it lacks access to improved sanitation (i.e., a flush toilet, latrine, ventilated improved pit, or composting toilet and the facility is not shared).[4]

Figure 3.1 identifies each of the countries included in the Global MPI and illustrates their relative MPI values. We can easily see that the large majority of counties included in the Global MPI are located in Africa, Asia, and Latin America and the Caribbean. To provide additional information and to facilitate ease of reference, Table 3.4, which is located in the appendix, provides an alphabetical listing of the 101 countries and six broad geographic regions that are included in the 2019 Global MPI. The table presents MPI values, headcount ratios, and average deprivation intensity values (i.e., average censored deprivation scores).

Among the countries that are included in the Global MPI, the population-weighted average values for the headcount ratio and average deprivation intensity are 23.1 percent and 0.4936, respectively. The

[3] Similarly, individuals are classified as deprived if the survey from which the information is drawn when constructing the Global MPI adopts a different definition for phrase "safe" drinking water.

[4] In some instances, based on the survey from which the information is drawn to construct the Global MPI, other definitions of "adequate" sanitation are used to classify individuals as deprived.

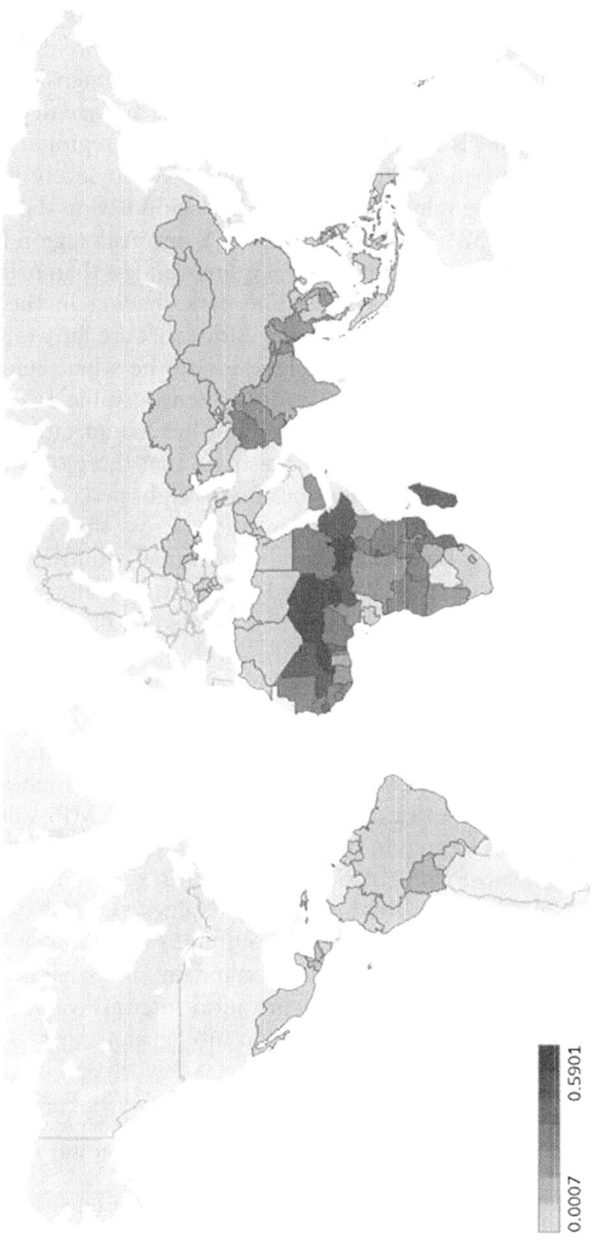

Fig. 3.1 Global Multidimensional Poverty Index, 2019. Note: Author's illustration based on data from the UNDP and OPHI (2019). Countries without shading are not included in the Global MPI

corresponding MPI value is 11.39. Comparing across regions, we see that sub-Saharan Africa has the highest headcount ratio with more than half of the region's population (57.5 percent) suffering multidimensional poverty. Compounding this high incidence rate is that the average deprivation intensity value (0.5488) is higher than that of any other region and is, in fact, so high that the typical deprived individual lives in severe multidimensional poverty. These values translate to the region having the world's highest MPI value (31.53). By comparison, the South Asia region has the second highest MPI value which at 14.15 is quite a bit less than half of the value observed for sub-Saharan Africa. The dark shading in the figure depicts levels of deprivation in sub-Saharan Africa that are far worse than what is seen in other areas of the world. Looking to the other regions, we find the second highest average deprivation intensity value is equal to 0.4844 (in the Arab states). The second highest headcount ratio is equal to 31 percent (South Asia); however, we also see that three of the other four regions listed in Table 3.4 have values below eight percent.

To further illustrate the extent of deprivation across the sub-Saharan Africa region, we can look at the values for the individual countries included in the Global MPI. We see that 39 of the 101 countries that are included in the index are located in sub-Saharan Africa. Ranking all 101 countries from highest to lowest MPI value, we see the 20 countries with the highest MPI values are all located in sub-Saharan Africa. Additionally, the headcount ratio values for these 20 countries are all higher than 50 percent, and the average deprivation intensity values among these countries are all greater than 0.5.[5] Further, 28 of the 30 countries with the highest MPI values are in sub-Saharan Africa, and 36 of the 50 highest MPI values are found among countries located in the region. To emphasize, 36 of the 39 countries located in sub-Saharan Africa that appear in the Global MPI are among the 50 countries with the highest MPI values.[6] Of the countries included in the Global MPI, 28 have headcount ratio values above 50 percent, and 26 of these 28 countries are located in sub-Saharan Africa. Twenty-seven countries have average deprivation intensity values higher than 0.5. Of these countries, 24 are located in sub-Saharan Africa.

[5] Mauritania (ranked 26th in terms of MPI value) is also in sub-Saharan Africa and has a headcount ratio value above 50 percent and an average deprivation intensity value that is greater than 0.5.

[6] The three countries located in sub-Saharan Africa that are not among the 50 highest MPI value countries are Eswatini (ranked 56th), Gabon (58th), and South Africa (67th).

While, across regions, sub-Saharan Africa has the highest headcount ratio, average deprivation intensity, and MPI values, and the difference between sub-Saharan Africa and other regions is stark, looking to the individual countries is even more telling. Five countries—South Sudan (91.9 percent), Niger (90.5 percent), Chad (85.7 percent), Burkina Faso (83.8 percent), and Ethiopia (83.5 percent)—have headcount ratio values greater than 80 percent. Another 23 countries also have headcount ratio values greater than 50 percent with 21 of these countries located in sub-Saharan Africa. Continuing to focus on the five countries with the highest headcount ratio values, we see that four (i.e., Niger (0.6523), South Sudan (0.6315), Chad (0.6226), and Burkina Faso (0.6191)) also have the highest average deprivation intensity values.[7] Of course, the countries with the highest headcount ratio values and the highest average deprivation intensity values have the highest MPI values. Niger holds the unenviable position as the country with the highest MPI value at 59.01. South Sudan has a similar MPI value (58.02), after which there is a slight gap with Chad, Burkina Faso, and Ethiopia ranking third through fifth with respective MPI values of 53.34, 51.91, and 48.88.

The magnitudes of the values that are illustrated in Fig. 3.1 and of the corresponding indicators of deprivation that are identified in Table 3.1 clearly illustrate that deprivation in developing economies is much different—both in scale/magnitude and in form—as compared to deprivation in a developed economy such as the U.S. Beyond the methodology that is employed to measure multidimensional poverty, the differences in the forms of deprivation that are employed as indicators are so different as to not truly be comparable. The differences in deprivation across societies at different stages of economic and social development may beg the question: Why should we examine deprivation in a developed economy such as the U.S. when there is such worse deprivation elsewhere in the world?

A simple answer to this question is that the alleviation of deprivation is beneficial and desirable regardless of its relative severity. Further, if deprivation in a developed economy is addressed it does not necessarily hinder efforts to reduce deprivation in developing societies. This is because resources allocated to reducing deprivation in one locale need not reduce the level of resources that are available and, ideally, allocated to counter

[7] The Central African Republic has the fifth highest average deprivation intensity value (0.5858) and Ethiopia, which has the fifth highest headcount ratio value, has the sixth highest average deprivation value (0.5854).

deprivation elsewhere. In other words, it is simply not an either/or proposition. One only need to look to the most recent half century to see simultaneous reductions in income poverty both in developed economies such as the U.S. and in much of the developing world. Additionally, it is important to recognize that extreme poverty persists even in developed economies. For example, Azpitarte (2012) finds incidences of multidimensional poverty in both the U.S. and in Spain, particularly among younger individuals, minorities, and those with lower levels of education. Whelan et al. (2014) examine 20 non-monetary indicators of deprivation in 28 European countries and document poverty in each country despite there being fluctuation consistent with national income levels. Variation in the incidence and intensity of multidimensional poverty in the U.S. is also identified by Brucker et al. (2015) who report differences in poverty across demographic cohorts with Hispanics, blacks, single-parent households, immigrants, disabled persons, and persons who live within metropolitan areas being most likely to experience multiple deprivations. Similarly, White and Yamasaki (2017) report that foreign-born individuals in the U.S. are significantly more likely to experience multidimensional poverty as compared to the native-born and that there is considerable heterogeneity in terms of deprivation incidence and intensity across immigrants when grouped by their home countries.

In the chapters that follow, we examine multidimensional poverty using annual data from the American Community Survey (ACS) for the years 2008 through 2018 (U.S. Census 2019). Each observation in the Public Use Microdata Sample (PUMS) person-level file represents a single individual, and each observation in the household-level file in the data represents a single housing unit. For our purposes, we have merged the files such that each observation in the person-level file has been matched to the corresponding household-level data. The resulting data file contains information for 34,291,600 individuals which is an average of 3,117,418 observations per year during our reference period. Effectively, the data for each year represent a one percent sample of the U.S. population. Unless otherwise noted, to generate accurate estimates and standard errors, we employ the ACS-provided population weight variable when calculating MPI and related values. We note that, in addition to identifying individual observations as being multidimensionally poor, we categorize the observations as experiencing severe multidimensional poverty, moderate multidimensional poverty, being vulnerable to multidimensional poverty, or as neither suffering from multidimensional poverty nor being vulnerable to it. This categorization both allows for a more complete understanding of multidimensional poverty in the U.S. and affords deeper empirical examination in later chapters.

3.3 Dimensions, Indicators, and the U.S. MPI

Crucial to a multidimensional analysis of poverty is the choice of the dimensions and indicators that represent deprivation. The choice of indicators must be made with consideration of how each indicator is related to deprivation, the extent to which the indicators collectively represent deprivation, and whether data are available for each indicator for every household or individual (depending on the unit of analysis). The choice of indicators and any related thresholds, in cases where the indicator is not dichotomous, to be met or exceeded to indicate deprivation is the first of the two cut-offs in the dual cut-off approach of the AF method.

The capability approach (Sen 1980; Alkire 2009) is often referred to when discussing the selection of indicators and cut-off values. The capability approach considers what individuals are able to achieve which, of course, is a relative determination since what can be achieved, and the resources necessary to achieve, vary across individuals. An example is that of a disabled individual perhaps requiring equipment to be as mobile as an otherwise comparable able-bodied person. A similar example would be a worker who requires a higher daily caloric intake as compared to someone who is not in the labor force (Clark 2005). This level of relativity can become significantly more complicated when we consider dimensions of culture and/or societal freedoms that may hinder access to resources. It is because of this relativity that assessing an individual's ability to achieve, and thus, well-being at a societal level is most comprehensively determined through a multidimensional analysis of well-selected dimensions and indicators.

As noted, when calculating the MPI for the U.S., we identify four dimensions of deprivation that are comprised, in total, by nine indicators. The four dimensions are (1) Economic Security, (2) Education, (3) Health, and (4) Housing. From the ACS data, we have selected the indicators that we believe best represent each corresponding dimension. By design, the dimensions and the indicators we choose to evaluate are similar to those employed by Dhongde and Haveman (2015), White and Yamasaki (2017), and White and Bailleul (2019); however, our reference period, dimensions, and indicators and, thus, our headcount ratio, average deprivation intensity, and MPI values differ to a certain degree. Figure 3.1 identifies the dimensions and indicators that we employ in the form of a schematic that illustrates the construction of the MPI.

Alkire (2009) notes that explanations and justifications for selected indicators and dimensions are often missing from studies of multidimensional poverty. To avoid this pitfall, we now discuss the indicators and dimensions that are presented in Fig. 3.2 and detailed in Table 3.2.

The Economic Security dimension consists of two indicators that identify individuals who suffer income poverty and/or who are unemployed. We identify individuals (i.e., observations) as being deprived in terms of the income poverty indicator if their reported household income is less than the poverty threshold that corresponds to their household size and composition. Regarding the unemployment indicator, an individual is considered to be deprived concerning employment status (i.e., unemployed) if they report that they are at least 16 years of age, are not currently employed, and are looking for work.

For the Education dimension, the indicators we use include the individual's level of educational attainment and whether the individual resides in a household that is characterized by limited English-speaking (that is

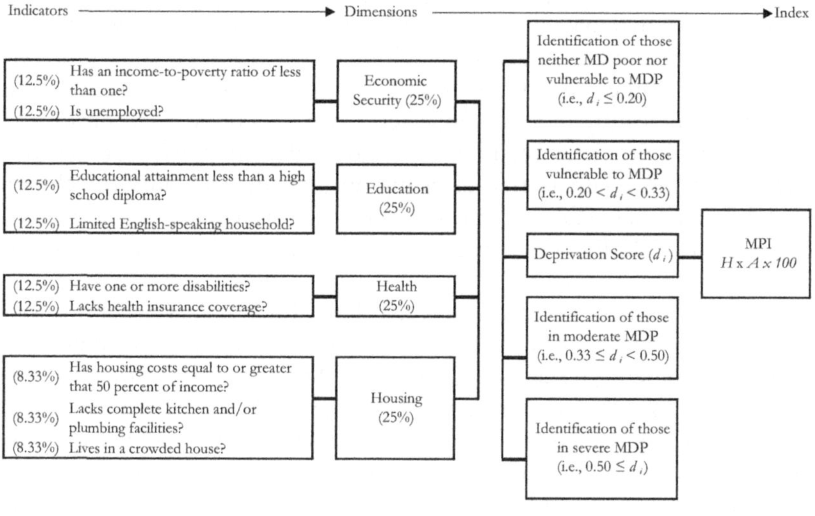

Fig. 3.2 Indicators, Dimensions, and Construction of the MPI for Empirical Example of U.S.

Table 3.2 Relative Deprivation in the United States, Dimensions and Indicators

Dimensions	*Indicators*	*Deprived if...*	*Weight*
Economic Security	Income poor	The total income of the householder's family is below the appropriate poverty threshold. (For non-family householders, their own income is compared with the appropriate threshold.)	1/8
	Unemployed	The individual 1) was unemployed during the corresponding reference week. Specifically, the individual (or householder, as applicable) was neither "at work" nor "with a job but not at work", and 2) was actively looking for work during the last 4 weeks, and 3) was available to start a job. Also included as unemployed are civilians who a) did not work at all during the reference week, and b) were waiting to be called back to a job from which they had been laid off, and c) were available for work except for temporary illness. Note that the indicator is set equal to zero for all individuals less than 16 years of age as such individuals are not counted as part of the labor force.	1/8
Education	High school diploma	The individual has not completed either a regular high school diploma or attained a General Equivalency Diploma (GED). Note, however, that the indicator is set equal to zero for individuals who are below six years of age and for those who are at least six years of age, who report being currently enrolled in school, and who have earned a high school diploma or equivalent degree.	1/8
	Limited English speaking household	No member 14 years old and over 1) speaks only English at home or 2) speaks a language other than English at home and speaks English "Very well."	1/8
Health	Disability status	The individual's interactions among their body; their physical, emotional, and mental health; and the physical and social environment in which they live, work, or play results in limitations of activities and restrictions to full participation at school, at work, at home, or in the community.	1/8
	Health insurance	The individual reported no health coverage.	1/8

(*continued*)

Table 3.2 (continued)

Dimensions	*Indicators*	*Deprived if...*	*Weight*
Housing	Lives in a crowded house	The number of individuals who reside in the individual's housing unit exceeds the number of room in the unit.	1/12
	Housing costs ≥ 50% of monthly income	Monthly housing costs are equal to or greater than 50 percent of the monthly household income.	1/12
	Incomplete kitchen or bathroom facilities	The individual's housing unit lacks (1) a sink with a faucet, (2) a stove or a range, (3) a refrigerator, (4) hot and cold running water, and (5) a bathtub or shower.	1/12

linguistically isolated). In terms of educational attainment, an individual is considered deprived if they are not a student, not under six years of age, and have not earned a high school diploma or a General Equivalency Degree (i.e., a GED). We also consider an individual to be deprived if they live in a household where there is no one 14 years of age or older who only speaks English at home or who speaks another language at home but cannot speak English "very well".

Indicators for the Health dimension indicate whether the individual is disabled and/or lacks health insurance. An individual is considered deprived due to disability if they are experiencing at least one of the following: self-care difficulty, hearing difficulty, vision difficulty, independent living difficulty, ambulatory difficulty, or cognitive difficulty. For the health insurance indicator, any individual that lacks insurance coverage is considered to be deprived.

Unlike the first three dimensions, which are each comprised of two indicators, the Housing dimension includes three indicators. For this dimension, the indicators identify whether an individual lives in a crowded house, lives in a house with incomplete housing amenities, and/or has high housing costs relative to their income. The crowded house indicator refers to the number of persons who reside in the household relative to the number of rooms. Deprivation in this indicator means that there are more people in the household than there are rooms. Incomplete housing amenities refers to incomplete kitchen facilities (i.e., the lack of a stove/range, refrigerator, and/or a sink with faucet) and/or incomplete plumbing facilities (i.e., the absence of hot and cold running water, a flush toilet, and/or a bathtub/shower). The housing costs indicator is based on the annual sum of monthly rent (if the residence is not owner-occupied) or of monthly owner costs (if owner-occupied) as a percentage of household income in the last year. Individuals are considered deprived in this indicator if their housing costs are equal to or greater than 50 percent of their income.

To consider the possibility that any of the chosen dimensions and/or indicators are overly related to any other dimension or indicator, we can look to the corresponding correlation coefficient values. Beginning with the six pairwise correlation coefficients across the four dimensions, we find a considerably strong correlation value of 0.3891 for the Economic Security and Housing dimensions. However, the next strongest correlation ($\rho = 0.2201$) is between the Education and Health dimensions, and the remaining four correlation values range from 0.0844 to 0.1591 in absolute value. Looking at the 36 pairwise correlation coefficient across the 9 indicators, we again find a strong pairwise correlation ($\rho = 0.4489$) between the indicators that represent housing costs being equal to or greater than 50 percent of household income and the income-to-poverty ratio being less than 1. As with the dimensions, all other correlation coefficients are considerably smaller in value. The next strongest correlation among the set of indicators is between the high school graduate indicator and that which identifies the observation/indicator as disabled ($\rho = 0.1739$). All other correlation coefficient values are equal to 0.1511 or lower in absolute value, with 23 correlation values between 0 and 0.10 and 10 of the values falling between 0.10 and 0.1511.

3.4 Weights, Thresholds, and an Illustrative Example

Following the AF method, the first cut-off to identify is that which identifies an individual as deprived in a particular indicator. Since all of our indicators are dichotomous, it is merely a case of "either/or" for each indicator. Thus, we code any indicator for which an individual is deemed to be deprived as one and those indicators for which the individual does not suffer deprivation as zero. As noted, since we employ four dimensions when calculating the MPI, we assign each dimension an equal weight of 0.25 (i.e., 1/4). The indicators that comprise each dimension are also weighted equally within each dimension. Therefore, each of the two indicators in the Economic Security, Education, and Health dimensions is assigned a weight of 0.125 (i.e., 0.25/2). Similarly, each of the three indicators in the Housing dimension is assigned a weight of 0.0833 (i.e., 0.25/3). Thus, within each dimension, the indicator weights sum to 0.25 and the sum of all dimension weights and, thus, the sum of the indicator weights, is equal to 1. The second of the two cut-offs refers to whether or not an individual's deprivation score meets or exceeds the specific threshold that corresponds with multidimensional poverty. We adopt the threshold value of 0.3333 that is employed by the United Nations (UNDP, 2015), as well as in numerous studies, as our secondary cut-off.

To both illustrate the calculation of the MPI using the dimensions and indicators that we have chosen for our examination of the U.S. and to offer greater clarity on MPI calculation, the remainder of this chapter provides a detailed example of MPI calculation and related values for a fictitious society. Table 3.3 provides the information that is employed to perform the calculations.

To begin, we can see that the population of this hypothetical society is represented by ten observations, listed left to right in the table.[8] In the row immediately below the observation number is the population weight value that has been assigned to each observation. The sum of the population weights is 1070; thus, surveyed individuals represent nearly a one percent sample of the population (i.e., 10/1070 = 0.93 percent). The left two columns indicate each of the four dimensions and the corresponding nine indicators. The third column from the left identifies the weights that are applied to each indicator. In all instances except the Housing dimension, the indicator weights equal 1/8 and sum to 25 percent. For the Housing dimension, as there are three indicators, the indicator weights are each equal to 1/12, and, as with the indicators associated with the other dimensions, the weights of the Housing dimension indicators sum to 25 percent. The final two rows in the table indicate the number of indicators for which each observation is deprived and the deprivation score for the observation. The series of 0 and 1 values correspond to each observation and indicator, with a value of 1 indicating deprivation in that indicator and a value of zero indicating no deprivation in that indicator. For a given observation, the deprivation score is constructed as the sum of the

[8] Of course, as this is a hypothetical situation, for simplicity and expedience we set aside concerns related to the small sample size assuming there is no related bias.

Table 3.3 Multidimensional Poverty Index Calculation Example

		Obs. #:	*1*	*2*	*3*	*4*	*5*	*6*	*7*	*8*	*9*	*10*
Dimensions	Indicators	Pop. wgt.:	104	109	106	91	114	110	118	98	103	117
Economic Security	Income-poor	1/8	0	1	0	0	0	0	0	1	0	0
""""	Unemployed	1/8	0	0	0	0	0	0	0	1	1	0
Education	High school incomplete	1/8	0	0	1	0	1	0	0	0	0	0
""""	Linguistic isolation	1/8	0	0	0	0	1	0	0	1	0	0
Health	At least one disability	1/8	0	0	0	1	0	0	0	0	1	0
""""	Lacks health insurance	1/8	0	0	0	0	0	0	0	1	0	1
Housing	Crowded house	1/12	0	0	1	0	0	0	1	1	0	0
""""	Housing costs ≥ 50% of income	1/12	0	0	0	1	0	1	0	0	1	0
""""	Incomplete kitchen or bathroom facilities	1/12	0	0	1	0	0	0	1	0	0	0
		N indicators deprived	0	1	3	2	2	1	2	5	3	1
		Deprivation Score:	0.0000	0.1250	0.2917	0.2083	0.2500	0.0833	0.1667	0.5833	0.3333	0.1250

indicator-specific weights for which the binary indicator values are equal to one (i.e., the sum of the weights that correspond to the indicator(s) for which the individual suffers deprivation).

Beginning with observation 1, we see that this individual does not suffer deprivation in any of the listed indicators. Thus, the deprivation score for observation 1 is equal to 0. Observation 2, by comparison, is income poor but is not deprived in any of the other eight indicators. Given the weight associated with the income poverty indicator, the deprivation score for this individual is equal to 0.1250 (i.e., the weight associated with the income poverty indicator: 1/8). Similarly, observations 6 and 10 are each deprived in only one indicator. Observation 6 has housing costs that are equal to or greater than 50 percent of their household income, while observation 10 is deprived by a lack of health insurance. Thus, the deprivation score for individual 6 is equal to 0.0833 and the deprivation score for individual 10 is 0.1250. Observation 7 is deprived in two indicators—namely, this individual lives in a crowded house that lacks complete kitchen or bathroom facilities—and has a deprivation score equal to 0.1667. Here, the deprivation score is equal to the sum of the two weights associated with the indicators in which deprivation exists: 1/12 + 1/12. What is common across these five individuals is that their deprivation scores are less than 0.20. Thus, these observations are classified as neither being multidimensionally poor nor as vulnerable to multidimensional poverty.

Looking to observation 3, we see the individual lacks a high school diploma and lives in a house that is both crowded and that lacks complete kitchen or bathroom facilities. Thus, this individual is deprived in three indicators. Given the associated indicator weights, the deprivation score for this individual is equal to 0.2917. This is calculated as 1/8 + 1/12 + 1/12 for the incomplete high school, crowded house, and incomplete kitchen or household indicators, respectively. Given our cut-off of 0.3333 to identify multidimensional poverty, this observation is not categorized as being multidimensionally poor. However, because the deprivation score is between 0.20 and 0.3333, this individual is categorized as being vulnerable to multidimensional poverty. Observations 4 and 5 also have deprivation scores within the 0.20 to 0.3333 range and, thus, are also classified as being vulnerable to multidimensional poverty. In the case of observation 4, the individual is disabled and has monthly housing costs equal to or greater than 50 percent of their monthly income. Observation 5 lacks a high school diploma and is linguistically isolated (i.e., no one in the individual's household is at least 14 years of age and speaks English well). As a result, the deprivation scores for observations 4 and 5 are equal to 0.2083 and 0.25, respectively.

The sum of the population weight values for observations 1, 2, 6, 7, and 10 is equal to 558. Thus, we can say that 52.15 percent of this society's population is neither multidimensionally poor nor vulnerable to multidimensional poverty (i.e., 558/1070). Similarly, as the sum of the population weights assigned to observations 3, 4, and 5 is equal to 311, we can say that 29.07 percent of this society's population (i.e., 311/1070) is vulnerable to multidimensional poverty. Collectively, these two categories indicate that 81.22 percent of the society's population does not live in multidimensional poverty. In turn, this means that 18.78 percent of the society's population does live in multidimensional poverty.[9] This is the headcount ratio value. These individuals are represented by observations 8 and 9 whose population weight values sum to 201 (i.e., 201/1070).

Focusing on observation 8, we see the individual is linguistically isolated, lacks health insurance, lives in a crowded house, is income poor, and is unemployed. The sum of the weights for these indicators is equal to 0.5833 (i.e., 1/8 + 1/8 +1/12 + 1/8 + 1/8). Somewhat similarly, observation 9 is disabled, unemployed, and has monthly housing costs equal to or greater than 50 percent of their monthly income. The corresponding deprivation score for observation 9 is equal to 0.33 (i.e., 1/8 + 1/12 + 1/8). While 18.78 percent of the society's population lives in multidimensional poverty, we can be even more specific by noting that deprivation scores ranging from 0.33 to 0.50 correspond with moderate multidimensional poverty while deprivation scores equal to or greater than 0.50 indicate severe multidimensional poverty. Considering the population weights, we can say that 9.16 percent of this society's population (i.e., 98/1070) is experiencing moderate multidimensional poverty, while 9.63 percent of the population (i.e., 103/1070) is experiencing severe multidimensional poverty.

To calculate the MPI value for this society, we need to know the average deprivation intensity value among those identified as multidimensionally poor. The average intensity, also known as the censored deprivation score, is calculated as the population-weighted average of deprivation scores among those who live in multidimensional poverty. Here, that value is equal to (0.5833 x 98/201) + (0.3333 x 103/201), which is equal to 0.2844 + 0.1708 = 0.4552. Multiplying the headcount ratio (H) of 18.78

[9] By comparison, since observations 2 and 8 are identified as income poor, the income poverty rate for this society is equal to 19.35 percent (i.e., 207/1070).

percent by the average deprivation intensity value (A) of 0.4552 and factoring by 100 results in an MPI value that is equal to 8.55.

If, as an alternative to using the dual cut-off method, we employ the counting method, we would arrive at a considerably different MPI value. Since there are nine indicators, if we continue to use one-third as the threshold for identification as multidimensionally poor, any observation that is deprived in three or more indicators would be categorized as living in multidimensional poverty. Returning to the information provided in Table 3.3, we see that observations 3, 8, and 9 are deprived in 3, 5, and 3 indicators and have deprivation scores of 0.3333, 0.5833, and 0.3333, respectively. Note the difference here, relative to identification of the multidimensionally poor when using the dual cut-off method is that observation 3 is now included among the multidimensionally poor. Given the population weights for these three observations, the corresponding headcount ratio (H) is equal to 28.69 percent (i.e., 307/1070). Calculating the average deprivation intensity (A), we find a value that is equal to (0.3333 x 106/307) + (0.5833 x 98/307) + (0.3333 x 103/307), which is equal to 0.1151 + 0.1862 + 0.1118 = 0.4131. Basing the calculation on the counting method results in an MPI value that is equal to 11.85.

In this case, the counting method results in an MPI value that is nearly 40 percent higher than the value that is calculated when using the dual cut-off method. However, the difference in values is generally attributable to the counting method providing a higher headcount ratio as compared to the dual cut-off method. In other words, the average deprivation intensity values are not very dissimilar. In the first case (i.e., the AF method), the value is equal to 0.4552, while in the second case (i.e., the counting method) the value is equal to 0.4131. The headcount ratios are equal to 18.78 percent and 28.69 percent when the AF method and the counting method, respectively, are employed.

Now that we have introduced the construction of the Global MPI and the MPI measure that we use for the U.S., we can shift gears to focus on the extent and magnitude of multidimensional poverty in the U.S. This is the focus of the following three chapters which offer a detailed reporting of multidimensional poverty in the U.S. during our reference period. Effectively, we provide a census of sorts of the multidimensionally poor. In the chapters that follow, we rely on the dual cut-off method for our analysis, but we also utilize the counting method in the next chapter as a form of robustness check.

Appendix

Table 3.4 MPI, Headcount Ratios (H), and Average Intensity Values (A)

Cohort	*Year and Survey*	*Population in Multidimensional Poverty*		*MPI*
		H	*A*	
Developing countries	..	23.07%	0.4936	11.39
Regions	..			
Arab States	..	15.72%	0.4844	7.61
East Asia and the Pacific	..	5.60%	0.4227	2.37
Europe and Central Asia	..	1.15%	0.3793	0.44
Latin America and Caribbean	..	7.55%	0.4308	3.25
South Asia	..	31.02%	0.4562	14.15
Sub-Saharan Africa	..	57.46%	0.5488	31.53
Countries	..			
Afghanistan	2015/2016	55.91%	0.4860	27.17
Albania	2017/2018	0.70%	0.3906	0.27
Algeria	2012/2013	2.10%	0.3881	0.82
Angola	2015/2016	51.10%	0.5527	28.24
Armenia	2015/2016	0.19%	0.3621	0.07
Bangladesh	2014	41.70%	0.4746	19.79
Barbados	2012	2.49%	0.3423	0.85
Belize	2015/2016	4.30%	0.3976	1.71
Benin	2017/2018	66.80%	0.5504	36.77
Bhutan	2010	37.34%	0.4683	17.49
Bolivia	2008	20.40%	0.4596	9.37
Bosnia and Herzegovina	2011/2012	2.19%	0.3793	0.83
Brazil	2015	3.84%	0.4255	1.63
Burkina Faso	2010	83.83%	0.6191	51.91
Burundi	2016/2017	74.25%	0.5430	40.32
Cambodia	2014	37.19%	0.4581	17.03
Cameroon	2014	45.33%	0.5354	24.27
Central African Republic	2010	79.36%	0.5858	46.49
Chad	2014/2015	85.67%	0.6226	53.34
China	2014	3.86%	0.4132	1.60
Colombia	2015/2016	4.85%	0.4056	1.97
Comoros	2012	37.26%	0.4851	18.08
Congo	2014/2015	24.27%	0.4602	11.17
Congo, DRC	2013/2014	74.05%	0.5254	38.90
Côte d'Ivoire	2016	46.07%	0.5120	23.59

(*continued*)

Table 3.4 (continued)

Cohort	*Year and Survey*	*Population in Multidimensional Poverty*		*MPI*
		H	*A*	
Dominican Republic	2014	3.88%	0.3893	1.51
Ecuador	2013/2014	4.49%	0.3999	1.80
Egypt	2014	5.16%	0.3761	1.94
El Salvador	2014	7.86%	0.4130	3.25
Eswatini	2014	19.21%	0.4230	8.13
Ethiopia	2016	83.50%	0.5854	48.88
Gabon	2012	14.85%	0.4431	6.58
Gambia	2013	55.24%	0.5174	28.58
Ghana	2014	30.07%	0.4584	13.79
Guatemala	2014/2015	28.88%	0.4623	13.35
Guinea	2016	61.86%	0.5431	33.60
Guinea-Bissau	2014	67.29%	0.5533	37.23
Guyana	2014	3.37%	0.4181	1.41
Haiti	2016/2017	41.27%	0.4836	19.96
Honduras	2011/2012	19.30%	0.4638	8.95
India	2015/2016	27.91%	0.4395	12.27
Indonesia	2012	7.01%	0.4033	2.83
Iraq	2018	8.64%	0.3786	3.27
Jamaica	2014	4.69%	0.3873	1.82
Jordan	2017/2018	0.43%	0.3539	0.15
Kazakhstan	2015	0.45%	0.3556	0.16
Kenya	2014	38.68%	0.4599	17.79
Kyrgyzstan	2014	2.28%	0.3632	0.83
Lao PDR	2017	23.07%	0.4695	10.83
Lesotho	2014	33.57%	0.4343	14.58
Liberia	2013	62.94%	0.5079	31.97
Libya	2014	2.00%	0.3712	0.74
Madagascar	2008/2009	77.76%	0.5820	45.26
Malawi	2015/2016	52.62%	0.4621	24.31
Maldives	2016/2017	0.77%	0.3438	0.27
Mali	2015	78.09%	0.5849	45.68
Mauritania	2015	50.57%	0.5155	26.06
Mexico	2016	6.30%	0.3922	2.47
Moldova	2012	0.94%	0.3745	0.35
Mongolia	2013	10.16%	0.4167	4.23
Montenegro	2013	0.38%	0.4570	0.17
Morocco	2011	18.57%	0.4568	8.48
Mozambique	2011	72.45%	0.5669	41.07
Myanmar	2015/2016	38.32%	0.4589	17.58

(*continued*)

Table 3.4 (continued)

Cohort	*Year and Survey*	*Population in Multidimensional Poverty*		*MPI*
		H	*A*	
Namibia	2013	38.00%	0.4512	17.14
Nepal	2016	33.99%	0.4362	14.83
Nicaragua	2011/2012	16.26%	0.4520	7.35
Niger	2012	90.47%	0.6523	59.01
Nigeria	2016/2017	51.43%	0.5661	29.12
North Macedonia	2011	2.53%	0.3774	0.96
Pakistan	2017/2018	38.33%	0.5172	19.82
Palestine	2014	0.96%	0.3754	0.36
Paraguay	2016	4.50%	0.4188	1.88
Peru	2012	12.66%	0.4161	5.27
Philippines	2017	5.80%	0.4184	2.42
Rwanda	2014/2015	54.42%	0.4753	25.87
Saint Lucia	2012	1.92%	0.3749	0.72
Sao Tome and Principe	2014	22.06%	0.4169	9.20
Senegal	2017	53.17%	0.5416	28.80
Serbia	2014	0.34%	0.4247	0.14
Sierra Leone	2017	57.93%	0.5122	29.67
South Africa	2016	6.26%	0.3978	2.49
South Sudan	2010	91.86%	0.6315	58.02
Sudan	2014	52.33%	0.5340	27.94
Suriname	2010	9.38%	0.4340	4.07
Syrian Arab Republic	2009	7.39%	0.3893	2.88
Tajikistan	2017	7.44%	0.3896	2.90
Tanzania	2015/2016	55.45%	0.4931	27.34
Thailand	2015/2016	0.79%	0.3910	0.31
Timor-Leste	2016	45.82%	0.4575	20.96
Togo	2013/2014	48.15%	0.5164	24.87
Trinidad and Tobago	2011	0.64%	0.3798	0.24
Tunisia	2011/2012	1.32%	0.3969	0.53
Turkmenistan	2015/2016	0.40%	0.3608	0.15
Uganda	2016	55.09%	0.4880	26.88
Ukraine	2012	0.24%	0.3448	0.08
Vanuatu	2007	38.76%	0.4486	17.39
Viet Nam	2013/2014	4.90%	0.3950	1.93
Yemen	2013	47.70%	0.5047	24.07
Zambia	2013/2014	53.24%	0.4908	26.13
Zimbabwe	2015	31.80%	0.4293	13.65

Source: UNDP and OPHI (2019)

References

Alkire, Sabina. 2009. The Human Development and Capability Approach. In *An Introduction to the Human Development and Capability Approach: Freedom and Agency*, ed. Séverine Deneulin and Lila Shahani. London, UK and Sterling, Virginia: Earthscan.

Alkire, Sabina, and James Foster. 2011. Counting and Multidimensional Poverty Measurement. *Journal of Public Economics* 95 (7–8): 476–487.

Alkire, Sabina, and Selim Jahan. 2018. *The New Global MPI 2018: Aligning with the Sustainable Development Goals.* HDRO Occasional Paper, United Nations Development Programme (UNDP).

Azpitarte, Francisco. 2012. Measuring Poverty Using Both Income and Wealth: A Cross-Country Comparison Between the US and Spain. *Review of Income and Wealth* 58 (1): 24–50.

Brucker, Debra L., Sophie Mitra, Navena Chaitoo, and Joseph Mauro. 2015. More Likely to Be Poor Whatever the Measure: Working-Age Persons with Disabilities in the United States. *Social Science Quarterly* 96 (1): 273–296.

Clark, David A. 2005. *The Capability Approach: Its Development, Critiques and Recent Advances.* GPRG Working Paper 32. Universities of Manchester and Oxford.

Dhongde, Shatakshee, and Robert Haveman. 2015. *Multi-Dimensional Poverty Index: An Application to the United States.* IRP Discussion Paper No. 1427–15.

Foster, James, Joel Greer, and Erik Thorbecke. 1984. A Class of Decomposable Poverty Measures. *Econometrica* 52 (3): 761–766.

Sen, Amartya K. 1980. Equality of What. In *The Tanner Lectures on Human Value*, ed. Sterling M. McMurrin. Salt Lake City: University of Utah Press.

U.S. Bureau of the Census/American Factfinder (U.S. Census). 2019. *American Community Survey (Annual Data, 2008–2018).* U.S. Census Bureau's American Community Survey Office. http://factfinder.census.gov.

United Nations Development Programme (UNDP) and Oxford Poverty and Human Development Initiative (OPHI). 2019. *Global Multidimensional Poverty Index 2019: Illuminating Inequalities.* United Nations Development Programme and Oxford Poverty and Human Development Initiative. Online. http://hdr.undp.org/sites/default/files/mpi_2019_publication.pdf. Accessed May 2020.

Weziak-Bialowolska, Dorota Maria, and Lewis Dijkstra. 2014. *Monitoring Multidimensional Poverty in the Regions of the European Union.* Science and Policy Report by the Joint Research Centre of the European Commission.

Whelan, Christopher T., Brian Nolan, and Bertrand Maitre. 2014. Multidimensional Poverty Measurement in Europe: An Application of the Adjusted Headcount Approach. *Journal of European Social Policy* 24 (2): 183–197.

White, Roger, and Thomas Bailleul. 2019. Multidimensional Poverty Across the Life Cycle: The United States as an Empirical Example, with Thomas Bailleul, in *Routledge International Handbook of Poverty*, Bent Greve (ed.), Oxfordshire, UK: Routledge.

White, Roger, and Stacy Yamasaki. 2017. Multidimensional Poverty Among the Native- and Foreign-born in the United States: Evidence from the 2010-2014 American Community Surveys. In *Measuring Multidimensional Poverty and Deprivation: Incidence and Determinants in Developed Countries*, ed. Roger White. New York, NY: Palgrave Macmillan.

PART II

America's Multidimensionally Poor

CHAPTER 4

A Profile of Multidimensional Poverty in America

Building on the material presented in the first part of this book—namely, the introduction to multidimensional poverty, the review of the related literature, and the details related to the construction of the Multidimensional Poverty Index (MPI)—we now begin a more deliberate discussion of multidimensional poverty measurement for the U.S. Using annual data from the 2008–2018 American Community Survey (ACS) Public Use Microdata Sample (PUMS) (U.S. Census 2019), we construct MPI values, headcount ratios, and average censored deprivation intensity values at the national level, and we consider the paths of these series over our reference period. To gain a more complete understanding of our topic, we focus on the incidence of deprivation at the dimension and indicator levels while also detailing the extent of deprivation based on the numbers of dimensions and indicators for which individuals are deprived. In addition to the categorization and summation of individuals who experience multidimensional poverty, we also report corresponding values for four segments of the population: those who are neither multidimensionally poor nor vulnerable to multidimensional poverty, those who are vulnerable to multidimensional poverty, those experiencing moderate multidimensional poverty, and those who suffer severe multidimensional poverty. Lastly, to consider the robustness of our primary measures, we explore several alternative constructions of the MPI and the associated incidence and intensity series and draw relevant comparisons.

R. White, *Multidimensional Poverty in America*,
https://doi.org/10.1007/978-3-030-45916-1_4

4.1 The Multidimensional Poverty Index, Headcount Ratio, and Average Deprivation Intensity Values

We begin our profile of multidimensional poverty in America by illustrating the paths of the MPI and its component series at the aggregate/national level during our reference period. These series are presented in Fig. 4.1. What may be most striking are the noticeable peaks in the series that occur during the initial portion of the period and the consistent declines that follow through 2018.[1] To more completely illustrate, Table 4.1 presents the annual values for the series that are depicted in Fig. 4.1. From the table, we see that each series reached its highest value in 2010. This timing corresponds with the Great Recession and the subsequent recovery. The recession began in December 2007 and continued until June 2009; however, the national unemployment rate did not reach its highest value during the period until September 2010. It is also noteworthy that the average deprivation intensity series (i.e., the average

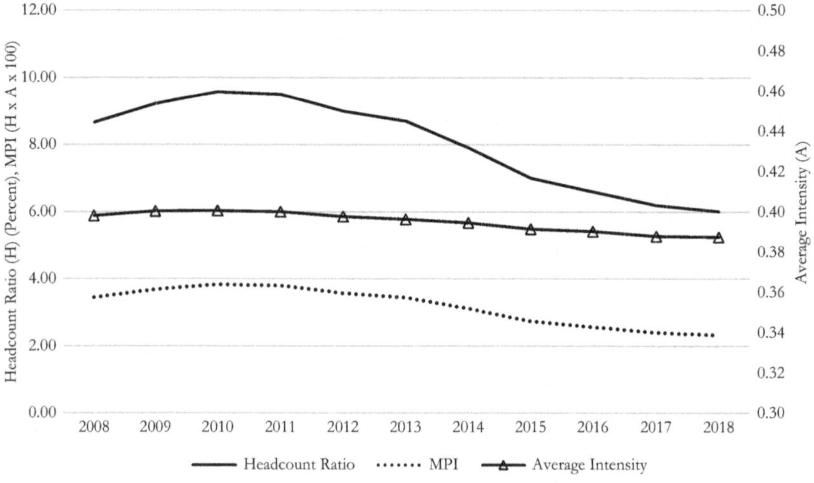

Fig. 4.1 Multidimensional Poverty Index, frequency, and intensity, 2008–2018

[1] Likewise, the Official Poverty Measure and the Supplemental Poverty Measure both decreased during this period (Fontenot et al. 2018; Meyer and Sullivan 2018).

Table 4.1 Multidimensional poverty index, frequency, and intensity, annual values, 2008–2018

Year/period	*MPI (H × A × 100)*	*Headcount ratio (H)*	*Average intensity (A)*
2008	3.4524	8.67%	0.3983
2009	3.6957	9.23%	0.4005
2010	3.8380	9.58%	0.4007
2011	3.8049	9.51%	0.4001
2012	3.5826	9.01%	0.3978
2013	3.4505	8.70%	0.3964
2014	3.1220	7.91%	0.3947
2015	2.7444	7.01%	0.3916
2016	2.5789	6.60%	0.3905
2017	2.4067	6.20%	0.3881
2018	2.3356	6.02%	0.3877
2008–2018	3.1715	8.01%	0.3958

Note: Author's illustration based on ACS data

censored deprivation score series) remains quite stable, somewhat horizontal, throughout the reference period. On the contrary, the headcount ratio exhibits considerable variation, thus influencing the path of the MPI series to a much greater degree than does the average deprivation intensity series.

From the values presented in Table 4.1, we can see that over the full reference period the value of the average deprivation intensity series is equal to 0.3958, with the series ranging from an annual high value of 0.4007 in 2010 to a low of 0.3877 in 2018. Although the series values do not change markedly over time, there is a pattern of consistent increases from 2008 through 2010 which is followed by consistent, albeit admittedly minor, annual decreases through 2018. By contrast, the variation in the headcount ratio is much more pronounced. The headcount ratio series reaches a maximum value of 9.58 percent in 2010 but declines substantially to barely more than 6 percent by 2018. Proportionally, the headcount ratio decreases by more than one-third from its peak value through the end of the period, while the average intensity series declines by only about three percent over the same period.

Largely a result of the observed variation in the headcount ratio and much lesser a consequence of the post-2010 decline in the average deprivation intensity series, the MPI series value decreases by nearly 40 percent from 3.84 in 2010 to 2.34 in 2018. To better interpret the meaning of such a change, recall from Chap. 3 that, in addition to being equal to the scaled product of the headcount ratio and the average deprivation intensity value among those categorized as being multidimensionally poor, the MPI is equal to the mean censored deprivation score across the entire population and that it represents the share of weighted deprivations experienced by those who are identified as multidimensionally poor divided by the maximum possible deprivations that could be experienced if all people were identified as multidimensionally poor and suffered deprivation in all indicators. Thus, we can interpret the change in the MPI value as indicative of a significant decrease in deprivation that was experienced at the aggregate/national level. We can also see that this decrease is largely due to a decline in multidimensional poverty incidence since the censored deprivation score largely remained unchanged during the reference period. Lastly, because throughout the period fewer than 10 percent of the population was multidimensionally poor in any particular year and because the headcount ratio decreased by nearly 40 percent from 2010 through 2018, we can see that the decrease in deprivation that is measured at the national level is concentrated among a relatively small subset of the population. For these individuals, the observed decrease in deprivation represents a significant improvement in well-being.

4.2 Dimensions and Indicators

To more completely examine the MPI, headcount ratio, and average deprivation intensity values, we turn our attention to the corresponding dimension and indicator series. Given the pronounced influence of changes in the headcount ratio series on the MPI relative to that of the average deprivation intensity series, we limit the focus of our discussion to the headcount ratios of the dimension and indicator series which we refer to as the deprivation frequencies. Figure 4.2 presents the path of the deprivation frequencies for each of the four dimensions that comprise the MPI, while Fig. 4.3 includes four graphs, one representing each dimension, that illustrate the deprivation frequency paths of the associated indicator values.[2]

Beginning at the dimension level of detail, as one may anticipate the Economic Security dimension is perhaps most indicative of the economic turmoil associated with the 2007–2009 recession and the subsequent

[2] The underlying values for all series presented in Figs. 4.2 and 4.3 are provided in the Appendix as Table 4.5.

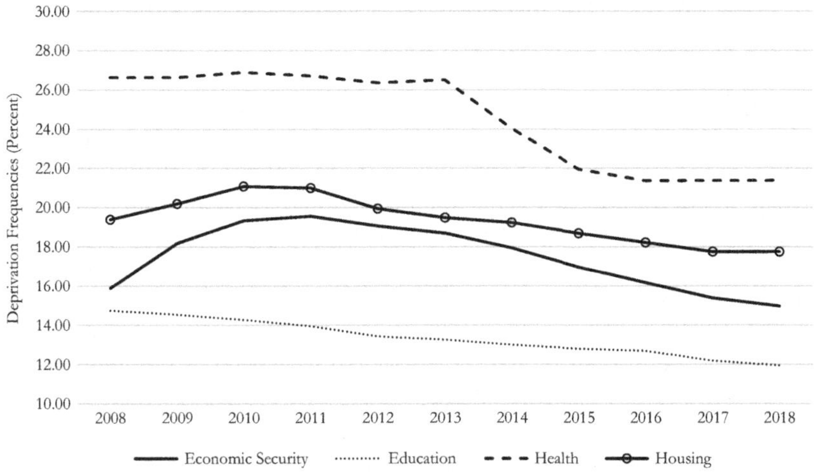

Fig. 4.2 Deprivation frequencies, by dimension, 2008–2018

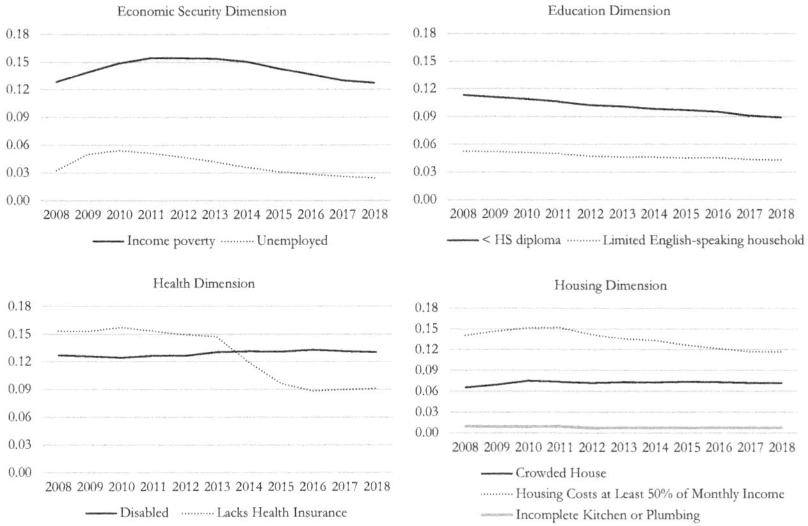

Fig. 4.3 Deprivation frequencies across indicators, grouped by dimension, 2008–2018

recovery. We see a stark increase in series values from 2008 through 2010, which is followed by a further increase in 2011 and then a consistent decline in values through 2018. A similar path, although less pronounced and without the minor uptick in 2011, is observed for the Housing dimension. This is not at all surprising given the strong correlation ($\rho = 0.3891$) between the Economic Security and Housing dimensions that we noted in Chap. 3. On the contrary, while the Education dimension exhibits a steady decrease, it is characterized by a slope that is rather shallow and quite steady. The path of the Education dimension does not exhibit variation of the extent observed for the paths of the other dimensions. Likewise, it is not characterized by strong inflection points. This most surely is a consequence of the indicators that are associated with each of the dimensions. Neither indicator is likely to change drastically from year to year; as a consequence, the series remains quite stable over time.

The path of the Health dimension is sufficiently distinct from the paths of the three other dimensions that it requires additional discussion. From 2008 through 2013, the Health dimension series remains nearly flat, ranging from a high value of 26.91 percent in 2010 to a low value of 26.38 percent observed two years later. During the final five years of our reference period, however, the series sharply declines to annual values that are only slightly greater than 21 percent. In fact, the Health dimension value for 2014 was 24.05 percent, a decrease of nearly 2.5 percentage points from the 26.52 percent value observed in the prior year. The value declines by more than two additional percentage points to 21.97 percent in 2015 before successive years during which the value was equal to 21.38 percent and then a near-identical value of 21.4 percent followed in 2018. On the first impression, it appears that the path of the Health dimension may have been significantly altered by the Affordable Care Act (ACA). Specifically, the timing of the change in deprivation frequency value for this dimension corresponds with the Medicaid expansion that occurred under the ACA and which was effective as of January 1, 2014. While employing difference techniques to identify multidimensional deprivation and/or examining different data, Dhongde and Haveman (2019) and Mitra and Brucker (2019) both find that ACA implementation coincided with a decrease in multidimensional poverty incidence. Mitra and Brucker also attribute an increase in deprivation in the Health dimension that begins in 2017 to a higher deprivation frequency value for the health insurance indicator relative to preceding years.

In Chap. 8, we examine the relationship between multidimensional poverty and the expansion of Medicaid due to the ACA in considerable detail. Here, we can further explore the relationship, in a descriptive sense, by looking at the paths of the deprivation frequencies for the two indicators that comprise the Health dimension. The first indicator identifies those individuals who suffer deprivation due to being disabled. The second indicator, which is directly relevant for a discussion of Medicaid expansion and the ACA, identifies individuals as deprived if they lack health insurance. In the lower-left panel of Fig. 4.3, we see the paths of the indicators associated with the Health dimension. First, the deprivation frequency of the disabled indicator is nearly constant. This series varies in value by less than one percentage point over the reference period, from a low value of 12.45 percent in 2010 to a high of 13.3 percent in 2016. The deprivation frequency values for the health insurance indicator also remain stable over the period from 2008 through 2013, ranging from a low of 14.76 percent in 2013 to 15.77 percent in 2010. In 2014, however, as the majority of U.S. states expanded Medicaid coverage, the deprivation frequency value declined sharply to 11.97 percent before falling further to range between 8.87 percent and 9.7 percent during the 2015–2018 period. As noted, the path of the Health dimension is the most striking of the dimension-specific series illustrated in Fig. 4.2. From the paths depicted in Fig. 4.3 and the corresponding values presented in the chapter Appendix as Table 4.5, we see that the path of the Health dimension is closely linked to changes in deprivation frequency values of the health insurance indicator.

The paths of the remaining deprivation frequencies that are presented in Fig. 4.3 may appear rather pedestrian, especially when compared to the path of the health insurance indicator; however, interesting patterns are found. For example, both indicators associated with the Economic Security dimension—that is, the unemployed and income poverty indicators—follow paths that somewhat resemble inverted U-shapes. As may be expected, given the connection to economic welfare, the indicator which identifies deprivation due to housing costs being equal to or greater than 50 percent of income follows a path similar to those observed for the income poverty and unemployment indicators. The paths of the deprivation frequency values for the two remaining indicators of the Housing dimension—that which identifies individuals who live in crowded housing units and that which indicates if the individual lives in a household that lacks complete kitchen and/or plumbing facilities—are nearly horizontal and relatively low in value throughout the reference period. By contrast, both indicators that comprise the Education dimension follow steady downward-sloping paths.

Notably, beyond the increases that are observed during the initial years of our reference period, we do not see marked increases in the deprivation frequency values of any indicator or dimension over the period. In fact, the 2018 value of each dimension is lower than the corresponding 2008 value. The Health dimension decreased the most, declining 5.25 percentage points (i.e., 19.7 percent) from 26.65 percent to 21.4 percent. The Education dimension also decreased considerably from 14.76 percent in 2008 to 11.96 percent in 2018, a decrease of 2.79 percentage points (i.e., 18.9 percent). The indicators that experienced the largest decreases in deprivation frequencies are the health insurance indicator (a 6.23 percentage point decline (40.6 percent)), the lack of a high school diploma indicator (2.43 percentage points (21.4 percent)), and the indicator that identifies those individuals who have housing costs equal to or above one-half of their household income (2.39 percentage points (16.9 percent)). Only two indicator values increased during the period. The disabled indicator increased by 0.34 percentage points from 12.7 percent to 13.04 percent (2.7 percent), and the indicator that identifies individuals who live in crowded housing units increased by 0.65 percentage points (9.8 percent) from 6.57 percent to 7.22 percent.

While understanding the relationships between each dimension and indicator and the MPI is important and informative, a different perspective can be obtained by examining the estimated numbers of individuals and the corresponding percentages of the population who suffered deprivation across different numbers of dimensions and indicators. Table 4.2 presents values for the full 2008–2018 period along with annual average values. In Table 4.3, we provide year-specific percentages of the population that experienced deprivation by numbers of dimensions and indicators.

Beginning with the values that are presented in Table 4.2, we see that the majority of the population (54 percent) were fortunate to have not suffered deprivation in any indicator or dimension. This equates, based on the ACS population weights, to an estimated 170.8 million individuals in the average year during our reference period. Another 79.5 million individuals (25.2 percent of the population), again during the average year, suffered deprivation in only a single dimension.[3] Since each dimension carries a weight of 25 percent and the threshold for categorization as multidimensionally poor is set equal to 0.3333, we know that these 250.3 million individuals—nearly four in five members of the population—did not experience multidimensional poverty in the typical year during our

[3] Note that an individual is determined to suffer deprivation in a dimension if they suffer deprivation in any indicator associated with that dimension. It is not necessary to meet any threshold other than having a non-zero deprivation score at the dimension level to be considered deprived in that dimension.

Table 4.2 Number of persons deprived by N dimensions and N indicators, 2008–2018

	2008–2018	*Average year*	*% of Population*	*Cummulative %*
	N	*N*		
Deprived in...				
0 dimensions	1,879,321,776	170,847,434	54.03%	54.03%
1 dimension	874,860,564	79,532,779	25.15%	79.18%
2 dimensions	494,394,939	44,944,994	14.21%	93.39%
3 dimensions	186,921,201	16,992,836	5.37%	98.77%
4 dimensions	42,842,311	3,894,756	1.23%	100.00%
Deprived in...				
0 indicators	1,879,321,776	170,847,434	54.03%	54.03%
1 indicator	840,260,796	76,387,345	24.16%	78.19%
2 indicators	454,569,313	41,324,483	13.07%	91.25%
3 indicators	206,488,135	18,771,649	5.94%	97.19%
4 indicators	73,925,828	6,720,530	2.13%	99.32%
5 indicators	19,646,521	1,786,047	0.56%	99.88%
6 indicators	3,742,705	340,246	0.11%	99.99%
7 indicators	373,558	33,960	0.01%	100.00%
8 indicators	11,847	1077	0.00%	100.00%
9 indicators	111	10	0.00%	100.00%

Values generated using 34,291,600 ACS observations and corresponding population weights

reference period. However, nearly 45 million individuals (14.2 percent) were categorized as having suffered deprivation in exactly two dimensions while another 17 million individuals (5.4 percent) suffered deprivation in three dimensions. Finally, in the typical year, a small portion of the population (i.e., only an estimated 3.9 million individuals (1.2 percent)) were deprived in all four dimensions.

When considering the estimated number of deprived individuals by the number of indicators in which they are deprived, we see that very few individuals (only 0.68 percent of the population) suffered deprivation in five or more indicators. This equates to an estimated 2.16 million individuals in the typical year, all of whom would be considered as suffering multidimensional poverty given the weights that correspond with the indicators and the cut-off threshold for being categorized as multidimensionally poor.[4]

[4] Specifically, the minimum deprivation score that is possible for an individual who is deprived in five indicators is 0.50. This value would apply to an individual who is deprived in all three Housing dimension indicators and two indicators from any of the other three dimensions. Thus, such an individual is not only multidimensionally poor, they are experiencing severe multidimensional poverty.

Table 4.3 Percent of population deprived by N dimensions and N indicators, annual values, 2008–2018

	2008	*2009*	*2010*	*2011*	*2012*	*2013*	*2014*	*2015*	*2016*	*2017*	*2018*
Population	304,059,744	307,006,519	309,349,699	311,591,921	313,913,991	316,128,868	318,857,073	321,418,812	323,127,538	325,719,155	327,167,448
Percent deprived in…											
0 dimensions	53.39%	52.25%	51.31%	51.47%	52.47%	52.54%	54.20%	55.62%	56.41%	57.01%	57.20%
1 dimension	25.12%	25.08%	25.22%	25.20%	25.01%	25.41%	25.07%	25.05%	25.04%	25.18%	25.27%
2 dimensions	14.32%	15.02%	15.55%	15.48%	15.11%	14.88%	14.22%	13.58%	13.13%	12.72%	12.57%
3 dimensions	5.74%	6.12%	6.35%	6.30%	6.00%	5.84%	5.29%	4.75%	4.49%	4.25%	4.15%
4 dimensions	1.43%	1.53%	1.56%	1.55%	1.41%	1.33%	1.22%	1.00%	0.93%	0.84%	0.81%
Percent deprived in…											
0 indicators	53.39%	52.25%	51.31%	51.47%	52.47%	52.54%	54.20%	55.62%	56.41%	57.01%	57.20%
1 indicator	24.06%	24.07%	24.22%	24.16%	24.01%	24.41%	24.08%	24.08%	24.10%	24.22%	24.32%
2 indicators	13.27%	13.75%	14.10%	14.06%	13.74%	13.59%	13.04%	12.54%	12.18%	11.90%	11.77%
3 indicators	6.17%	6.51%	6.79%	6.77%	6.53%	6.39%	5.95%	5.43%	5.15%	4.93%	4.82%
4 indicators	2.32%	2.53%	2.64%	2.61%	2.45%	2.33%	2.08%	1.80%	1.69%	1.54%	1.50%
5 indicators	0.65%	0.72%	0.76%	0.75%	0.66%	0.63%	0.55%	0.45%	0.40%	0.35%	0.33%
6 indicators	0.13%	0.16%	0.16%	0.16%	0.13%	0.11%	0.10%	0.07%	0.07%	0.05%	0.05%
7 indicators	0.01%	0.02%	0.02%	0.02%	0.01%	0.01%	0.01%	0.01%	0.00%	0.00%	0.00%
8 indicators	0.00%	0.00%	0.00%	0.00%	0.00%	0.00%	0.00%	0.00%	0.00%	0.00%	0.00%
9 indicators	0.00%	0.00%	0.00%	0.00%	0.00%	0.00%	0.00%	0.00%	0.00%	0.00%	0.00%

Values generated using 34,291,600 ACS observations and corresponding population weights

The large majority of individuals in the typical year (288.6 million individuals or 91.25 percent of the population) suffered deprivation in two or fewer indicators. Again, given the weights assigned to the indicators, an individual who is deprived in two or fewer indicators would have, at a maximum, a deprivation score of 0.25 and, thus, would not be categorized as multidimensionally poor. The remaining 8.07 percent of the population were deprived in either three or four indicators. This equates to just fewer than 25.5 million individuals. From the headcount ratio value for the full 2008–2018 period that is presented in Table 4.1 (i.e., 8.01 percent), we know that an estimated 25,328,644 individuals lived in multidimensional poverty during the typical year in our reference period. Accounting also for the individuals who suffered deprivation in five or more indicators, we have that nearly all of those who experienced deprivation in three or four indicators were categorized as multidimensionally poor (i.e., 7.33 percent of the 8.07 percent of the total population, or 23.1 million individuals). From these values, we see that although the percentage of the population that suffers multidimensional poverty may appear small, when expressed in more concrete terms such as the number of multidimensionally poor individuals, it is quite a large and significant number.

Table 4.3 identifies the portion of the population for each year during our reference period who were deprived. Again, the values are organized based on the number of dimensions and indicators in which deprivation is observed. Given the decrease in the headcount ratio over the period and, accordingly, the decline in the MPI value, it is not at all surprising to see the percentage of individuals who did not suffer deprivation in any dimension increase by 3.8 percentage points over the period. Considering the values for the four dimensions, we see that this increase is almost entirely accounted for by decreases in the percentages of individuals who suffered deprivation in either two dimensions (a decrease of 1.75 percentage points) or three dimensions (a decline of 1.59 percentage points). Looking to the indicator series for additional information, we see the increase is largely attributable to decreases in the percentages of individuals who suffered deprivation in two indicators (a decrease of 1.49 percentage points), three dimensions (a 1.35 percentage point decline), or four indicators (a decline of 0.82 percentage points over the reference period.

4.3 Alternative Constructions of the MPI

To this point, when calculating the MPI series and its associated values, we have relied solely on the AF method. While the AF method is widely accepted and commonly used when examining developing economies, the somewhat limited literature on multidimensional poverty in developed economies involves the use of a somewhat uniform set of dimensions and indicators. This raises the question of whether MPI values that are calculated for developed economies are robust.

To consider the robustness of our primary methodology, we employ three alternative constructions to calculate the MPI and related values for the U.S. and then compare each to the methodology that we have employed thus far. First, only a small percentage of households lack complete kitchen or plumbing facilities. The inclusion of this indicator, all else equal, results in lower weights being assigned to other indicators within the same dimension and, thus, may result in the classification of significantly fewer individuals as living in multidimensional poverty. Accordingly, using our primary methodology (i.e., the stated weighting process and the threshold for classification as multidimensionally poor) we calculate the MPI value, the headcount ratio, and the average deprivation intensity value with this variable excluded. A second related issue is that we may see differences in results—and, again, a possible downward bias in values—due to the assignment of different weights to indicators based solely on the number of indicators that fall within a given dimension.[5] To consider such a possibility, we calculate the MPI, the headcount ratio, and the average deprivation intensity values under a scenario where no weights are assigned to individual indicators (or, if one prefers, no variation in weights exists across indicators) and an individual is categorized as suffering multidimensional poverty if they are deprived in three or more indicators.[6] Third, because the inclusion of the limited English-speaking household indicator may inaccurately identify linguistic isolation, especially in locales where English is not the predominant language or another language is also frequently used, we exclude this indicator and calculate the MPI, headcount ratio, and average deprivation intensity values using our primary methodology. Results are presented in Panel A of Table 4.4.

[5] A criticism of assigning different weights to indicators based on the total number of indicators within the corresponding dimension is that such unevenness in weights treats some deprivations as more (or less) impactful than other deprivations.

[6] By setting the threshold for classification at three indicators we maintain the cut-off of one-third that we employ with our primary method.

Table 4.4 Robustness checks, 2008–2018

	Robustness Measures			
	Primary Measure	*Incomplete Kitchen or Plumbing Indicator Removed*	*Primary Measure Without Weights*	*Limited English-speaking Household Indicator Removed*
	(a)	*(b)*	*(c)*	*(d)*
Panel A: Multidimensional Poverty Index, Headcount Ratio, and Average Intensity				
Headcount Ratio (H)	0.0801	0.0855	0.1045	0.0875
Average Intensity (A)	0.3958	0.4253	0.4201	0.3794
MPI	3.1715	3.6377	4.3898	3.3176
Panel B: Correlation Matrix, Deprivation Scores				
(a)	1.0000			
(b)	0.9921	1.0000		
(c)	0.9564	0.9427	1.0000	
(d)	0.9936	0.9966	0.9435	1.0000
Panel C: Comparison of Multidimensional Poverty Categorizations				
N obs. MDP=0	31,923,760	31,785,510	30,944,937	31,721,673
N obs. MDP=1	2,367,840	2,506,090	3,346,663	2,569,927
% Match		99.43%	95.87%	99.41%

Values generated using 34,291,600 ACS observations and corresponding population weights

We see that the average deprivation intensity values are somewhat dissimilar across measures, ranging in value from 0.3794 to 0.4253, and fall both above and below the average deprivation intensity value (0.3958) that is obtained when we calculate our primary measure. However, greater proportional variation is found across values for the headcount ratio. This may be expected given the changes made to produce the robustness measures. The primary headcount ratio has a value of 8.01 percent. Across robustness measures, the headcount ratio value ranges from 8.55 percent to as much as 10.45 percent. Coinciding mainly with the observed differences in headcount ratios, the MPI values vary from 3.32, which is nearly identical to the primary value of 3.17, to a high value of 4.39. Even so, across all robustness checks, the results are somewhat consistent and, to a degree, are comparable in value. Additionally, as our primary measure has a lower headcount ratio and MPI value as compared to the alternative constructions, we can say that the primary measure produces more conservative estimates of multidimensional poverty.

An intermediate step that is performed when constructing the values that are reported in Panel A is the calculation of deprivation scores for each individual in our sample. As an additional means of comparison across alternative constructions, in Panel B, we present the correlation coefficients for all four deprivation score series. Of greatest interest for the determination of robustness are the values presented in column (a). Here, we see very strong positive pairwise correlation values—ranging from 0.9564 to 0.9936—for the three robustness check measures. In other words, the deprivation score series produced when completing the robustness checks are quite similar to the series produced when we use our primary methodology. While this finding may be anticipated based on the mean average deprivation intensity values that are presented in Panel A, the very high positive correlation coefficient values indicate that the similarities between the primary series and the robustness checks extend beyond similar mean values.

Finally, the values presented in Panel C indicate differences across our alternative constructions in terms of the number of observations that would be categorized as being multidimensionally poor. We have checked to see what percentage of observations have matching categorizations with that of our primary calculation method, finding that the removal of the incomplete kitchen and/or plumbing facilities indicator results in an increase of 138,250 in the number of individuals categorized as being multidimensionally poor during our 11-year reference period; however, 99.4 percent of the classifications in this scenario match those from our primary measure. When we abandon indicator weights and identify observations as multidimensionally poor if they are categorized as suffering deprivation in three or more indicators, we find that 95.9 percent of the classifications match those of our primary measure and that the number of individuals categorized as being multidimensionally poor rises by 978,823. Lastly, when the limited English-speaking ability indicator is removed from the calculation, we find that 99.4 percent of the classifications match those from our primary measure and that the estimated number of individuals who are multidimensionally poor rises by 202,087.

Based on the values presented in Table 4.4 and especially those presented in Panel C of the table, a strong case can be made for the robustness of our primary measure. As we proceed, we rely on our primary methodology but we do so with the understanding that no method is perfect. Knowing, however, that the alternative calculations we have presented do not deviate greatly in terms of classifying individuals as multidimensionally poor from those of our primary measure adds credence and support for our choice of methodology and our set of indicators. In fact, the similarities in values that are presented in the table, along with the intuitive justifications for the choice of indicators and use of dimension-linked indicator weights, strongly suggest that the choice of indicators is subject to data availability and what researchers believe best represents deprivation. While differences in MPI calculation—stemming from the choice of weights or the indicators that are employed—runs counter to the promotion of uniformity in measurement across studies, it does allow for the consideration of alternative/additional forms of deprivation. This, in turn, suggests the need for robustness checks and reporting to ensure that variation in methodologies do not produce major differences in results.

4.4 Summary

Beginning at the national level of detail, our examination of ACS data for the years 2008–2018 has revealed a number of interesting results and insights. Application of the AF method to our data indicates that 8.01 percent of U.S. residents lived in multidimensional poverty during our reference period. The pattern of multidimensional poverty incidence varied considerably while that of multidimensional poverty intensity remained largely constant over time. We also identified interesting variation in the deprivation frequency values of our dimension and indicator series, with the Health dimension and the health insurance indicators exhibiting what may be the most interesting time paths. We also observe that a majority of U.S. residents were not deprived in any indicator or dimension. Lastly, considering several alternative construction methods for our multidimensional poverty measures, we find values that are similar to what is obtained when we employ our primary measurement method.

In the following two chapters, we continue to document and detail multidimensional poverty in America. Specifically, in Chap. 5 we consider variation across geographic units at the sub-national level and in Chap. 6 we examine variation across several socio-demographic cohorts.

Appendix

Table 4.5 Deprivation frequencies by dimension and indicator, annual and aggregate values, 2008–2018

	2008	*2009*	*2010*	*2011*	*2012*	*2013*	*2014*	*2015*	*2016*	*2017*	*2018*	*2008–2018*
Economic Security	15.89%	18.20%	19.34%	19.57%	19.07%	18.71%	17.96%	16.98%	16.17%	15.39%	14.98%	17.46%
Suffers Income Poverty	12.84%	13.92%	14.90%	15.47%	15.45%	15.40%	15.07%	14.34%	13.68%	13.02%	12.73%	14.25%
Is Unemployed	3.28%	5.04%	5.45%	5.15%	4.72%	4.23%	3.63%	3.15%	2.88%	2.65%	2.48%	3.86%
Education	14.76%	14.55%	14.30%	13.97%	13.45%	13.27%	13.01%	12.82%	12.70%	12.20%	11.96%	13.34%
Lacks High School Diploma	11.35%	11.13%	10.92%	10.64%	10.26%	10.14%	9.86%	9.73%	9.55%	9.13%	8.93%	10.13%
Lives in a Limited English-speaking Household	5.28%	5.24%	5.14%	5.02%	4.76%	4.67%	4.68%	4.56%	4.60%	4.41%	4.34%	4.78%
Health	26.65%	26.65%	26.91%	26.72%	26.38%	26.52%	24.05%	21.97%	21.38%	21.38%	21.40%	24.50%
Is Disabled	12.70%	12.59%	12.45%	12.65%	12.66%	13.06%	13.13%	13.10%	13.30%	13.15%	13.04%	12.90%
Lacks Health Insurance	15.37%	15.36%	15.77%	15.37%	14.99%	14.76%	11.97%	9.70%	8.87%	9.02%	9.14%	12.70%
Housing	19.39%	20.21%	21.09%	21.00%	19.96%	19.49%	19.24%	18.70%	18.24%	17.76%	17.77%	19.33%
Incomplete Kitchen or Plumbing	0.96%	0.88%	0.90%	0.93%	0.70%	0.74%	0.71%	0.74%	0.72%	0.72%	0.71%	0.79%
Housing Costs at Least 50% of Monthly Income	14.13%	14.75%	15.21%	15.27%	14.24%	13.61%	13.37%	12.66%	12.17%	11.73%	11.74%	13.51%
Lives in a Crowded House	6.57%	6.97%	7.52%	7.38%	7.24%	7.34%	7.32%	7.41%	7.33%	7.23%	7.22%	7.23%

Values generated using 34,291,600 ACS observations and corresponding population weights

References

Dhongde, Shatakshee, and Robert Haveman. 2019. *A Decade-long View of Multidimensional Poverty in the United States.* IRP Discussion Paper No. 1440-19.

Fontenot, Kayla, Jessica Semega, and Melissa Kollar. 2018. *Income and Poverty in the United States: 2017.* Washington, DC: U.S. Census Bureau.

Meyer, Bruce D., and James X. Sullivan. 2018. *Annual Report on U.S. Consumption Poverty: 2017.* Chicago: University of Chicago.

Mitra, Sophie, and Debra Brucker. 2019. Monitoring Multidimensional Poverty in the United States. *Economics Bulletin* 39 (2): 1272–1293.

U.S. Bureau of the Census/American Factfinder (U.S. Census). 2019. *American Community Survey (Annual Data, 2008–2018).* U.S. Census Bureau's American Community Survey Office. http://factfinder.census.gov.

CHAPTER 5

Variation in Multidimensional Poverty Across Geographic Locales

An insight from the previous chapter that is well worth stressing here is that most people do not experience multidimensional poverty. The incidence rate (i.e., the headcount ratio) during the typical year in our 2008–2018 reference period is only 8.01 percent; this equates to roughly one in every dozen or so U.S. residents. Similarly, again in the typical year, more than one-half of all individuals (54 percent) did not experience deprivation in any of the nine indicators that we use to measure multidimensional poverty, and roughly another quarter (24.2 percent) of the U.S. population only experienced deprivation in terms of a single indicator. Put simply, if you were to randomly select an individual from the U.S. population, there is a high likelihood that the individual would not be multidimensionally poor, and the odds are that the individual would not be deprived in any of the indicators that we consider. Even so, we estimate that more than 25.3 million U.S. residents were multidimensionally poor during the typical year in our reference period. This is not, by any means, a small or an inconsequential number. In fact, it is such a large number that the relative infrequence of deprivation suggests a need for a sub-national accounting of deprivation as it may better identify the multidimensionally poor population of the U.S.

Given the abundance of available data, we are fortunate in being able to accomplish much more than a national-level examination of our topic. The volume of data affords opportunities to work at increasingly finer levels of detail. As a result, we can explore variation in multidimensional

R. White, *Multidimensional Poverty in America*,
https://doi.org/10.1007/978-3-030-45916-1_5

poverty across time periods and across geographic and/or socio-demographic cohorts. This ability to improve our understanding of multidimensional poverty is sufficient reason to continue our analysis; however, by providing a more detailed documentation of our topic, we can produce useful background information and important foundational knowledge that motivates the work that is presented in later chapters. Along the same lines, the information that we provide in this chapter, as well as in the preceding chapter and the subsequent chapters, serves as a bridge from the material presented at the outset to the examples of multidimensional analysis that we later present.

Throughout this chapter, we continue our examination of data from the 2008–2018 American Community Survey (ACS) Public Use Microdata Sample (PUMS) (U.S. Census 2019). We begin with an exploration of possible variation in the Multidimensional Poverty Index (MPI) and its associated measures across geographic regions, divisions, and states. We then continue with our theme of increasing specificity by focusing our efforts on Public Use Microdata Areas (PUMAs).[1] Following the geographic delineations that are provided by the U.S. Census Bureau, the U.S. is divided into four regions—the Northeast, Midwest, South, and West. Within these regions, there are nine divisions. The divisions consist of the 50 states and the District of Columbia, and, during the 2012–2018 portion of our reference period, the states and Washington, DC, are comprised of 2351 2010 census-based PUMAs.[2]

This chapter is structured as follows. As noted, we begin by documenting variation in MPI values and related measures at the region, division, and state levels. This provides opportunities to identify the extent of multidimensional poverty and to consider variation across relatively large geographic units. The remainder of the chapter is then focused on multidimensional poverty incidence and intensity, and corresponding variation, at the PUMA level of detail. This general pattern of working from the aggregate/national level of detail to the examination of regions, divisions, states, and then PUMAs is continued in the following chapter, where we focus on potential variation across individual characteristics (i.e.,

[1] PUMAs are state-specific decennial census-based statistical geographic areas. Generally, each PUMA has a population of at least 100,000 persons but not more than 200,000 persons. PUMAs are aggregated from census tracts and approximate Community Districts (or combinations of Community Districts).

[2] For all geographic areas other than PUMAs, we examine the 2008–2018 period; however, due to changes in the geographic boundaries of PUMAs following the 2010 decennial census, our examination of PUMAs is limited to the period from 2012 through 2018.

by age, gender, nativity, race, ethnicity, educational attainment, etc.). Here, at the outset, we can state unequivocally that considerable variation is observed across geographic levels in terms of headcount ratios, average deprivation intensity values (i.e., average censored deprivation scores), MPI values, and average (uncensored) deprivation scores. Further, we are able to identify the forms of deprivation (i.e., dimensions and indicators) that contribute to a higher (or lower) incidence and/or intensity of deprivation at each geographic level and again see significant variation across dimension- and indicator-level deprivation frequency values.

5.1 Examining Regions, Divisions, and States

Evaluating the data for our full 2008–2018 reference period, we identify clear and pronounced commonalities and differences across the four regions in both the incidence and the intensity of multidimensional poverty. Specifically, the values for the Northeast and Midwest regions are considerably different from the values observed for the South and West regions. Looking first to the most basic, general measure of deprivation—the average uncensored deprivation scores (i.e., the average deprivation score values across all observations in our sample)—we see that the values of the Northeast and the Midwest regions are quite similar, being equal to 0.0749 and 0.0720, respectively. While the average scores for the South (0.0906) and the West (0.0944) are also similar, they also are significantly higher. This pattern, or ordering, of values is also observed when we look at the average deprivation intensity values (i.e., the censored deprivation scores). Here, we see that the values for the Northeast (0.3914) and the Midwest (0.3895) are again comparable and are lower, while the corresponding values for the South (0.3972) and the West (0.3997) regions are again similar and considerably higher.

Even more noteworthy differences are found when comparing headcount ratio values across the regions, where we see the same ordering that is observed for the average uncensored deprivation scores and the average deprivation intensity values. More specifically, the Midwest region has the lowest headcount ratio value at 6.15 percent, and the value for the Northeast region, 6.87 percent, is quite similar. The headcount ratio for the South region, however, is about two percentage points higher at 8.76 percent, and the headcount ratio value for the West region is yet higher still at 9.35 percent. Given the higher average deprivation intensity and headcount ratio values, it follows that the MPI values for the South and the West regions, being equal to 3.48 and 3.74, respectively, are much higher than the corresponding values for the Northeast and Midwest regions (i.e., 2.69 and 2.40, respectively). We present these values in Fig. 5.1 to further illustrate the variation across regions.

While the variation in percentage values may appear neither here nor there, when considered in terms of the numbers of individuals who experience deprivation the differences in values becomes much more meaningful. A few simple calculations help to illustrate the practical significance of the variation that is reported across the four regions. Looking to the regions with the lowest and highest MPI values, we see that, at 6.15 percent, the Midwest region has the lowest headcount ratio while the West region has the highest value at 9.35 percent. Applying these rates to the mid-2018 population estimates (U.S. Census 2020) for the corresponding regions, we estimate that 4.2 million individuals in the Midwest region suffered multidimensional poverty in 2018 while 7.3 million individuals

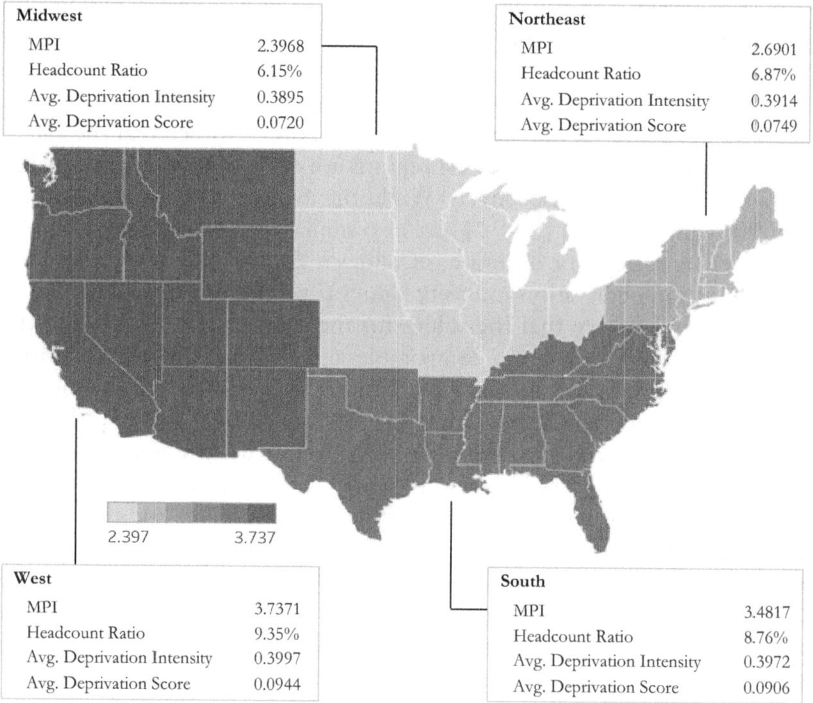

Fig. 5.1 MPI values by region, 2008–2018. Not shown: Alaska and Hawaii. Both states are part of the West region

were multidimensionally poor in the West region. Comparison of these values simply provides the difference in estimated numbers across the two regions. If instead we apply the headcount ratio for the West region to the Midwest population, we estimate that 6.4 million individuals in the Midwest would live in multidimensional poverty. Similarly, application of the headcount ratio for the Midwest region to the West region results in an estimate of 4.8 million individuals being identified as multidimensionally poor. The differences between these values and the estimates obtained when factoring the observed headcount ratios by the corresponding regions' population estimates are 2.2 million fewer individuals being identified as multidimensionally poor in the Midwest region relative to a scenario in which the headcount ratio for both the West region and the Midwest region equal 9.35 percent (i.e., the West region headcount ratio value) and 2.5 more individuals being categorized as multidimensionally poor in the West region relative to the scenario in which the West and Midwest regions have identical headcount ratios that are equal to 6.15 percent (i.e., the Midwest region headcount ratio value).

To further explore the differences in deprivation across regions, we can look to the dimension-level deprivation frequency values. Considering the forms of deprivation that are most-commonly (or, alternatively, least-frequently) experienced provides a more nuanced understanding of deprivation at the region level. A review of the frequency values—defined as the percentage of the population that is identified as suffering deprivation in one or more of the indicators that correspond to a given dimension—results in several interesting findings. Much like the observed cleavage in MPI values, with the exception of the Housing dimension, the South and West regions have the two highest values for each of the four dimensions while the Northeast and Midwest regions have the two lowest values. The Midwest region has the lowest headcount ratio and average deprivation intensity value. It also has the lowest deprivation frequency values for the Education dimension (10.2 percent) and the Housing dimension (15 percent). The Midwest also has the second lowest values for the Economic Security dimension (16.5 percent) and the Health dimension (22 percent). Similarly, the Northeast region has the lowest deprivation frequency values for the Economic Security and Health dimensions (15.7 percent and 20.6 percent, respectively). The Northeast region also has the second lowest value for the Education dimension (12.7 percent) and has the third lowest (i.e., second highest) value for the Housing dimension (19.2 percent). The South region, by contrast, has the third highest (i.e., second lowest) deprivation frequency value for the Housing dimension, the second highest value for the Education dimension (14.1 percent), and the highest values for the Economic Security dimension (18.6 percent) and the Health dimension (28.1 percent). Finally, the West region, which has the highest headcount ratio and average deprivation intensity values, also has the highest values for the Education dimension (15.4 percent) and the Housing dimension (25.6 percent) and the second highest values for the Economic Security dimension (17.8 percent) and the Health dimension (24 percent).

Among the four regions, the West has the highest average uncensored deprivation score, the highest average deprivation intensity value, and the highest headcount ratio. Thus, as noted, the West region has a higher MPI value than any other region. The West region also consists of two divisions—the Mountain division and the Pacific division. Figure 5.2 includes summary values for these and all other divisions. The values presented in the figure reveal clear differences between the Mountain and Pacific divisions. Similar to the values observed for the West region relative to all other regions, the Pacific division has higher values relative to the Mountain division for the average uncensored deprivation score, the average deprivation intensity, and the headcount ratio. Thus, the Pacific division has a higher MPI value than the Mountain division. In fact, the Pacific division is an outlier of sorts as it has the highest MPI value, and the highest values for all other series presented in the figure, among all divisions in the country.

As we see when comparing MPI and related values across regions, when we compare across divisions we see a similar degree of variation. Just as the Pacific division differs from the remainder of the country in its relatively higher values for the MPI and the associated measures, the New England division and the West North Central division differ from the remaining divisions due to their values being much lower. Similar to the relatively higher values of the West region being influenced by the Pacific division, the lower values for the New England and West North Central divisions contribute to the low values that are observed for the Northeast and Midwest regions, respectively. More specifically, the differences between values for the New England division and the Middle Atlantic division, which together comprise the Northeast region, are quite large. In fact, driven largely by variation across divisions in headcount ratio values, the MPI value for the Middle Atlantic division (3.0313) is closer to the MPI values of the South Atlantic (3.2494), East South Central (3.1020), and East North Central (2.5446) divisions than it is to the value of the New England division (2.0178). Likewise, the MPI value of the East North Central division is nearly the same difference from the MPI value of the Middle Atlantic division (i.e., a difference of 0.4867) as it is from the MPI

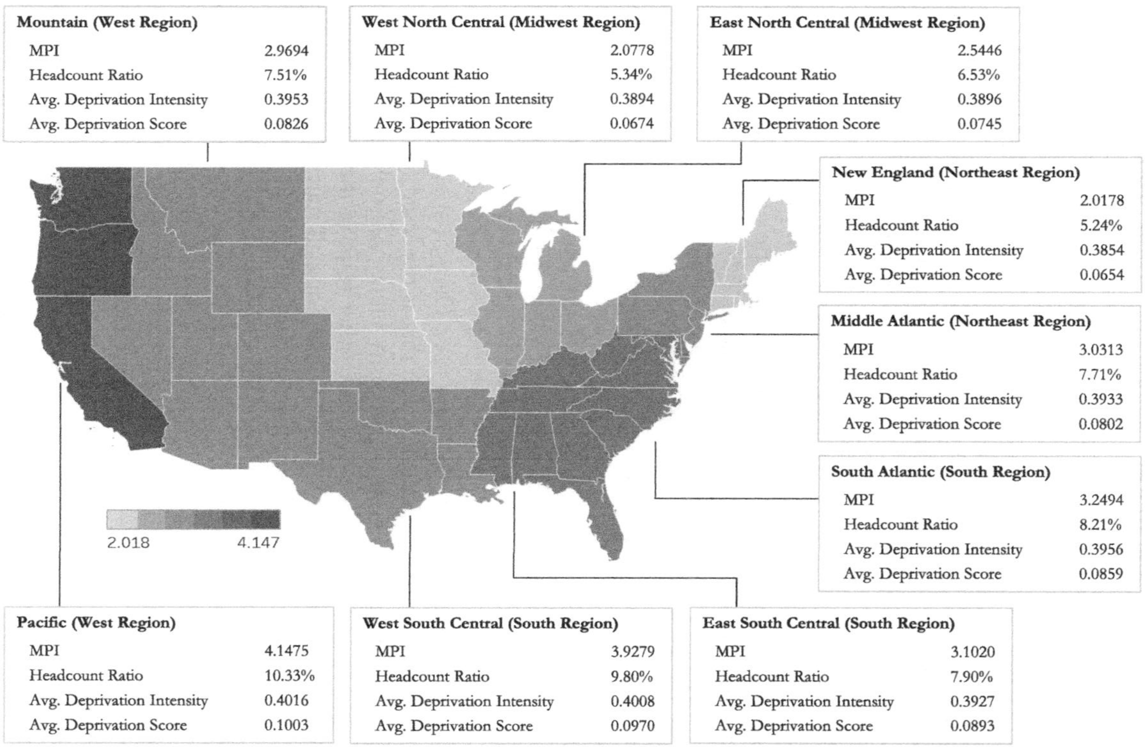

Fig. 5.2 MPI values by division, 2008–2018. Not shown: Alaska and Hawaii. Both states are part of the Pacific division

value of the West North Central division (i.e., a difference of 0.4668) with which it comprises the Midwest region. Lastly, the MPI values for the West South Central division and the Mountain division (i.e., a difference of 0.2196) are much nearer to each other than to the MPI values of the East South Central division and the Pacific division, respectively. This pattern of relative differences in division values underscores the presence of variation in values across the four regions.

Returning our focus to the Pacific division, as it is the division with the highest levels of multidimensional poverty, it is comprised of the five states of Alaska, California, Hawaii, Oregon, and Washington. By a substantial margin, however, California has the largest population among the states in this division, accounting for nearly three of every four Pacific division residents. As a result, California has a sizable weight in the division-level statistics and, although to a somewhat lesser extent, the state exerts significant influence on the statistics of the West region. Table 5.1 presents the MPI values, headcount ratios, and average deprivation scores (censored and uncensored) for each state during the 2008–2018 period. While the average intensity values (i.e., censored deprivation scores) are similar across states within the division, we see much larger differences in the average uncensored deprivation score, headcount ratio, and MPI values.

Beginning with the headcount ratio values for the states within the Pacific division, the value for California (11.35 percent) is not only higher than that of any other state it is more than 50 percent greater than the next highest value within the division (i.e., Oregon at a rate of 7.56 percent) and is more than twice the value that is observed for Hawaii (5.06 percent). Turning to the average intensity values, not only do we see that California has a higher value than any other state in the Pacific division (0.4033), it has the second highest value among all states in the country. As a result of having the highest headcount ratio value and the second highest average intensity value, California has the highest MPI value (i.e., 4.5756) of any state in the country. In fact, if we were to exclude California from the Pacific division calculations, all else equal, the result would be a division MPI value that would rank as the fourth highest among the nine divisions, behind the New England, West North Central, and East North Central divisions.

Extending from the region and division levels, Fig. 5.3 illustrates the relative MPI values across states. Consistent with the earlier mappings, with few exceptions, we see lower MPI values (i.e., lighter shading) among the states that are located in the Northeast, the Midwest, and the more

Table 5.1 Multidimensional poverty measures by state, 2008–2018

	Deprivation score (Avg.)	*Headcount ratio*	*Average intensity*	*MPI*		*Deprivation score (Avg.)*	*Headcount ratio*	*Average intensity*	*MPI*
Northeast Region, New England Division					South Region (Continued), South Atlantic Division				
Connecticut	0.0659	5.84%	0.3920	2.2894	Delaware	0.0695	5.31%	0.3843	2.0416
Maine	0.0738	5.10%	0.3786	1.9310	District of Columbia	0.0760	7.14%	0.3817	2.7244
Massachusetts	0.0638	5.23%	0.3850	2.0128	Florida	0.0965	9.70%	0.3968	3.8508
New Hampshire	0.0578	3.92%	0.3814	1.4944	Georgia	0.0916	9.06%	0.3971	3.5992
Rhode Island	0.0760	7.26%	0.3929	2.8519	Maryland	0.0653	5.38%	0.3880	2.0868
Vermont	0.0603	3.84%	0.3743	1.4358	North Carolina	0.0850	8.19%	0.3974	3.2547
Northeast Region, Middle Atlantic Division					South Carolina	0.0869	7.82%	0.3949	3.0865
New Jersey	0.0756	7.38%	0.3956	2.9215	Virginia	0.0676	5.73%	0.3900	2.2362
New York	0.0876	8.94%	0.3954	3.5352	West Virginia	0.0872	6.57%	0.3849	2.5292
Pennsylvania	0.0692	5.73%	0.3854	2.2066	South Region, West South Central Division				
Midwest Region, East North Central Division					Arkansas	0.0933	7.81%	0.3900	3.0444
Illinois	0.0753	7.14%	0.3927	2.8029	Louisiana	0.0953	8.22%	0.3908	3.2146
Indiana	0.0781	6.57%	0.3909	2.5687	Oklahoma	0.0947	7.62%	0.3920	2.9885
Michigan	0.0761	6.53%	0.3862	2.5237	Texas	0.1022	11.23%	0.4050	4.5485
Ohio	0.0741	6.12%	0.3874	2.3713	West Region, Mountain Division				
Wisconsin	0.0620	4.87%	0.3855	1.8784	Arizona	0.0958	9.02%	0.3962	3.5755
Midwest Region, West North Central Division					Colorado	0.0686	6.18%	0.3941	2.4343
Iowa	0.0586	4.24%	0.3846	1.6326	Idaho	0.0794	6.18%	0.3897	2.4082
Kansas	0.0695	5.79%	0.3934	2.2789	Montana	0.0759	5.35%	0.3806	2.0363
Minnesota	0.0565	4.49%	0.3879	1.7435	Nevada	0.0965	9.64%	0.4000	3.8572

(*continued*)

Table 5.1 (continued)

	Deprivation score (Avg.)	*Headcount ratio*	*Average intensity*	*MPI*		*Deprivation score (Avg.)*	*Headcount ratio*	*Average intensity*	*MPI*
Missouri	0.0792	6.41%	0.3907	2.5049	New Mexico	0.1075	9.80%	0.3976	3.8974
Nebraska	0.0621	5.26%	0.3916	2.0588	Utah	0.0626	5.25%	0.3913	2.0535
North Dakota	0.0580	3.61%	0.3734	1.3481	Wyoming	0.0672	4.44%	0.3878	1.7200
South Dakota	0.0685	5.10%	0.3882	1.9815	West Region, Pacific Division				
South Region, East South Central Division					Alaska	0.1112	6.29%	0.3912	2.4614
Alabama	0.0901	8.03%	0.3943	3.1643	California	0.1068	11.35%	0.4033	4.5756
Kentucky	0.0861	7.61%	0.3917	2.9826	Hawaii	0.0767	5.06%	0.3830	1.9363
Mississippi	0.1040	9.31%	0.3921	3.6505	Oregon	0.0811	7.56%	0.3909	2.9551
Tennessee	0.0862	7.69%	0.3931	3.0231	Washington	0.0742	6.50%	0.3918	2.5474

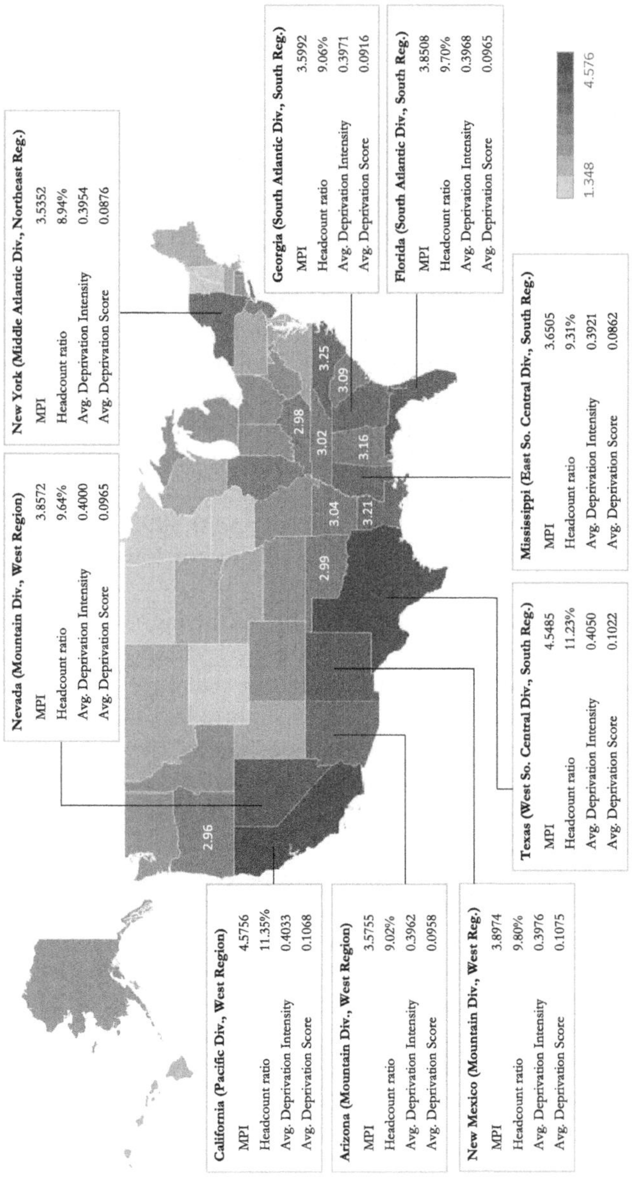

Fig. 5.3 MPI values by state, select states identified, 2008–2018

northern portion of the Mountain division. The South region, southern Mountain division, and California and Oregon have relatively higher MPI values. In the figure, we also identify nine states for which MPI values are greater than 3.5. For each of these states, the MPI value and values for associated measures are presented. Lastly, the states for which MPI values range between 2.95 and 3.50 are noted in the figure. We can see that, with the exception of New York, the set of states is contiguous, beginning in the Pacific division with Oregon and California, continuing south and east through the Mountain division states of Nevada, Arizona, and New Mexico, continuing eastward to include all of the states in the West South Central and the East South Central divisions, and to the south and east to include the four southernmost states in the South Atlantic division. All states located to the north of this cohort, with the exception of New York, have MPI values lower than 2.95.[3] Collectively, these 18 states have a headcount ratio of 9.67 percent, an average deprivation intensity value of 0.3990, and an MPI value of 3.86. By contrast, the remaining 32 states plus the District of Columbia have collective headcount ratio and average deprivation intensity values of 5.98 percent and 0.3893, respectively, and an MPI value (i.e., 2.33) that is nearly 40 percent lower than the value calculated for the group of 18 states.

If we focus only on the nine states that have the highest MPI values, we are able to further demonstrate the state-level variation in multidimensional poverty. In the typical year during our reference period, the combined population of these nine states is slightly less than 128.8 million individuals. This is equivalent to 40.7 percent of the U.S. population. Thus, even though nine states may seem a small portion of the country, these particular states are home to sizeable shares of U.S. residents. Further, when calculating the MPI and related values for this group of states, we find a headcount ratio of 10.3 percent. Likewise, the average deprivation intensity value for this group is 0.4005. Thus, the MPI for this group of nine states is 4.12. This value is higher than the MPI value of any state with the two exceptions of California (4.58) and Texas (4.55), thus illustrating both and the extent of deprivation within this group of states relative to the remainder of the U.S. and the relative population sizes and the high MPI and headcount ratio values of these two states.

In Table 5.2, we list the deprivation frequency values for the U.S. and for each of the nine states that have MPI values greater than 3.5. Since

[3] Among these states, New Jersey has the highest MPI value at 2.92.

Table 5.2 Comparison of select states in terms of dimension and indicator frequency values, 2008–2018

	U.S.	*Arizona*	*California*	*Florida*	*Georgia*	*Mississippi*	*Nevada*	*New Mexico*	*New York*	*Texas*
Economic security	14.8%	17.8%	16.1%	15.6%	17.1%	21.6%	15.8%	22.2%	15.3%	16.0%
Income poverty	12.7%	15.7%	13.5%	13.5%	15.0%	19.5%	13.1%	20.1%	13.0%	14.1%
Unemployed	3.1%	3.2%	3.7%	3.2%	3.3%	3.6%	3.9%	3.5%	3.2%	2.7%
Education	12.0%	12.6%	17.9%	13.5%	12.3%	13.6%	13.8%	14.5%	14.2%	16.0%
HS diploma	9.5%	10.2%	12.5%	9.7%	10.6%	13.1%	10.2%	12.1%	10.2%	12.0%
English	3.6%	3.8%	8.1%	5.3%	2.4%	0.7%	5.2%	4.2%	5.8%	6.4%
Health	23.4%	25.8%	21.7%	27.6%	27.0%	31.2%	25.6%	29.2%	19.8%	29.3%
Disabled	14.8%	14.8%	12.4%	15.7%	14.8%	19.7%	14.2%	17.0%	13.7%	14.2%
Health insurance	9.6%	12.1%	10.0%	13.3%	13.8%	13.3%	12.6%	13.3%	6.5%	16.7%
Housing	16.6%	19.5%	28.1%	18.6%	15.2%	15.5%	19.4%	19.8%	21.7%	17.7%
Crowded house	6.1%	9.3%	14.3%	5.5%	4.3%	5.3%	8.1%	9.5%	8.1%	8.5%
House amenities	0.7%	1.6%	0.9%	0.6%	0.5%	0.7%	0.6%	2.5%	0.7%	0.7%
Housing costs	11.2%	10.7%	16.3%	13.7%	11.3%	10.4%	12.1%	9.7%	15.3%	9.9%

these states are all characterized by higher than average levels of deprivation, it is not surprising that about 80 percent of the listed state-specific deprivation frequency values exceed the corresponding U.S. values. Comparing the values for the individual states to the values of the U.S. across the four dimensions and the nine indicators helps to show the differences in the forms of deprivation across states. For example, as indicated earlier, the state with the highest MPI value is California. All indicators that are associated with the Economic Security, Education, and Housing dimensions (and, of course, the related dimension values) are greater than the corresponding U.S. values. Similarly, the health insurance indicator value for California is marginally higher than the U.S. value. To the contrary, however, California has a sufficiently low value for the disability indicator relative to the U.S. value that the Health dimension value for the state is lower than the national value. Texas has a near identical MPI value to California and all of the dimension values for Texas are greater than the corresponding U.S. values; however, Texas has values for three of the nine indicators—specifically, unemployment, disability status, and housing costs—that are below the U.S. levels. Still another example is provided jointly by Georgia and Mississippi. Both states experience more frequent deprivation than others in terms of the Economic Security, Education, and Health dimensions but both also have values below the U.S. level for the Housing dimension. The takeaway from these values, and more broadly from this section, to the extent that there is only a single message to convey, is that while we see variation in the incidence and intensity of deprivation across regions, divisions, and states, we also find considerable variation in the forms of deprivation that are experienced.

5.2 Examining Public Use Microdata Areas

To further explore multidimensional poverty in the U.S., we now turn to the highest level of geographic disaggregation that we consider. Public Use Microdata Areas (i.e., a PUMAs) are defined by the U.S. Census Bureau and are updated following each decennial census. PUMAs are statistical geographic units that are built on census tracts and counties, are geographically contiguous and nested within states, and include at least 100,000 people but, generally, fewer than 200,000 people. Figure 5.4 illustrates the variation in headcount ratio values across the 2351 PUMAs that comprise the U.S. To a large degree, the shading in the figure resembles that in Fig. 5.3, even as the former illustrates the distribution of headcount ratio values while the latter illustrates MPI values. However, Fig. 5.4

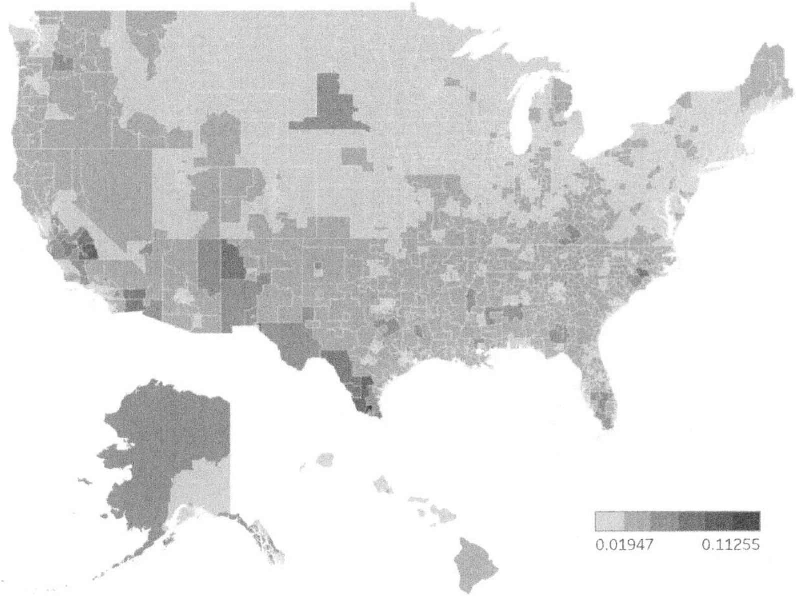

Fig. 5.4 Headcount ratio values by PUMA, 2012–2018

affords the opportunity to see the large amount variation in headcount ratio values within states.

Table 5.3 provides another indication of the extent to which multidimensional poverty varies across PUMAs. We present MPI, headcount ratio, and average deprivation intensity values, along with deprivation frequency values at the dimension and indicator levels, for different quantiles of the MPI distribution across PUMAs.[4] These values are presented in columns while the rows indicate the range of the distribution over which the values apply. For example, the first row lists values for the top one percent of PUMAs. This quantile includes the 24 least-deprived PUMAs in the country. At the opposing end of the spectrum, we have the bottom one percent of PUMAs. This quantile includes the 24 most-deprived PUMAs in the U.S. Between these two endpoints, we consider a number of other quantiles, including quintile-specific values. Finally, we include values for the mean and median PUMAs as points of comparison, and we

[4] The values presented are non-weighted averages taken across the population-weighted PUMA-specific values included in each corresponding quantile.

Table 5.3 Mean values across PUMA quantiles, ranked by MPI values, 2012–2018

	MPI	*Headcount ratio*	*Average deprivation intensity*	*Dimensions*				*Indicators, by dimension*									
								Economic security		*Education*		*Health*		*Housing*			
				Economic security	*Education*	*Health*	*Housing*	*Income poverty*	*Unemployed*	*Educational attainment*	*English*	*Disability*	*Health insurance*	*Crowded house*	*Housing costs*	*Amenities*	
Top 1%	0.4844	1.31%	0.3686	5.76%	3.58%	11.46%	8.67%	3.86%	1.89%	2.70%	0.99%	8.35%	3.37%	1.64%	7.21%	0.27%	
Top 5%	0.6744	1.80%	0.3742	6.53%	4.52%	12.82%	9.63%	4.40%	2.15%	3.40%	1.31%	9.71%	3.40%	1.83%	8.02%	0.34%	
Top 10%	0.8086	2.15%	0.3754	7.20%	5.05%	14.05%	9.93%	5.03%	2.22%	3.92%	1.35%	10.44%	3.96%	2.07%	8.11%	0.36%	
Top 20%	1.0114	2.68%	0.3769	8.31%	5.71%	15.48%	10.42%	6.10%	2.31%	4.53%	1.45%	11.24%	4.65%	2.36%	8.35%	0.40%	
Next 20%	1.7236	4.51%	0.3826	11.66%	8.06%	20.42%	12.53%	9.23%	2.68%	6.69%	1.79%	13.99%	7.18%	3.57%	9.43%	0.55%	
Middle 20%	2.4099	6.23%	0.3867	14.85%	10.47%	24.05%	14.62%	12.27%	3.03%	8.66%	2.45%	15.71%	9.36%	4.76%	10.56%	0.68%	
Second 20%	3.2836	8.39%	0.3914	17.85%	13.48%	27.14%	16.74%	15.21%	3.31%	11.18%	3.32%	16.88%	11.61%	6.08%	11.62%	0.71%	
Bottom 20%	5.9721	14.84%	0.4006	24.05%	22.75%	29.50%	27.84%	20.91%	4.14%	16.41%	10.04%	15.30%	15.52%	13.81%	16.90%	1.01%	
Bottom 10%	7.4126	18.24%	0.4052	26.55%	27.71%	31.17%	32.80%	23.28%	4.31%	19.27%	13.72%	14.60%	17.91%	17.99%	18.73%	1.16%	
Bottom 5%	8.8043	21.46%	0.4095	28.58%	32.72%	33.34%	36.27%	25.43%	4.22%	22.18%	17.51%	14.18%	20.62%	21.39%	19.63%	1.12%	
Bottom 1%	11.6213	27.81%	0.4176	32.86%	40.42%	35.76%	44.10%	29.71%	4.11%	26.70%	23.75%	13.74%	23.60%	28.77%	22.70%	1.51%	
Mean PUMA	2.8816	7.17%	0.4020	14.68%	13.93%	25.94%	11.00%	12.07%	3.27%	12.16%	2.53%	16.94%	10.34%	3.91%	7.52%	0.49%	
Median PUMA	2.3983	6.05%	0.3966	9.33%	11.68%	16.11%	15.81%	6.37%	3.07%	8.00%	5.01%	9.59%	7.06%	5.71%	10.83%	0.49%	
90:10 Ratio	9.17	8.47	1.08	3.69	5.49	2.22	3.30	4.63	1.94	4.92	10.17	1.40	4.52	8.69	2.31	3.26	
80:20 Ratio	5.90	5.53	1.06	2.89	3.98	1.91	2.67	3.43	1.79	3.63	6.90	1.36	3.34	5.85	2.02	2.50	

90:10 (80:20) ratios are constructed as Bottom 10% (Bottom 20%) value divided by Top 10% (Top 20%) value (i.e., ordered in terms of more over less deprivation). Mean PUMA, based on MPI values, is the Catawba County—Hickory City PUMA in North Carolina. Median PUMA, again based on MPI values, is the DuPage County (Northwest)—Bloomingdale (South), Wayne & Winfield (North) Townships PUMA in Illinois

include a 90:10 ratio and an 80:20 ratio as a further demonstration of the distribution of deprivation in the U.S.

Beginning with a comparison of the least- and the most-deprived cohorts of PUMAs—that is, the top one percent and the bottom one percent—we see that the average MPI value among the most-deprived cohort was nearly 25 times higher than the average MPI value for the least-deprived cohort. Likewise, the difference in headcount ratio values is equal to a factor of more than 20. Looking to the mean deprivation frequency values at the dimension level, the greatest gaps between the most- and least-deprived cohorts is seen for the Education and the Housing dimensions. With respect to the Education dimension, only 3.6 percent of those within the cohort of least-deprived PUMAs are deprived while an astounding 40.4 percent of those within the most-deprived cohort are deprived. Stated differently, the typical individual in the most-deprived PUMA cohort is 11.3 times more likely to be deprived in the Education dimension. A similar gap, equal to 35.4 percentage points, is found for the Housing dimension deprivation frequency values. In this case, 44.1 percent of individuals in the most-deprived PUMA cohort suffer deprivation in this dimension as compared to only 8.7 percent of those in the least-deprived cohort. Likewise, there are exceptionally large differences in terms of the Economic Security and the Health dimensions.

To gain a slightly different perspective on the relative levels of deprivation frequency, we can look to the 90:10 and 80:20 ratios. The 90:10 ratio is simply equal to the bottom 10 percent cohort value divided by the top 10 percent cohort value. For example, the 90:10 ratio of MPI values is equal to 9.17 (i.e., 7.4126 divided by 0.8086). From this, we can say that the MPI value of the bottom 10 percent cohort is about 9.2 times the MPI value of the top 10 percent cohort value. Looking to the indicator values, we see a wide range of magnitudes. The lowest ratio is found for the disability indicator (1.4) while the highest value is observed for the English language indicator (10.17). Other large differences are found for the crowded house indicator (8.69), the high school diploma indicator (4.92), the income poverty indicator (4.63), and the health insurance indicator (4.52). When we look at deprivation frequency values for the indicators while using the 80:20 ratio, we see lower ratios, as expected, but no marked changes in the indicators for which the differences are greatest. Again, it is the English language (6.9), crowded house (5.85), high school diploma (3.63), income poverty (3.43), and health insurance (3.34) indicators where we see the greatest differences in deprivation frequency. In fact, comparison of deprivation frequency values for indicators across quantile pairings reveals that the highest ratio values are consistently found for, in the following order, the English language, crowded house, high school diploma, income poverty, and health insurance indicators.

To add a finer point to our exploration of PUMA-level variation in multidimensional poverty, we include three tables in our chapter appendix. Each of the three tables consists of two panels. Panel A provides information for the cohort of least-deprived PUMAs as ranked by MPI value (i.e., the top one percent of all PUMAs), while Panel B provides information for the cohort of most-deprived PUMAs (i.e., the bottom one percent of PUMAs). To facilitate comparison, the first row of each table presents the corresponding values for the entire U.S. Table 5.4 presents the MPI and related values as well as dimension-specific deprivation frequency values. The differences between the values that are presented in the panels of Table 5.4 are striking. In Table 5.5, we see a similar pattern with respect to the magnitudes of the indicator-specific deprivation frequency values. Admittedly, the cohorts are at the extreme ends of the PUMA-level MPI distribution; however, the values provided in Table 5.3 indicate that broad differences exist throughout the distribution. Additionally, looking to the PUMA locations is telling. In Panel A, we see that only five of the 24 PUMAs listed (20.8 percent) are located in one of the 18 states that are highlighted in Fig. 5.3 as having an MPI value greater than 2.95. By contrast, in Panel B, all 24 listed PUMAs are located in states with MPI values greater than 2.95, with 18 of the PUMAs (75 percent) located in either Texas or California, the two states with the highest MPI values.

Finally, Table 5.6 presents the same PUMAs that are listed in the previous two tables; however, the values presented provide a brief demographic summary of the residents of each PUMA. Again, for comparison, the national-level values are presented in the first row of each panel. Beginning with Panel A, we see that 22 of the 24 least-deprived PUMAs have populations that are characterized by a higher percentage of white residents as compared to the national value. Similarly, half of these PUMAs have Asian population shares that exceed the national level, and none of the least-deprived PUMAs are characterized by higher black, Hispanic, or "all other races" population shares relative to the national level. Only five of the 24 PUMAs have higher percentages of foreign-born residents than the national level. In terms of educational attainment, all 24 PUMAs have higher population shares for holders of four-year college degrees and post-graduate degrees relative to the national values.

Comparing the demographic representation of the cohort of most-deprived PUMAs to the corresponding national levels tells a much different story. First, in terms of race and ethnicity, this cohort of PUMAs is much more diverse relative to the group of least-deprived PUMAs. We see that only eight of the 24 PUMAs had white population shares above the national level. Likewise, only eight of the PUMAs had Asian population shares that were higher than the national level, and only 10 of the PUMAs had black shares in excess of the national level. We do see, however, that 20 of the 24 PUMAs have "all other race" population shares that exceed the national level and all 24 PUMAs have Hispanic population shares and foreign-born population shares that are greater than the national level. In terms of educational attainment, 23 of the 24 PUMAs have higher shares than the national level in the "less than a high school diploma" classification, while 18 of the 24 PUMAs have higher shares than the national level in the "high school diploma" classification.

The contrasting figures of the demographic compositions between the least- and most-deprived PUMAs is striking. Relative to the national population, those who live in the least-deprived PUMAs are more often found to be white, Asian, non-Hispanic, and native-born, and are generally more highly educated. On the other hand, the populations of the most-deprived PUMAs, again in comparison to the national population, are more likely to be black or of another race (i.e., self-identifying as neither white, black, nor Asian), Hispanic, or foreign-born, and are more likely to have not completed high school or to have only completed high school (i.e., to not have attended college). We also see that the residents of the most-deprived PUMAs are more likely to live in states with relatively high MPI values and, in particular, to live in either California or in Texas. The demographic differences are considerable across quantiles based on relative MPI values. The noted geographic differences across these quantiles link to state-, division-, and region-level variation in multidimensional deprivation. While the focus of this chapter has been largely aimed toward geographic variation, we continue in the following chapter with a more detailed exploration of variation across individual characteristics.

Appendix

Table 5.4 MPI, related measures, and dimension values, 2012–2018

Rank	*Name*	*Deprivation score*	*Headcount ratio*	*Average deprivation intensity*	*MPI*	*Dimensions*			
						Economic security	*Education*	*Health*	*Housing*
Panel A: Top 1 Percent of PUMAs, Least Deprived According to MPI Values									
	United States, 2012–2018	0.0810	7.2%	0.3925	2.84	16.5%	12.3%	23.3%	19.2%
1	Norfolk (Northeast) & Middlesex (Southeast) Counties (West of Boston City), MA	0.0285	0.8%	0.3747	0.31	4.6%	2.8%	8.9%	9.0%
2	Douglas (Northeast) & Elbert (West) Counties—Parker Town & The Pinery, CO	0.0345	1.0%	0.3539	0.34	5.4%	2.9%	11.8%	10.1%
3	Waukesha County (West), WI	0.0332	1.1%	0.3506	0.39	5.7%	3.1%	12.2%	7.6%
4	Loudoun County (East Central)—Ashburn (Southwest/Belmont Ridge) & Dulles Airport, VA	0.0271	1.1%	0.3690	0.40	3.9%	4.8%	7.3%	7.8%
5	Maricopa County—Scottsdale (North), Phoenix (Far Northeast) Cities & Cave Creek, AZ	0.0372	1.1%	0.3789	0.42	6.5%	2.8%	11.9%	11.7%
6	Hamilton County (Central)—Carmel City & Fishers Town (West), IN	0.0293	1.1%	0.3820	0.43	4.9%	3.0%	10.7%	6.2%
7	Douglas County (South)—Castle Rock Town, CO	0.0306	1.2%	0.3793	0.44	5.0%	2.7%	10.2%	8.9%

8	Douglas (West) & Jefferson (Southeast) Counties—Highlands Ranch & Chatfield Park, CO	0.0308	1.2%	0.3633	0.45	4.9%	2.9%	10.7%	7.8%
9	Waukesha County (East), WI	0.0362	1.3%	0.3610	0.47	5.5%	3.8%	13.7%	8.0%
10	Orange County (Southeast)—Rancho Santa Margarita City (East) & Ladera Ranch, CA	0.0380	1.3%	0.3680	0.48	5.5%	3.8%	8.2%	17.4%
11	Washtenaw County (West, Northeast & Southeast), MI	0.0406	1.4%	0.3598	0.50	5.9%	4.4%	15.7%	8.2%
12	Washington County (South)—Woodbury & Cottage Grove Cities, MN	0.0335	1.4%	0.3529	0.50	5.7%	3.9%	12.1%	6.7%
13	Arapahoe County (Southwest)—Centennial (West & Central) & Greenwood Village Cities, CO	0.0344	1.4%	0.3712	0.51	6.1%	2.9%	11.5%	9.4%
14	Maricopa County—Gilbert (South) & Queen Creek Towns, AZ	0.0378	1.3%	0.3807	0.51	6.8%	3.4%	11.8%	10.6%
15	Howard County (West)—Columbia (West) & Ellicott City (Northwest), MD	0.0335	1.4%	0.3659	0.51	4.9%	4.5%	11.0%	8.3%
16	El Paso County (North Central)—Colorado Springs City (North) & Monument Town, CO	0.0359	1.4%	0.3585	0.51	6.9%	2.4%	12.4%	9.3%
17	Erie County (Northeast), NY	0.0415	1.4%	0.3654	0.52	6.2%	5.4%	16.2%	6.9%
18	Kane County (West), IL	0.0334	1.4%	0.3719	0.53	5.8%	3.5%	10.1%	9.7%

(*continued*)

Table 5.4 (continued)

Rank	*Name*	*Deprivation score*	*Headcount ratio*	*Average deprivation intensity*	*MPI*	*Dimensions*			
						Economic security	*Education*	*Health*	*Housing*
19	Prince William County (North & West)—Linton Hall & Gainesville, VA	0.0338	1.5%	0.3718	0.56	4.5%	4.9%	11.0%	8.8%
20	Denton County (South Central)—Flower Mound Town & Highland Village City, TX	0.0299	1.4%	0.3929	0.57	4.8%	2.9%	10.7%	7.4%
21	Washington & Ozaukee Counties, WI	0.0388	1.5%	0.3735	0.57	6.3%	4.4%	14.2%	8.1%
22	Middlesex County (Outside Lowell City), MA	0.0367	1.5%	0.3704	0.57	6.3%	5.0%	10.9%	9.6%
23	Delaware County, OH	0.0336	1.6%	0.3621	0.57	5.8%	3.1%	12.2%	7.7%
24	Johnson County (Southeast)—Blue Valley Region, KS	0.0285	1.6%	0.3691	0.58	4.6%	2.7%	9.7%	7.4%
Panel B: Bottom 1 Percent of PUMAs, Most Deprived According to MPI Values									
	United States, 2012–2018	0.0810	7.2%	0.3925	2.84	16.5%	12.3%	23.3%	19.2%
2328	Orange County (Central)—Santa Ana City (East), CA	0.1771	23.9%	0.4181	9.97	20.9%	37.3%	29.7%	55.2%
2329	Los Angeles County (Central)—Bell Gardens, Bell, Maywood, Cudahy & Commerce Cities, CA	0.1962	24.7%	0.4137	10.21	27.9%	42.4%	30.3%	56.4%
2330	Dallas City (West Central)—East of Loop TX-12 & West of I-35E, TX	0.1727	25.1%	0.4094	10.28	26.4%	39.6%	36.5%	30.5%

2331	Houston City (North)—South of Aldine & Inside Beltway TX-8, TX	0.1532	25.0%	0.4117	10.29	24.5%	33.4%	35.8%	25.1%
2332	Los Angeles County (Central)—LA City (East Central/Central City & Boyle Heights), CA	0.1926	24.9%	0.4166	10.37	30.8%	38.9%	33.0%	48.3%
2333	NYC-Bronx Community District 7—Bedford Park, Fordham North & Norwood, NY	0.1862	25.4%	0.4104	10.43	34.4%	36.9%	26.9%	49.7%
2334	Los Angeles County—LA City (Central/Univ. of Southern California & Exposition Park), CA	0.1837	25.2%	0.4148	10.47	33.6%	33.9%	28.9%	48.6%
2335	South Texas Development Council (South) & Coastal Bend COG (West), TX	0.1855	24.8%	0.4236	10.50	30.3%	37.0%	47.3%	24.7%
2336	NYC-Bronx Community District 4—Concourse, Highbridge & Mount Eden, NY	0.1930	26.0%	0.4052	10.53	38.2%	35.8%	27.9%	52.8%
2337	Los Angeles County (South Central)—LA City (South Central/Watts), CA	0.2053	25.9%	0.4080	10.57	36.1%	38.2%	30.2%	61.1%
2338	El Paso City (Central), TX	0.1939	25.5%	0.4222	10.76	33.3%	40.1%	46.1%	24.0%
2339	NYC-Bronx Community District 5—Morris Heights, Fordham South & Mount Hope, NY	0.2010	26.8%	0.4078	10.91	42.8%	38.0%	25.9%	52.4%

(continued)

Table 5.4 (continued)

Rank	*Name*	*Deprivation score*	*Headcount ratio*	*Average deprivation intensity*	*MPI*	*Dimensions*			
						Economic security	*Education*	*Health*	*Housing*
2340	Miami-Dade County (Northeast)—Hialeah City (South Central), FL	0.1976	27.2%	0.4116	11.18	26.2%	51.1%	39.0%	34.4%
2341	South Texas Development Council (North)—Webb County—Laredo City (Central), TX	0.1940	27.5%	0.4175	11.47	34.9%	37.3%	43.2%	36.7%
2342	Los Angeles County (Central)—Huntington Park City, Florence-Graham & Walnut Park, CA	0.2068	28.0%	0.4156	11.64	29.5%	45.0%	29.2%	60.9%
2343	Hidalgo County (East)—Alamo & Donna Cities, TX	0.1950	27.8%	0.4310	12.00	36.6%	35.7%	43.0%	36.6%
2344	Los Angeles County—LA City (East Central/Silver Lake, Echo Park & Westlake), CA	0.1931	28.2%	0.4342	12.25	28.8%	36.3%	33.1%	52.0%
2345	NYC-Brooklyn Community District 7—Sunset Park & Windsor Terrace, NY	0.1834	29.7%	0.4216	12.53	26.8%	42.9%	23.0%	47.3%
2346	Miami-Dade County (Northeast Central)—Miami City (Downtown), FL	0.2095	30.8%	0.4198	12.93	31.6%	45.5%	44.0%	40.7%
2347	Los Angeles County (Central)—LA City (Central/Koreatown), CA	0.2109	31.8%	0.4177	13.26	28.1%	44.8%	34.3%	58.5%

2348	Hidalgo County (North & West), TX	0.2158	31.2%	0.4303	13.41	40.0%	36.7%	52.5%	35.5%
2349	Los Angeles County (Central)—LA City (Southeast/East Vernon), CA	0.2343	33.4%	0.4186	13.99	39.1%	46.7%	33.9%	65.0%
2350	Houston City (North) & Aldine—Between Loop I-610 & Beltway TX-8, TX	0.2185	34.3%	0.4204	14.44	34.9%	53.9%	42.6%	35.1%
2351	Houston City (West)—Westpark Tollway, Between Loop I-610 & Beltway TX-8, TX	0.2086	34.4%	0.4217	14.52	33.3%	42.9%	42.0%	43.7%

Table 5.5 Deprivation frequency values by indicator, 24 least- and 24 most-deprived PUMAs, 2012–2018

Rank	*Name*	*Economic security*		*Education*		*Health*		*Housing*		
		Income poverty	*Unemployed*	*Educational attainment*	*English*	*Disability*	*Health insurance*	*Crowded house*	*Housing costs*	*Amenities*
Panel A: Top 1 Percent of PUMAs, Least Deprived According to MPI Values										
	United States, 2012–2018	14.2%	3.4%	9.2%	4.6%	13.1%	11.2%	7.3%	12.8%	0.7%
1	Norfolk (Northeast) & Middlesex (Southeast) Counties (West of Boston City), MA	3.0%	1.9%	1.7%	1.2%	8.0%	1.0%	0.7%	8.0%	0.3%
2	Douglas (Northeast) & Elbert (West) Counties—Parker Town & The Pinery, CO	3.7%	1.8%	2.2%	0.8%	8.0%	4.0%	2.3%	7.9%	0.3%
3	Waukesha County (West), WI	4.2%	1.7%	2.9%	0.3%	9.7%	2.7%	0.8%	6.7%	0.1%
4	Loudoun County (East Central)—Ashburn (Southwest/Belmont Ridge) & Dulles Airport, VA	2.3%	1.7%	2.1%	2.8%	4.3%	3.2%	1.7%	6.1%	0.1%
5	Maricopa County—Scottsdale (North), Phoenix (Far Northeast) Cities & Cave Creek, AZ	4.8%	2.0%	2.3%	0.6%	8.9%	3.2%	1.4%	10.4%	0.2%

6	Hamilton County (Central)—Carmel City & Fishers Town (West), IN	3.4%	1.8%	1.8%	1.3%	7.1%	3.8%	1.0%	5.0%	0.3%
7	Douglas County (South)—Castle Rock Town, CO	3.4%	1.8%	2.1%	0.6%	7.1%	3.2%	1.7%	7.4%	0.2%
8	Douglas (West) & Jefferson (Southeast) Counties—Highlands Ranch & Chatfield Park, CO	3.2%	2.0%	2.0%	1.2%	7.1%	3.8%	1.5%	6.3%	0.4%
9	Waukesha County (East), WI	4.0%	1.6%	3.1%	0.8%	11.2%	2.7%	1.7%	6.3%	0.3%
10	Orange County (Southeast)—Rancho Santa Margarita City (East) & Ladera Ranch, CA	3.5%	2.3%	2.2%	1.8%	5.1%	3.2%	4.0%	14.0%	0.3%
11	Washtenaw County (West, Northeast & Southeast), MI	4.6%	1.6%	4.1%	0.3%	11.3%	5.0%	1.7%	6.6%	0.3%

(*continued*)

Table 5.5 (continued)

Rank	*Name*	*Economic security*		*Education*		*Health*		*Housing*		
		Income poverty	*Unemployed*	*Educational attainment*	*English*	*Disability*	*Health insurance*	*Crowded house*	*Housing costs*	*Amenities*
12	Washington County (South)—Woodbury & Cottage Grove Cities, MN	4.1%	1.8%	3.3%	0.6%	9.2%	3.2%	1.4%	5.3%	0.1%
13	Arapahoe County (Southwest)—Centennial (West & Central) & Greenwood Village Cities, CO	4.3%	2.0%	1.9%	1.1%	8.3%	3.4%	1.6%	7.8%	0.2%
14	Maricopa County—Gilbert (South) & Queen Creek Towns, AZ	5.2%	1.9%	2.8%	0.9%	7.3%	4.7%	3.2%	7.9%	0.1%
15	Howard County (West)—Columbia (West) & Ellicott City (Northwest), MD	3.5%	1.6%	2.7%	2.0%	8.6%	2.7%	1.3%	7.0%	0.3%
16	El Paso County (North Central)—Colorado Springs City (North) & Monument Town, CO	4.6%	2.6%	1.9%	0.6%	8.2%	4.5%	1.6%	7.5%	0.4%
17	Erie County (Northeast), NY	4.8%	1.7%	5.0%	0.4%	13.1%	3.5%	0.8%	5.8%	0.4%
18	Kane County (West), IL	3.7%	2.4%	2.9%	0.6%	7.1%	3.4%	1.6%	8.0%	0.3%

19	Prince William County (North & West)—Linton Hall & Gainesville, VA	2.6%	2.0%	3.4%	1.7%	7.0%	4.3%	1.9%	6.9%	0.2%
20	Denton County (South Central)—Flower Mound Town & Highland Village City, TX	3.1%	1.9%	2.1%	0.8%	7.1%	3.8%	1.1%	6.3%	0.3%
21	Washington & Ozaukee Counties, WI	4.9%	1.6%	3.9%	0.5%	11.1%	3.4%	1.9%	6.1%	0.4%
22	Middlesex County (Outside Lowell City), MA	4.0%	2.5%	3.9%	1.2%	9.7%	1.4%	1.8%	7.8%	0.4%
23	Delaware County, OH	4.5%	1.6%	2.6%	0.5%	8.8%	3.7%	1.5%	6.2%	0.2%
24	Johnson County (Southeast)—Blue Valley Region, KS	3.3%	1.5%	1.7%	1.1%	7.1%	3.0%	1.4%	5.8%	0.4%
Panel B: Bottom 1 Percent of PUMAs, Most Deprived According to MPI Values										
	United States, 2012–2018	14.2%	3.4%	9.2%	4.6%	13.1%	11.2%	7.3%	12.8%	0.7%
2328	Orange County (Central)—Santa Ana City (East), CA	18.6%	3.1%	27.6%	16.8%	10.3%	21.0%	45.4%	20.2%	0.8%

(*continued*)

Table 5.5 (continued)

Rank	*Name*	*Economic security*		*Education*		*Health*		*Housing*		
		Income poverty	*Unemployed*	*Educational attainment*	*English*	*Disability*	*Health insurance*	*Crowded house*	*Housing costs*	*Amenities*
2329	Los Angeles County (Central)—Bell Gardens, Bell, Maywood, Cudahy & Commerce Cities, CA	25.0%	4.5%	32.4%	19.2%	9.6%	21.7%	41.9%	24.1%	1.0%
2330	Dallas City (West Central)—East of Loop TX-12 & West of I-35E, TX	24.0%	3.9%	26.4%	23.1%	12.3%	26.0%	20.4%	12.5%	0.9%
2331	Houston City (North)—South of Aldine & Inside Beltway TX-8, TX	22.8%	2.6%	20.9%	20.8%	13.5%	23.5%	12.5%	14.2%	1.0%
2332	Los Angeles County (Central)—LA City (East Central/Central City & Boyle Heights), CA	28.7%	3.9%	29.4%	18.6%	15.5%	19.1%	31.8%	23.5%	3.1%
2333	NYC-Bronx Community District 7—Bedford Park, Fordham North & Norwood, NY	31.4%	5.5%	22.8%	21.9%	16.4%	11.0%	29.0%	29.9%	1.1%

2334	Los Angeles County—LA City (Central/Univ. of Southern California & Exposition Park), CA	30.3%	5.5%	23.1%	19.2%	11.2%	18.7%	30.7%	26.4%	1.3%
2335	South Texas Development Council (South) & Coastal Bend COG (West), TX	28.0%	3.9%	26.9%	20.8%	21.3%	29.4%	17.7%	7.5%	2.0%
2336	NYC-Bronx Community District 4—Concourse, Highbridge & Mount Eden, NY	35.5%	5.5%	23.0%	19.7%	17.6%	11.1%	29.1%	32.5%	1.1%
2337	Los Angeles County (South Central)—LA City (South Central/Watts), CA	33.3%	5.1%	30.0%	15.5%	11.1%	20.2%	39.0%	33.8%	0.8%
2338	El Paso City (Central), TX	31.5%	3.9%	27.7%	25.3%	23.2%	26.0%	12.8%	12.0%	1.4%
2339	NYC-Bronx Community District 5—Morris Heights, Fordham South & Mount Hope, NY	39.7%	6.1%	24.1%	21.7%	16.3%	10.2%	28.0%	34.9%	1.3%
2340	Miami-Dade County (Northeast)—Hialeah City (South Central), FL	24.3%	3.3%	27.5%	37.6%	17.5%	22.8%	12.2%	24.3%	1.0%

(*continued*)

Table 5.5 (continued)

Rank	*Name*	*Economic security*		*Education*		*Health*		*Housing*		
		Income poverty	*Unemployed*	*Educational attainment*	*English*	*Disability*	*Health insurance*	*Crowded house*	*Housing costs*	*Amenities*
2341	South Texas Development Council (North)—Webb County—Laredo City (Central), TX	33.4%	2.4%	24.9%	21.4%	16.8%	28.7%	24.6%	15.7%	1.2%
2342	Los Angeles County (Central)—Huntington Park City, Florence-Graham & Walnut Park, CA	26.7%	4.6%	34.5%	20.8%	9.0%	21.0%	45.1%	26.5%	1.6%
2343	Hidalgo County (East)—Alamo & Donna Cities, TX	34.6%	3.4%	24.9%	18.3%	15.5%	29.9%	27.2%	13.6%	3.2%
2344	Los Angeles County—LA City (East Central/Silver Lake, Echo Park & Westlake), CA	25.9%	4.8%	23.6%	24.0%	12.1%	22.1%	36.7%	23.8%	2.5%
2345	NYC-Brooklyn Community District 7—Sunset Park & Windsor Terrace, NY	24.5%	3.8%	26.1%	30.1%	9.6%	14.1%	29.7%	27.2%	0.9%

2346	Miami-Dade County (Northeast Central)—Miami City (Downtown), FL	29.5%	3.9%	25.0%	33.1%	17.6%	28.2%	16.0%	28.4%	1.1%
2347	Los Angeles County (Central)—LA City (Central/Koreatown), CA	25.1%	5.0%	21.2%	35.1%	8.0%	27.2%	40.3%	27.7%	2.6%
2348	Hidalgo County (North & West), TX	38.1%	3.9%	29.3%	15.4%	17.2%	40.4%	26.1%	13.2%	3.2%
2349	Los Angeles County (Central)—LA City (Southeast/East Vernon), CA	37.0%	4.2%	36.3%	20.7%	9.7%	25.2%	47.3%	32.7%	1.4%
2350	Houston City (North) & Aldine—Between Loop I-610 & Beltway TX-8, TX	33.1%	3.0%	31.6%	37.2%	10.7%	33.4%	19.4%	18.2%	1.1%
2351	Houston City (West)—Westpark Tollway, Between Loop I-610 & Beltway TX-8, TX	32.0%	2.7%	21.4%	33.7%	7.9%	35.5%	27.5%	22.0%	1.1%

Table 5.6 Race/ethnicity and educational attainment values, 24 least- and 24 most-deprived PUMAs, 2012–2018

Rank	*PUMA*	*Race/ethnicity*					*Age/nativity*		*Educational attainment*					
		White	*Black*	*Asian*	*All other races*	*Hispanic*	*Age*	*Foreign-born*	*< HS diploma*	*HS diploma*	*Some college*	*BA/BS degree*	*Post-graduate*
Panel A: Top 1 Percent of PUMAs, Least Deprived According to MPI Values													
	United States, 2012–2018	76.7%	10.3%	5.1%	7.9%	14.3%	41.01	11.6%	27.5%	22.2%	24.4%	14.2%	11.8%
1	Norfolk (Northeast) & Middlesex (Southeast) Counties (West of Boston City), MA	85.0%	2.0%	9.6%	3.3%	3.4%	39.79	14.2%	2.2%	9.4%	15.1%	31.4%	41.9%
2	Douglas (Northeast) & Elbert (West) Counties—Parker Town & The Pinery, CO	91.0%	1.0%	3.8%	4.2%	7.0%	36.79	5.5%	2.6%	15.9%	32.3%	33.3%	15.9%
3	Waukesha County (West), WI	96.1%	0.8%	0.9%	2.2%	2.6%	42.38	2.5%	3.2%	24.1%	30.3%	28.2%	14.2%
4	Loudoun County (East Central)—Ashburn (Southwest/Belmont Ridge) & Dulles Airport, VA	63.1%	6.3%	24.0%	6.7%	7.1%	32.96	22.9%	2.8%	8.3%	19.0%	39.0%	30.9%

5	Maricopa County—Scottsdale (North), Phoenix (Far Northeast) Cities & Cave Creek, AZ	91.9%	1.1%	4.0%	3.1%	5.4%	45.40	8.9%	2.4%	12.0%	27.4%	35.3%	22.9%
6	Hamilton County (Central)—Carmel City & Fishers Town (West), IN	86.3%	2.7%	7.8%	3.2%	3.0%	38.77	9.7%	1.9%	10.1%	21.3%	40.7%	26.0%
7	Douglas County (South)—Castle Rock Town, CO	91.2%	0.7%	3.8%	4.3%	6.9%	38.43	5.9%	2.4%	12.7%	28.7%	35.6%	20.6%
8	Douglas (West) & Jefferson (Southeast) Counties—Highlands Ranch & Chatfield Park, CO	89.7%	0.7%	5.1%	4.5%	7.7%	38.91	7.9%	2.2%	12.7%	27.3%	37.4%	20.5%
9	Waukesha County (East), WI	92.0%	1.1%	4.9%	2.0%	2.4%	44.00	6.0%	3.8%	22.6%	28.4%	29.4%	15.8%
10	Orange County (Southeast)—Rancho Santa Margarita City (East) & Ladera Ranch, CA	81.6%	0.8%	9.9%	7.6%	13.4%	36.96	13.9%	2.7%	10.9%	29.1%	37.1%	20.2%
11	Washtenaw County (West, Northeast & Southeast), MI	90.7%	2.9%	2.2%	4.2%	3.5%	42.80	4.7%	4.9%	20.3%	30.4%	23.9%	20.5%

(*continued*)

Table 5.6 (continued)

Rank	*PUMA*	*Race/ethnicity*					*Age/nativity*		*Educational attainment*				
		White	*Black*	*Asian*	*All other races*	*Hispanic*	*Age*	*Foreign-born*	*< HS diploma*	*HS diploma*	*Some college*	*BA/BS degree*	*Post-graduate*
12	Washington County (South)—Woodbury & Cottage Grove Cities, MN	88.1%	2.7%	5.8%	3.5%	3.5%	38.92	6.6%	4.1%	20.1%	32.4%	27.9%	15.4%
13	Arapahoe County (Southwest)—Centennial (West & Central) & Greenwood Village Cities, CO	88.8%	1.3%	5.4%	4.4%	6.6%	41.44	9.6%	2.1%	11.2%	22.7%	37.1%	26.9%
14	Maricopa County—Gilbert (South) & Queen Creek Towns, AZ	85.6%	3.1%	5.1%	6.2%	13.0%	33.71	8.2%	3.7%	16.1%	36.1%	28.8%	15.3%
15	Howard County (West)—Columbia (West) & Ellicott City (Northwest), MD	68.5%	9.3%	18.1%	4.2%	3.7%	41.36	17.9%	3.3%	11.2%	18.5%	30.8%	36.1%

16	El Paso County (North Central)—Colorado Springs City (North) & Monument Town, CO	88.4%	2.6%	3.3%	5.8%	8.4%	38.13	5.9%	2.1%	12.1%	30.7%	31.6%	23.5%
17	Erie County (Northeast), NY	94.2%	2.2%	1.6%	2.0%	1.8%	43.50	3.9%	6.0%	28.2%	30.7%	19.6%	15.4%
18	Kane County (West), IL	92.6%	2.0%	2.5%	3.0%	6.5%	39.79	6.3%	3.5%	21.4%	32.4%	27.6%	15.0%
19	Prince William County (North & West)—Linton Hall & Gainesville, VA	77.0%	8.8%	8.7%	5.5%	8.4%	37.27	13.1%	4.3%	16.1%	27.9%	30.5%	21.2%
20	Denton County (South Central)—Flower Mound Town & Highland Village City, TX	85.9%	2.8%	6.9%	4.4%	8.7%	37.75	9.3%	2.7%	12.4%	26.6%	39.4%	18.9%
21	Washington & Ozaukee Counties, WI	95.3%	1.0%	1.7%	2.0%	2.5%	42.50	3.3%	4.9%	28.5%	31.5%	23.2%	11.9%
22	Middlesex County (Outside Lowell City), MA	88.9%	1.2%	7.5%	2.4%	2.7%	41.07	9.1%	4.7%	22.2%	25.2%	27.8%	20.1%
23	Delaware County, OH	89.5%	2.9%	4.8%	2.9%	2.1%	37.76	5.8%	3.3%	20.1%	26.0%	32.3%	18.2%

(*continued*)

Table 5.6 (continued)

Rank	*PUMA*	*Race/ethnicity*					*Age/nativity*		*Educational attainment*				
		White	*Black*	*Asian*	*All other races*	*Hispanic*	*Age*	*Foreign-born*	*< HS diploma*	*HS diploma*	*Some college*	*BA/ BS degree*	*Post-graduate*
24	Johnson County (Southeast)—Blue Valley Region, KS	85.1%	2.8%	8.9%	3.2%	3.4%	39.43	10.5%	2.0%	8.8%	21.6%	41.3%	26.3%
Panel B: Bottom 1 Percent of PUMAs, Most Deprived According to MPI Values													
	United States, 2012–2018	76.7%	10.3%	5.1%	7.9%	14.3%	41.01	11.6%	27.5%	22.2%	24.4%	14.2%	11.8%
2328	Orange County (Central)—Santa Ana City (East), CA	54.8%	1.1%	6.2%	37.9%	78.3%	34.14	42.7%	38.6%	22.5%	23.5%	11.1%	4.3%
2329	Los Angeles County (Central)—Bell Gardens, Bell, Maywood, Cudahy & Commerce Cities, CA	71.8%	1.0%	0.7%	26.5%	94.7%	32.97	44.6%	47.3%	25.1%	21.7%	4.8%	1.1%
2330	Dallas City (West Central)—East of Loop TX-12 & West of I-35E, TX	75.9%	11.0%	0.9%	12.3%	68.2%	35.42	28.0%	36.6%	25.8%	19.7%	11.6%	6.2%
2331	Houston City (North)—South of Aldine & Inside Beltway TX-8, TX	71.5%	18.9%	1.0%	8.7%	53.6%	38.34	22.8%	27.9%	28.0%	22.0%	14.2%	7.8%

2332	Los Angeles County (Central)—LA City (East Central/Central City & Boyle Heights), CA	51.2%	6.6%	13.8%	28.4%	68.2%	37.16	42.1%	37.6%	20.1%	21.8%	14.0%	6.5%
2333	NYC-Bronx Community District 7—Bedford Park, Fordham North & Norwood, NY	20.5%	22.0%	7.8%	49.7%	66.3%	35.78	42.0%	30.8%	27.2%	24.4%	12.2%	5.3%
2334	Los Angeles County—LA City (Central/Univ. of Southern California & Exposition Park), CA	32.2%	15.1%	13.9%	38.9%	57.3%	34.06	43.7%	30.9%	19.7%	29.8%	14.2%	5.4%
2335	South Texas Development Council (South) & Coastal Bend COG (West), TX	92.3%	0.7%	0.4%	6.6%	87.3%	37.76	23.3%	37.5%	29.6%	22.5%	7.3%	3.1%
2336	NYC-Bronx Community District 4—Concourse, Highbridge & Mount Eden, NY	14.0%	38.0%	2.1%	45.9%	61.9%	35.16	42.2%	31.9%	25.5%	27.0%	11.5%	4.2%

(*continued*)

Table 5.6 (continued)

Rank	*PUMA*	*Race/ethnicity*					*Age/nativity*		*Educational attainment*				
		White	*Black*	*Asian*	*All other races*	*Hispanic*	*Age*	*Foreign-born*	*< HS diploma*	*HS diploma*	*Some college*	*BA/BS degree*	*Post-graduate*
2337	Los Angeles County (South Central)—LA City (South Central/Watts), CA	34.7%	23.1%	0.6%	41.6%	75.2%	31.83	36.6%	45.2%	26.5%	22.0%	5.0%	1.2%
2338	El Paso City (Central), TX	83.4%	1.7%	0.6%	14.3%	89.0%	43.58	34.7%	34.8%	22.7%	26.7%	10.2%	5.5%
2339	NYC-Bronx Community District 5—Morris Heights, Fordham South & Mount Hope, NY	14.2%	36.1%	1.8%	47.9%	65.7%	33.86	42.0%	34.3%	27.2%	25.8%	9.0%	3.7%
2340	Miami-Dade County (Northeast)—Hialeah City (South Central), FL	93.9%	2.5%	0.3%	3.4%	94.8%	46.78	74.7%	32.7%	33.7%	20.3%	9.9%	3.3%
2341	South Texas Development Council (North)—Webb County—Laredo City (Central), TX	92.9%	0.4%	0.3%	6.3%	96.4%	36.43	27.9%	35.6%	26.3%	25.0%	9.2%	4.0%

2342	Los Angeles County (Central)—Huntington Park City, Florence-Graham & Walnut Park, CA	56.3%	3.8%	0.6%	39.3%	93.9%	33.32	46.4%	50.2%	23.1%	20.3%	4.9%	1.4%
2343	Hidalgo County (East)—Alamo & Donna Cities, TX	90.8%	0.5%	0.0%	8.7%	91.9%	34.82	25.5%	37.7%	27.3%	23.4%	8.6%	3.0%
2344	Los Angeles County—LA City (East Central/Silver Lake, Echo Park & Westlake), CA	45.8%	3.5%	18.7%	32.1%	54.8%	37.64	45.9%	29.3%	17.0%	21.8%	22.4%	9.6%
2345	NYC-Brooklyn Community District 7—Sunset Park & Windsor Terrace, NY	41.8%	3.5%	33.4%	21.4%	33.9%	36.07	45.2%	34.2%	19.8%	15.3%	19.1%	11.6%
2346	Miami-Dade County (Northeast Central)—Miami City (Downtown), FL	82.4%	10.6%	0.9%	6.1%	81.8%	41.72	63.8%	29.7%	30.8%	19.6%	12.5%	7.4%
2347	Los Angeles County (Central)—LA City (Central/Koreatown), CA	26.7%	4.8%	35.3%	33.2%	49.1%	36.83	58.9%	26.1%	21.3%	22.0%	23.3%	7.2%
2348	Hidalgo County (North & West), TX	90.0%	1.3%	0.1%	8.5%	93.0%	32.82	31.0%	44.4%	26.2%	21.0%	6.1%	2.3%

(*continued*)

Table 5.6 (continued)

Rank	*PUMA*	*Race/ethnicity*					*Age/nativity*		*Educational attainment*				
		White	*Black*	*Asian*	*All other races*	*Hispanic*	*Age*	*Foreign-born*	*< HS diploma*	*HS diploma*	*Some college*	*BA/BS degree*	*Post-graduate*
2349	Los Angeles County (Central)—LA City (Southeast/East Vernon), CA	42.5%	8.2%	0.7%	48.6%	89.6%	31.31	46.2%	54.6%	21.8%	18.1%	4.2%	1.2%
2350	Houston City (North) & Aldine—Between Loop I-610 & Beltway TX-8, TX	77.1%	12.3%	0.8%	9.7%	78.4%	33.17	34.5%	47.0%	29.8%	19.1%	3.2%	1.0%
2351	Houston City (West)—Westpark Tollway, Between Loop I-610 & Beltway TX-8, TX	59.5%	14.1%	13.1%	13.3%	53.6%	33.00	51.7%	28.9%	23.7%	20.4%	17.6%	9.5%

All other races include American Indian, Alaskan Native, Native Hawaiian, Pacific Islander, other race, and multiple race categories

References

U.S. Bureau of the Census/American Factfinder (U.S. Census). 2019. *American Community Survey (Annual Data, 2008–2018)*. U.S. Census Bureau's American Community Survey Office. http://factfinder.census.gov.

U.S. Bureau of the Census (U.S. Census). 2020. *Table 2. Cumulative Estimates of Resident Population Change for the United States, Regions, States, and Puerto Rico and Region and State Rankings: April 1, 2010 to July 1, 2018 (NST-EST2018-02)*. Population Division. Online. Accessed July 2020. http://www2.census.gov/programs-surveys/popest/tables/2010-2018/national/totals/nst-est2018-02.xlsx?#.

CHAPTER 6

Variation in Multidimensional Poverty Across Socio-Demographic Cohorts

We now complete our descriptive overview of multidimensional poverty in the U.S. In this chapter, we present the Multidimensional Poverty Index (MPI), the headcount ratio, and the average deprivation intensity values of a variety of socio-demographic cohorts. More specifically, we detail multidimensional poverty incidence and intensity for several categories that identify individuals by gender, age, race, ethnicity, nativity, level of educational attainment, marital status, and labor market status. Each of these categories is comprised of two to seven cohorts, and comparison across the cohorts allows for a more detailed depiction of multidimensional poverty. To this end, we also discuss estimates of the number of multidimensionally poor for each cohort and for the corresponding categories.

The treatment presented here extends from our discussions of national and sub-national geographic units that are provided in Chaps. 4 and 5. Chapter 4 began this part of the book by placing an emphasis on the national level. We then broadened our discussion in Chap. 5 to include the examination of possible variation across regions, divisions, states, and Public Use Microdata Areas. We again examine data from the 2008–2018 American Community Survey (ACS) Public Use Microdata Sample (PUMS) (U.S. Census 2019). However, we now deviate from our earlier process of examining geographic units first at an aggregate level and then at the sub-national level. Instead,

R. White, *Multidimensional Poverty in America*,
https://doi.org/10.1007/978-3-030-45916-1_6

we follow a path from the aggregate/national level to the individual level of detail via the examination of our socio-demographic cohorts.

The structure of the chapter is as follows. We first provide a discussion of the levels of and the variation in MPI values and related measures across our cohorts. This is followed by a comparison, again across cohorts, of the distribution of individuals across four groups: those who are neither multidimensionally poor nor vulnerable to multidimensional poverty, those who are vulnerable to multidimensional poverty, those experiencing moderate multidimensional poverty, and those who are severely multidimensionally poor. We then turn our attention to deprivation frequency values at the dimension and indicator levels of detail before offering concluding thoughts.

6.1 Cohort-specific Variation in Multidimensional Poverty Incidence and Intensity

Table 6.1 presents headcount ratio, average deprivation intensity, and MPI values for the entire U.S. population during our 2008–2018 reference period and for each of the cohorts that we examine. Looking first to the Gender category, we see that by a slight margin women experience multidimensional poverty more frequently than do their male counterparts (i.e., a rate of 8.07 percent as compared to 7.96 percent). We also see that, because the average deprivation intensity value for the female cohort (0.3946) is marginally lower in value than the corresponding value for the male cohort (0.3970), the difference in the MPI values across the two cohorts is rather negligible. By comparison, there is much more pronounced variation in the values of the MPI and its related measures across the three age cohorts. Additionally, across the age cohorts, the values follow a consistent ordering, with the highest values observed for individuals 18–64 years of age (i.e., the working age cohort) while the 0–17 years of age cohort (i.e., the child cohort) has the lowest values. The differences in values are quite large, particularly in terms of the headcount ratio, which is evident when the MPI value for the working age cohort (3.84) is compared to that of the child cohort (1.69). The values for the third age cohort, that which includes individuals who are at least 65 years of age, fall between the values observed for the other two cohorts.

Unlike the Gender category, the Race category includes seven cohorts, two of which serve as umbrella cohorts (i.e., the other race and the

Table 6.1 MPI and related measures, 2008–2018

Category	*Cohort*	*Headcount ratio (%)*	*Average intensity*	*MPI*
All (full sample)		8.01%	0.3958	3.1715
Gender	Female	8.07%	0.3946	3.1836
	Male	7.96%	0.3970	3.1590
Age	0–17 years of age	4.56%	0.3696	1.6870
	18–64 years of age	9.56%	0.4018	3.8429
	65 years of age and above	6.85%	0.3875	2.6552
Race	American Indian And Alaskan native	14.60%	0.3996	5.8353
	Asian	9.16%	0.3950	3.6177
	Black	10.73%	0.3868	4.1499
	Native Hawaiian and Pacific Islander	9.75%	0.3913	3.8151
	White	6.45%	0.3944	2.5441
	Multiple races	7.27%	0.3891	2.8302
	Other race	22.80%	0.4138	9.4348
Ethnicity	Hispanic	19.29%	0.4118	7.9423
	Non-hispanic	5.70%	0.3846	2.1922
Nativity	Foreign-born	22.14%	0.4187	9.2707
	Native-born	5.88%	0.3827	2.2488
Educational attainment	Less than a high school diploma	14.68%	0.4103	6.0235
	High school graduate	6.87%	0.3731	2.5627
	Some college	4.59%	0.3676	1.6866
	Bachelor's degree	2.17%	0.3684	0.7985
	Master's degree	1.36%	0.3660	0.4966
	Professional degree	1.38%	0.3688	0.5078
	Doctorate	1.26%	0.3683	0.4657
Marital status	Married	6.00%	0.4051	2.4320
	Single	8.25%	0.3911	3.2257
	Divorced, Separated, or Widowed	12.43%	0.3935	4.8902
Labor market status	Employed	4.72%	0.3925	1.8541
	Unemployed	39.66%	0.4245	16.8357
	Not in the Labor force	8.66%	0.3872	3.3534

multiple races cohorts). When considering variation in values across the seven cohorts, we find quite large differences in terms of the headcount ratio and MPI values. As is common, less variation is found among the average deprivation intensity values. That being said, it is noteworthy that the average deprivation intensity value of the other race cohort (0.4138) is considerably higher than the values of the remaining cohorts, which range from 0.3868 to 0.3996. Looking to the headcount ratio series, the value of the other race cohort (22.8 percent) is more than 35 percent higher than the next highest value. This results in the MPI value for the other race cohort (9.43) being more than twice the value of any other cohort with the single exception of the American Indian and Alaskan Native (AIAN) cohort (5.84). The AIAN cohort also has the second highest headcount ratio value (14.6 percent), while the black cohort has the next highest headcount ratio (10.7 percent), followed closely by the Native Hawaiian and Pacific Islander (NHPI) cohort (9.75 percent) and the Asian cohort (9.16 percent). Due to the minor variation in average deprivation intensity values, the ordering of cohort-specific MPI values follows that of the headcount ratio series. Following the other race and AIAN cohorts, the MPI for the black cohort (4.15) is somewhat higher than that of the NHPI cohort (3.82) which is only slightly higher than the value of the Asian cohort (3.62). Interestingly, the MPI values for these cohorts all exceed the level that is observed for the entire U.S. population. Thus, the headcount ratio and MPI values of the multiple race cohort and the white cohort are all well below the respective national values.

The high incidence of multidimensional poverty among those within the other race cohort is interesting. Our full sample contains 34,291,600 observations, of which 1,265,208 (3.7 percent) self-identify as being of "some other race" (i.e., neither white, black or African American, AIAN, Asian, NHPI, nor two or more races). Of the observations in the other race cohort, 95.2 percent also identify as Hispanic. However, it is obviously not the case that all who identify as Hispanic also report being part of the other race cohort. There are 4,771,449 observations in the full sample that self-identified as Hispanic; however, a large majority of these individuals (65.9 percent) reported their race as being white. Given the large white population in the U.S., Hispanic individuals comprise only 11.9 percent of the country's white population. Thus, there is a low pairwise correlation value (ρ = -0.10) between the Hispanic series and the white series. To the contrary, the correlation coefficient value for the pairing of the other race and the Hispanic series is much higher (ρ = 0.46).[1]

[1]The other race cohort and the white cohort combine to account for 91.1 percent of Hispanic individuals in our data. The majority of the remaining Hispanic individuals (i.e., 5.1

Looking at the Ethnicity category, we see that the headcount ratio for the Hispanic cohort (19.3 percent) is similar to that observed for the other race cohort (22.8 percent). The average deprivation intensity values between the two cohorts are even more similar, differing by only 0.002. This produces an MPI value for the Hispanic cohort (7.94) that, although lower than the MPI value of the other race cohort, is still more than twice the national MPI figure. To the contrary, both the headcount ratio value (5.7 percent) and the MPI value (2.19) of the non-Hispanic cohort fall below the corresponding national values.

When comparing the cohort of native-born individuals to their foreign-born counterparts, we see differences that are similar to what is reported for the Ethnicity category. However, the pairwise correlation coefficient between the Hispanic series and the foreign-born series is only equal to 0.29; thus, while the values may be similar there appears to be only a minor overlap of observations across cohorts. Among the foreign-born in the U.S., the MPI value is equal to 9.27. This is more than triple the value reported for the native-born cohort (2.25). As we have observed when comparing many cohorts, there is not a great amount of variation in the average deprivation intensity values. Instead, it is the difference in the headcount ratio series (i.e., 22.1 percent for the foreign-born cohort as compared to 5.7 percent for the native-born cohort) that accounts for most of the difference in the cohorts' MPI values.

Turning our attention to the Educational Attainment category, we find a clear and largely consistent pattern in the magnitudes of the MPI and its related measures. In particular, the headcount ratio and the MPI values generally decrease as we move from lower to higher levels of educational attainment. For example, the cohort that includes adults (and the children of household heads) who did not earn a high school diploma (or an equivalent credential) has significantly higher headcount ratio (14.7 percent) and MPI values (6.02) relative to the cohort of individuals who did complete high school (6.9 percent and 2.56, respectively). We see the headcount ratio values decrease still further to 4.6 percent for the cohort of individuals who completed some college coursework, and then further declines, this time by more than half, to 2.2 percent for those who completed a bachelor's degree. The headcount ratio remains largely constant across the cohorts that identify the three highest levels of education

percent of the remaining 8.9 percent) identify as being of two or more races (i.e., multiple races).

attainment (i.e., the values range from 1.26 percent to 1.38 percent). While we do not see the same pattern or magnitudes of decreases in values among the average deprivation intensity series, the decreases in the headcount ratio values contribute to a sufficient degree that MPI values decline as the level of educational attainment increases. Additionally, it is of note that the MPI value for the cohort of individuals who did not complete high school is higher than the corresponding national value, while the MPI values for all other cohorts are less than the national value.

The final two categories that we consider are Marital Status and Labor Market Status. Both of these categories are comprised of three cohorts, and in each case two of the cohorts have MPI values that exceed the national level. Beginning with the Marital Status category, the headcount ratio (6.0 percent) and MPI value (2.43) for the married cohort are below the national level; however, the headcount ratio (12.4 percent) and MPI value (4.89) for the cohort of divorced, separated, or widowed individuals both far exceed the respective national values. Interestingly, the values for the cohort of single individuals are not terribly dissimilar from the national values. Likewise, among the cohorts in the Labor Market Status category, we see that the values for individuals who are not in the labor force cohort are similar to the national values; however, the values for those who are employed are less than the national values, and the values for those who are unemployed are significantly higher than the corresponding national values.

Given the relatively minimal variation in average deprivation intensity values across cohorts, it is the observed differences in headcount ratio values that contribute the most to variation in MPI values across cohorts. The headcount ratio values, however, are based on the binary outcome of either being multidimensionally poor or of not being multidimensionally poor. The classification of being multidimensionally poor is determined by the level of the deprivation score (i.e., an observation is classified as multidimensionally poor if the corresponding deprivation score is equal to or above 0.3333). By applying a population weight series to the individual observations, aggregating to estimate both the number of individuals who are multidimensionally deprived and the size of the population, and then dividing the former value by the latter, we arrive at the headcount ratio.[2]

[2] See Chap. 3 for more specifics on the calculation of the deprivation score and its use to identify multidimensional poverty.

To provide a more complete depiction of deprivation, we further categorize the observations that are identified as multidimensionally poor into two groups: those that are experiencing moderate multidimensional poverty (i.e., a deprivation score ranging from 0.3333 to 0.5) and those who are suffering severe multidimensional poverty (i.e., a deprivation score that is equal to or above 0.5). Similarly, we categorize the cohort of observations who are not multidimensionally poor into two groups: those who are vulnerable to multidimensional poverty (i.e., a deprivation score of at least 0.2 but less than 0.3333) and those who are neither deprived nor vulnerable to multidimensional poverty (i.e., a deprivation score that is less than 0.2). With appropriate population weights applied, Table 6.2 presents the share of individuals in each cohort, grouped by category, who are identified in each of these four groups. Table 6.3 lists the corresponding population counts.

Table 6.2 presents the population shares of each cohort that fall within each of the four groups (i.e., neither deprived nor vulnerable, vulnerable, experiencing moderate multidimensional poverty, or suffering severe multidimensional poverty). All cohort-specific population shares that are greater than the corresponding value for the full sample are identified by bold font. An example may help to illustrate. We see that 13.66 percent of women are identified as vulnerable to multidimensional poverty while 13.62 percent of the full sample (i.e., the combined male and female population) are classified as vulnerable. Thus, and admittedly by only a small degree, women are more likely to be vulnerable to multidimensional deprivation. We also see that women are more likely to experience moderate multidimensional poverty. Men, on the other hand, are more likely to neither be deprived nor vulnerable to multidimensional poverty and are more likely to suffer severe multidimensional poverty. That men are more likely than women to suffer severe deprivation is of particular interest as the headcount ratio values that are presented in Table 6.1 indicate only the relative frequencies of multidimensional poverty (i.e., a binary outcome) without regard to the severity of deprivation.

If we focus on the four groups and those cohorts that have higher population share values than observed for the full sample, we see a number of interesting values. A large majority of the full sample (78.4 percent) are neither deprived nor vulnerable to multidimensional poverty. A number of cohorts are disproportionately represented among this group. Specifically, we see that males, those 0–17 years of age, white individuals, those who are not Hispanic, the native-born, individuals with at least a high school

Table 6.2 Population shares by multidimensionally poor category, 2008–2018

Category	*Cohort*	*Population share within cohort*	*Neither deprived nor vulnerable*	*Vulnerable to MD poverty*	*Moderate MD poverty*	*Severe MD poverty*
			(d_i < 0.20)	*(0.20 ≤ d_i < 0.33)*	*(0.33 ≤ d_i < 0.50)*	*(0.50 ≤ d_i)*
All (full sample)		100.00%	78.37%	13.62%	7.05%	0.96%
Gender	Female	50.79%	78.26%	**13.66%**	**7.13%**	0.95%
	Male	49.22%	**78.46%**	13.57%	6.99%	**0.98%**
Age	0–17 years of age	23.31%	**80.44%**	**15.02%**	4.38%	0.17%
	18–64 years of age	62.48%	77.69%	12.74%	**8.24%**	**1.33%**
	65 years of age and above	14.21%	77.97%	**15.20%**	6.19%	0.63%
Race	American Indian and Alaskan native	0.82%	63.41%	**21.95%**	**12.20%**	**2.44%**
	Asian	5.08%	75.98%	**14.76%**	**8.07%**	**1.18%**
	Black	12.61%	69.71%	**19.59%**	**9.83%**	0.87%
	Native Hawaiian and Pacific Islander	0.16%	75.00%	**18.75%**	6.25%	0.00%
	White	73.56%	**81.89%**	11.66%	5.70%	0.75%
	Multiple races	2.93%	77.47%	**15.36%**	6.48%	0.68%
	Other race	4.83%	53.42%	**23.81%**	**18.63%**	**4.14%**
Ethnicity	Hispanic	17.03%	58.95%	**21.79%**	**15.91%**	**3.35%**
	Non-hispanic	82.97%	**82.36%**	11.94%	5.23%	0.47%
Nativity	Foreign-born	13.14%	57.76%	**20.09%**	**17.81%**	**4.34%**
	Native-born	86.87%	**81.48%**	12.64%	5.43%	0.45%
Educational attainment	Less than a high school diploma	33.55%	64.05%	**20.92%**	**12.52%**	**2.50%**
	High school graduate	21.67%	**79.70%**	13.43%	6.55%	0.32%
	Some college	23.83%	**84.68%**	10.74%	4.41%	0.17%
	Bachelor's degree	13.35%	**91.84%**	5.99%	2.10%	0.07%

(*continued*)

Table 6.2 (continued)

Category	*Cohort*	*Population share within cohort*	*Neither deprived nor vulnerable*	*Vulnerable to MD poverty*	*Moderate MD poverty*	*Severe MD poverty*
			($d_i < 0.20$)	*($0.20 \le d_i < 0.33$)*	*($0.33 \le d_i < 0.50$)*	*($0.50 \le d_i$)*
	Master's degree	5.39%	**94.62%**	4.08%	1.30%	0.00%
	Professional degree	1.34%	**94.78%**	3.73%	1.49%	0.00%
	Doctorate	0.87%	**95.40%**	3.45%	1.15%	0.00%
Marital status	Married	38.87%	**85.03%**	8.98%	5.09%	0.90%
	Single	45.83%	75.78%	**15.97%**	**7.38%**	0.87%
	Divorced, Separated, or Widowed	15.29%	69.26%	**18.31%**	**11.05%**	**1.37%**
Labor market status	Employed	46.85%	**86.92%**	8.37%	4.20%	0.51%
	Unemployed	3.86%	30.31%	**30.05%**	**31.09%**	**8.55%**
	Not in the labor force	49.29%	74.01%	**17.33%**	**7.87%**	0.79%

Values presented in bold font are greater than the corresponding "all (full sample)" category value

education, those who are married, and the employed all have population share values in excess of the national value. Additionally, for this group, it is the cohort of doctoral degree holders (i.e., the highest of the Educational Attainment categories) that has the highest population share (95.4 percent). We also see large proportions of those who have earned a bachelor's degree (91.8 percent), a master's degree (94.6 percent), or a professional degree (94.8 percent) in the neither deprived nor vulnerable to multidimensional poverty group. Of course, since the population shares sum to 100 percent, it follows that when a cohort is overrepresented in a group it must also be underrepresented in one or more of the remaining groups.

For the group that includes those who are vulnerable to multidimensional poverty, we see a larger number of cohorts with population share values that are greater than the value presented for the full sample. Namely,

Table 6.3 Population counts by multidimensionally poor category, 2008–2018

Category	*Cohort*	*Neither deprived nor vulnerable*	*Vulnerable to MD poverty*	*Moderate MD poverty*	*Severe MD poverty*	*MD poor*
		($d_i < 0.20$)	($0.20 \le d_i < 0.33$)	($0.33 \le d_i < 0.50$)	($0.50 \le d_i$)	($0.33 \le d_i$)
All (full sample)		247,815,976	43,068,184	22,293,003	3,035,643	25,328,646
Gender	Female	125,694,590	**21,945,169**	**11,446,904**	1,517,821	12,964,725
	Male	**122,121,386**	21,123,015	10,877,721	**1,517,821**	12,395,542
Age	0–17 years of age	**59,289,901**	**11,067,448**	3,225,371	126,485	3,351,856
	18–64 years of age	153,489,696	25,170,539	**16,284,959**	**2,624,566**	18,909,526
	65 years of age and above	35,036,379	**6,830,197**	2,782,673	284,592	3,067,264
Race	American Indian and Alaskan native	1,644,307	**569,183**	**316,213**	**63,243**	379,455
	Asian	12,205,814	**2,371,596**	**1,296,473**	**189,728**	1,486,200
	Black	27,795,106	**7,810,456**	**3,921,039**	347,834	4,268,873
	Native Hawaiian and Pacific Islander	379,455	**94,864**	31,621	0	31,621
	White	**190,486,594**	27,131,059	13,249,317	1,739,170	14,988,487
	Multiple races	7,178,031	**1,422,958**	600,804	63,243	664,047
	Other race	8,158,290	**3,636,447**	**2,845,915**	**632,426**	3,478,341
Ethnicity	Hispanic	31,747,766	**11,731,495**	**8,569,367**	**1,802,413**	10,371,780
	Non-hispanic	**216,068,210**	31,336,689	13,723,636	1,233,230	14,956,866
Nativity	Foreign-born	24,000,552	**8,348,018**	**7,399,380**	**1,802,413**	9,201,793
	Native-born	**223,815,424**	34,720,166	14,925,244	1,233,230	16,158,474

Educational attainment	Less than a High school diploma	67,954,132	**22,198,139**	**13,280,938**	**2,656,188**	15,937,125
	High school graduate	**54,609,952**	9,201,793	4,490,222	221,349	4,711,571
	Some college	**63,811,744**	8,095,048	3,320,234	126,485	3,446,720
	Bachelor's degree	**38,767,690**	2,529,702	885,396	31,621	917,017
	Master's degree	**1,61,26,853**	695,668	221,349	0	221,349
	Professional degree	**4,015,903**	158,106	63,243	0	63,243
	Doctorate	**2,624,566**	94,864	31,621	0	31,621
Marital status	Married	**104,508,332**	11,035,827	6,261,014	1,106,745	7,367,758
	Single	109,820,707	**23,146,777**	**10,687,993**	1,264,851	11,952,844
	Divorced, Separated, or Widowed	33,486,936	**8,853,959**	**5,343,996**	**664,047**	6,008,043
Labor market status	Employed	**128,761,855**	12,395,542	6,229,392	758,911	6,988,303
	Unemployed	3,699,690	**3,668,069**	**3,794,554**	**1,043,502**	4,838,056
	Not in the labor force	115,354,432	**27,004,574**	**12,269,057**	1,233,230	13,502,287

Values presented in bold font corresponding to population shares that are greater than the value for the "all (full sample)" category. See Table 6.2 for population shares

13.6 percent of the full sample is vulnerable to multidimensional deprivation, and more than half of the cohorts included in Table 6.2 (i.e., 15 of 29) have higher population share values. By far, the cohort that is comprised of unemployed individuals has the highest population share (30.1 percent) in this group. Other cohorts that are more likely to be vulnerable to deprivation include women; those who are under 18 years of age and those who are at least 65 years of age; individuals who are American Indian or Alaskan native; Asians; blacks; native Hawaiians and Pacific Islanders; those who identify as some other race or as multiple races; Hispanic individuals; those who are foreign-born; those who did not complete high school; those who are single; and those who are not in the labor force.

A review of Table 6.1 allows for the identification of cohorts that have headcount ratio values greater than the 8.01 percent value that is reported for the full sample. Comparing each cohort's population shares for the moderate multidimensional poverty and the severe multidimensional poverty groups to the corresponding values that are reported for the full sample yields a number of interesting results. First, while the headcount ratio of men is less than the value of the full sample, we still find that men are slightly more likely to suffer severe multidimensional poverty. Second, with respect to the moderate multidimensional poverty group, the population shares of the cohorts that include women, blacks, the single, and those who are not in the labor force are all greater than the corresponding value for the full sample. Lastly, the remaining cohorts have population share values for both the moderate and severe multidimensionally poor groups that are greater than the corresponding full sample values.[3]

Table 6.3 presents population counts for each cohort during the typical year in our reference period. Based on the full sample values, the multidimensionally poor population of the U.S. totals slightly more than 25.3 million individuals. This total is near-evenly split between men and women. However, a very large majority (74.7 percent) of those who are multidimensionally poor are 18–64 years of age. A majority of the multidimensionally poor population are white (59.2 percent), and a near-equal proportion (59.1 percent) are non-Hispanic. More than one-third of the multidimensionally poor are foreign-born (36.2 percent).

[3] These specific cohorts are those 18–64 years of age; the race cohorts of American Indians and Alaskan natives, Asians, and individuals who identify as some other race; those who are Hispanic; the foreign-born; individuals who did not complete high school; those who are divorced, separated, or widowed; and the unemployed.

Likewise, more than half of the multidimensionally poor lack a high school diploma (62.9 percent). A plurality (47.2 percent) of the multidimensionally deprived are single, and slightly more than half (53.5 percent) are not in the labor force. Now, with these shares being stated, a caveat is in order: It is important to remember that there is great variation in population shares across cohorts. For example, to say that a majority (59.2 percent) of the multidimensionally poor are white, while true, is also somewhat misleading since white individuals account for 73.6 percent of the population. Since white individuals are underrepresented, relative to their population share, among the multidimensionally poor, it follows that one or more of the other race cohorts is overrepresented among the multidimensionally poor.

6.2 Cohort-specific Variation in Deprivation Frequency Values

To better understand the forms of deprivation that are faced by the individuals that comprise the various socio-demographic cohorts we have introduced, we can look to the deprivation frequency values at both the dimension and indicator levels of detail. Recall that the deprivation frequency value is simply the proportion of population-weighted observations that have been identified as facing deprivation in the corresponding dimension or indicator. Table 6.4 presents the deprivation frequency values at the dimension level, while Table 6.5 presents the values at the indicator level. As before, we use bold font to identify those values that are greater than the corresponding full sample value.

Beginning with the Gender category in Table 6.4 and noting that the headcount ratio values presented in Table 6.1 for the female and male cohorts are quite similar, we can see that women are more likely, relative to the full population, to suffer deprivation in terms of the Economic Security and Housing dimensions. Men, on the other hand, are more likely to experience deprivation in the Education and Health dimensions. Looking at the values for the female and male cohorts in Table 6.5, we see that higher frequencies of income poverty and facing housing costs that are greater than 50 percent of income are the driving indicators that cause the dimension-level deprivation frequency values experienced by women to exceed the full sample values. For men, we see that the educational

Table 6.4 Deprivation frequency values by dimension, 2008–2018

Category	*cohort/dimension*	*Economic security*	*Education*	*Health*	*Housing*
All (full sample)		16.92%	12.87%	24.50%	19.82%
Gender	Female	**17.80%**	12.33%	23.35%	**20.76%**
	Male	16.02%	**13.43%**	**25.68%**	18.84%
Age	0–17 years of age	**20.64%**	5.89%	10.63%	**28.15%**
	18–64 years of age	**17.16%**	**13.64%**	**26.51%**	17.84%
	65 years of age and above	9.80%	**20.95%**	**38.38%**	14.83%
Race	American Indian and Alaskan native	**29.28%**	**16.57%**	**39.59%**	**29.89%**
	Asian	14.03%	**24.34%**	17.62%	**25.87%**
	Black	**28.24%**	12.41%	**28.43%**	**27.16%**
	Native Hawaiian and Pacific Islander	**21.87%**	**13.04%**	23.00%	38.01%
	White	14.21%	10.66%	23.57%	16.34%
	Multiple races	**20.85%**	8.69%	21.73%	**24.35%**
	Other race	**27.00%**	**37.70%**	**34.67%**	**42.17%**
Ethnicity	Hispanic	**25.07%**	**32.23%**	**32.58%**	**36.37%**
	Non-hispanic	15.25%	8.90%	22.85%	16.42%
Nativity	Foreign-born	**20.11%**	**41.28%**	**35.93%**	**32.44%**
	Native-born	16.44%	8.58%	22.77%	17.91%
Educational attainment	Less than a high school diploma	**23.35%**	**36.01%**	**26.12%**	**28.68%**
	High school graduate	**18.12%**	4.00%	**35.48%**	18.54%
	Some college	15.34%	2.04%	**25.16%**	16.53%
	Bachelor's degree	8.34%	2.46%	14.42%	11.28%
	Master's degree	5.66%	2.12%	11.46%	8.68%
	Professional degree	4.95%	2.10%	11.89%	9.15%
	Doctorate	4.65%	3.25%	11.81%	8.24%
Marital status	Married	8.45%	**13.92%**	21.43%	13.41%
	Single	**22.99%**	9.78%	21.43%	**24.82%**
	Divorced, Separated, or Widowed	**20.29%**	**19.51%**	**41.49%**	**21.10%**
Labor market status	Employed	6.77%	10.84%	18.82%	13.86%
	Unemployed	**100.00%**	**17.25%**	**45.68%**	**31.33%**
	Not in the labor force	**20.07%**	**14.47%**	**28.23%**	**24.57%**

Values presented in bold font are greater than the corresponding "all (full sample)" category value

Table 6.5 Deprivation frequency values by indicator, 2008–2018

Category	*Dimension*	*Economic security*		*Education*		*Health*		*Housing*		
	Cohort/ indicator	*Income poverty*	*Unemployed*	*Educational attainment*	*Limited English HH*	*Disability status*	*Health insurance*	*Crowded house*	*Housing costs*	*House amenities*
All (full sample)		14.25%	3.86%	10.13%	4.78%	12.90%	12.70%	7.23%	13.51%	0.79%
Gender	Female	**15.52%**	3.46%	9.66%	4.57%	**13.15%**	11.13%	7.15%	**14.61%**	0.78%
	Male	12.94%	**4.28%**	**10.62%**	**5.00%**	12.64%	**14.31%**	**7.32%**	12.38%	**0.80%**
Age	0–17 years of age	**20.07%**	0.73%	1.40%	**5.89%**	4.15%	6.67%	**13.97%**	**17.10%**	0.69%
	18–64 years of age	13.26%	**5.72%**	**11.37%**	4.48%	10.52%	**17.61%**	6.00%	12.35%	0.73%
	65 years of age and above	9.07%	0.82%	**18.99%**	4.32%	**37.71%**	0.95%	1.60%	12.72%	**1.22%**
Race	American Indian and Alaskan native	**25.87%**	**5.91%**	**15.41%**	3.89%	**17.21%**	**25.32%**	**16.79%**	**13.70%**	**3.33%**
	Asian	11.61%	3.14%	**10.15%**	**18.33%**	6.91%	11.24%	**12.36%**	**15.05%**	**1.00%**
	Black	**24.49%**	**6.38%**	**11.87%**	1.61%	**14.51%**	**15.48%**	**7.89%**	**20.61%**	**0.89%**
	Native Hawaiian and Pacific Islander	**18.18%**	**5.29%**	9.88%	**5.00%**	10.27%	**13.93%**	**25.32%**	**16.23%**	**1.42%**
	White	11.75%	3.39%	8.87%	3.38%	**13.36%**	11.22%	5.31%	11.52%	0.71%
	Multiple races	**18.04%**	**4.13%**	7.13%	3.27%	11.38%	11.62%	**9.31%**	**16.36%**	**0.83%**
	Other race	**24.01%**	**4.70%**	**25.68%**	**21.19%**	8.19%	**27.88%**	**25.89%**	**21.75%**	**0.99%**

(*continued*)

Table 6.5 (continued)

Category	*Dimension*	*Economic security*		*Education*		*Health*		*Housing*		
	Cohort/ indicator	*Income poverty*	*Unemployed*	*Educational attainment*	*Limited English HH*	*Disability status*	*Health insurance*	*Crowded house*	*Housing costs*	*House amenities*
Ethnicity	Hispanic	**22.26%**	**4.26%**	**21.70%**	**18.31%**	8.90%	**25.03%**	**21.00%**	**19.40%**	**0.89%**
	Non-hispanic	12.61%	3.78%	7.76%	2.01%	**13.72%**	10.16%	4.41%	12.30%	0.77%
Nativity	Foreign-born	**17.16%**	**4.38%**	**27.43%**	**24.87%**	9.61%	**27.69%**	**16.81%**	**18.37%**	**1.03%**
	Native-born	13.81%	3.78%	7.52%	1.75%	**13.40%**	10.43%	5.78%	12.77%	0.75%
Educational attainment	Less than a high school diploma	**21.70%**	2.75%	**33.96%**	**8.89%**	**12.96%**	**14.42%**	**13.44%**	**17.73%**	**0.93%**
	High school graduate	14.20%	**5.80%**	0.00%	4.00%	**19.07%**	**18.14%**	5.63%	13.21%	**0.90%**
	Some college	11.79%	**5.01%**	0.00%	2.04%	**13.27%**	**13.05%**	3.95%	12.68%	0.71%
	Bachelor's degree	5.75%	3.20%	0.00%	2.46%	8.09%	6.74%	2.36%	8.77%	0.58%
	Master's degree	3.70%	2.33%	0.00%	2.12%	8.23%	3.48%	1.67%	6.78%	0.53%
	Professional degree	3.52%	1.74%	0.00%	2.10%	8.33%	3.81%	1.53%	7.39%	0.51%
	Doctorate	3.22%	1.74%	0.00%	3.25%	9.20%	2.90%	1.57%	6.28%	0.74%
Marital status	Married	6.01%	3.00%	**11.33%**	4.76%	12.44%	9.81%	5.20%	8.66%	0.54%
	Single	**20.05%**	**4.47%**	6.68%	**5.06%**	7.72%	**14.69%**	**10.33%**	**16.24%**	**0.81%**

	Divorced, Separated, or Widowed	**17.81%**	**4.22%**	**17.42%**	4.04%	**29.61%**	**14.05%**	3.12%	**17.65%**	**1.37%**
Labor market status	Employed	6.77%	0.00%	8.50%	4.27%	5.62%	**13.97%**	5.17%	8.88%	0.62%
	Unemployed	**30.79%**	**100.00%**	**16.02%**	4.32%	11.63%	**37.77%**	**8.92%**	**24.04%**	**1.02%**
	Not in the labor force	**20.07%**	0.00%	**11.22%**	**5.31%**	**19.92%**	9.52%	**9.07%**	**17.09%**	**0.94%**

Values presented in bold font are greater than the corresponding “all (full sample)” category value

attainment indicator (i.e., lack of a high school diploma or equivalent credential) and the limited English-speaking household indicator drive the high deprivation frequency values for the Education dimension. We also see that the health insurance indicator accounts for the Health dimension's deprivation frequency value being greater than the full sample value.

A similar pattern is found when we consider the cohorts within the Age category. We see that the 0–17 years of age cohort is more likely to be deprived in the Economic Security and Housing dimensions, while the 65 years of age and above cohort is more likely to experience deprivation in the Education dimension and the Health dimension. The working age cohort (i.e., those individuals 18–64 years of age) are more likely to suffer deprivation in the Economic Security, Education, and Health dimensions but not with respect to the Housing dimension. In terms of the factors that account for the dimension-level deprivation, the indicators that represent income poverty and housing costs greater than 50 percent of income underlie the high dimension-level deprivation frequency values of the 0–17 years of age cohort. For those individuals in the 18–64 years of age cohort, it is the unemployment, educational attainment (i.e., incomplete high school), and the lack of health insurance indicators that result in deprivation frequency values at the dimension level that exceed the national values. Finally, for the 65 years of age and above cohort, the high deprivation frequency values that are found at the dimension level are attributable to the educational attainment and the disability status indicators. Note that the differences in the forms of deprivation across the age cohorts suggests variation over the life cycle. We explore this topic in depth as our third example of multidimensional analysis in Chap. 10.

A review of the cohorts that comprise the Race category reveals a number of significant differences. To begin with, relative to the full sample, the white cohort is less likely to be deprived in any of the four dimensions. The Asian cohort, however, is more likely to be deprived in terms of the Education dimension and the Housing dimension. The indicator-level deprivation frequency values that are presented in Table 6.5 shows that the high dimension-level deprivation frequency values of the Asian cohort are attributable to deprivation in the educational attainment (i.e., incomplete high school), limited English-speaking household indicators, and all three indicators that correspond to the Housing dimension. The black cohort is more likely to be deprived in the Economic Security, Health, and Housing dimensions, with levels of deprivation frequency above the full sample levels found for all indicators except the limited English-speaking household indicator. The AIAN cohort and the other race cohort are both more likely to be deprived in terms of all four dimensions and in all indicators except for the limited English-speaking household (for AIAN) and the disability status indicator (for the other race cohort). Likewise, looking to the Ethnicity and the Nativity categories, we see that the Hispanic cohort and the foreign-born cohort are both more likely to be deprived in all four dimensions, while the non-Hispanic and native-born cohorts are less likely to be deprived regardless of the dimension considered. A check of Table 6.5 shows the foreign-born cohort and the Hispanic cohort have indicator-level deprivation frequency values greater than the full sample values for all indicators except disability status. In Chap. 9, we provide a detailed analysis of variation in multidimensional poverty across native- and foreign-born residents of the U.S. and across immigrant populations in the U.S. that are grouped by their home countries. This is the second of our three examples of multidimensional analysis.

The Educational Attainment category provides additional interesting information. The cohort that includes adults who did not complete their high school diploma (or earn an equivalent diploma), children less than six years of age, children above the age of six who are neither enrolled in school nor report having earned a high school diploma or the equivalent is more likely, relative to the full sample, to be deprived in each of the four categories. The indicator-level deprivation frequency values for this cohort are all greater than those reported for the full sample with the single exception being the unemployment indicator. The dimension-level deprivation frequency values for the cohort of High school graduates are greater than those of the full sample for the Economic Security and Health dimensions, while the cohort of individuals who have completed some college coursework are more likely to be deprived in the Health dimension. The indicator-level deprivation frequency values for these two cohorts exceed the full sample values for the unemployment, disability status, and health insurance indicators. All other educational attainment cohorts (i.e., Bachelor's degree and above) are found less likely than the full sample to suffer deprivation in each of the four dimensions.

The remaining two categories are Marital Status and Labor Market Status. Compared to the full sample, individuals in the divorced, separated, or widowed cohort are more likely to be deprived in all dimensions. Likewise, individuals who are in the unemployed cohort and the not in the labor force cohort of the Labor Market Status category are more likely to be deprived in all dimensions. Each of these cohorts, as well as the cohort that includes single (i.e., never married) individuals, has seven indicator-level deprivation frequency values that exceed the corresponding full sample values; however, the single cohort is only more likely to be deprived in two dimensions: Economic Security and Housing. Those who are employed are found less likely to be deprived regardless of the dimension considered, while those who are in the married cohort are only more likely to experience deprivation in the Education dimension, and this appears to be driven by deprivation above the national value in the educational attainment indicator.

Taken collectively, the information that is presented in Chaps. 4 and 5, plus the information presented in this chapter, provide what may be viewed as a census of sorts of America's multidimensionally poor population. In this chapter, we have identified considerable variation across socio-demographic cohorts in the incidence and intensity of multidimensional deprivation. We continue our empirical examination in the next chapter where we seek to identify the determinants of multidimensional poverty.

Reference

U.S. Bureau of the Census/American Factfinder (U.S. Census). 2019. *American Community Survey (Annual Data, 2008–2018)*. U.S. Census Bureau's American Community Survey Office. http://factfinder.census.gov.

CHAPTER 7

Identifying the Determinants of Multidimensional Poverty

In the preceding three chapters, we have documented the incidence and intensity of multidimensional poverty at the national level, at several sub-national geographic levels (i.e., regions, divisions, states, and PUMAs), and for an even larger number of cohorts based on individual characteristics (e.g., age, gender, educational attainment, etc.). This information provides an enhanced understanding of the observed variation in multidimensional poverty in the U.S. during recent years. The work also serves to both extend and buttress the discussions of multidimensional poverty that are presented in the first part of this book. These initial discussions focus on the relationship between deprivation and income poverty, on the findings of prior studies of multidimensional poverty both in the U.S. and elsewhere, and on the measurement of multidimensional poverty. To further develop our understanding of the topic, we now turn our attention to the identification of the potential determinants of multidimensional poverty.

In this chapter, we again examine data from the 2008–2018 American Community Survey (ACS) Public Use Microdata Sample (PUMS) (U.S. Census 2019). We present the results of a series of related estimations where we consider the relationships between a number of individual- and household-specific variables and three dependent variable measures, each of which represents the incidence or intensity of multidimensional poverty. The first measure is the uncensored deprivation score. This series represents the intensity of deprivation. It is continuous, and it ranges in

R. White, *Multidimensional Poverty in America*,
https://doi.org/10.1007/978-3-030-45916-1_7

value from zero to one (i.e., not at all deprived to deprived in all measured forms, respectively). Our second dependent variable series is the "MD Poor" (Multidimensionally Poor) series. This is a binary variable that is equal to one if the deprivation score value for an observation is equal to or greater than one-third (i.e., if the observation is categorized as multidimensionally poor) and is otherwise equal to zero. The third dependent variable that we examine is the "MD Poor Category" series. This final measure is a categorical variable that effectively decomposes the dichotomous MD Poor series. It takes one of four values based on the level of the deprivation score variable: neither multidimensionally poor nor vulnerable to multidimensional poverty (coded as 0), vulnerable to multidimensional poverty (1), suffering moderate multidimensional poverty (2), and experiencing severe multidimensional poverty (3). The latter two categories cleave the group of observations that the MD Poor variable identifies as multidimensionally poor, while the former two categories are a decomposition of the group of observations that are identified as not suffering multidimensional poverty.

Throughout this chapter, we utilize data from the 2008–2018 American Community Survey for the years 2008 through 2018. Our set of explanatory variables is informed by the variation in multidimensional poverty incidence and intensity that is documented in Chaps. 5 and 6. The choice of explanatory variables includes indicators of each observation's gender, their educational attainment, race/ethnicity, nativity, age, marital status, and employment status. We also control for household size (in members) and the primary household language. Lastly, to absorb variation in the dependent variable series that may be attributable to unobserved time- and location-specific fixed effects, respectively, each of our estimation equations includes a series of variables that identify the survey year and each observation's state of residence.

In the next section, we present our data and discuss the descriptive statistics for the full sample and several sub-samples. We follow, in Sect. 7.2, by detailing our empirical model and estimation strategy. Results are presented and discussed in Sects. 7.3 and 7.4, and we summarize and conclude in Sect. 7.5.

7.1 Descriptive Statistics

Table 7.1 presents descriptive statistics for the full sample (column (a)) and for the cohorts that comprise the MD Poor series (columns (b) and (c)) and the MD Poor Category series (columns (d) through (g)). Looking first to the full sample, we see the average deprivation score is equal to 0.0847. This is the uncensored deprivation intensity value; thus, it is the average deprivation score across the nearly 34.3 million observations in our data set. Because we estimate binomial and ordered logit models as part of our analysis, we do not employ population weights to scale our observations. As a result, the sample and sub-sample values that are presented in the table correspond to the number of observations that fall within a given category. They should not be viewed as estimates of the numbers of individuals or of population shares; however, they can be considered as approximations of such estimates.

Working from the left to the right across the columns in Table 7.1 and maintaining focus on the sub-sample sizes and average deprivation scores, we first see that 93.1 percent of all observations are categorized as not suffering multidimensional poverty. This equates to 31.9 million individual observations (column (b)). Based on the deprivation score criteria/cut-off value of 0.3333 used to categorize observations, the remaining 2.4 million observations, or 6.9 percent of the full sample, have deprivation scores greater than or equal to 0.3333 and, thus, are categorized as experiencing multidimensional poverty (column (c)). The average deprivation score for the observations that are not categorized as multidimensionally poor is 0.0618 which is much smaller, as expected, than the average deprivation score of 0.3935 that is listed for the observations that are categorized as multidimensionally poor.

Focusing on those observations that are not categorized as multidimensionally poor (i.e., the observations for which descriptive statistics are presented in column (b)), we divide the observations into two sub-samples based on deprivation scores. The summary values for these sub-samples are presented in columns (d) and (e). We see that 80.5 percent of the observations in the full sample have deprivation scores less than 0.2. These observations are categorized as being neither multidimensionally poor nor vulnerable to multidimensional poverty. Accordingly, the average deprivation score for this sub-sample is equal to 0.035 and is the lowest among the four MD Poor Categories. Turning our attention to the values presented in column (e), we see that 12.6 percent of the full sample is

Table 7.1 Descriptive Statistics

N = Variables	*Full Sample* *3,42,91,600* *(a)*	*Not MD Poor* *3,19,23,760* *(b)*	*MD Poor* *23,67,840* *(c)*	*Not Deprived* *(d_i < 0.20)* *2,75,92,514* *(d)*	*Vulnerable* *(0.20 ≤ d_i < 0.33)* *43,31,246* *(e)*	*Moderate Poverty* *(0.33 ≤ d_i < 0.50)* *21,02,275* *(f)*	*Severe Poverty* *(0.50 ≤ d_i)* *2,65,565* *(g)*
Dependent variables…							
Deprivation score (0–1)	0.0847	0.0618	0.3935	0.035	0.2323	0.3723	0.5615
	(0.119)	(0.0847)	(0.0773)	(0.0541)	(0.0242)	(0.0476)	(0.0601)
Explanatory variables…							
Gender							
Female	0.5122	0.5115	0.5215	0.5114	0.5127[a]	0.5233	0.5069
	(0.4999)	(0.4999)	(0.4995)	(0.4999)	(0.4998)	(0.4995)	(0.5)
Age category							
Under 20 years	0.2436	0.2506	0.1489	0.2498	0.2554	0.1588	0.0704
	(0.4292)	(0.4334)	(0.356)	(0.4329)	(0.4361)	(0.3655)	(0.2558)
20–29 years	0.1177	0.1145	0.1609	0.1101	0.1423	0.1573	0.1898
	(0.3222)	(0.3184)	(0.3675)	(0.313)	(0.3493)	(0.3641)	(0.3921)
30–39 years	0.1177	0.1145	0.1607	0.1156	0.1079	0.1521	0.2295
	(0.3223)	(0.3184)	(0.3673)	(0.3197)	(0.3103)	(0.3591)	(0.4205)
40–49 years	0.1299	0.1281	0.1546	0.1309	0.1101	0.151	0.1833
	(0.3362)	(0.3342)	(0.3615)	(0.3373)	(0.313)	(0.358)	(0.3869)
50–59 years	0.1473	0.1465	0.1582	0.1502	0.1229	0.1581	0.1594
	(0.3544)	(0.3536)	(0.3649)	(0.3573)	(0.3283)	(0.3648)	(0.3661)
60 or more years	0.2438	0.2458	0.2166	0.2433	0.2614	0.2228	0.1676
	(0.4294)	(0.4306)	(0.4119)	(0.4291)	(0.4394)	(0.4161)	(0.3735)
Race and ethnicity							
Asian	0.0486	0.0478	0.0597	0.0466	0.0551	0.0593	0.0624
	(0.215)	(0.2133)	(0.2369)	(0.2108)	(0.2281)	(0.2363)	(0.2419)

Black	0.1039	0.0996	0.1607	0.0899	0.1618	0.1662	0.1173
	(0.3051)	(0.2995)	(0.3673)	(0.286)	(0.3683)	(0.3723)	(0.3217)
White	0.7707	0.7823	0.614	0.8014	0.6606	0.6174	0.5865
	(0.4204)	(0.4127)	(0.4868)	(0.3989)	(0.4735)	(0.486)	(0.4925)
Other race	0.0769	0.0703	0.1657	0.0621	0.1225	0.1571	0.2338
	(0.2664)	(0.2556)	(0.3718)	(0.2413)	(0.3279)	(0.3638)	(0.4232)
Hispanic	0.1391	0.123	0.3569	0.1057	0.2329	0.3324	0.5506
	(0.3461)	(0.3284)	(0.4791)	(0.3075)	(0.4227)	(0.4711)	(0.4974)
Foreign-born	0.1143	0.0989	0.3228	0.0869	0.1749	0.2937	0.5524
	(0.3182)	(0.2985)	(0.4675)	(0.2817)	(0.3799)	(0.4555)	(0.4972)
Educational attainment							
Less than high school	0.2838	0.2595	0.6106	0.2241	0.4852	0.5793	0.8584
	(0.4508)	(0.4384)	(0.4876)	(0.417)	(0.4998)	(0.4937)	(0.3487)
High school graduate	0.2231	0.2259	0.185	0.2279	0.2131	0.1987	0.0768
	(0.4163)	(0.4182)	(0.3883)	(0.4195)	(0.4095)	(0.399)	(0.2663)
Some college	0.2409	0.2485	0.1384	0.2591	0.1815	0.1502	0.0447
	(0.4277)	(0.4322)	(0.3453)	(0.4381)	(0.3855)	(0.3573)	(0.2067)
4-year college degree	0.137	0.1444	0.0372	0.1578	0.0593	0.0404	0.0117
	(0.3439)	(0.3515)	(0.1893)	(0.3646)	(0.2361)	(0.197)	(0.1075)
Post-graduate degree	0.1152	0.1216	0.0287	0.1311	0.0609	0.0313	0.0084
	(0.3192)	(0.3268)	(0.167)	(0.3375)	(0.2391)	(0.1741)	(0.0912)
Marital status							

(continued)

Table 7.1 (continued)

N = Variables	*Full Sample* *3,42,91,600* *(a)*	*Not MD Poor* *3,19,23,760* *(b)*	*MD Poor* *23,67,840* *(c)*	*Not Deprived* *($d_i < 0.20$)* *2,75,92,514* *(d)*	*Vulnerable* *($0.20 \le d_i < 0.33$)* *43,31,246* *(e)*	*Moderate Poverty* *($0.33 \le d_i < 0.50$)* *21,02,275* *(f)*	*Severe Poverty* *($0.50 \le d_i$)* *2,65,565* *(g)*
Divorced or separated	0.1026	0.0971	0.1775	0.0911	0.135	0.1785	0.1696
	(0.3035)	(0.2961)	(0.3821)	(0.2878)	(0.3417)	(0.3829)	(0.3752)
Married	0.4278	0.437	0.3038	0.4611	0.2838	0.2953	0.3717
	(0.4948)	(0.496)	(0.4599)	(0.4985)	(0.4508)	(0.4562)	(0.4833)
Single	0.4142	0.4126	0.4355	0.4007	0.4881	0.4409	0.3929
	(0.4926)	(0.4923)	(0.4958)	(0.49)	(0.4999)	(0.4965)	(0.4884)
Widowed	0.0554	0.0533	0.0832	0.0471	0.0931	0.0854	0.0658
	(0.2287)	(0.2247)	(0.2761)	(0.2118)	(0.2906)	(0.2794)	(0.248)
Employment status							
Employed	0.457	0.4724	0.249	0.5048	0.2658	0.2522	0.2232
	(0.4981)	(0.4992)	(0.4324)	(0.5)	(0.4418)	(0.4343)	(0.4164)
Unemployed	0.0352	0.0238	0.1893	0.0145	0.0824	0.1681	0.3566
	(0.1842)	(0.1523)	(0.3917)	(0.1197)	(0.275)	(0.374)	(0.479)
Not in labor force	0.3191	0.3088	0.4576	0.2866	0.4502	0.467	0.3836
	(0.4661)	(0.462)	(0.4982)	(0.4522)	(0.4975)	(0.4989)	(0.4863)
Household size							
1 person	0.1496	0.1447	0.2154	0.1345	0.2099	0.221	0.1708
	(0.3567)	(0.3518)	(0.4111)	(0.3412)	(0.4072)	(0.4149)	(0.3763)
2 people	0.2816	0.2871	0.2072	0.2976	0.2207	0.2096	0.1877
	(0.4498)	(0.4524)	(0.4053)	(0.4572)	(0.4147)	(0.407)	(0.3905)
3–4 people	0.3689	0.3752	0.2844	0.3861	0.3061	0.2851	0.2783
	(0.4825)	(0.4842)	(0.4511)	(0.4868)	(0.4609)	(0.4515)	(0.4482)

5–7 people	0.1789	0.1747	0.2358	0.1682	0.216	0.2283	0.2952
	(0.3833)	(0.3797)	(0.4245)	(0.3741)	(0.4115)	(0.4197)	(0.4561)
8 or more people	0.0209	0.0182	0.0573	0.0136	0.0472	0.056	0.068
	(0.1431)	(0.1337)	(0.2325)	(0.116)	(0.2121)	(0.2299)	(0.2517)
Primary household language							
Asian or Pacific Island	0.0386	0.0375	0.0521	0.0361	0.0468	0.0517	0.0546
	(0.1925)	(0.1901)	(0.2221)	(0.1865)	(0.2111)	(0.2215)	(0.2272)
English	0.7307	0.749	0.4847	0.7727	0.5981	0.5103	0.2821
	(0.4436)	(0.4336)	(0.4998)	(0.4191)	(0.4903)	(0.4999)	(0.45)
Indo-European	0.0467	0.0459	0.0577	0.045	0.0516	0.0572	0.0619
	(0.2111)	(0.2093)	(0.2333)	(0.2074)	(0.2212)	(0.2323)	(0.241)
Spanish	0.1293	0.1132	0.3461	0.0977	0.2119	0.3208	0.5462
	(0.3356)	(0.3169)	(0.4757)	(0.297)	(0.4087)	(0.4668)	(0.4979)
Other language	0.0123	0.0113	0.0247	0.01	0.0196	0.0238	0.0319
	(0.11)	(0.1058)	(0.1552)	(0.0996)	(0.1387)	(0.1524)	(0.1758)

Standard deviations in parentheses. All mean values presented in columns (b)-(g) are statistically significant from the corresponding mean value presented in column (a) at the 1 percent level of significance unless indicated by a superscript “a” which indicates a statistically significant difference at the 5 percent level

categorized as being vulnerable to multidimensional poverty. The average deprivation score among these 4.3 million observations is equal to 0.2323.

Shifting our focus to those observations that are identified as multidimensionally poor (column (c)), we further categorize observations as experiencing moderate multidimensional poverty (column (f)) if their deprivation score is equal to greater than 0.3333 but less than 0.5 and as suffering severe multidimensional poverty (column (g)) if their deprivation score is equal to or greater than one-half. A very large majority of the observations who are found to experience multidimensional poverty fall within the moderate poverty sub-sample. These observations account for slightly more than 6.1 percent of the full sample. The remaining observations, 0.8 percent of the full sample, face severe multidimensional poverty. The average deprivation scores for these two groups are equal to 0.3723 for those categorized as experiencing moderate multidimensional poverty and 0.5615 for those suffering severe multidimensional poverty.

Having gained a sense of the relative frequencies and the numbers of observations that correspond with the dependent variable series, we can turn our attention to the explanatory variables. To gain a measure of the difference between observations categorized as being multidimensionally poor and those not identified as multidimensionally poor, we look to the mean values of the explanatory variables that are listed in columns (b) and (c). A comparison of mean values for the two sub-samples produces a number of interesting insights. First, while women represent a larger portion of both sub-samples, they comprise a slightly larger portion of the multidimensionally poor sub-sample. Higher percentages of observations categorized as multidimensionally poor are within the ages of 20 to 59 years, while observations that represent younger individuals (i.e., those below age 20) and older individuals (i.e., those age 60 years and above) comprise larges shares of the non-multidimensionally poor sub-sample. In terms of race and ethnicity, observations that are categorized as being multidimensionally poor are significantly more likely to represent individuals who are Asian, black, or some other race(s) (i.e., non-white and/or another race or multiple races) and who identify as Hispanic. Accordingly, a considerably higher proportion of the sub-sample identified as not being multidimensionally poor are white (78.2 percent) as compared to the multidimensionally poor cohort (61.4 percent). We also see a much higher percentage of the multidimensionally poor sub-sample is foreign-born (32.3 percent) relative to their non-poor counterparts (9.9 percent).

Perhaps not surprisingly, the majority of observations (61.1 percent) that are categorized as multidimensionally poor represent individuals who did not complete high school. This far exceeds the corresponding value of 26 percent for the sub-sample of observations not categorized as multidimensionally poor. It also leads to higher percentages for the sub-sample of observations not identified as experiencing multidimensional poverty in terms of all other educational attainment categories. Married individuals comprise a larger portion of the sub-sample of observations not categorized as multidimensionally poor, while those who are divorced or separated, are single, or who are widowed comprise a higher percentage of the multidimensionally poor sub-sample. Not surprisingly, the multidimensionally poor sub-sample includes higher proportions of observations that represent individuals who report being either unemployed or who are not in the labor force as compared to the not multidimensionally poor sub-sample which includes a higher percentage of individuals who are employed.

Focusing on household characteristics, we see that single-person households and households that include five or more individuals comprise larger shares of the multidimensionally poor sub-sample and that households that consist of two to four people are more frequently represented in the not multidimensionally poor sub-sample. Lastly, mirroring the pattern observed for race and ethnicity, we see a higher proportion of households for which English is the primary language are categorized as not being multidimensionally poor. To the contrary, higher percentages of households for which the primary language is Asian or Pacific Island, Indo-European, Spanish, or another language are found among the multidimensionally poor sub-sample.

Separating the multidimensionally poor cohort into two sub-samples based on whether the observations represent individuals who are experiencing moderate multidimensional poverty or who are suffering severe multidimensional poverty provides additional insights. Looking to columns (f) and (g) in Table 7.1, we see that a higher percentage of the observations categorized as experiencing moderate multidimensional poverty is female relative to the share identified as facing severe multidimensional poverty. And as is observed when comparing the multidimensionally poor to their non-poor counterparts, among those in the former category a higher percentage of observations representing individuals age 20 to 59 years is categorized as suffering severe poverty, while higher percentages are found for those under 20 years of age and 60 years of age or older among the moderately multidimensionally poor. Similar to the results presented in columns (b) and (c), we see that higher percentages of observations identified as facing severe poverty are Asian, some other race(s), or Hispanic. To the contrary, smaller percentages of the sub-samples that are identified as being severely poor are black or white individuals as compared to the share who are facing moderate multidimensional poverty. While the multidimensionally poor are much more likely to be foreign-born, by nearly a two-to-one margin the percentage of foreign-born within the severe poverty category exceeds that found for the moderate poverty category.

With respect to educational attainment, the severely poor classification is overwhelmingly comprised of observations representing individuals who did not complete their high school education (85.8 percent). Even so, more than half (57.9 percent) of the observations identified as moderately poor did not complete high school. For all other education classifications, we see lower values for the severely poor relative to those observed for the moderately poor. Interestingly, the differences between the moderately poor and those who are severely poor in terms of marital status is not particularly striking. Among the observations classified as severely multidimensionally poor, we see a higher frequency of unemployment and lower values for the employment and not in the labor force variables as compared to the moderately poor sub-sample.

Finally, turning to the household characteristic variables, we see higher percentages of the moderately poor among household sizes of four or fewer individuals. Larger households—that is, those with five or more people—are more frequently represented among the severely poor sub-sample. Consistent with the findings for the dichotomous categorization of observations as multidimensionally poor, we see the severely poor more often use a language other than English as their primary household language. Even so, of the observations that represent individuals who are classified as moderately poor only about one-half identify English as their primary household language. Nearly a third of the moderately multidimensionally poor list Spanish as their primary household language, and more than half of those who are severely poor rely on Spanish as their primary household language.

In the next section, we present the results of our estimations of the determinants of multidimensional poverty.

7.2 Empirical Model and Estimation Strategy

Throughout this and the following two chapters, our estimation equations are constructed based on intuition, the findings reported in earlier chapters, the specifications employed in earlier studies, and available data; thus, admittedly, our regression models are *ad hoc*. At the same time, our models closely resemble the estimation equations that have been employed in earlier studies of multidimensional poverty. As we are examining potential determinants of multidimensional poverty, each of our estimations employs the same set of explanatory variables. What varies across estimations is the dependent variable series and, based on the form of the dependent variable, the estimation techniques we employ. As noted earlier, our three dependent variable series include uncensored deprivation scores, the MD Poor variable, and the MD Poor Category variable. As these measures are continuous, dichotomous, and categorical, respectively, we employ the ordinary least squares (OLS), binomial logit, and ordered logit techniques in turn. In general terms, eq. (7.1) presents our empirical model.

$$M_{ijkt} = \alpha_0 + \beta_\Theta \Theta_i + \beta_\Phi \Phi_j + \beta_\Psi \Psi_k + \beta_\Omega \Omega_t + \varepsilon_{ijkt} \tag{7.1}$$

The dependent variable, M, represents the three dependent variable series that we employ in our analysis. The subscripts i, j, k, and t denote the observation, corresponding household, state of residence, and year of survey, respectively. Θ includes a set of variables that indicate each observation's gender, educational attainment, race, ethnicity, nativity, age, marital status, and employment status. Similarly, Φ includes the variables that represent household size (in members) and the primary household language. Ψ and Ω control for otherwise unobserved location and time fixed effects that are related to state of residence and survey year. α represents our constant term (or cut points when we estimate our model using the ordered logit technique) and ε is our assumed i.i.d. error term (when we estimate our model using the OLS technique).

General expectations regarding the signs of the coefficient estimates are based on the results of prior studies, the descriptive statistics that are presented in Table 7.1, and the information related to variation in multidimensional poverty across demographic cohorts that we present in Chap. 6. Based on the values presented in Table 7.1, we may expect women, individuals between the ages of 20 and 59 years, non-white individuals, Hispanics, and those who are foreign-born to more likely be categorized as multidimensionally poor. Similarly, we see an inverse relationship between educational attainment and the frequency of multidimensional poverty; thus, the probability that an individual is categorized as multidimensionally poor would be expected to decrease as we move to higher levels of educational attainment. Observations that are identified as divorced or separated, single, or widowed and those who are unemployed or as not in the labor force may also be more likely identified as multidimensionally poor. Generally speaking, the same characteristics that correspond with classification as being multidimensionally poor appear to contribute, albeit in a more pronounced fashion, to being severely poor as compared to moderately poor.

7.3 Determinants of the Intensity of Multidimensional Poverty

Results obtained when eq. (7.1) is estimated and the uncensored deprivation score is regressed on our set of explanatory variables are presented in Table 7.2. It is both useful and informative to examine the determinants of uncensored deprivation scores and to see the relative magnitude of the resulting coefficients. The results inform us about the extent of deprivation throughout the entire population. We first note that all coefficient estimates are significantly different from zero at the one-percent level. We also see that slightly more than 40 percent of the variation in the dependent variable series is explained by the model.

A review of the estimated coefficients reveals that the typical female individual, all else constant, has a marginally lower deprivation score as compared to the typical male individual. Comparing across age categories, and relative to the excluded "under 20 years of age" cohort, we see a consistent increase in the uncensored deprivation score for all listed age categories. For example, the estimated score for individuals between the ages of 40 and 49 years, all else held constant, is 0.1075 units higher than the score of a comparable individual who is below 20 years of age. The magnitudes of the estimated coefficients across the age categories are quite similar, ranging from a low value of 0.094 for those individuals 60 years of age and older to a high value of 0.1107 for individuals who are 30 to 39 years of age. We also see that estimated deprivation scores for blacks, individuals categorized as being of some other race(s) (i.e., neither Asian, black, nor white), and those who identify as Hispanic have deprivation

Table 7.2 Determinants of Deprivation Scores, OLS Technique

Dependent variable:	*Dep. Score*	*Dependent variable:*	*Dep. Score*
Gender (excluded: Male)		Marital status (excluded: Single)	
Female	-0.0032***	Married	-0.0326***
	(0.00003)		(0.00006)
Age category (excluded: Under 20 years of age)		Widowed	0.0014***
20–29 years of age	0.1070***		(0.00009)
	(0.00008)	Divorced or separated	0.0056***
30–39 years of age	0.1107***		(0.00008)
	(0.00009)	Employment status (excluded: Employed)	
40–49 years of age	0.1075***	Unemployed	0.1951***
	(0.00009)		(0.0001)
50–59 years of age	0.1077***	Not in labor force	0.0524***
	(0.00009)		(0.00004)
60 or more years of age	0.0940***	Household size (excluded: 1 person in household)	
	(0.00009)	2 people	-0.0112***
Race and ethnicity (excluded: White and non-Hispanic)			(0.00006)
Asian	-0.0040***	3–4 people	-0.0181***
	(0.0001)		(0.00006)
Black	0.0252***	5–7 people	-0.0033***
	(0.00006)		(0.00007)
Other race	0.0163***	8 or more people	0.0496***
	(0.00008)		(0.0002)
Hispanic	0.0239***	Primary household language (excluded: English)	
	(0.00008)	Asian or Pacific Island	0.0237***
Nativity (excluded: Native-born)			(0.0001)
Foreign-born	0.0352***	Indo-European	0.0151***
	(0.00007)		(0.00009)
Educational attainment (excluded: Less than high school)		Spanish	0.0333***
			(0.00008)

(*continued*)

Table 7.2 (continued)

Dependent variable:	*Dep. Score*	*Dependent variable:*	*Dep. Score*
High school graduate	-0.1085***	Other language	0.0352***
	(0.00006)		(0.0002)
Some college	-0.1218***	Constant	0.0857***
	(0.00006)		(0.0002)
4-year college degree	-0.1382***		
	(0.00007)		
Post-graduate degree	-0.1077***		
	(0.00007)		
.	.	N	34,291,600
.	.	R^2	0.4044
.	.	F statistic	99,999***

Robust standard errors in parentheses. All estimations include year and state fixed effects terms, which are not reported here due to space limitations. "***", "**", and "*" denote statistical significance at the 1%, 5%, and 10% levels, respectively

scores that are 0.0163 to 0.0252 units higher than those of white and non-Hispanic individuals. Foreign-born individuals, relative to their native-born counterparts, are found to have significantly higher uncensored deprivation scores. Specifically, all else held constant, the uncensored deprivation score of the typical foreign-born individual is estimated to be 0.0352 units higher than the score of an otherwise comparable native-born individual.

As expected, higher levels of educational attainment correspond generally with lower uncensored deprivation scores. We see that the estimated coefficients for all education classifications are negative in sign. As the excluded group is those individuals who lack a high school diploma or equivalent credential, we can say that completion of high school corresponds with an estimated deprivation score that is 0.1085 units lower than that of a comparable individual who did not complete their high school education. Likewise, completing some college course work results in a 0.1218 unit decrease in the estimated deprivation score relative to those who did not complete high school, and those who complete a four-year college degree see their deprivation score decreased by an estimated 0.1382 units relative to the excluded cohort. Finally, those individuals with a post graduate degree, which includes professional degrees, master's degrees, and doctorates, are estimated to have a deprivation score that is 0.1077 units lower than the excluded cohort.

When looking at individual's marital status we see that widowers and those who are divorced or who are separated have higher estimated deprivation scores relative to single/never married individuals, and those individuals who are married have a significantly lower deprivation score relative to their single counterparts. Perhaps least surprising of all is that employment status is both significantly related to deprivation scores and that the estimated coefficient for the variable that identifies individuals as unemployed is quite large. This is likely unsurprising since unemployment is an indicator within the Economic Security dimension of the Multidimensional Poverty Index and factors directly into the calculation of the index. In addition, relative to the excluded group of employed individuals, those who are not in the labor force are estimated to have higher deprivation scores.

Turning to the household characteristics, relative to single-person households, we see that individuals who live in households which contain two to seven individuals are estimated to have lower uncensored deprivation scores, but those who live in households that consist of eight or more people are estimated to have significantly higher deprivation scores than single-person households. The final group of results in this table pertain to the primary language used in individuals' households. The excluded group are those individuals who have identified English as their primary household language. The estimated coefficients for the four included categories are positive and significantly different from zero. This indicates that individuals who use a language other than English as their primary household language, all else constant, are estimated to have higher deprivation scores. Similar to what is observed for the coefficient of the variable that identifies individuals as unemployed, we include a measure of English-speaking ability within the household (i.e., of potential linguistic-isolation) as part of our Education dimension that follows directly into the calculation of the deprivation score.

7.4 Determinants of the Incidence of Multidimensional Poverty

While our analysis of uncensored deprivation scores provides a large amount of information on the relative intensity of deprivation, we also wish to examine the factors which determine the incidence of multidimensional poverty. To do so, we estimate eq. (7.1), using the binomial logit technique to regress the binary MD Poor dependent variable on our set of explanatory variables. The resulting estimated log-odds coefficients are presented in Table 7.3. Before focusing in the coefficients, we can note that model fits the data quite well. The Count R^2 value is equal to 0.9370; thus, the model correctly predicts 93.7 percent of observed outcomes. To complement our estimation results that are presented in Table 7.4, we note the corresponding changes in the estimated probability of being multidimensionally poor.

Beginning with the values presented in Table 7.3, we see that women are more likely to be multidimensionally poor, all else equal, relative to men. Individuals who 20 years of age and older are more likely to be multidimensionally poor as compared to individuals who are below the age of 20. Looking to the race and ethnicity classifications, we do not see a statistically significant difference in the probabilities of being multidimensionally poor between Asian and white individuals; however, we do see that black individuals, individuals who identify as being of some other race(s), and those who identify as Hispanic all have higher estimated probabilities of being multidimensionally poor relative to white and non-Hispanic individuals. We also see that foreign-born individuals have a

Table 7.3 Determinants of Multidimensional Poverty Incidence, Binomial Logit Technique

Dependent variable:	*Binomial Logit*	*Dependent variable:*	*Binomial Logit*
	MD Poor (0, 1)		*MD Poor (0, 1)*
	(a)		*(b)*
Gender (excluded: Male)		Marital status (excluded: Single)	
Female	0.0793***	Divorced or separated	0.2512***
	(0.0016)		(0.0029)
Age category (excluded: Under 20 years of age)		Married	-0.7405***
20–29 years	1.9523***		(0.0026)
	(0.0033)	Widowed	-0.1542***
30–39 years	2.2055***		(0.004)
	(0.0036)	Employment status (excluded: Employed)	
40–49 years	2.0857***	Unemployed	2.9533***
	(0.0037)		(0.0027)
50–59 years	2.0232***	Not in labor force	0.9988***
	(0.0038)		(0.0019)
60 or more years	1.3263***	Household size (excluded: 1 person in household)	
	(0.004)	2 people	-0.2513***
Race and ethnicity (excluded: White and non-Hispanic)			(0.0027)
Asian	0.0048	3–4 people	-0.5708***
	(0.0052)		(0.0027)
Black	0.4257***	5–7 people	-0.1966***
	(0.0024)		(0.003)
Other race	0.1893***	8 or more people	0.4196***
	(0.0027)		(0.0046)
Hispanic	0.2804***	Primary household language (excluded: English)	
	(0.0032)	Asian or Pacific Island	0.8147***
			(0.0055)

(*continued*)

Table 7.3 (continued)

Dependent variable:	*Binomial Logit*	*Dependent variable:*	*Binomial Logit*
	MD Poor (0, 1)		*MD Poor (0, 1)*
	(a)		*(b)*
Nativity (excluded: Native-born)		Indo-European	0.7223***
Foreign-born	0.6772***		(0.0037)
	(0.0024)	Spanish	0.9938***
Educational attainment (excluded: Less than high school)			(0.0031)
High school graduate	-1.9316***	Other language	1.0167***
	(0.0023)		(0.0057)
Some college	-2.2759***	Constant	-3.16***
	(0.0025)		(0.0072)
4-year college degree	-2.881***		
	(0.004)		
Post-graduate degree	-2.4978***		
	(0.0047)		
.	.	N	34,291,600
.	.	Wald Chi^2	3,899,580***
.	.	Pseudo R^2	0.3060
.	.	Log pseudolikelihood	-5,977,602
.	.	Count R^2	0.9370

Robust standard errors in parentheses. All estimations include year and state fixed effects terms, which are not reported here due to space limitations. "***", "**", and "*" denote statistical significance at the 1%, 5%, and 10% levels, respectively

Table 7.4 Estimated Changes in Predicted Probabilities, Binomial Logit Estimations

Dependent variable:	*MD Poor*	*Dependent variable:*	*MD Poor*
Gender (excluded: Male)		Educational attainment (continued)	
Female	0.0016	Post-graduate degree	-0.0260
Age category (excluded: 18–29 years of age)		Marital status (excluded: Single)	
20–29 years	0.0786	Divorced or separated	0.0040
30–39 years	0.1116	Married	-0.0140
40–49 years	0.1023	Widowed	-0.0039
50–59 years	0.0927	Employment status (excluded: Employed)	
60 or more years	0.0430	Unemployed	0.2691
Race and ethnicity (excluded: White and non-Hispanic)		Not in labor force	0.0266
Asian	-0.0016	Household size (excluded: 1 person in household)	
Black	0.0069	2 people	-0.0054
Other race	0.0039	3–4 people	-0.0129
Hispanic	0.0034	5–7 people	-0.0067
Nativity (excluded: Native-born)		8 or more people	0.0059
Foreign-born	0.0143	Primary household language (excluded: English)	
Educational attainment (excluded: Less than high school)		Asian or Pacific Island	0.0260
High school graduate	-0.0264	Indo-European	0.0259
Some college	-0.0311	Spanish	0.0279
4-year college degree	-0.0289	Other language	0.0374

higher estimated probability of being multidimensionally poor as compared to their native-born counterparts, all else constant. We also see that individuals who are divorced or separated are more likely to be multidimensionally poor than single individuals; however, those who are widowed or are married are significantly less likely to be multidimensionally poor relative to their single counterparts. Relative to employed individuals, those who are unemployed and those individuals who are not in labor force are estimated to be more likely multidimensionally poor. Individuals who live in households that contain two to seven individuals are less likely multidimensionally poor compared to those in single-person households, and members of households that contain eight or more people are significantly more likely to be multidimensionally poor as compared to their single-person household counterparts. We also see, compared to households in which English is commonly used, all other language categories have estimated log-odds coefficients that are positive and significantly different from zero.

To gain a more intuitive understanding of the determinants of multidimensional poverty, we can look to the changes in estimated probabilities that are presented in Table 7.4. These values correspond to the log-odds coefficients that are provided in Table 7.3. There are a number of interesting findings, including a few very large effects, among the mix of larger and smaller effects. We see, for example, that the estimated probability of suffering multidimensional poverty increases until we reach the ages of 40–49 years when we begin to see decreasing values. Even so, across all age categories the estimated probability of being multidimensionally poor is higher than that which is observed for a similar individual who is below the age of 20 years. Of somewhat similar magnitudes, compared to an individual who has not completed high school, a high school graduate is 2.64 percent less likely to be multidimensionally poor and an individual who has completed a four-year college degree is 2.89 percent less likely to be multidimensionally poor. Likewise, the estimated probability of a foreign-born individual being multidimensionally poor is 1.43 percent higher than the estimated probability of a comparable native-born individual. Individuals who use a language other than English in their household are estimated to be 2.59 percent to 3.74 percent more likely to be multidimensionally poor, dependent on the language used, than their counterparts who primarily use English. These values correspond to statistically significant log-odds coefficients and are sufficiently large in magnitude to also be of practical significance. By contrast, unemployed individuals are 26.9 percent more likely, relative to their employed counterparts, to be multidimensionally poor. Additional coefficient estimates, while statistically significant from zero, are much less pronounced in value. For example, individuals who are female, Asian, Hispanic, or who live in households that consist of five to seven people are estimated to have lower uncensored deprivation scores as compared to their male, white, or non-Hispanic counterparts and relative to individuals who live in single-person households, respectively. In each instance, however, the estimated coefficient is so small in value as to not hold much, if any, practical significance.

To gain a more nuanced understanding of multidimensional poverty, we estimate eq. (7.1) using the ordered logit technique while employing the MD Poor Category variable as our dependent variable series. The MD

Poor Category variable is an extension of the binary MD Poor variable in that it categorizes each observation into one of four categories based on the corresponding deprivation score: neither multidimensionally poor nor vulnerable to multidimensional poverty (i.e., outcome category 0, where the deprivation score, d_i, < 0.2), as vulnerable to multidimensional poverty (outcome 1, where $0.2 \leq d_i < 0.3333$), as experiencing moderate multidimensional poverty (outcome 2, where $0.3333 \leq d_i < 0.5$), and those who are suffering severe multidimensional poverty (outcome 1, where $0.5 \leq d_i$). Estimation results are presented in Table 7.5, and the corresponding changes in estimated probabilities over the four categories for each of explanatory variables are presented in Table 7.6.

Beginning with the log-odds coefficients that are reported in Table 7.5, we see a number of results are similar to those reported from our binomial logit estimation. This is largely to be expected as our ordered logit estimation is an extension of the binomial estimation. Before discussing specific coefficient estimates, we can note that all coefficients presented in the table are significantly different from zero at the one-percent level. We also can see from the Count R^2 value that the model correctly predicts 82.2 percent of the observed outcomes. Since we are using the ordered logit estimation technique, the coefficients represent the estimated changes in the logs of the odds ratios of moving to a higher category of the dependent variable series given a change in the corresponding explanatory variable holding all else constant. Given the ordering of the MD Poor Category series, where the lowest category corresponds with being neither multidimensionally poor nor vulnerable to multidimensional poverty and the highest category indicates experiencing severe multidimensional poverty, a positive coefficient indicates an increased probability of being in a higher category and, correspondingly, a reduced probability of being in a lower category.

The positive coefficient of the foreign-born variable indicates that, relative to their native-born counterparts, foreign-born individuals are more likely to be in a higher dependent variable category and, in as noted, less likely to be in a lower category. Likewise, women are more likely to be in a higher dependent variable category. Considering the effect of educational attainment, we see that there is an inverse relationship with multidimensional poverty. We also see that, relative to the excluded category of individuals who are less than 20 years of age, older individuals are significantly more likely to be in a higher dependent variable category. The same is true for unemployed individuals and for those who are not in the labor force as compared to their counterparts who are employed. We also see

Table 7.5 Determinants of Multidimensional Poverty Incidence, Ordered Logit Technique

Dependent variable:	*MD Poor (0–3)*	*Dependent variable:*	*MD Poor (0–3)*
	(a)		*(b)*
Gender (excluded: Male)		Marital status (excluded: Single)	
Female	0.0389***	Divorced or separated	0.1726***
	(0.001)		(0.0019)
Age category (excluded: Under 20 years of age)		Married	-0.8299***
20–29 years	1.9662***		(0.0017)
	(0.0022)	Widowed	-0.1017***
30–39 years	2.063***		(0.0024)
	(0.0024)	Employment status (excluded: Employed)	
40–49 years	1.9512***	Unemployed	2.9924***
	(0.0025)		(0.0021)
50–59 years	1.8993***	Not in labor force	1.0323***
	(0.0025)		(0.0012)
60 or more years	1.4328***	Household size (excluded: 1 person in household)	
	(0.0026)	2 people	-0.2154***
Race and ethnicity (excluded: White and non-Hispanic)			(0.0017)
Asian	0.009***	3–4 people	-0.4687***
	(0.0033)		(0.0017)
Black	0.5535***	5–7 people	-0.074***
	(0.0015)		(0.0019)
Other race	0.269***	8 or more people	0.7313***
	(0.0018)		(0.0031)
Hispanic	0.3899***	Primary household language (excluded: English)	
	(0.0021)	Asian or Pacific Island	0.6229***
Nativity (excluded: Native-born)			(0.0035)
Foreign-born	0.6456***	Indo-European	0.4937***
	(0.0017)		(0.0024)

Educational attainment (excluded: Less than high school)		Spanish	0.7351***
High school graduate	-2.0464***		(0.002)
	(0.0016)	Other language	0.8255***
Some college	-2.3361***		(0.004)
	(0.0017)	/ cut 1	1.5587
4-year college degree	-2.8677***		(0.0044)
	(0.0023)	/ cut 2	3.2133
Post-graduate degree	-2.2403***		(0.0045)
	(0.0026)	/ cut 3	5.9566
			(0.0049)
.	.	N	34,291,600
.	.	Wald Chi^2	7,845,998***
.	.	Pseudo R^2	0.2308
.	.	Log pseudolikelihood	-17,014,819
.	.	Count R^2	0.8220

Robust standard errors in parentheses. All estimations include year and state fixed effects terms, which are not reported here due to space limitations. "***", "**", and "*" denote statistical significance at the 1%, 5%, and 10% levels, respectively

Table 7.6 Estimated Changes in Predicted Probabilities, Ordered Logit Estimations

Dependent variable category:	*Not Deprived*	*Vulnerable*	*Moderate Poverty*	*Severe Poverty*
	($d_i < 0.20$)	($0.20 \leq d_i < 0.33$)	($0.33 \leq d_i < 0.50$)	($0.50 \leq d_i$)
	(a)	*(b)*	*(c)*	*(d)*
Gender (excluded: Male)				
Female	-0.0043	0.0034	0.0009	0.0001
Age category (excluded: 18–29 years of age)				
20–29 years	-0.2977	0.2131	0.0792	0.0054
30–39 years	-0.3385	0.2379	0.0941	0.0065
40–49 years	-0.3193	0.2264	0.0869	0.0060
50–59 years	-0.3021	0.2165	0.0801	0.0054
60 or more years	-0.1906	0.1438	0.0439	0.0028
Race and ethnicity (excluded: White and non-Hispanic)				
Asian	0.0034	-0.0026	-0.0007	0.0000
Black	-0.0510	0.0395	0.0108	0.0007
Other race	-0.0251	0.0196	0.0052	0.0003
Hispanic	-0.0301	0.0234	0.0063	0.0004
Nativity (excluded: Native-born)				
Foreign-born	-0.0619	0.0478	0.0132	0.0008
Educational attainment (excluded: Less than high school)				
High school graduate	0.1341	-0.1057	-0.0267	-0.0017
Some college	0.1539	-0.1209	-0.0310	-0.0019
4-year college degree	0.1428	-0.1130	-0.0281	-0.0017
Post-graduate degree	0.1239	-0.0983	-0.0241	-0.0015
Marital status (excluded: Single)				
Divorced or separated	-0.0128	0.0100	0.0026	0.0002
Married	0.0743	-0.0581	-0.0152	-0.0010
Widowed	0.0120	-0.0094	-0.0024	-0.0002

Employment status (excluded: Employed)				
Unemployed	-0.5891	0.3232	0.2449	0.0210
Not in labor force	-0.1216	0.0936	0.0263	0.0017
Household size (excluded: 1 person in household)				
2 people	0.0250	-0.0196	-0.0050	-0.0003
3–4 people	0.0529	-0.0415	-0.0107	-0.0007
5–7 people	0.0199	-0.0156	-0.0040	-0.0003
8 or more people	-0.0692	0.0533	0.0150	0.0010
Primary household language (excluded: English)				
Asian or Pacific Island	-0.0785	0.0603	0.0171	0.0011
Indo-European	-0.0696	0.0536	0.0151	0.0010
Spanish	-0.0818	0.0629	0.0177	0.0011
Other language	-0.1124	0.0854	0.0254	0.0016

positive coefficients, relative to white and non-Hispanic individuals, for those who are Hispanic and/or are of another race, and we again see that individuals who live in households where English is not the primary language have higher probabilities of being multidimensionally poor. To the contrary, individuals who live in households that have two to seven members are less likely than individuals in single-person households to be in a higher dependent variable category while those individuals who live in households with eight or more members are more likely to be in a higher dependent variable category. Lastly, as compared to single individuals, those who have been divorced or separated are more likely to be multidimensionally poor while those that are married or widowed are found to have a lower probability of multidimensional poverty relative to individuals who are single.

Table 7.6 presents that estimated changes in predicted probabilities that correspond to the estimation results that are presented in Table 7.5. Contrary to the changes in the predicted probabilities that follow from the binomial estimation (i.e., that are presented in Table 7.4), here we gain a more nuanced view of the relationship between the potential determinants and the four dependent variable categories. Because there are four categories and, thus, four potential classifications, the combined sum of estimated probabilities across the four outcomes must equal one. Similarly, a change in the estimated probability for any category necessitates a change in the estimated probabilities for one or more other categories to keep the sum equal to one. For example, looking at the variable which represents foreign-born individuals, relative to the excluded category of an otherwise comparable native-born individual, we see that the typical foreign-born individual is 4.78 percentage points more likely to be vulnerable to multidimensional poverty (outcome 1), 1.32 percentage points more likely to experience moderate multidimensional poverty (outcome 2), and 0.08 percentage points more likely to suffer severe multidimensional poverty (outcome 3). The sum of these three values is equivalent to the 6.19 percentage point decrease in the probability of being neither multidimensionally poor nor vulnerable to multidimensional poverty (outcome 0).

Looking to some of the remaining values in the table, we see there is considerable variation in the estimated changes in predicted probabilities. Changes in the employment status, age category, and to a lesser extent educational attainment variables produce the largest changes in predicted probabilities. For example, becoming unemployed increases the probability of being severely multidimensionally poor by 2.1 percentage points. It also is estimated to increase the probability of being moderately multidimensionally poor by 24.49 percentage points and the probability of being vulnerable to multidimensional poverty by 32.32 percentage points. Given the large increases in outcomes 1–3, it follows that there is a corresponding decrease of 59.91 percentage points in the value for outcome 0 (i.e., the predicted probability of being neither multidimensionally poor nor vulnerable to multidimensional poverty). Similarly, we see very large changes in predicted probabilities—particularly across outcomes 0 and 1—for the age category variables and educational attainment categories.

For many of the explanatory variables, we see estimated change values that are quite small and, in certain cases, the changes are so small as to be of questionable practical significance. Two examples for which the changes are of rather minor magnitudes are the female variable and the Asian variable. In both cases, not only are changes small in magnitude, they also are largely restricted to outcomes 0 and 1; thus, there is very little influence on the predicted probability of being multidimensionally poor. By contrast, the changes in the predicted probabilities that correspond to the black, other race, and Hispanic variables are greater in magnitude and the changes estimated for the primary household language, household size, and marital status variables are, generally, even greater in magnitude.

From the estimations that have been performed and the estimated changes in the predicted probabilities that result from these estimations, we have obtained a much greater understanding of the relationships between our explanatory variables and our three measures of deprivation. Given the similarities in our estimation equations—namely, that all three equations utilize the same set of explanatory variables and that the differences across estimations are restricted to the measure of deprivation employed as a dependent variable series and the corresponding estimation technique—we also can consider our estimation results and corresponding probability estimates as pseudo-robustness checks. This robustness, however, only applies in general terms, such as consistency in the signs of coefficient estimates across estimations and the relative magnitudes of predicted probabilities and estimated changes in those probabilities. Because the sample size is so large, our standard errors are quite small in value and we see near-universal statistical significance of coefficient estimates.

7.5 Summary and Conclusions

Extending from the more descriptive treatment of our data that is presented in earlier chapters, here we have employed three related measures of deprivation and a common set of individual- and household-specific explanatory variables to examine the determinants of multidimensional poverty incidence and intensity. Our data includes nearly 34.3 million observations from the 2008–2018 American Community Surveys, each of which represents a unique individual. The set of explanatory variables includes each observation's gender, level of educational attainment, race, ethnicity, nativity, age, marital status, and employment status. We also control for household size (in members) and the primary household language, and all estimations include year and state of residence fixed effects terms. The three measures of deprivation are the uncensored deprivation score, which is a continuous variable that measures deprivation intensity, a binary variable that identifies observations that are classified as multidimensionally poor, and a categorical variable that allows for the identification of moderate and severe multidimensional poverty as well as vulnerability to multidimensional poverty. Given the different forms of our dependent variables, we utilize the Ordinary Least Squares, binomial logit, and ordered logit estimation techniques as appropriate.

Across our estimations, we have consistently identified statistically significant relationships between our deprivation intensity measure and our measures of deprivation incidence (i.e., the dependent variable series) and the explanatory variables. Additionally, the empirical models have performed quite well in terms of their goodness of fit and ability to correctly predict observed outcomes. With respect to the specific determinants of deprivation, we see that those who are the foreign-born, black and/or Hispanic, lesser educated, older, unemployed or not in the labor force, and who have a primary household language other than English tend to have higher deprivation scores, higher estimated probabilities of being multidimensionally poor, and are more likely to be vulnerable to multidimensional poverty than their otherwise comparable counterparts. We also find that the magnitudes of the estimated coefficients often vary considerably. In fact, we find that the variables which identify women and Asian individuals, while statistically significant from zero, are of such a low magnitude to be of questionable practical significance. This is particularly noticeable when estimates of changes in predicted probabilities are considered.

Reference

U.S. Bureau of the Census/American Factfinder (U.S. Census). 2019. American Community Survey (Annual Data, 2008–2018). U.S. Census Bureau's American Community Survey Office. Retrieved from http://factfinder.census.gov.

PART III

Three Studies of Multidimensional Poverty

CHAPTER 8

Exploring the Effects of the Affordable Care Act on Multidimensional Poverty

Building on the descriptive analyses that are provided in Chaps. 4 through 6 and the examination of the determinants of multidimensional poverty that is detailed in Chap. 7, we now further our examination of multidimensional poverty by presenting the first of three examples of multidimensional poverty analysis. Here, we consider the influence of the Medicaid expansion that was enacted in 2014 as part of the Patient Protection and Affordable Care Act (ACA) on multidimensional poverty. The expansion of Medicaid eligibility was intended to be national in scope; however, the June 2012 U.S. Supreme Court ruling in the case of the *National Federation of Independent Business v. Sebelius* effectively made the expansion optional for individual states. As a result, on January 1, 2014, when the expansion went into effect, only 24 states and the District of Columbia had implemented the expansion. Another seven states expanded their Medicaid programs by July 2016; thus, through the end of our reference period (i.e., 2018), 31 states and the District of Columbia had chosen to expand their programs and 19 states had chosen not to do so.[1]

Because some states chose to expand Medicaid eligibility while others did not, we have a natural experiment through which we can analyze the influence of the ACA on the incidence of deprivation. Medicaid expansion

[1] For simplicity, for the remainder of this chapter we refer to the 31 states and Washington, DC simply as "32 states".

R. White, *Multidimensional Poverty in America*,
https://doi.org/10.1007/978-3-030-45916-1_8

is associated with the health insurance indicator and, in turn, the Health dimension. By extension, the expansion may affect both the incidence and intensity of multidimensional poverty. Using the difference-in-difference (DID) estimation technique, we isolate the effects of the ACA-related Medicaid expansion on multidimensional poverty. Since our data span the period from 2008 through 2018, we have a six-year pre-treatment period (2008–2013) during which neither our control group nor our treatment group were exposed to the treatment (i.e., the expansion of Medicaid eligibility as of January 1, 2014). We also have a five-year post-treatment period (2014–2018) during which 19 states were not exposed to the treatment while 32 states were exposed.[2,3] The states that were not exposed to Medicaid expansion are our control group, and the 32 states that chose to expand eligibility are our treatment group. The effects of the Medicaid expansion on multidimensional poverty incidence and deprivation frequencies at the Health dimension and health insurance indicator levels is the difference in the average outcome for our treatment group prior to and following the treatment less the difference in the average outcome for our control group before and following the treatment.

A brief explanation of the process through which Medicaid expansion may affect multidimensional poverty incidence is as follows. An expansion of Medicaid eligibility may significantly reduce the probability that a given individual is deprived in terms of the health insurance indicator series. If so, then this reduction in deprivation frequency for the health insurance indicator will correspond with a reduction in the deprivation frequency of the Health dimension, which consists of the health insurance and disability indicators. If the deprivation frequencies of the health insurance indicator and the Health dimension are lower, then we may see a corresponding decrease in the headcount ratio value. If the headcount ratio value

[2] The 19 states that chose to not expand Medicaid eligibility by the end of our reference period are Alabama, Florida, Georgia, Idaho, Kansas, Maine, Mississippi, Missouri, Nebraska, North Carolina, Oklahoma, South Carolina, South Dakota, Tennessee, Texas, Utah, Virginia, Wisconsin, and Wyoming.

[3] The 25 states that chose to expand Medicaid eligibility on January 1, 2014 are Arizona, Arkansas, California, Colorado, Connecticut, Delaware, Hawaii, Illinois, Iowa, Kentucky, Maryland, Massachusetts, Minnesota, Nevada, New Jersey, New Mexico, New York, North Dakota, Ohio, Oregon, Rhode Island, Vermont, West Virginia, Washington, and Washington, DC. Another seven states implemented Medicaid expansions by July 2016: Alaska (Sep. 2015), Indiana (Feb. 2015), Louisiana (Jul. 2016), Michigan (Apr. 2014), Montana (Jan. 2016), New Hampshire Aug. 2014), and Pennsylvania (Jan. 2015). We include these seven states with the initial 25 states as part of our treatment group.

decreases, then the Multidimensional Poverty Index (MPI) will decrease proportionally.

Informed by this intuition and the structure of the MPI, the expansion of Medicaid provides three related hypotheses that we are able to address:

Hypothesis 1: The expansion of the Medicaid program resulted in a reduction in the deprivation frequency of the health insurance indicator;
Hypothesis 2: Conditional on Hypothesis 1, there is a corresponding decrease in the deprivation frequency of the Health dimension; and
Hypothesis 3: Conditional on Hypotheses 1 and 2, there is a corresponding decrease in the headcount ratio.

Because multidimensional poverty incidence and deprivation frequency are binary outcomes, we use the binomial logit and the ordered logit regression techniques in conjunction with the DID technique to generate probability estimates for both our control group and our treatment groups during the pre-treatment and post-treatment periods. Comparison of the differences in estimated probabilities allows for the effects of Medicaid expansion to be determined. While we do compare predicted probability values to measure the differences in predicted probabilities across periods and between groups, our estimations follow the standard DID framework. We again examine data from the 2008–2018 American Community Survey (ACS) Public Use Microdata Sample (PUMS) (U.S. Census 2019).

In the next section, we detail the DID technique and explain its application to our topic and hypotheses. This is followed in Sect. 8.2 with the presentation of our empirical model and discussions of our data and descriptive statistics. Section 8.3 details our estimation strategy and presents the findings of our analysis. Section 8.4 concludes.

8.1 An Explanation of the Difference-in-Difference Approach

The difference-in-difference (DID) technique uses observational study data to mimic an experimental research design. The technique estimates the differential effect of some treatment on two groups in a natural experiment. In such an experiment, one group (i.e., the treatment group) is exposed to a treatment while the other group (i.e., the control group) is not exposed. The technique estimates the effect of the treatment (i.e., an explanatory variable that represents exposure) on an outcome (i.e., a response variable or dependent variable) by comparing the difference in average changes over time that are attributable to the outcome variable for the treatment group relative to the average change over time for the control group.

One definition of the DID estimator is that it is the difference in the average outcome for a treatment group prior to and following some treatment less the difference in the average outcome for the control group before and following the treatment. A slightly more formal/technical explanation of the estimator is as follows.

In Eqs. (8.1) and (8.2), $\hat{\delta}_T$ and $\hat{\delta}_C$ are the average differences in outcome Y_i for the treatment group and the control group, respectively, before and after the treatment to which only the treatment group is exposed. The subscripts and superscripts T and C identify the treatment and control groups, respectively, and the subscripts 0 and 1 indicate the pre-treatment and post-treatment periods, respectively.

$$\hat{\delta}_T = \overline{Y}_1^T - \overline{Y}_0^T \tag{8.1}$$

$$\hat{\delta}_C = \overline{Y}_1^C - \overline{Y}_0^C \tag{8.2}$$

In Table 8.1, $\hat{\delta}_T$ is located at the rightmost end of the first row, and $\hat{\delta}_C$ is found at the rightmost end of the second row. Subtracting the latter from the former results in the difference-in-difference value, which appears in the bottom right corner of the table and is noted in Eq. (8.3) as $\hat{\delta}_{DID}$. Here, we see that $\hat{\delta}_{DID}$ is equal to the difference in the average differences over the pre- and post-treatment periods across the groups.

$$\hat{\delta}_{DID} = \overline{Y}_1^T - \overline{Y}_0^T - \left(\overline{Y}_1^C - \overline{Y}_0^C\right) \tag{8.3}$$

Table 8.1 An illustration of the difference-in-difference technique

	Pre-treatment	*Post-treatment*	*Post-pre difference*
Treatment group (T)	$\overline{Y}_0^T$	$\overline{Y}_1^T$	$\overline{Y}_1^T - \overline{Y}_0^T$
Control group (C)	$\overline{Y}_0^C$	$\overline{Y}_1^C$	$\overline{Y}_1^C - \overline{Y}_0^C$
T - C difference	$\overline{Y}_0^T - \overline{Y}_0^C$	$\overline{Y}_1^T - \overline{Y}_1^C$	$\overline{Y}_1^T - \overline{Y}_0^T - \left(\overline{Y}_1^C - \overline{Y}_0^C\right)$

We also can see from the table and from Eq. (8.3) that $\hat{\delta}_{DID}$ is equal to the difference in the average difference between the groups across the pre- and post-treatment periods. These differences are presented in the bottom rows of the columns that are labelled "Pre-Treatment" and "Post-Treatment".[4]

The DID technique is based on the Classical Assumptions that apply to the Ordinary Least Squares technique plus the key parallel trend assumption. The parallel trend assumption ensures internal validity of DID models. For the assumption to be fulfilled, in the absence of a treatment (i.e., during the pre-treatment period), the difference between the treatment and control group must remain constant.[5] There is no statistical test for this assumption and, as a result, visual inspection is relied upon for verification of the assumption. To this end, Fig. 8.1 presents pre-treatment comparisons for each of our dependent variable series. While the series are not perfectly parallel, the series do seem to follow quite similar paths. Calculation of the pairwise correlation coefficients supports this position. Specifically, the correlation coefficient values for the series are 0.97, 0.98, and 0.90 for the series presented in Panels A, B, and C, respectively. Given the high correlation coefficient values and an assertion that the paths of the series pass the "eyeball test", we move forward with the belief that the parallel trend assumption is not violated.

8.2 Empirical Model and Descriptive Statistics

To test the first two of our three hypotheses, we estimate a variant of the empirical model that is introduced in Chap. 7. The third hypothesis is addressed using the results obtained when testing the first two hypotheses. The modifications we make to the model involves the incorporation of the difference-in-difference technique and our choice of dependent variable series. More specifically, as we seek to discern a potential relationship between the expansion of Medicaid eligibility as part of the ACA, we first regress the deprivation frequency series for the health insurance indicator on our set of explanatory variable. We then repeat the estimation with the

[4] One final definition of the DID estimator is that it is the difference estimator between the actual $\overline{Y}_1^T$ value and the $\overline{Y}_1^T$ value that would be observed in the treatment group during the post-treatment period if there had been no treatment: $\overline{Y}_{cf}^T = \overline{Y}_0^T - \left(\overline{Y}_1^C - \overline{Y}_0^C\right)$.

[5] Failure of the parallel trend assumption is among the most common problems with DID estimators. If the assumption is not fulfilled, the estimator may be biased (upward or downward) and the bias can even cause the estimator to exhibit the incorrect sign.

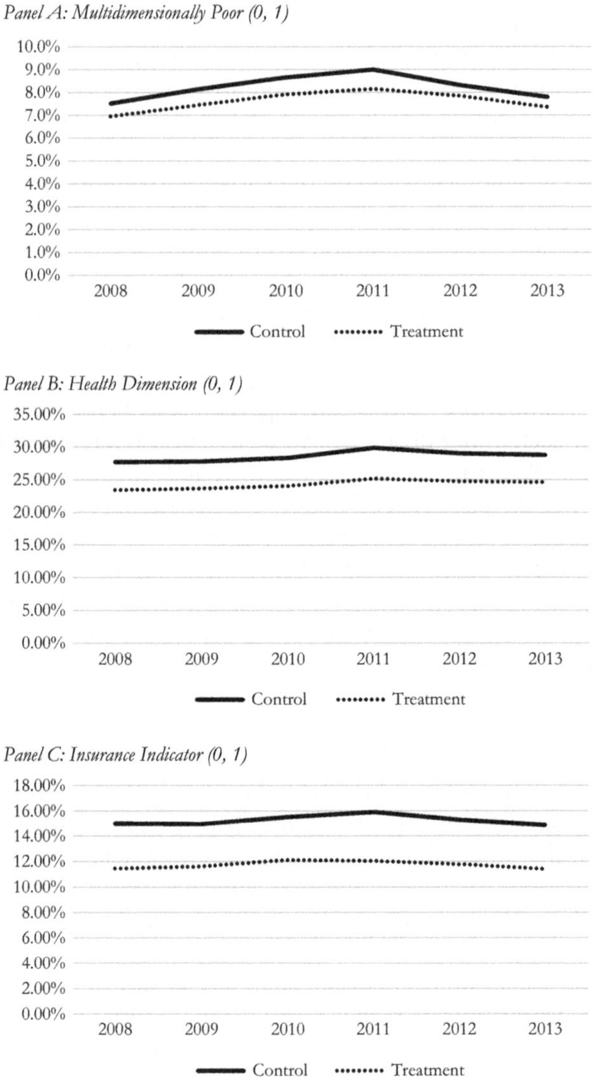

Fig. 8.1 Time paths of dependent variable series, control and treatment groups: 2008–2013

deprivation frequency series of the Health dimension variable employed as the dependent variable. Finally, we estimate our model using the MD Poor series and then the MD Poor Category series as our dependent variable. We use the binomial logit technique in all instances where the dependent variable series is binary and we used the ordered logit technique when the MD Poor Category is employed as our dependent variable series. These estimations address our first two hypotheses, in turn. Our empirical model, in general form, is given as Eq. (8.4).

$$M_{ijkt} = \alpha_0 + \beta_{DID}\left(\mathrm{T}_{ijk} \times \mathrm{Y}_t\right) + \beta_1 \mathrm{T}_{ijk} + \beta_2 \mathrm{Y}_t + \beta_\Theta \Theta_i + \beta_\Phi \Phi_j + \beta_\Psi \Psi_k \quad (8.4)$$

The dependent variable, M, represents the three dependent variable series that we employ in our analysis. It includes the deprivation frequencies of the health insurance indicator and of the Health dimension and it includes the headcount ratio series. As before, the subscripts i, j, k, and t denote the observation, corresponding household, state of residence, and year of survey, respectively. T is a dummy variable that identifies the treatment group, and Y is a dummy variable that identifies the post-treatment time period. The interaction of these two dummy variables, $(T_{ijk} \times Y_t)$, is our difference-in-difference term. We have no *a priori* expectation regarding the sign of the coefficient of the T variable. For the Y variable, due to the general decrease in multidimensional poverty incidence over our reference period, we anticipate a negative coefficient. Similarly, we expect the estimated coefficient of the difference-in-difference term to be negative. The sign of the interaction term indicates an increase (if of positive sign) or decrease (if negative in sign) in the dependent variable series that cannot be attributed to either the post-treatment period or the treatment group generally. In our case, a negative coefficient would indicate that expansion of Medicaid eligibility under the ACA significantly reduced the value of the corresponding dependent variable series.

Looking to the remaining explanatory variables in Eq. (8.4), we see that Θ includes a set of variables that indicate each observation's gender, educational attainment, race, ethnicity, nativity, age, marital status, and employment status. Similarly, Φ includes the variables that represent household size (in members) and the primary household language. Ψ controls for otherwise unobserved location fixed effects that are related to state of residence, and α represents our constant term (or cut points when we employ the ordered logit technique).

In column (a) of Table 8.2, we present the descriptive statistics for our full data sample. In columns (b) and (c) and in columns (d) and (e), respectively, we present the descriptive statistics for our control and treatment groups during both the pre- and post-treatment periods. We see that, in both periods, the treatment group has lower values for the MD Poor variable as compared to the control group. Similarly, both groups have MD Poor values during the post-treatment period (2014–2018) that are lower than the overall mean value (6.91 percent) and their corresponding pre-treatment period values. The treatment group appears to be marginally more educated, on average, than is the control group. Similarly, the treatment group is considerably more likely, as compared to the control group, to be foreign-born. Likely due to the higher foreign-born value for the treatment group, we also see that the treatment group is less likely to use English or Spanish as their primary household language. Members of the treatment group are also less likely to be black but are more likely to be Asian or some other race(s) or of multiple race(s).

In many other respects, the control and treatment groups are, on average, quite similar. For example, the gender composition of the two groups are quite similar. Likewise, the value for the Hispanic variable is nearly the same between the two groups, and there are no great differences across groups in the values of the employment status variables. The values of the age, marital status, and household size variables are also quite similar across groups.

8.3 Logit Estimations Involving the Health Insurance Indicator and the Health Dimension Series

Given the assumed mechanism through which expansion of Medicaid eligibility under the Affordable Care Act would affect multidimensional poverty incidence, we begin our examination by performing our difference-in-difference estimation technique with the health insurance indicator employed as our dependent variable series. Estimation results are presented in Table 8.3.

The first three coefficient values in column (a) are related to the difference-in-difference technique. We see that the coefficients on our difference-in-difference term, the treatment cohort dummy variable, and the time dummy variable are all negative and statistically significant from

Table 8.2 Descriptive statistics

Cohort:	*All*	*Control*		*Treatment*	
Period:	*2008–2018*	*2008–2013*	*2014–2018*	*2008–2013*	*2014–2018*
N=	*34,291,600*	*6,998,521*	*6,067,583*	*11,452,398*	*9,773,098*
Dependent variables...					
Multidimensionally poor (0,1)	0.0691 (0.2535)	0.0825 (0.2752)	0.0623 (0.2417)	0.0763 (0.2655)	0.055 (0.2281)
Multidimensionally poor category (0–3)	0.2722 (0.6059)	0.3119 (0.6492)	0.2527 (0.5827)	0.2929 (0.6293)	0.2315 (0.555)
Gender...					
Female	0.5122 (0.4999)	0.5141 (0.4998)	0.5122 (0.4999)	0.5128 (0.4998)	0.5103 (0.4999)
Male	0.4878 (0.4999)	0.4859 (0.4998)	0.4878 (0.4999)	0.4872 (0.4998)	0.4897 (0.4999)
Age category...					
Under 20 years of age	0.2436 (0.4292)	0.2527 (0.4346)	0.2393 (0.4266)	0.2492 (0.4326)	0.2331 (0.4228)
20–29 years of age	0.1177 (0.3222)	0.1156 (0.3198)	0.1155 (0.3196)	0.1178 (0.3224)	0.1203 (0.3254)
30–39 years of age	0.1177 (0.3223)	0.1171 (0.3215)	0.117 (0.3214)	0.1171 (0.3215)	0.1194 (0.3242)
40–49 years of age	0.1299 (0.3362)	0.1356 (0.3424)	0.1208 (0.3259)	0.1383 (0.3452)	0.1217 (0.327)
50–59 years of age	0.1473 (0.3544)	0.1464 (0.3535)	0.1441 (0.3512)	0.15 (0.3571)	0.1468 (0.3539)
60 years and older	0.2438 (0.4294)	0.2325 (0.4224)	0.2633 (0.4404)	0.2276 (0.4193)	0.2587 (0.4379)
Race/ethnicity...					
Asian	0.0486 (0.215)	0.0247 (0.1551)	0.0291 (0.1682)	0.0583 (0.2342)	0.0664 (0.2491)
Black	0.1039 (0.3051)	0.1408 (0.3478)	0.1337 (0.3403)	0.0842 (0.2777)	0.0819 (0.2742)
White	0.7707 (0.4204)	0.7771 (0.4162)	0.7772 (0.4162)	0.7731 (0.4188)	0.7593 (0.4275)
Other/multiple race(s)	0.0769 (0.2664)	0.0574 (0.2326)	0.06 (0.2375)	0.0844 (0.278)	0.0924 (0.2896)
Hispanic	0.1391 (0.3461)	0.1321 (0.3386)	0.1423 (0.3494)	0.1373 (0.3441)	0.1444 (0.3515)
Non-Hispanic	0.8609 (0.3461)	0.8679 (0.3386)	0.8577 (0.3494)	0.8627 (0.3441)	0.8556 (0.3515)

(*continued*)

Table 8.2 (continued)

Cohort:	*All*	*Control*		*Treatment*	
Period:	*2008–2018*	*2008–2013*	*2014–2018*	*2008–2013*	*2014–2018*
N=	*34,291,600*	*6,998,521*	*6,067,583*	*11,452,398*	*9,773,098*
Nativity...					
Foreign-born	0.1143	0.0902	0.096	0.1252	0.1302
	(0.3182)	(0.2864)	(0.2946)	(0.331)	(0.3365)
Native-born	0.8857	0.9098	0.904	0.8748	0.8698
	(0.3182)	(0.2864)	(0.2946)	(0.331)	(0.3365)
Educational attainment...					
Less than high school	0.2838	0.304	0.2773	0.2906	0.2653
diploma	(0.4508)	(0.46)	(0.4477)	(0.4541)	(0.4415)
High school diploma	0.2231	0.2272	0.2233	0.2237	0.2192
or equivalent	(0.4163)	(0.419)	(0.4165)	(0.4167)	(0.4137)
Some college	0.2409	0.2406	0.248	0.2366	0.2419
	(0.4277)	(0.4275)	(0.4319)	(0.425)	(0.4282)
B.A./B.S. degree	0.137	0.1252	0.1392	0.1335	0.1483
	(0.3439)	(0.331)	(0.3462)	(0.3401)	(0.3554)
Post-graduate	0.1152	0.103	0.1121	0.1156	0.1253
	(0.3192)	(0.304)	(0.3155)	(0.3197)	(0.3311)
Marital status...					
Divorced or separated	0.1026	0.1075	0.1094	0.0983	0.1001
	(0.3035)	(0.3098)	(0.3121)	(0.2977)	(0.3001)
Married	0.4278	0.436	0.4328	0.4249	0.4222
	(0.4948)	(0.4959)	(0.4955)	(0.4943)	(0.4939)
Single	0.4142	0.3986	0.4015	0.4215	0.4247
	(0.4926)	(0.4896)	(0.4902)	(0.4938)	(0.4943)
Widowed	0.0554	0.0578	0.0563	0.0553	0.0531
	(0.2287)	(0.2334)	(0.2305)	(0.2286)	(0.2243)
Employment status...					
Employed	0.457	0.4461	0.4532	0.4564	0.4679
	(0.4981)	(0.4971)	(0.4978)	(0.4981)	(0.499)
Unemployed	0.0352	0.0402	0.0248	0.044	0.0278
	(0.1842)	(0.1963)	(0.1555)	(0.205)	(0.1643)
Not in labor force	0.3191	0.3157	0.3365	0.3068	0.3251
	(0.4661)	(0.4648)	(0.4725)	(0.4612)	(0.4684)
Household size...					
1 person	0.1496	0.1458	0.1552	0.1451	0.1542
	(0.3567)	(0.3529)	(0.3621)	(0.3522)	(0.3611)
2 people	0.2816	0.2904	0.2952	0.2724	0.2777
	(0.4498)	(0.4539)	(0.4562)	(0.4452)	(0.4478)

(*continued*)

Table 8.2 (continued)

Cohort:	*All*	*Control*		*Treatment*	
Period:	*2008–2018*	*2008–2013*	*2014–2018*	*2008–2013*	*2014–2018*
N=	*34,291,600*	*6,998,521*	*6,067,583*	*11,452,398*	*9,773,098*
3–4 people	0.3689 (0.4825)	0.3721 (0.4834)	0.3601 (0.48)	0.3746 (0.484)	0.3656 (0.4816)
5–7 people	0.1789 (0.3833)	0.1745 (0.3796)	0.1724 (0.3778)	0.1845 (0.3879)	0.1796 (0.3839)
8 or more people	0.0209 (0.1431)	0.0173 (0.1302)	0.017 (0.1294)	0.0235 (0.1514)	0.0229 (0.1496)
Household language...					
Asian	0.0386 (0.1925)	0.0203 (0.141)	0.0228 (0.1494)	0.047 (0.2115)	0.0515 (0.2211)
English	0.7307 (0.4436)	0.7696 (0.4211)	0.7565 (0.4292)	0.7158 (0.451)	0.7043 (0.4564)
Indo-European	0.0467 (0.2111)	0.0329 (0.1784)	0.032 (0.1759)	0.0568 (0.2314)	0.0541 (0.2262)
Spanish	0.1293 (0.3356)	0.1324 (0.3389)	0.1341 (0.3408)	0.1276 (0.3336)	0.1262 (0.332)
Other language	0.0123 (0.11)	0.0071 (0.0841)	0.0087 (0.0927)	0.014 (0.1177)	0.0161 (0.1257)

Standard deviations in parentheses

zero. The time dummy variable identifies the post-treatment period and the coefficient estimate is applicable to both the treatment and a control group. We interpret the coefficient as the difference in the predicted value of our dependent variable series in the post-treatment period relative to the pre-treatment period. The coefficient estimate of the treatment group dummy variable identifies the extent to which the predicted value of the dependent variable series differs for the treatment group relative to the control group regardless of the time period considered. Finally, concerning our variable of primary interest, the coefficient estimate of our difference-in-difference term indicates the difference between the treatment and control groups during the post-treatment period that is not explained by the remaining explanatory variables. In our analysis, this coefficient estimate indicates the influence of the expansion of Medicaid eligibility due to the ACA on the respective dependent variable series.

Table 8.3 Difference-in-difference estimation results, insurance indicator and Health dimension, binomial logit estimations

Dependent variable:	*Insurance indicator (0, 1)*	*Health dimension (0, 1)*	*Dependent variable:*	*Insurance indicator (0, 1)*	*Health dimension (0, 1)*
	(a)	*(b)*		*(a)*	*(b)*
Difference-in-difference variables			Educational attainment (continued)		
DID (Treatment × Time Dummies)	-0.3173***	-0.0756***	4-year college degree	-1.2636***	-1.3278***
	(0.0025)	(0.0018)		(0.0027)	(0.0018)
Treatment cohort dummy	-0.4021***	-0.2561***	Post-graduate degree	-1.4172***	-1.4226***
	(0.0015)	(0.0012)		(0.0034)	(0.0021)
Time dummy (2014–2018)	-0.3648***	-0.1953***	Marital status (excluded: Single)		
	(0.0018)	(0.0014)	Divorced or separated	0.1123***	-0.024***
Gender (excluded: Male)				(0.0022)	(0.0017)
Female	-0.2411***	-0.2876***	Married	-0.6911***	-0.7203***
	(0.0012)	(0.0009)		(0.0019)	(0.0015)
Age category (excluded: under 20 years of age)			Widowed	-0.6947***	0.0422***
20–29 years	1.6866***	1.5494***		(0.0046)	(0.0022)
	(0.0025)	(0.002)	Employment status (excluded: Employed)		
30–39 years	1.6943***	1.745***	Unemployed	1.2409***	1.1666***
	(0.0027)	(0.0022)		(0.0023)	(0.0021)
40–49 years	1.4551***	1.7518***	Not in labor force	0.3908***	1.1527***
	(0.0028)	(0.0023)		(0.0015)	(0.001)
50–59 years	1.1754***	1.8198***	Household size (excluded: 1 person in household)		
	(0.003)	(0.0023)	2 people	-0.1359***	-0.1808***
60 or more years	-0.3955***	1.7312***		(0.0021)	(0.0015)
	(0.0038)	(0.0024)	3–4 people	-0.2324***	-0.235***
Race and ethnicity (excluded: White and Non-Hispanic)				(0.002)	(0.0015)
Asian	-0.2206***	-0.2712***	5–7 people	-0.1039***	-0.1722***
	(0.0042)	(0.0034)		(0.0023)	(0.0018)

Black	0.2023***	0.1642***	8 or more people	0.2383***	0.1208***
	(0.0018)	(0.0014)		(0.004)	(0.0035)
Other race	0.2278***	0.2472***	Primary household language (excluded: English)		
	(0.0021)	(0.0018)	Asian or Pacific Island	0.1262***	-0.0237***
Hispanic	0.3643***	0.1751***		(0.0045)	(0.0037)
	(0.0024)	(0.002)	Indo-European	0.2573***	0.0944***
Nativity (excluded: Native-born)				(0.003)	(0.0024)
Foreign-born	0.8242***	0.2833***	Spanish	0.3222***	0.245***
	(0.002)	(0.0017)		(0.0024)	(0.0021)
Educational attainment (excluded: Less than High School)			Other language	0.3929***	0.1715***
High school graduate	-0.1266***	-0.391***		(0.005)	(0.0042)
	(0.0019)	(0.0014)	Constant	-2.1132***	-1.7177***
Some college	-0.5909***	-0.7589***		(0.0026)	(0.002)
	(0.002)	(0.0015)			
.	.	.	N	34,291,600	34,291,600
.	.	.	Wald Chi^2	3,235,129***	4,674,875***
.	.	.	Pseudo R^2	0.1833	0.1586
.	.	.	Log pseudolikelihood	-9,639,241	-15,987,937
.	.	.	Count R^2	0.8960	0.7860

Robust standard errors in parentheses. "***", "**", amd "*" denote statistical significance from zero at the 1%, 5%, and 10% levels, respectively. All estimations include year and state of residence fixed effects

Regarding our first two hypotheses, the coefficient estimates on the difference-in-difference variables that are presented in columns (a) and (b) are both negative and statistically significant from zero. The dependent variable series in these estimations are the deprivation frequencies of the health insurance indicator and the Health dimension, respectively. Given the coefficient signs, we can state that the expansion of Medicaid eligibility under the ACA led to a reduction in the deprivation frequency of the health insurance indicator. That is, the Medicaid expansion resulted in an increased probability that the typical individual, all else held constant, will have health insurance coverage. We can also say that the Medicaid expansion led to a reduction in the deprivation frequency associated with the Health dimension. Thus, a higher incidence of health insurance coverage has led to a reduction in deprivation for the corresponding dimension. The interpretation of the coefficient signs is interesting; however, the magnitudes of these effects will provide additional insights.

Figure 8.2 illustrates the results of our difference-in-difference estimation and demonstrates the extents to which the expansion of Medicaid eligibility reduced the deprivation frequencies. In Panel A of the figure, we see that during the pre-treatment period the difference between the control group and the treatment group in terms of the probability of lacking health insurance that is 3.07 percent. During the post-treatment period, this gap is estimated to have increased to 3.46 percent. The difference between these differences is 0.39 percent. Thus, the expansion of Medicaid eligibility under the ACA led to a 0.39 percent reduction in the probability that the typical individual lacked health insurance. The corresponding increase in health insurance coverage, in turn, would be expected to decrease the deprivation frequency value for the Health dimension, the headcount ratio, and the MPI value.

A similar depiction of the effects of the Medicaid expansion on the deprivation frequency for the Health dimension is provided in Panel B of the figure. During the pre-treatment period, the control group is estimated to have a probability of deprivation that is 4.66 percent higher than that of the treatment group. By comparison, during the post-treatment period, the difference between the control and treatment groups is equal to 5.22 percent. As a result, the difference in these differences is equal to 0.56 percent. Stated more deliberately, the expansion of Medicaid eligibility under the ACA led to a 0.56 percent reduction in the probability that the typical individual will experience deprivation in terms of the Health dimension. Note that the effect at the dimension level is larger than that

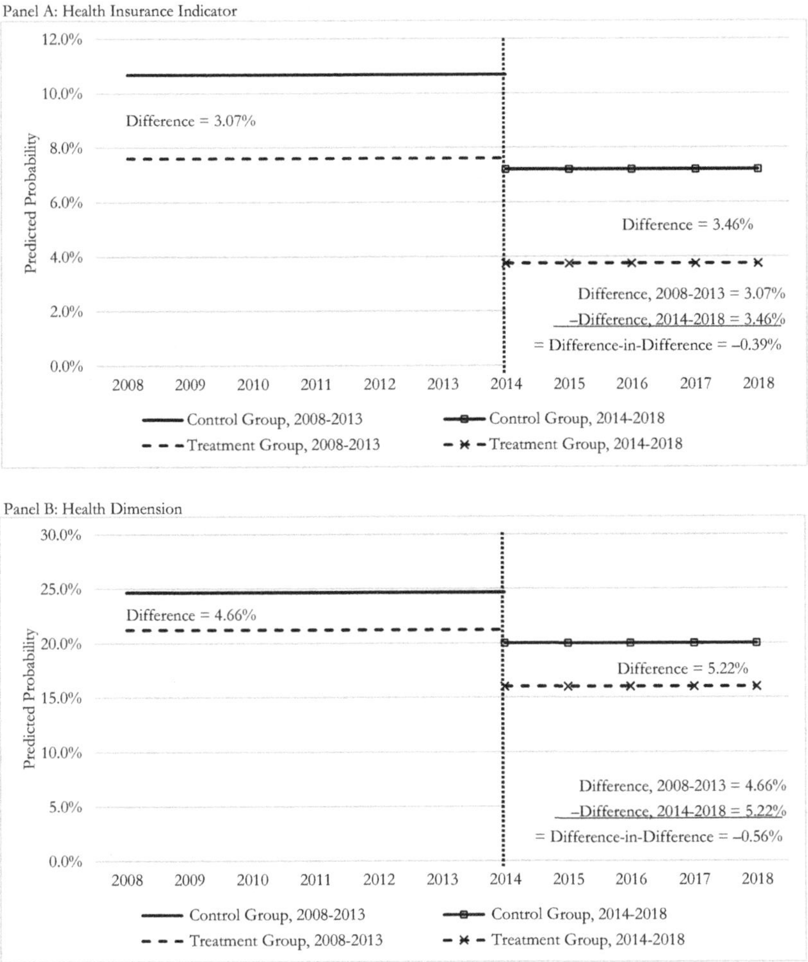

Fig. 8.2 Difference-in-difference estimates for indicator and dimension deprivation frequencies

reported at the indicator level. This is likely attributable to those who are deprived in the Health dimension being more likely, relative to the general population, to lack health insurance.

The results presented so far verify our first two hypotheses. Our findings are consistent with the expansion of Medicaid eligibility under the

ACA resulting in a statistically significant reduction in the deprivation frequencies of the health insurance indicator and of the Health dimension. To complete our analysis, we can now examine our final hypothesis: Conditional on Hypotheses 1 and 2, there is a corresponding decrease in the headcount ratio. The corresponding estimation results and discussion are presented in the following section.

8.4 Binomial and Ordered Logit Estimations Involving the MD Poor and MD Poor Category Series

To examine our third hypothesis, we continue our application of the difference-in-difference technique with the sole alterations being that we now estimate Eq. (8.4) while employing the MD Poor series as our dependent variable and we perform an additional estimation in which the MD Poor Category variable is employed as our dependent variable series and, accordingly as the variable is categorical, we utilize the ordered logit estimation technique. Given our *a priori* expectations and the results reported in the previous section, for both estimations, we anticipate that the coefficient estimate of our difference-in-difference term will be negative. Our estimation results are presented in Table 8.4, while Fig. 8.3 illustrates the extent to which expansion of Medicaid eligibility reduced the headcount ratio.

Beginning with the difference-in-difference variables that are presented in Table 8.4, we again see that all coefficient estimates are negative and statistically significant from zero. Looking first to the values presented in column (a), where the dependent variable is the MD Poor series, the negative coefficient indicates a statistically significant reduction in the frequency of multidimensional poverty. Our earlier findings that the expansion of Medicaid under the ACA led to reductions in the deprivation frequencies of the health insurance indicator and the Health dimension series implies a corresponding reduction in the average deprivation intensity series. Thus, the reductions in multidimensional poverty incidence and intensity result in a decrease in the MPI value. We can turn to Fig. 8.3 to identify the extent of the decrease in estimated probability that the typical individual is multidimensionally poor.

During the pre-treatment period, the difference in the estimated probabilities for the control and treatment groups is equal to 0.45 percent. In

Table 8.4 Difference-in-difference estimation results, binomial and ordered logit techniques

	Binomial logit	*Ordered logit*		*Binomial logit*	*Ordered logit*
Dependent variable:	*MD poor (0, 1)*	*MDP category (0–3)*	*Dependent variable:*	*MD poor (0, 1)*	*MDP category (0–3)*
	(a)	*(b)*		*(a)*	*(b)*
Difference-in-difference variables			Educational attainment (continued)		
DID (Treatment × Time Dummies)	-0.0681***	-0.0341***	Post-graduate degree	-2.5273***	-2.2644***
	(0.0033)	(0.002)		(0.0047)	(0.0026)
Treatment cohort dummy	-0.169***	-0.1277***	Marital status (excluded: Single)		
	(0.0021)	(0.0013)	Divorced or separated	0.271***	0.1903***
Time dummy (2014–2018)	-0.2461***	-0.2077***		(0.0029)	(0.0019)
	(0.0025)	(0.0016)	Married	-0.7246***	-0.8167***
Gender (excluded: Male)				(0.0026)	(0.0017)
Female	0.079***	0.0382***	Widowed	-0.1346***	-0.0875***
	(0.0016)	(0.001)		(0.004)	(0.0024)
Age category (excluded: under 20 years of age)			Employment status (excluded: Employed)		
20–29 years	1.9598***	1.9698***	Unemployed	2.9559***	2.9951***
	(0.0033)	(0.0022)		(0.0027)	(0.0021)
30–39 years	2.21***	2.065***	Not in labor force	1.0065***	1.0407***
	(0.0036)	(0.0024)		(0.0019)	(0.0012)
40–49 years	2.0858***	1.9502***	Household size (excluded: 1 person in household)		
	(0.0037)	(0.0025)	2 people	-0.2435***	-0.209***
50–59 years	2.0198***	1.8963***		(0.0027)	(0.0017)
	(0.0038)	(0.0025)	3–4 people	-0.5663***	-0.4661***
60 or more years	1.3137***	1.4223***		(0.0027)	(0.0017)
	(0.004)	(0.0026)	5–7 people	-0.1937***	-0.0728***
Race and ethnicity (excluded: White and Non-Hispanic)				(0.003)	(0.0019)
Asian	-0.0076	0.0024	8 or more people	0.4209***	0.7349***
	(0.0051)	(0.0033)		(0.0046)	(0.003)

(continued)

Table 7.5 (continued)

	Binomial logit	*Ordered logit*		*Binomial logit*	*Ordered logit*
Dependent variable:	*MD poor (0, 1)*	*MDP category (0–3)*	*Dependent variable:*	*MD poor (0, 1)*	*MDP category (0–3)*
	(a)	*(b)*		*(a)*	*(b)*
Black	0.4298***	0.5538***	Primary household language (excluded: English)		
	(0.0024)	(0.0015)	Asian or Pacific Island	0.7774***	0.6057***
Other race	0.1879***	0.2741***		(0.0054)	(0.0035)
	(0.0026)	(0.0018)	Indo-European	0.6789***	0.4606***
Hispanic	0.2563***	0.3832***		(0.0036)	(0.0024)
	(0.0031)	(0.002)	Spanish	0.9818***	0.7292***
Nativity (excluded: Native-born)				(0.0031)	(0.002)
Foreign-born	0.6599***	0.6294***	Other language	1.0022***	0.8252***
	(0.0024)	(0.0017)		(0.0056)	(0.0039)
Educational attainment (excluded: Less than high school)			Constant	-3.2655***	.
High school graduate	-1.9404***	-2.0524***		(0.0035)	.
	(0.0023)	(0.0016)	/ Cut 1	.	1.6175
Some college	-2.2904***	-2.3443***		.	(0.0021)
	(0.0025)	(0.0017)	/ Cut 2	.	3.2682
4-year college degree	-2.9076***	-2.8883***		.	(0.0022)
	(0.004)	(0.0023)	/ Cut 3	.	6.0074
				.	(0.003)
.	.	.	N	34,291,600	34,291,600
.	.	.	Wald Chi^2	3,886,470***	7,790,959***
.	.	.	Pseudo R^2	0.3042	0.2289
.	.	.	Log pseudolikelihood	-5,994,910	-17,055,621
.	.	.	Count R^2	0.9370	0.8220

Robust standard errors in parentheses. All estimations include year and state fixed effects terms, which are not reported here due to space limitations. "***", "**", and "*" denote statistical significance at the 1%, 5%, and 10% levels, respectively

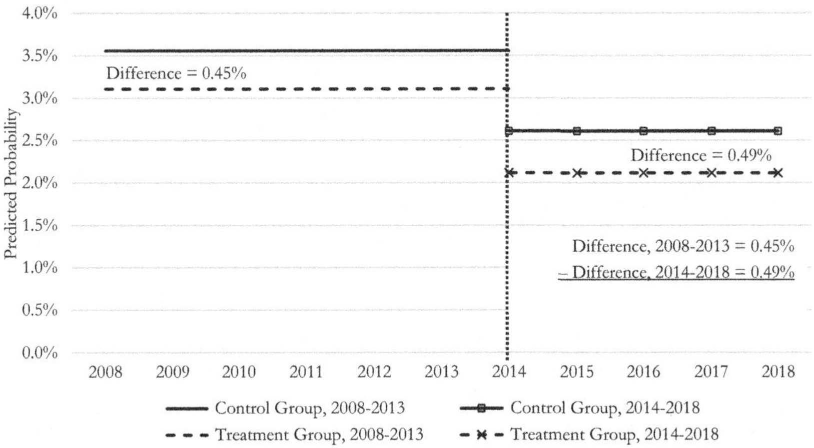

Fig. 8.3 Difference-in-difference estimates for headcount ratio

the post-treatment period, this difference increased only slightly to a value of 0.49 percent. Thus, the difference in these differences is equal to 0.04 percent. While the change in estimated probabilities that is attributable to the expansion of Medicaid eligibility is rather small in magnitude, we can gauge the practical significance of the effect through some simple calculations. Based on the ACS data, the U.S. population in 2018 was equal to 327,167,422 individuals. In Chap. 4, the 2018 headcount ratio is listed as being equal to 6.02 percent. If we assume that without the expansion of Medicaid eligibility the headcount ratio would equal 6.06 percent, then factoring the population value by 6.06 percent results in an estimated 19,826,346 U.S. residents living in multidimensional poverty during 2018. If instead the same calculation is performed using the observed headcount ratio of 6.02 percent, then our estimate of the number of multidimensionally poor individuals in the U.S. in 2018 would decrease by 130,867. Thus, the estimated reduction in the number of multidimensionally poor U.S. residents is considerable.

8.5 Conclusions

In this chapter, we have presented the first of three examples of multidimensional poverty analysis. More specifically, we have considered the influence of the Medicaid expansion that was enacted in 2014 as part of the Patient Protection and Affordable Care Act (ACA) on multidimensional poverty. The rationale for this relationship is straightforward. If an expansion of Medicaid eligibility reduces the probability that an individual lacks health insurance, then it also will reduce the deprivation frequency for the Health dimension. Likewise, a reduction in the deprivation frequencies of the health insurance indicator and the Health dimension will result in a decrease in the average deprivation intensity value and a reduced headcount ratio, thus lowering the incidence and intensity of multidimensional poverty.

We modify the empirical model that is introduced in Chap. 7 to allow for application of the difference-in-difference approach. This allows for the isolation of the effects of the expansion of Medicaid eligibility. Our results indicate that the expansion led to a 0.39 percentage point decrease in the deprivation frequency for the health insurance indicator, a 0.56 percentage point decrease in the deprivation frequency for the Health dimension, and a 0.04 percentage point decrease in the headcount ratio. This decrease in the headcount ratio equates to 130,867 fewer individuals suffering multidimensional poverty in the U.S. during 2018.

Reference

U.S. Bureau of the Census/American Factfinder (U.S. Census). 2019. American Community Survey (Annual Data, 2008–2018). U.S. Census Bureau's American Community Survey Office. http://factfinder.census.gov

CHAPTER 9

Nativity, Immigrant Home Countries, and Multidimensional Poverty

In this, our second of three examples of multidimensional poverty analysis, we examine potential variation in deprivation across cohorts of native- and foreign-born residents of the U.S. and, separately, across the immigrants' specific home countries. This builds upon a portion of the descriptive analysis that is presented in Chap. 6, where we identified considerable differences between the native- and foreign-born populations of the U.S. in terms of headcount ratios, average deprivation intensity values, and Multidimensional Poverty Index (MPI) values. A small number of works have examined such variation, broadly, with White and Yamasaki (2017), being most closely related to the analysis that is presented here.[1,2] This chapter also extends from the analysis presented in Chap. 7 where we identify the factors that contribute to multidimensional poverty. Specifically, we interact dummy variables that identify observations based on nativity with the explanatory variables used in that analysis to consider variation in the determinants of multidimensional poverty across the

[1] See also Brucker et al. (2015), Dhongde and Haveman (2015), and Mitra and Brucker (2014).

[2] White and Yamasaki (2017) provides a similar examination and, thus, serves as the basic structure/framework for the work that is presented in this chapter; however, their study considered two additional indicators that we forgo (i.e., access to a private vehicle for transportation and receipt of benefits via the Supplemental Nutrition Assistance Program). Their study was also limited to a shorter reference period (i.e., 2010 through 2014) than the 2008 through 2018 period that we examine.

R. White, *Multidimensional Poverty in America*,
https://doi.org/10.1007/978-3-030-45916-1_9

native- and foreign-born cohorts. Still further, we extend our analysis in a similar fashion to consider variation across groupings of immigrants' home countries that are defined based on the relative headcount ratio and average deprivation intensity values of the home country. Collectively, the information gained from this study facilitates a deeper understanding of our topic.

As in earlier chapters, we again examine data from the 2008–2018 American Community Survey (ACS) Public Use Microdata Sample (PUMS) (U.S. Census 2019).[3] We measure multidimensional poverty, as we have throughout this work, by employing the methodology of Alkire and Foster (2009) and the dimensions, indicators, weights, and threshold that are detailed in Chap. 3. Our findings are largely consistent with those of earlier studies in that we report considerable variation across immigrant home countries in terms of headcount ratio (i.e., the incidence, or frequency) and average deprivation intensity values and, thus, across MPI values. In our empirical analysis, we utilize the binomial logit and the ordered logit estimation techniques as appropriate.

Consistent with the more general, descriptive finding that is presented in Chap. 7, we find that, once we control for other factors, foreign-born individuals are significantly more likely than their comparable native-born counterparts to suffer multidimensional poverty. We build upon this finding to consider potential variation in the relationships between the determinants and measures of multidimensional poverty across native- and foreign-born cohorts and across immigrants' home country groupings that are defined based on the relative headcount ratio and average deprivation intensity values of the home countries. A brief summary of results includes that gender, race and ethnicity, age, education, marital and employment statuses, household size, and primary household language and, most importantly for the topic at hand, nativity are all significant determinants of multidimensional poverty. Further, while the signs of the

[3] To facilitate examination at the home country level of detail and to allow for more accurate categorization of home countries based on relative headcount ratio and average deprivation intensity values, we exclude from our analysis all observations that indicate a foreign place of birth but do not identify a particular foreign country as the place of birth (e.g., observations for which the place of birth is listed as "Other Europe, Not Specified" or "South America"). The effect on our sample composition is the exclusion of 102,108 observations which results in a sample size of 34,189,492 observations. An additional consequence is that summary values in this chapter differ slightly from the values that are provided in Chap. 4 where the full sample is examined.

estimated coefficients are largely the same across the native- and foreign-born cohorts and across home country groupings defined by relative values of the multidimensional poverty measures, we find statistically significant differences in the magnitudes of the coefficient estimates.

The structure of this chapter is as follows. In the next section, we provide a detailed descriptive portrait of multidimensional poverty in the U.S. among native- and foreign-born cohorts and the individual home countries of the foreign-born population. This is followed in Sect. 9.2 with a more complete discussion of our methodology than has been presented here and a presentation of MPI values and related findings for the native- and foreign-born cohorts and for the specific home countries of the foreign-born population. In Sect. 9.3, we present the results of our econometric analysis in which we identify the determinants of multidimensional poverty while allowing for variation that may correspond with nativity and we explore potential variation in the identified determinants across native- and foreign-born cohorts and across groupings of immigrants' home countries. In Sect. 9.4, we summarize and offer concluding thoughts.

9.1 Multidimensional Poverty in the U.S. Among the Native- and the Foreign-born

During our full 2008–2018 reference period, 8.05 percent of U.S. residents were multidimensionally poor. The average censored deprivation score across these individuals was equal to 0.3958. These values are presented in panel A of Table 9.1. Given these headcount ratio and average deprivation intensity values, the MPI value for the full sample is 3.19. As a point of comparison, White and Yamasaki (2017) adopt the same deprivation threshold that we employ (i.e., 0.3333) when examining ACS data for the period from 2010 through 2014. Since this period includes the initial recovery period following the Great Recession, it is reasonable that the authors report headcount ratio (9.5 percent), average deprivation intensity (0.4164), and MPI (3.95) values that are greater in magnitude than what we report here. Because our data span a lengthier reference period, including more recent years during which a sustained economic expansion occurred, the relative magnitudes of the values appear reasonable. Somewhat less similar, Dhongde and Haveman (2015) adopt a deprivation score threshold of 0.25 for categorization as multidimensionally poor. At this cut-off, for the year 2014, Dhongde and Haveman report

Table 9.1 Multidimensional poverty, deprivation, and dimensions/indicators

	Full sample	*Native-born*	*Foreign-born*
Panel A: Frequency, intensity, and multidimensional poverty indices			
Percentage of population that are multidimensionally poor (H)	8.05%	5.91%	21.46%
Average intensity across the poor (A)	0.3958	0.3827	0.4186
MPI (H × A × 100)	3.1866	2.2625	8.9835
Panel B: Breakdown of non-deprived, near-deprived, deprived, and severely deprived			
Not deprived (Deprivation score (DS) < 0.20)	78.31%	81.41%	58.84%
Vulnerable (0.20 ≤ DS < 0.33)	13.64%	12.68%	19.70%
Moderate poverty (0.33 ≤ DS < 0.50)	7.08%	5.47%	17.23%
Severe poverty (0.50 ≤ DS)	0.97%	0.45%	4.23%
Panel C: Dimensions and indicators (indented), mean values (0, 1)			
Economic security (25%)	17.09%	16.62%	20.05%
Income-to-poverty ratio < 1.0 (12.5%)	14.43%	14.00%	17.09%
Unemployed (12.5%)	3.86%	3.78%	4.37%
Education (weight = 25%)	13.33%	9.07%	40.03%
Educational attainment < High school diploma (12.5%)	10.13%	7.52%	26.51%
Limited English-speaking household (12.5%)	4.76%	1.72%	23.86%
Health (25%)	24.49%	22.78%	35.24%
Disabled (12.5%)	12.91%	13.43%	9.61%
Lacks health insurance coverage (12.5%)	12.69%	10.41%	26.99%
Housing costs (25%)	19.80%	17.88%	31.84%
Housing costs ≥ 50% of household income (8.33%)	13.50%	12.77%	18.07%
Lacks complete kitchen and/or plumbing facilities (8.33%)	0.79%	0.75%	1.02%
Lives in a crowded house (8.33%)	7.02%	5.76%	16.42%
Number of observations (*N*)	34,189,492	30,079,348	4,110,144

a headcount ration value of 20.1 percent, an average deprivation intensity value of 0.3283, and an MPI value of 6.6. As expected, since we employ a higher threshold for categorization as multidimensionally poor, our headcount ratio and MPI values are lower while our average deprivation intensity value is higher.

Comparing across the cohorts of native- and foreign-born observations, we see stark differences. The headcount ratio for the native-born cohort (5.91 percent) is only slightly more than one-quarter of the value that is observed for the foreign-born cohort (21.46 percent). Somewhat similarly, the average deprivation intensity value for the native-born (0.3827) is lower than the value for their foreign-born counterparts

(0.4186). The lower incidence and intensity values for the native-born cohort indicates that the MPI value for the native-born is considerably lower than the MPI value of the foreign-born. Comparing the values, we see that the MPI value for the foreign-born in the U.S. (8.98) is higher than the value observed for the native-born population (2.26) by nearly a factor of four.

Looking to panel B, we see that the vast majority of individuals in the U.S. (91.95 percent) are not multidimensionally deprived. Among these individuals, 78.31 percent have a deprivation score (d_i) below 0.20, which results in the classification of these individuals as neither multidimensionally poor nor vulnerable to multidimensional poverty. A sizeable portion of the sample (13.64 percent) is, however, categorized as being vulnerable to multidimensional poverty (i.e., $0.20 \leq d_i < 0.33$). Among those who are multidimensionally poor, 7.08 percent are classified as moderately poor (i.e., $0.3333 \leq d_i < 0.50$). The remaining 0.97 percent of all individuals are categorized as suffering severe multidimensional poverty (i.e., $0.50 \leq d_i$). Comparing across the native- and foreign-born cohorts, we again see pronounced differences. Members of the native-born cohort are about 1.2 times more likely to not be multidimensionally poor, while those within the foreign-born cohort are 3.2 times more likely to suffer moderate multidimensional poverty and 9.5 times more likely to experience severe multidimensional poverty.

In panel C, for the full sample, we see that the Health dimension has the highest deprivation frequency value, with 24.49 percent of all individuals deprived in this area. The Health dimension is followed by the Housing (19.8 percent), Economic Security (17.09 percent), and Education (13.33 percent) dimensions. The indicator with the highest deprivation frequency value falls within the Economic Security dimension; 14.43 percent of the sample are income poor. However, many are also found to be deprived due to having housing costs that are equal to or greater than 50 percent of household income (13.5 percent) and/or because they suffer one or more disabilities (12.91 percent). The indicator with the smallest impact is housing amenities; those who lack complete kitchen or plumbing facilities make up only 0.79 percent of the sample.

Comparing across native- and foreign-born cohorts in panel C, we again see tremendous differences. By a margin of more than four-to-one, foreign-born individuals (40.03 percent) are more likely to be deprived in terms of the Education dimension relative to their native-born counterparts (9.07 percent). This difference is driven by a near 19 percent gap in deprivation incidence for the indicator related to the completion of high school (26.51 percent as compared to 7.52 percent) and a more than 22 percent differential in deprivation incidence for the linguistic isolation (i.e., English language) indicator (23.86 percent versus 1.72 percent). Similarly, a much higher percentage of foreign-born individuals (35.24 percent) were deprived in the Health dimension as compared to native-born individuals (22.78 percent). Unlike the Education dimension where the foreign-born cohort was found to be more frequently deprived in both indicators, the nearly 12.5 percent difference between cohorts that is witnessed for the Health dimension is driven by a disparity in the health insurance indicator. In fact, members of the foreign-born cohort are less frequently categorized as being disabled (9.61 percent) relative to native-born individuals (13.43 percent). Thus, there is a 16.59 percentage point gap between the deprivation frequencies of the native-born (10.41 percent) and foreign-born individuals (26.99 percent) in terms of the health insurance coverage indicator. There are lesser differences between cohorts in terms of the Housing dimension (13.95 percent) and the Economic Security dimension (3.43 percent). The former is largely the result of 10.66 and 5.3 percentage point gaps in values for the crowded house and housing costs relative to household income indicators, respectively. The latter is mostly attributable to a difference in income poverty incidence: 17.09 percent for foreign-born individuals as compared to 14 percent for the native-born.

In addition to calculating the MPI and related values for native- and foreign-born cohorts, we disaggregate the foreign-born cohort by home country and calculate these values for each immigrant home country. A scatter plot of the headcount ratio and average deprivation intensity series is presented as Fig. 9.1, and a map that identifies the MPI values for U.S. foreign-born populations, identified by their home countries, is provided as Fig. 9.2. Interestingly, the home countries can be grouped into three cohorts based on their positioning within the figure. Group 1 includes the home countries that have headcount ratio values below 25 percent and average deprivation intensity values below the full sample mean of 0.3935.[4] The average values for countries in group 1 are quite similar to those of the native-born cohort: 7.9 percent for the headcount ratio, 0.3806 for the average deprivation intensity, and 3.02 for the MPI. In panel A of Table 9.1, we see similar values for the full sample;

[4]The choice of 25 percent to segment the headcount ratio series is chosen as there is a break in the series between 24.36 percent and 26.61 percent.

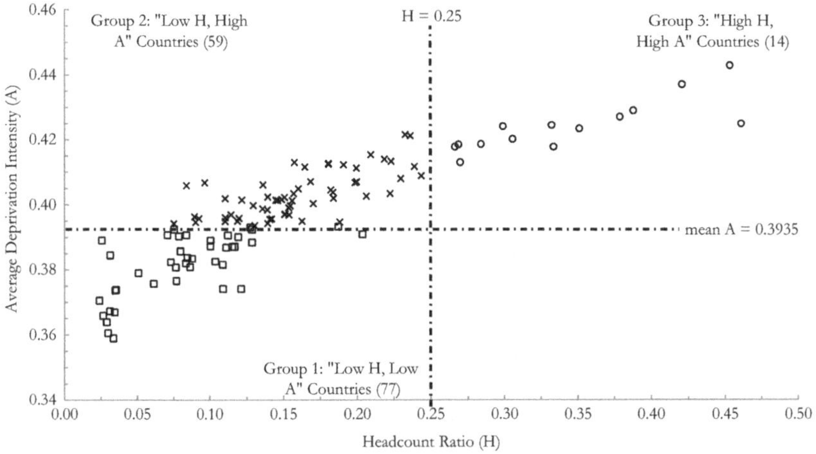

Fig. 9.1 Immigrant home country groups, categorized by relative frequency and intensity measures

8.1 percent for the headcount ratio, an average deprivation intensity value of 0.3958, and an MPI value that is equal to 3.19. The countries within group 1 tend to have lower MPI values, on average, relative to other home country groups. For example, group 2 includes home countries with somewhat higher headcount ratios (15.9 percent, on average) and higher than average values for the average deprivation intensity series (0.4031). This second group has an average MPI value of 6.42, which is still lower than the MPI value of 8.98 that is observed for the full foreign-born cohort. Lastly, home countries with higher headcount ratios (34.4 percent, on average) and higher than average poverty intensities (0.4242, again, on average) are included in group 3. This third group is rather small in number, consisting of the 14 home countries of the immigrant cohorts with the highest MPI values (14.62, on average). These differences are especially noteworthy since, in our econometric analysis, we examine variation in the determinants of multidimensional poverty not only across native- and foreign-born cohorts but also across the three identified home country groups.

The countries that comprise group 3 are identified in Fig. 9.2. For each of the noted countries, we have listed both the 2018 MPI value for the cohort of immigrants in the U.S. from the respective country and the

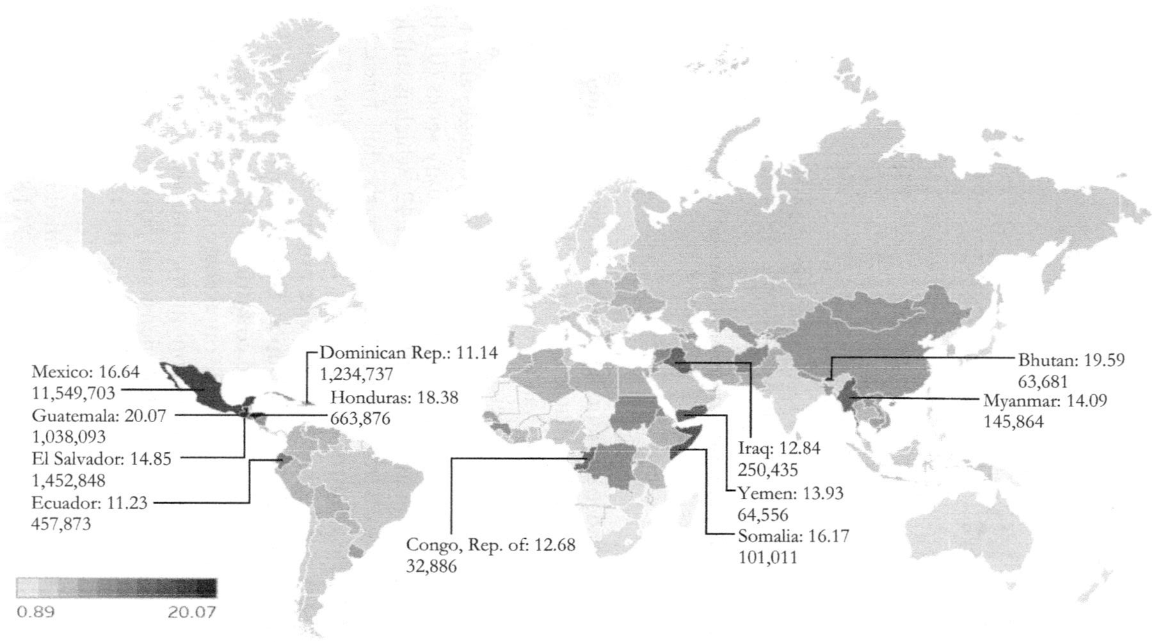

Fig. 9.2 MPI values for U.S. foreign-born populations by home country, 2008–2018. Group 3 countries not shown: Marshall Islands (MPI = 11.12; 27,890) and Micronesia (MPI = 11.88; 32,438)

estimated immigrant population from each country who resided the U.S. during 2018. For example, we see that in 2018 an estimated 11.5 million immigrants from Mexico lived in the U.S. and the MPI value for this cohort of immigrants was equal to 16.64. Immigrants from Mexico have the fourth highest MPI value among the 150 immigrant groups, categorized by their home countries, for which data are available. We also see that the headcount ratio among immigrants from Mexico is equal to 38.8 percent and that the average deprivation intensity value for this cohort is equal to 0.429.

Immigrants from Mexico present a unique case as they comprise such a large proportion of the foreign-born population of the U.S. In total, in 2018 there were an estimated 47,963,031 immigrants in the U.S.[5] This is equal to 14.66 percent of the total population of the U.S. Immigrants from Mexico accounted for 24.1 percent of the U.S. foreign-born population in this year; thus, they represented about 0.44 percent of the U.S. population. Stated in different terms, it is estimated that one in every 225 U.S. residents in 2018 was an immigrant from Mexico. In total, the 14 home countries that comprise group 3 account for slightly more than 17.1 million immigrants in the U.S. This is equal to 35.7 percent of the U.S. foreign-born population and, as can be seen from a review of the immigrant populations from other home countries, immigrants from Mexico account for a very large proportion of the 17.1 million immigrants.

There is considerable diversity in terms of the geographic locations of the group 3 home countries. Beyond the cluster of six countries in Latin America and the Caribbean, we have pairs of home countries in each of Africa, the Middle East, East Asia, and the Pacific Islands. Looking to the immigrant population values, however, we see that the six home countries in Latin America and the Caribbean collectively account for 16.4 million of the 17.1 million group 3 immigrants in the U.S. Expressed as a percentage, Mexico, Guatemala, Honduras, El Salvador, the Dominican Republic, and Ecuador account for 95.8 percent of the group 3 immigrant population, 34.2 percent of the total U.S. foreign-born population, and slightly above 0.5 percent of the entire U.S. population.

To further illustrate the extent of multidimensional poverty among the foreign-born cohort, Table 9.7 presents the headcount ratio, average deprivation intensity, and MPI values for each immigrant home country.

[5] The 2018 immigrant population estimates and the estimate of the total U.S. population have been made using ACS data.

Countries are ranked in descending order by MPI value, and we identify each home country by group (i.e., group 1, 2, or 3, from Fig. 9.1, based on their respective headcount ratio and average deprivation intensity values). To further compare across immigrants based on their respective home countries, in Table 9.8, we present the shares of immigrant populations in the U.S. that are classified as neither deprived nor vulnerable to multidimensional poverty, vulnerable to multidimensional poverty, facing moderate poverty, or in severe poverty. Both Tables 9.7 and 9.8 are available in the chapter appendix.

It is important to note that, for most home countries, the majority of immigrants are categorized as neither deprived nor vulnerable to deprivation and a very small percentage are considered severely deprived. In fact, 45 of the 150 home countries listed have MPI values below our full sample value of 3.19, and 29 home countries have MPI values that are less than that of the native-born cohort (i.e., below 2.26). Even so, 70 percent of the listed home countries have MPI values that are greater than that of the full sample. Nearly one-third of the home countries (28.7 percent) have MPI values more than two times the full sample value, and 12 percent have values more than three times that of the full sample. In short, there is considerable variation across immigrant cohorts when grouped by home country in terms of MPI values, the component measures (i.e., headcount ratio and poverty intensity measure), and shares of immigrant populations that are categorized as neither deprived nor vulnerable, vulnerable, facing moderately poverty poor, or/and experiencing severe poverty.

9.2 Variation in the Determinants of Multidimensional Poverty

Having identified the extent of multidimensional poverty for the full sample, for both the native- and the foreign-born cohorts, and for immigrant groups based on their home countries, we turn our attention to the identification of potential variation in the determinants of multidimensional poverty across native- and foreign-born cohorts. Specifically, we estimate a pair of regression models using data for the full 2008–2018 reference period and two related measures of multidimensional poverty, separately, as our dependent variable series. The first dependent variable is the “MD Poor” series. It is a binary variable that is equal to one if the deprivation score value is equal to or greater than 0.3333 (i.e., if the observation is categorized as multidimensionally poor) and is otherwise equal to zero. Our second dependent variable is the "MD Poor Category" series. This latter measure is a categorical variable that takes one of four values (labelled as 0 through 3) based on the level of the deprivation score variable (i.e., neither deprived nor vulnerable to deprivation (coded as 0), vulnerable to multidimensional poverty (1), suffering moderate multidimensional poverty (2), and experiencing severe poverty (3)). These latter two categories cleave the group of observations that are categorized as being multidimensionally poor.

Equations (9.1) and (9.2) illustrate the estimation equations.

$$M_{ijkt} = \alpha_0 + \beta_1 \mathrm{F}_i + \beta_{F\Theta}\left(\mathrm{F}_i x \Theta_i\right) + \beta_{F\Phi}\left(\mathrm{F}_i x \Phi_j\right) + \beta_{N\Theta}\left(\mathrm{N}_i x \Theta_i\right) + \beta_{N\Phi}\left(\mathrm{N}_i x \Phi_j\right) + \beta_\Psi \Psi_k + \beta_\Omega \Omega_t \tag{9.1}$$

$$M_{ijkt} = \alpha_0 + \beta_1 \mathrm{G1}_i + \beta_2 \mathrm{G2}_i + \beta_3 \mathrm{G3}_i + \beta_{\mathrm{G1}\Theta}\left(\mathrm{G1}_i x \Theta_i\right) + \beta_{\mathrm{G1}\Phi}\left(\mathrm{G1}_i x \Phi_j\right) + \beta_{\mathrm{G2}\Theta}\left(\mathrm{G2}_i x \Theta_i\right) + \beta_{\mathrm{G2}\Phi}\left(\mathrm{G2}_i x \Phi_j\right) + \beta_{\mathrm{G3}\Theta}\left(\mathrm{G3}_i x \Theta_i\right) + \beta_{\mathrm{G3}\Phi}\left(\mathrm{G3}_i x \Phi_j\right) + \beta_{N\Theta}\left(\mathrm{N}_i x \Theta_i\right) + \beta_{N\Phi}\left(\mathrm{N}_i x \Phi_j\right) + \beta_\Psi \Psi_k + \beta_\Omega \Omega_t \tag{9.2}$$

The dependent variables in Eqs. (9.1) and (9.2), noted as M, represent the two dependent variable series that are employed in our analysis (i.e., the MD Poor series (0, 1) and the MD Poor Category series (0–3)). The subscripts *i*, *j*, *k*, and *t* denote the observation, corresponding household, state of residence, and year of survey, respectively. *F* and *N* are dummy variables that identify observations are being either foreign-born or native-born, respectively. Similarly, G1, G2, and G3 are dummy variables that identify foreign-born observations based on their home countries' respective characterization in group 1, group 2, or group 3. Θ includes a set of variables that indicate each observation's gender, educational attainment, race, ethnicity, age, marital status, and employment status. Similarly, Φ includes the variables that represent household size (in members) and the primary household language. Ψ and Ω control for otherwise unobserved location and time fixed effects related to state of residence and survey year. α represents our constant term (or cut points when we estimate our model using the ordered logit technique).

For these estimations, we use data only for the final year in our reference period. Based on our results, we calculate the estimated changes in the predicted probability that correspond with each pairing of explanatory variables and interaction terms. This facilitates the comparison of differences in predicted probabilities, given discrete, isolated changes in explanatory variables, across foreign- and native-born individuals and across the home country groups. Descriptive statistics are discussed in the next section and are presented in Table 9.2.

9.3 Descriptive Statistics

Beginning with the two dependent variable series, we see striking differences between the native- and foreign-born cohorts. The headcount ratios are presented in Table 9.1. We see that the value for the foreign-born cohort is equal to 21.46 percent while the corresponding value for the native-born cohort is only 5.91 percent. Moreover, in Table 9.2 we see that the mean value of the uncensored deprivation score variable for the foreign-born cohort (0.1522) is more than double the value that is reported for the native-born cohort (0.0754). Similarly, the foreign-born cohort has a mean value of the MD Poor Category variable that is nearly three times that of the native-born cohort: 0.6686 as compared to 0.2495.[6] Considerable differences are also found with respect to the mean values of the three groupings of immigrants' home countries. Specifically, as noted earlier, here we see that the mean deprivation score values for group 1 are often quite similar to those of the full sample while the mean values for group 2 are near the values that we observe for the entire foreign-born cohort.

The mean values for group 3, however, reflect a much more pronounced deprivation than is observed for the other two groups. The mean deprivation score value for this group (0.2386) is nearly three times the corresponding values of group 1 (0.0842). It is more than three times the value of the native-born cohort (0.0754), more than 1.6 times the group 2 value (0.1433), and nearly twice that of the foreign-born cohort (0.2146). Looking to the mean values of the explanatory variables, we again see pronounced differences. Individuals from countries in group 3 differ from the native-born and from individuals in group 1 or group 2 countries. They are more likely to be Hispanic (95.77 percent), male (50.96 percent), younger, less educated (e.g., 55.66 percent lack a high school diploma, while only 5.16 percent have completed a four-year college degree and 2.45 percent have completed graduate study), more likely to use Spanish as their primary household language (90.93 percent), and

[6] These values are calculated as the weighted value of the category frequencies that are presented in panel B of Table 9.1.

Table 9.2 Descriptive statistics

	Native-born	*Foreign-born*					
	All	*All*	*Not MDP*	*MDP*	*Group 1*	*Group 2*	*Group 3*
N =	*30,079,348*	*4,110,144*	*3,338,558*	*771,586*	*1,630,307*	*1,082,226*	*1,397,611*
Variables	*(a)*	*(b)*	*(b)*	*(c)*	*(d)*	*(e)*	*(f)*
Deprivation score (0–1)	0.0754	0.1522	0.0912	0.4186	0.0842	0.1433	0.2386
	(0.1095)	(0.1579)	(0.0943)	(0.0916)	(0.1143)	(0.1468)	(0.1686)
Gender							
Female	0.5107	0.5236	0.5237	0.5231	0.5471	0.5309	0.4904
	(0.4999)	(0v.4994)	(0.4994)	(0.4995)	(0.4978)	(0.499)	(0.4999)
Male	0.4893	0.4764	0.4763	0.4769	0.4529	0.4691	0.5096
	(0.4999)	(0.4994)	(0.4994)	(0.4995)	(0.4978)	(0.499)	(0.4999)
Age category							
Under 20 years	0.2649	0.0909	0.0950	0.0731	0.0941	0.0895	0.0891
	(0.4413)	(0.2875)	(0.2932)	(0.2603)	(0.2919)	(0.2854)	(0.2849)
20–29 years	0.1165	0.1270	0.1214	0.1510	0.1556	0.1168	0.1092
	(0.3208)	(0.3329)	(0.3266)	(0.3581)	(0.3625)	(0.3212)	(0.3119)
30–39 years	0.1083	0.1859	0.1767	0.2258	0.2289	0.1621	0.1649
	(0.3107)	(0.3891)	(0.3814)	(0.4181)	(0.4201)	(0.3686)	(0.3711)
40–49 years	0.1202	0.2000	0.2027	0.1881	0.1983	0.1811	0.2231
	(0.3252)	(0.4000)	(0.4020)	(0.3908)	(0.3988)	(0.3851)	(0.4163)
50–59 years	0.1440	0.1709	0.1781	0.1398	0.1827	0.1769	0.1549
	(0.3511)	(0.3765)	(0.3826)	(0.3468)	(0.3864)	(0.3816)	(0.3618)
60 or more years	0.2462	0.2253	0.2260	0.2221	0.2506	0.2787	0.1434
	(0.4308)	(0.4178)	(0.4183)	(0.4157)	(0.4334)	(0.4484)	(0.3505)

(*continued*)

Table 9.2 (continued)

	Native-born	*Foreign-born*					
	All	*All*	*Not MDP*	*MDP*	*Group 1*	*Group 2*	*Group 3*
N =	*30,079,348*	*4,110,144*	*3,338,558*	*771,586*	*1,630,307*	*1,082,226*	*1,397,611*
Race and ethnicity							
Asian	0.0179	0.2731	0.3000	0.1567	0.4075	0.4099	0.0104
	(0.1324)	(0.4456)	(0.4583)	(0.3635)	(0.4914)	(0.4918)	(0.1015)
Black	0.1076	0.0741	0.0790	0.0526	0.1139	0.0880	0.0168
	(0.3098)	(0.2619)	(0.2698)	(0.2233)	(0.3177)	(0.2833)	(0.1286)
White	0.8094	0.4898	0.4806	0.5297	0.4292	0.4318	0.6054
	(0.3928)	(0.4999)	(0.4996)	(0.4991)	(0.495)	(0.4953)	(0.4888)
Other race	0.0652	0.1630	0.1404	0.2610	0.0494	0.0703	0.3674
	(0.2468)	(0.3694)	(0.3474)	(0.4392)	(0.2166)	(0.2557)	(0.4821)
Hispanic	0.1025	0.4101	0.3459	0.6880	0.0300	0.2756	0.9577
	(0.3033)	(0.4919)	(0.4757)	(0.4633)	(0.1706)	(0.4468)	(0.2013)
Educational attainment							
Less than high school	0.2793	0.3194	0.2286	0.7123	0.1564	0.2586	0.5566
	(0.4486)	(0.4663)	(0.4200)	(0.4527)	(0.3633)	(0.4379)	(0.4968)
High school graduate	0.2264	0.2000	0.2134	0.1418	0.1765	0.2026	0.2253
	(0.4185)	(0.4000)	(0.4097)	(0.3488)	(0.3813)	(0.402)	(0.4177)
Some college	0.2466	0.1993	0.2265	0.0818	0.2357	0.2186	0.1420
	(0.4310)	(0.3995)	(0.4185)	(0.2741)	(0.4244)	(0.4133)	(0.349)
4-year college degree	0.1337	0.1597	0.1866	0.0436	0.2406	0.1775	0.0516
	(0.3403)	(0.3664)	(0.3896)	(0.2041)	(0.4274)	(0.3821)	(0.2213)
Post-graduate degree	0.1141	0.1216	0.1449	0.0205	0.1908	0.1427	0.0245
	(0.3179)	(0.3268)	(0.3520)	(0.1418)	(0.3929)	(0.3497)	(0.1546)

Marital status							
Divorced or separated	0.1032	0.0987	0.0947	0.1159	0.1026	0.0954	0.0996
	(0.3042)	(0.2983)	(0.2928)	(0.3201)	(0.3034)	(0.2937)	(0.2994)
Married	0.4063	0.5820	0.5991	0.5081	0.5894	0.5979	0.5579
	(0.4911)	(0.4932)	(0.4901)	(0.4999)	(0.4919)	(0.4903)	(0.4966)
Single	0.4348	0.2674	0.2585	0.3058	0.2522	0.2435	0.3069
	(0.4957)	(0.4426)	(0.4378)	(0.4607)	(0.4343)	(0.4292)	(0.4612)
Widowed	0.0558	0.0519	0.0477	0.0701	0.0558	0.0632	0.0356
	(0.2296)	(0.2218)	(0.2130)	(0.2554)	(0.2295)	(0.2434)	(0.1853)
Employment status							
Employed	0.4410	0.5715	0.6071	0.4178	0.5648	0.5619	0.5867
	(0.4965)	(0.4949)	(0.4884)	(0.4932)	(0.4958)	(0.4961)	(0.4924)
Unemployed	0.0343	0.0418	0.0240	0.1187	0.0349	0.0416	0.0499
	(0.1819)	(0.2001)	(0.1531)	(0.3234)	(0.1835)	(0.1998)	(0.2178)
Not in labor force	0.3175	0.3300	0.3095	0.4187	0.3426	0.3411	0.3067
	(0.4655)	(0.4702)	(0.4623)	(0.4933)	(0.4746)	(0.4741)	(0.4611)
Household size							
1 person	0.1551	0.1090	0.1081	0.1129	0.1095	0.1405	0.0718
	(0.3620)	(0.3116)	(0.3105)	(0.3165)	(0.3123)	(0.3475)	(0.2582)
2 people	0.2893	0.2245	0.2362	0.1742	0.2343	0.2969	0.1325
	(0.4534)	(0.4173)	(0.4247)	(0.3793)	(0.4236)	(0.4569)	(0.3391)
3–4 people	0.3660	0.3913	0.4097	0.3120	0.4136	0.3923	0.3729
	(0.4817)	(0.4880)	(0.4918)	(0.4633)	(0.4925)	(0.4883)	(0.4836)
5–7 people	0.1714	0.2349	0.2144	0.3236	0.2113	0.1510	0.3510
	(0.3768)	(0.4239)	(0.4104)	(0.4679)	(0.4082)	(0.3581)	(0.4773)
8 or more people	0.0183	0.0403	0.0318	0.0773	0.0313	0.0193	0.0717
	(0.1339)	(0.1967)	(0.1753)	(0.2671)	(0.1741)	(0.1377)	(0.2581)

(*continued*)

Table 9.2 (continued)

	Native-born	*Foreign-born*					
	All	*All*	*Not MDP*	*MDP*	*Group 1*	*Group 2*	*Group 3*
N =	*30,079,348*	*4,110,144*	*3,338,558*	*771,586*	*1,630,307*	*1,082,226*	*1,397,611*
Primary household language							
Asian or Pacific Island	0.0163	0.2016	0.2175	0.1325	0.3283	0.2816	0.0101
	(0.1265)	(0.4012)	(0.4126)	(0.339)	(0.4696)	(0.4498)	(0.1001)
English	0.8089	0.1650	0.1931	0.0431	0.0816	0.3377	0.0280
	(0.3932)	(0.3712)	(0.3948)	(0.203)	(0.2737)	(0.4729)	(0.165)
Indo-European	0.0290	0.1710	0.1869	0.1022	0.2405	0.2657	0.0067
	(0.1677)	(0.3765)	(0.3898)	(0.303)	(0.4274)	(0.4417)	(0.0818)
Spanish	0.0936	0.3928	0.3267	0.6790	0.2598	0.0384	0.9093
	(0.2913)	(0.4884)	(0.4690)	(0.4669)	(0.4385)	(0.1921)	(0.2872)
Other language	0.0082	0.0391	0.0405	0.0332	0.0602	0.0439	0.0173
	(0.0904)	(0.1939)	(0.1971)	(0.1791)	(0.2378)	(0.2048)	(0.1303)

Standard deviations in parentheses

more likely to live in a larger household. Comparing across native- and foreign-born cohorts, we again see Spanish is more commonly used in the households of the foreign-born (39.28 percent), while English is the primary language in most households of the native-born (80.89 percent). This makes sense considering immigration trends during the past 60 years. The typical foreign-born individual is more likely to be Hispanic (41.01 percent) as compared to the typical native-born individual (10.25 percent). The foreign-born are also more likely to be Asian (27.31 percent) relative to the native-born (1.79 percent) and, generally, a higher share of foreign-born adults are employed.

9.4 Potential Variation across Native- and Foreign-born Cohorts

Given the observation from Table 9.2 that there is a greater incidence of multidimensional poverty among the foreign-born relative to the native-born, our regression models are structured such that each explanatory variable is interacted, separately, with dummy variables that identify individuals as being native- or foreign-born. This allows us to isolate the cohort-specific effect of each explanatory variable on the likelihood of being multidimensionally poor. Results obtained when using the binary MD Poor series as our dependent variable are presented in column (a) of Table 9.3. In column (b), we present results obtained from the estimation of an ordered logistic regression, where the MD Poor Category variable is the dependent variable series.

Beginning with the coefficients of the dummy variable that identify individuals as being foreign-born, results presented in column (a) indicate that, all else equal, being foreign-born corresponds with an increase of 1.19 in the log-odds ratio. Likewise, the results in column (b) reveal that, again all else equal, being foreign-born increases the log-odds that the deprivation score is sufficiently high to be categorized as either vulnerable to multidimensional poverty or more likely to suffer moderate or severe poverty by 0.90. To better depict these findings, the estimated changes in the corresponding predicted probabilities are reported in Table 9.4. We find that, all else equal, evaluated at the mean values of the explanatory variables, the typical foreign-born individual has an estimated likelihood of being multidimensionally poor that is 4.15 percent higher than the likelihood of the typical native-born individual. This cleavage in predicted

Table 9.3 Determinants of deprivation scores and of multidimensional poverty, native- and foreign-born cohorts, 2008–2018

	Binomial logit		*Ordered logit*	
Dependent variable:	*MD Poor (0, 1)*		*MD Poor (0–3)*	
Explanatory variable interacted with:	*Foreign-born*	*Native-born*	*Foreign-born*	*Native-born*
	(a)		*(b)*	
Nativity (excluded: Native-born)				
Foreign-born	1.1899***	.	0.8985***	.
	(0.0104)	.	(0.0074)	.
Gender (excluded: Male)				
Female	-0.0906***	0.1511***	-0.1284***	0.0718***
	(0.0033)	(0.0019)	(0.0026)	(0.0011)
Age category (excluded: 18–29 years of age)				
20–29 years	1.6644***	1.9316***	1.9728***	1.9204***
	(0.0073)	(0.0038)	(0.0063)	(0.0024)
30–39 years	1.75***	2.1994***	2.0186***	1.9964***
	(0.0075)	(0.0042)	(0.0064)	(0.0027)
40–49 years	1.3106***	2.2609***	1.6138***	1.9906***
	(0.0077)	(0.0043)	(0.0066)	(0.0027)
50–59 years	1.0399***	2.255***	1.3669***	1.9803***
	(0.008)	(0.0044)	(0.0068)	(0.0028)
60 or more years	0.8423***	1.3994***	1.192***	1.448***
	(0.0081)	(0.0048)	(0.0069)	(0.0029)
Race and ethnicity (excluded: White and Non-Hispanic)				
Asian	-0.0224***	0.087***	-0.008	0.0909***
	(0.0079)	(0.0088)	(0.0055)	(0.0050)
Black	0.2073***	0.4652***	0.2449***	0.5978***
	(0.0078)	(0.0026)	(0.0057)	(0.0016)
Other race	0.0588***	0.2847***	0.0743***	0.3471***
	(0.004)	(0.0035)	(0.0035)	(0.0021)
Hispanic	0.0381***	0.3326***	0.1619***	0.3975***
	(0.0091)	(0.0036)	(0.0066)	(0.0023)
Educational attainment (excluded: Less than high school)				
High school graduate	-1.8559***	-1.9563***	-2.1089***	-2.0242***
	(0.0043)	(0.0027)	(0.0034)	(0.0018)
Some college	-2.4202***	-2.2283***	-2.653***	-2.2547***
	(0.0054)	(0.0029)	(0.0039)	(0.0019)
4-year college degree	-2.7241***	-2.9397***	-2.9894***	-2.8419***
	(0.0069)	(0.0049)	(0.0047)	(0.0027)
Post-graduate degree	-3.0687***	-2.2658***	-3.3608***	-1.9707***
	(0.0094)	(0.0054)	(0.0061)	(0.0029)

(*continued*)

Table 9.3 (continued)

	Binomial logit		*Ordered logit*	
Dependent variable:	*MD Poor (0, 1)*		*MD Poor (0–3)*	
Explanatory variable interacted with:	*Foreign-born*	*Native-born*	*Foreign-born*	*Native-born*
	(a)		*(b)*	
Marital status (excluded: Single)				
Divorced or separated	-0.0208***	0.2727***	-0.0026	0.1783***
	(0.0063)	(0.0033)	(0.0051)	(0.0020)
Married	-0.4457***	-0.8943***	-0.4918***	-0.9593***
	(0.0046)	(0.0033)	(0.0037)	(0.0020)
Widowed	-0.1574***	-0.1692***	-0.1072***	-0.1165***
	(0.0081)	(0.0045)	(0.0066)	(0.0026)
	(0.0038)	(0.0023)	(0.0031)	(0.0013)
Employment status (excluded: Employed)				
Unemployed	2.5036***	3.0733***	2.7975***	3.0539***
	(0.0069)	(0.003)	(0.0057)	(0.0022)
Not in labor force	0.7822***	1.0919***	0.8919***	1.0837***
	(0.0038)	(0.0023)	(0.0031)	(0.0013)
Household size (excluded: 1 person in household)				
2 people	-0.5784***	-0.1957***	-0.533***	-0.164***
	(0.0067)	(0.003)	(0.0051)	(0.0018)
3–4 people	-1.0245***	-0.4648***	-0.9661***	-0.3902***
	(0.0065)	(0.003)	(0.005)	(0.0018)
5–7 people	-0.6881***	-0.0716***	-0.5813***	0.0053**
	(0.0067)	(0.0034)	(0.0052)	(0.0021)
8 or more people	-0.3395***	0.6798***	-0.1597***	0.9336***
	(0.0086)	(0.0055)	(0.0068)	(0.0034)
Primary household language (excluded: English)				
Asian or Pacific Island	1.7227***	0.431***	1.4801***	0.2996***
	(0.0102)	(0.0088)	(0.0066)	(0.0051)
Indo-European	1.5136***	0.7018***	1.2554***	0.4479***
	(0.0088)	(0.0051)	(0.0055)	(0.0031)
Spanish	2.1173***	0.7992***	1.7759***	0.5824***
	(0.0098)	(0.0035)	(0.0066)	(0.0022)
Other language	1.8016***	0.9852***	1.5346***	0.8444***
	(0.0114)	(0.0077)	(0.0079)	(0.0050)
Constant	-3.4018***	.	.	.
	(0.0075)	.	.	.
/ Cut 1	.	.	1.6755	.
	.	.	(0.0045)	.

(*continued*)

Table 9.3 (continued)

	Binomial logit		*Ordered logit*	
Dependent variable:	*MD Poor (0, 1)*		*MD Poor (0–3)*	
Explanatory variable interacted with:	*Foreign-born*	*Native-born*	*Foreign-born*	*Native-born*
	(a)		*(b)*	
/ Cut 2	.	.	3.345	.
	.	.	(0.0046)	.
/ Cut 3	.	.	6.1051	.
	.	.	(0.005)	.
N	34,189,492	.	34,189,492	.
Wald Chi^2	4,003,990***	.	8,049,353***	.
Pseudo R^2	0.3123	.	0.2354	.
Log pseudolikelihood	-5,902,199	.	-16,858,274	.
Count R^2	0.938	.	0.8230	.

Robust standard errors in parentheses. All estimations include year and state fixed effects terms, which are not reported here due to space limitations. "***", "**", and "*" indicate statistical significance from zero at the 1%, 5%, and 10% levels, respectively

probabilities persists when the results presented in column (b) of Table 9.3 are used to calculate predicted probabilities. Compared to the typical native-born individual, the typical foreign-born individual is 11.84 percent less likely to not be deprived, 9.06 percent more likely to be vulnerable to poverty, 2.62 percent more likely to live in moderate poverty, and 0.17 percent more likely to experience severe poverty.

Turning attention to the estimated coefficients of the remaining explanatory variables that are presented in Table 9.3, with few exceptions we see considerable similarity across the two estimations. For example, women who are foreign-born are less likely to be multidimensionally poor as compared to native-born women. We also see that, as expected, additional educational attainment generally reduces the likelihood of experiencing multidimensional poverty. Relative to the white non-Hispanic control group, Hispanics, those who are black, and individuals of other races (i.e., that are neither Asian, black, nor white) are estimated to have higher probabilities of being multidimensionally poor. This stands in contrast to Asians who have lower estimated probabilities. Not surprisingly, individuals who are employed tend to have lower likelihoods of being multidimensionally

Table 9.4 Estimated changes in predicted probabilities

Explanatory variable interacted with:	*Foreign-born*	*Native-born*	*Foreign-born*				*Native-born*			
Outcome:	*MDP ($d_i \geq 0.33$)*		*Not deprived ($d_i < 0.20$)*	*Vulnerable ($0.20 \leq d_i < 0.33$)*	*MD poor ($0.33 \leq d_i < 0.50$)*	*Severe poverty ($d_i \geq 0.50$)*	*Not deprived ($d_i < 0.20$)*	*Vulnerable ($0.20 \leq d_i < 0.33$)*	*MD poor ($0.33 \leq d_i < 0.50$)*	*Severe poverty ($d_i \geq 0.50$)*
Variable	*(a)*	*(b)*	*(c)*	*(d)*	*(e)*	*(f)*	*(g)*	*(h)*	*(i)*	*(j)*
Foreign-born	0.0415	.	-0.1184	0.0906	0.0262	0.0017	.	.	.	.
Female	-0.0014	0.003	0.0101	-0.0080	-0.0020	-0.0001	-0.0075	0.0059	0.0015	0.0001
20–29 years	0.0623	0.0777	-0.3195	0.2240	0.0893	0.0061	-0.2938	0.2114	0.0773	0.0052
30–39 years	0.08	0.1108	-0.3543	0.2440	0.1031	0.0072	-0.3312	0.2341	0.0910	0.0062
40–49 years	0.0472	0.1225	-0.2632	0.1900	0.0687	0.0046	-0.3357	0.2365	0.0929	0.0064
50–59 years	0.0285	0.1215	-0.1920	0.1426	0.0464	0.0030	-0.3356	0.2373	0.0920	0.0063
60 or more years	0.0233	0.0492	-0.1700	0.1273	0.0401	0.0026	-0.2024	0.1525	0.0469	0.0030
Asian	-0.0014	-0.0011	0.0063	-0.0050	-0.0013	-0.0001	-0.0020	0.0016	0.0004	0.00002
Black	0.0005	0.0081	-0.0132	0.0104	0.0027	0.0002	-0.0573	0.0445	0.0121	0.0008
Other race	0.0017	0.0054	-0.0098	0.0076	0.0020	0.0001	-0.0315	0.0246	0.0065	0.0004
Hispanic	0.0004	0.0044	-0.0114	0.0089	0.0023	0.0001	-0.0324	0.0253	0.0067	0.0004
High school graduate	-0.0169	-0.0245	0.0948	-0.0759	-0.0178	-0.0011	0.1269	-0.1005	-0.0248	-0.0015
Some college	-0.0184	-0.028	0.1010	-0.0810	-0.0189	-0.0011	0.1429	-0.1130	-0.0282	-0.0017
4-year college degree	-0.0188	-0.0265	0.1032	-0.0828	-0.0192	-0.0012	0.1344	-0.1069	-0.0259	-0.0016
Post-graduate degree	-0.0191	-0.0231	0.1050	-0.0842	-0.0195	-0.0012	0.1127	-0.0898	-0.0215	-0.0013
Divorced or separated	-0.001	0.0044	0.0003	-0.0002	-0.0001	-0.000003	-0.0126	0.0099	0.0026	0.0002
Married	-0.0075	-0.0151	0.0392	-0.0311	-0.0077	-0.0005	0.0804	-0.0633	-0.0161	-0.0010
Widowed	-0.0034	-0.0041	0.0074	-0.0058	-0.0015	-0.0001	0.0139	-0.0110	-0.0028	-0.0002
Unemployed	0.1852	0.2902	-0.5475	0.3175	0.2128	0.0172	-0.6022	0.3259	0.2544	0.0219
Not in labor force	0.0251	0.0296	-0.1253	0.0953	0.0282	0.0018	-0.1314	0.1011	0.0285	0.0018
2 people	-0.009	-0.0041	0.0424	-0.0336	-0.0083	-0.0005	0.0209	-0.0165	-0.0042	-0.0003
3–4 people	-0.0142	-0.0097	0.0708	-0.0564	-0.0135	-0.0008	0.0432	-0.0341	-0.0086	-0.0005
5–7 people	-0.0118	-0.0037	0.0546	-0.0434	-0.0105	-0.0006	0.0100	-0.0078	-0.0020	-0.0001
8 or more people	-0.0092	0.0156	0.0302	-0.0239	-0.0059	-0.0004	-0.1048	0.0801	0.0232	0.0015
Asian or Pacific Island	0.0781	0.0109	-0.2237	0.1642	0.0558	0.0037	-0.0339	0.0264	0.0070	0.0004
Indo-European	0.0654	0.0269	-0.1814	0.1353	0.0434	0.0028	-0.0652	0.0504	0.0139	0.0009
Spanish	0.0994	0.0203	-0.2535	0.1842	0.0650	0.0043	-0.0632	0.0490	0.0134	0.0008
Other language	0.098	0.0325	-0.2491	0.1805	0.0643	0.0043	-0.1104	0.0842	0.0246	0.0016

Values presented in columns (a) and (b) are derived from estimation results presented in Table 9.5. Values presented in columns (c) through (j) are derived from estimation results in Table 9.6

poor as compared to the unemployed and individuals who are not in the labor force. Relative to individuals who are less than 20 years of age, the likelihood of being multidimensionally poor is typically increasing for foreign-born individuals who are 20 to 39 years of age, after which the likelihood decreases but remains significantly higher than that of the under 20 years of age cohort. Being married or widowed, relative to being single, corresponds with a lower probability of being multidimensionally poor; however, being divorced or separated is largely non-consequential for foreign-born individuals but corresponds with a higher probability among the native-born. Compared to households with only one resident, those with more members have lower likelihoods of being multidimensionally poor. Lastly, generally speaking, predominant use of a language other than English in one's household is positively related to multidimensional poverty.

Looking to the variation in poverty intensity and incidence that is depicted in Fig. 9.1 and indicated by the differences in mean values across the three foreign-born group presented in Table 9.2, we further modify our regression model to interact dummy variables for each of the three foreign-born groups, and a dummy variable that represents native-born individuals, with each of the explanatory variables. The results obtained when the binary MD Poor variable is employed as the dependent variable series are presented in Table 9.5 and the results obtained with the MD Poor Category variables is used as the dependent variable series are provided in Table 9.6.

Focusing first on the group-specific dummy variables, in both tables we see positive and statistically significant coefficients for groups 2 and 3. Considering the relative headcount ratio and MPI values of each group, it is unsurprising to see the coefficients increase in absolute magnitude as we move from group 1 to group 2 to group 3. Likewise, given the similarity in multidimensional poverty incidence between the native-both and immigrants from group 1, it is not entirely surprising to see that the coefficient of the group 1 cohort dummy is not significantly different from zero. Throughout Table 9.5, with variation in coefficient magnitudes noted, there are not great differences across the three groups and the native-born cohort in terms of coefficient signs and statistical significance. The variation in coefficient magnitudes are, however, considerable in a number of cases. To examine these differences in greater detail, we can look to Table 9.6 to compare

Table 9.5 Determinants of MDP poor, by foreign-born groups and native-born (binomial logit estimations), 2018

Explanatory var. interacted with:	*Group 1*	*Group 2*	*Group 3*	*Native-born*
	(a)	*(b)*	*(c)*	*(d)*
Group (excluded: Native-born)				
Group dummy	-0.0286	0.4631***	0.6833***	.
	(0.0719)	(0.0768)	(0.0862)	.
Gender (excluded: Native-born, Male)				
Female	-0.0781***	-0.0969***	-0.0373**	0.1301***
	(0.0289)	(0.0225)	(0.0162)	(0.0069)
Age category (excluded: Native-born, under 20 years of age)				
20–29 years	1.6873***	1.2132***	1.6562***	1.7282***
	(0.0761)	(0.0569)	(0.0398)	(0.0141)
30–39 years	1.8274***	1.44***	1.9058***	2.0709***
	(0.0782)	(0.0575)	(0.038)	(0.015)
40–49 years	1.7396***	1.1362***	1.3618***	2.1624***
	(0.0795)	(0.0583)	(0.0387)	(0.0158)
50–59 years	1.5752***	0.8857***	0.8938***	2.1866***
	(0.08)	(0.0583)	(0.0405)	(0.0156)
60 or more years	1.4213***	0.7654***	0.7758***	1.4274***
	(0.0761)	(0.0565)	(0.0415)	(0.0168)
Race and ethnicity (excluded: Native-born, Non-Hispanic White)				
Asian	0.2075***	0.1844***	0.1187	-0.1915***
	(0.0411)	(0.0476)	(0.1051)	(0.0328)
Black	0.5114***	0.0322	-0.1368**	0.3291***
	(0.0509)	(0.0435)	(0.0644)	(0.0098)
Other race	0.2854***	0.2029***	0.0356**	0.2329***
	(0.0652)	(0.0428)	(0.0157)	(0.0126)
Hispanic	0.1427	0.3012***	0.0346	0.1361***
	(0.0954)	(0.0705)	(0.0674)	(0.0135)
Educational attainment (excluded: Native-born, less than high school)				
High school graduate	-1.7461***	-1.7613***	-1.969***	-2.0497***
	(0.0397)	(0.0303)	(0.0218)	(0.0098)
Some college	-2.1682***	-2.2244***	-2.5666***	-2.2963***
	(0.0422)	(0.0346)	(0.0322)	(0.0106)
4-year college degree	-2.4713***	-2.4503***	-2.7208***	-3.0099***
	(0.0455)	(0.0387)	(0.0513)	(0.0174)
Post-graduate degree	-2.927***	-2.8962***	-2.6039***	-2.5921***
	(0.0572)	(0.0501)	(0.0778)	(0.0201)
Marital status (excluded: Native-born, Single)				
Divorced or separated	0.1977***	0.0743*	-0.1536***	0.216***
	(0.0563)	(0.0444)	(0.0294)	(0.0118)

(*continued*)

Table 9.5 (continued)

Explanatory var. interacted with:	*Group 1*	*Group 2*	*Group 3*	*Native-born*
	(a)	*(b)*	*(c)*	*(d)*
Married	-0.3521***	-0.1978***	-0.5626***	-0.8364***
	(0.0496)	(0.0359)	(0.0209)	(0.0122)
Widowed	-0.0653	0.0441	-0.3059***	-0.2329***
	(0.0618)	(0.0509)	(0.0414)	(0.016)
Employment status (excluded: Native-born, Employed)				
Unemployed	2.7322***	2.6142***	2.3208***	3.149***
	(0.055)	(0.0498)	(0.0451)	(0.0121)
Not in labor force	1.0721***	1.0426***	0.7464***	1.1261***
	(0.0339)	(0.0256)	(0.0186)	(0.0082)
Household size (excluded: Native-born, 1 person in household)				
2 people	-0.6612***	-0.7695***	-0.5801***	-0.3307***
	(0.045)	(0.0392)	(0.0375)	(0.0106)
3–4 people	-1.2172***	-1.4511***	-1.1693***	-0.7096***
	(0.046)	(0.039)	(0.0358)	(0.0106)
5–7 people	-0.9448***	-1.3687***	-0.8859***	-0.3923***
	(0.0506)	(0.042)	(0.0363)	(0.0124)
8 or more people	-1.0819***	-1.0525***	-0.6667***	0.4381***
	(0.0932)	(0.0645)	(0.0445)	(0.0194)
Primary household language (excluded: Native-born, English-speaking)				
Asian or Pacific Island	1.3107***	2.1981***	2.2211***	0.3438***
	(0.05)	(0.0683)	(0.1214)	(0.033)
Indo-European	1.4006***	2.2101***	2.269***	0.8253***
	(0.0413)	(0.0693)	(0.1164)	(0.0184)
Spanish	0.9949***	1.9539***	2.3244***	0.7322***
	(0.0919)	(0.0771)	(0.0597)	(0.0137)
Other language	1.2881***	2.5455***	2.7688***	0.9335***
	(0.0646)	(0.0799)	(0.0981)	(0.0272)
Constant	-3.3447***	.	.	.
	(0.0253)	.	.	.
N	3,205,428	.	.	.
Count R^2	0.9520	.	.	.
Wald Chi^2	291,367***	.	.	.
Log pseudolikelihood	-458,129	.	.	.
Pseudo R^2	0.2916	.	.	.

Robust standard errors in parentheses. All estimations include year and state fixed effects terms, which are not reported here due to space limitations. "***", "**", and "*" indicate statistical significance from zero at the 1%, 5%, and 10% levels, respectively

Table 9.6 Determinants of MDP poor, by foreign-born groups and native-born (ordered logit estimations), 2018

Explanatory var. interacted with:	*Group 1*	*Group 2*	*Group 3*	*Native-born*
	(a)	*(b)*	*(c)*	*(d)*
Group (excluded: Native-born)				
Group dummy	-0.0702*	0.5578***	0.8895***	.
	(0.0403)	(0.0458)	(0.0641)	.
Gender (excluded: Native-born, Male)				
Female	-0.1003***	-0.1256***	-0.0641***	0.0668***
	(0.0167)	(0.0157)	(0.0136)	(0.0038)
Age category (excluded: Native-born, under 20 years of age)				
20–29 years	2.1337***	1.5457***	1.8679***	1.7954***
	(0.0451)	(0.0401)	(0.0351)	(0.0084)
30–39 years	2.0865***	1.6418***	2.1284***	1.9448***
	(0.0471)	(0.0417)	(0.0343)	(0.0091)
40–49 years	1.9751***	1.362***	1.6224***	1.9535***
	(0.0478)	(0.0419)	(0.0346)	(0.0097)
50–59 years	1.8871***	1.0919***	1.157***	1.9774***
	(0.0477)	(0.042)	(0.0356)	(0.0096)
60 or more years	1.7748***	1.0114***	1.0419***	1.4702***
	(0.0462)	(0.0415)	(0.0368)	(0.0099)
Race and ethnicity (excluded: Native-born, Non-Hispanic White)				
Asian	0.0854***	0.1297***	0.1556*	-0.0353**
	(0.0238)	(0.0321)	(0.0837)	(0.0169)
Black	0.3725***	0.1209***	-0.1126**	0.4988***
	(0.0294)	(0.0303)	(0.0525)	(0.0057)
Other race	0.1443***	0.1354***	0.0475***	0.2905***
	(0.0385)	(0.0307)	(0.0133)	(0.0072)
Hispanic	0.0188	0.2838***	-0.0347	0.2763***
	(0.0568)	(0.0452)	(0.0536)	(0.0078)
Educational attainment (excluded: Native-born, less than high school)				
High school graduate	-1.9478***	-1.9687***	-2.1907***	-2.0596***
	(0.0257)	(0.0221)	(0.0164)	(0.0062)
Some college	-2.2885***	-2.4051***	-2.7256***	-2.2908***
	(0.0261)	(0.0236)	(0.0213)	(0.0065)
4-year college degree	-2.5637***	-2.6447***	-2.988***	-2.8327***
	(0.0271)	(0.0256)	(0.0333)	(0.0089)
Post-graduate degree	-2.9637***	-3.1561***	-2.905***	-2.1991***
	(0.0318)	(0.0316)	(0.0524)	(0.0101)
Marital status (excluded: Native-born, Single)				
Divorced or separated	0.1776***	0.1421***	-0.1345***	0.131***
	(0.033)	(0.0316)	(0.0252)	(0.007)

(*continued*)

Table 9.6 (continued)

Explanatory var. interacted with:	*Group 1*	*Group 2*	*Group 3*	*Native-born*
	(a)	*(b)*	*(c)*	*(d)*
Married	-0.4501***	-0.2197***	-0.5694***	-0.911***
	(0.0278)	(0.0249)	(0.0178)	(0.0068)
Widowed	0.0349	0.1504***	-0.227***	-0.1542***
	(0.0367)	(0.038)	(0.0365)	(0.0088)
Employment status (excluded: Native-born, Employed)				
Unemployed	2.5979***	2.7081***	2.6848***	3.0332***
	(0.04)	(0.0435)	(0.0393)	(0.0091)
Not in labor force	1.0034***	1.024***	0.8279***	1.1208***
	(0.0192)	(0.018)	(0.016)	(0.0046)
Household size (excluded: Native-born, 1 person in household)				
2 people	-0.4961***	-0.6557***	-0.6177***	-0.2894***
	(0.0266)	(0.029)	(0.0321)	(0.0061)
3–4 people	-0.8955***	-1.276***	-1.2291***	-0.5752***
	(0.027)	(0.0287)	(0.0305)	(0.0061)
5–7 people	-0.6629***	-1.1233***	-0.887***	-0.2067***
	(0.0308)	(0.031)	(0.0311)	(0.0071)
8 or more people	-0.2881***	-0.7908***	-0.5483***	0.7256***
	(0.0492)	(0.047)	(0.037)	(0.0118)
Primary household language (excluded: Native-born, English-speaking)				
Asian or Pacific Island	1.0037***	1.8019***	1.7406***	0.2652***
	(0.028)	(0.0388)	(0.0923)	(0.0175)
Indo-European	0.9752***	1.7536***	1.8395***	0.5187***
	(0.0231)	(0.0391)	(0.0894)	(0.0112)
Spanish	0.7145***	1.5076***	1.9277***	0.5368***
	(0.0527)	(0.0458)	(0.0377)	(0.008)
Other language	0.9843***	2.0035***	2.3054***	0.8011***
	(0.0381)	(0.0485)	(0.0746)	(0.0169)
/ Cut 1	1.6565	.	.	.
	(0.0147)	.	.	.
/ Cut 2	3.3756	.	.	.
	(0.0149)	.	.	.
/ Cut 3	6.2665	.	.	.
	(0.017)	.	.	.
N	3,205,428	.	.	.
Count R^2	0.8490	.	.	.
Wald Chi^2	613,818***	.	.	.
Log pseudolikelihood	-1,401,247	.	.	.
Pseudo R^2	0.2207	.	.	.

Robust standard errors in parentheses. All estimations include year and state fixed effects terms, which are not reported here due to space limitations. "***", "**", and "*" indicate statistical significance from zero at the 1%, 5%, and 10% levels, respectively

9.5 Summary/Conclusions

We have examined data from the 2008–2018 American Community Survey Public Use Microdata Sample files (U.S. Census 2019) while employing the methodology of Alkire and Foster (2009) to measure multidimensional poverty. We have documented considerable variation across native- and foreign-born residents of the U.S. and across immigrant home countries in both the incidence and intensity of deprivation as reflected by their respective MPI values. Our empirical analysis, which examines data only from 2018, identifies factors that contribute to multidimensional poverty and, extending the literature, we have examined variation in the determinants across both native- and foreign-born cohorts and across groupings of immigrants' home countries. Our results confirm that, once other factors are controlled for, foreign-born individuals who reside in the U.S. are significantly more likely to be multidimensionally poor.

We hope that the detailed coverage that we provide in this chapter is of value to fellow researchers and for the formulation of public policies that aim to alleviate deprivation. To that end, our findings suggest that reductions in multidimensional poverty within the U.S. and, more directly, among members of the foreign-born population of the U.S. can be achieved via the creation and implementation of public policies that target individuals who are from the countries we classify as group 3.

Appendix

Table 9.7 Home country-specific frequency, intensity, and multidimensional poverty indices

Home country	*Group*	*N*	*H*	*A*	*MPI*	*Home country*	*Group*	*N*	*H*	*A*	*MPI*
Guatemala	3	72,509	45.32%	0.4428	20.0678	Korea	1	114,006	11.69%	0.3871	4.5253
Bhutan	3	2246	46.10%	0.4249	19.5896	Sierra Leone	1	3226	11.53%	0.3871	4.4648
Honduras	3	43,175	42.07%	0.4370	18.3847	Argentina	2	18,546	11.05%	0.4019	4.4429
Mexico	3	1,017,512	38.79%	0.4290	16.6426	Russia	1	41,782	11.24%	0.3907	4.3914
Somalia	3	5240	37.87%	0.4271	16.1737	Cameroon	2	3969	11.06%	0.3961	4.3795
El Salvador	3	105,488	35.08%	0.4234	14.8522	Bahamas	2	3385	11.05%	0.3949	4.3660
Myanmar	3	10,431	33.21%	0.4244	14.0942	Albania	1	7410	11.23%	0.3864	4.3383
Yemen	3	4704	33.34%	0.4177	13.9252	Turkey	1	12,897	11.13%	0.3869	4.3053
Iraq	3	16,118	30.55%	0.4202	12.8364	Italy	1	49,192	10.99%	0.3899	4.2866
Congo, Rep. of	3	1051	29.90%	0.4241	12.6787	St. Vincent & The Grenadines	1	2138	10.89%	0.3816	4.1565
Micronesia	3	2206	28.39%	0.4186	11.8819	Chile	1	9987	10.69%	0.3857	4.1242
Ecuador	3	36,051	26.85%	0.4184	11.2341	Saudi Arabia	1	6339	10.92%	0.3742	4.0865
Dominican Republic	3	79,761	26.96%	0.4131	11.1352	Tunisia	1	179	10.40%	0.3826	3.9790
Marshall Islands	3	1119	26.61%	0.4178	11.1195	Bosnia and Herzegovina	2	10,492	9.67%	0.4068	3.9320
Afghanistan	2	6933	24.36%	0.4089	9.9586	Kazakhstan	1	2952	10.08%	0.3891	3.9204
Syria	2	7942	23.60%	0.4212	9.9400	Poland	1	45,942	10.06%	0.3873	3.8971
Cuba	2	112,157	23.89%	0.4117	9.8354	Guyana	1	27,079	9.94%	0.3807	3.7849
Guinea	2	1159	23.26%	0.4215	9.8063	United Arab Emirates	2	1287	9.26%	0.3958	3.6644
Sudan	2	3395	22.97%	0.4080	9.3706	Jamaica	1	65,002	9.47%	0.3844	3.6389
Eritrea	2	2792	22.31%	0.4134	9.2201	Romania	2	17,932	9.04%	0.3947	3.5663
Nicaragua	2	23,063	21.85%	0.4140	9.0465	Kuwait	2	2674	8.95%	0.3964	3.5458
Democratic Rep. Of Congo	2	1778	22.25%	0.4035	8.9752	Hungary	1	8872	8.89%	0.3892	3.4617

Haiti	2	52,416	20.91%	0.4154	8.6870	Antigua & Barbuda	1	1889	8.98%	0.3854	3.4611
Uzbekistan	2	5460	20.62%	0.4027	8.3017	Grenada	1	3211	8.93%	0.3847	3.4354
Cambodia	2	15,707	19.93%	0.4113	8.1988	Kosovo	2	234	8.39%	0.4060	3.4067
Armenia	1	7928	20.79%	0.3915	8.1389	Kenya	1	10,017	8.79%	0.3835	3.3709
Azerbaijan	2	1918	19.95%	0.4071	8.1213	Trinidad & Tobago	1	22,850	8.64%	0.3809	3.2898
Bangladesh	2	19,425	19.85%	0.4069	8.0760	Lithuania	1	3820	8.38%	0.3907	3.2733
Senegal	1	1843	20.36%	0.3910	7.9595	St. Kitts-Nevis	1	605	8.45%	0.3838	3.2445
Laos	2	17,384	19.06%	0.4123	7.8602	Fiji	1	4287	8.31%	0.3900	3.2422
Uruguay	2	4574	18.07%	0.4127	7.4563	Uganda	1	2302	8.34%	0.3820	3.1847
Dominica	2	2609	18.07%	0.4125	7.4519	Panama	1	15,342	7.97%	0.3858	3.0759
Rwanda	2	198	18.82%	0.3948	7.4284	Sri Lanka	1	5069	7.86%	0.3904	3.0692
Vietnam	2	136,181	18.36%	0.4039	7.4131	Ghana	1	12,447	7.87%	0.3855	3.0341
Jordan	2	6901	18.40%	0.4020	7.3958	Indonesia	1	10,363	7.90%	0.3827	3.0245
China	2	196,535	18.22%	0.4046	7.3718	Slovakia	1	2225	7.54%	0.3925	2.9584
Nepal	1	8568	18.72%	0.3934	7.3645	Croatia	2	4653	7.50%	0.3943	2.9576
Gambia	2	696	16.86%	0.4071	6.8630	Barbados	1	5324	7.82%	0.3769	2.9471
Cape Verde	2	3598	17.03%	0.4005	6.8210	Nigeria	1	24,000	7.65%	0.3807	2.9110
Mongolia	2	225	16.46%	0.4117	6.7757	Hong Kong	1	27,044	7.45%	0.3889	2.8957
Togo	2	1158	15.74%	0.4130	6.5027	Latvia	1	2690	7.69%	0.3766	2.8949
Costa Rica	2	8419	16.02%	0.4049	6.4875	Israel	1	16,695	7.32%	0.3871	2.8341
Georgia	2	1693	16.27%	0.3950	6.4268	Taiwan	1	44,127	7.30%	0.3824	2.7917
Kyrgyzstan	2	220	15.70%	0.4035	6.3336	Spain	1	14,090	7.07%	0.3908	2.7627
Azores Islands	2	2969	15.58%	0.4013	6.253	Bermuda	1	1855	6.82%	0.3784	2.5801
Tonga	2	1632	15.46%	0.3997	6.1787	Serbia	1	2465	6.13%	0.3757	2.3017
Moldova	2	4121	15.36%	0.3991	6.1295	Cyprus	1	553	5.76%	0.3718	2.1406
Morocco	2	7205	15.39%	0.3969	6.1069	Bulgaria	1	6884	5.59%	0.3774	2.1109
Iran	2	37,851	15.07%	0.4023	6.0636	India	1	204,858	5.16%	0.3924	2.0265
Ukraine	2	34,804	15.11%	0.3972	6.0016	Estonia	1	441	5.73%	0.3455	1.9800
Thailand	2	25,033	15.07%	0.3971	5.9835	Czech Republic	1	3397	5.40%	0.3652	1.9723

(*continued*)

Table 9.7 (continued)

Colombia	2	65,548	14.88%	0.4016	5.9746	Philippines	1	217,175	5.08%	0.3790	1.9244
Libya	2	1067	14.61%	0.4014	5.8648	Japan	1	58,435	4.93%	0.3754	1.8509
Venezuela	2	23,194	14.47%	0.4015	5.8114	Germany	1	136,734	4.43%	0.3775	1.6740
Egypt	2	17,292	14.20%	0.3957	5.619	Finland	1	2531	4.25%	0.3810	1.6205
Belarus	2	6086	13.92%	0.4024	5.6029	France	1	25,531	4.08%	0.3763	1.5339
Ethiopia	2	16,839	14.07%	0.3955	5.5649	Iceland	1	1205	3.84%	0.3734	1.4348
Portugal	2	18,542	13.90%	0.3985	5.5376	Austria	1	6668	3.88%	0.3656	1.4195
Lebanon	2	13,191	13.60%	0.4062	5.5243	Canada	1	113,992	3.75%	0.3781	1.4168
Algeria	1	2008	14.19%	0.3882	5.5086	Belgium	1	5257	3.80%	0.3718	1.4121
Peru	2	40,227	13.92%	0.3944	5.4886	England	1	51,514	3.59%	0.3713	1.3334
Pakistan	2	33,007	13.57%	0.3988	5.4113	Singapore	1	4132	3.53%	0.3739	1.3204
Belize	1	4907	13.27%	0.3932	5.216	Scotland	1	8700	3.49%	0.3737	1.3035
Ivory Coast	2	373	12.93%	0.3998	5.1706	Netherlands	1	12,334	3.45%	0.3670	1.2647
Bolivia	2	7263	13.04%	0.3937	5.1326	Zimbabwe	1	2149	3.15%	0.3845	1.2105
Tanzania	1	2213	12.86%	0.3925	5.0481	Zambia	1	848	3.36%	0.3590	1.2046
Samoa	1	1369	12.74%	0.3931	5.0079	Ireland	1	16,046	3.23%	0.3650	1.1772
St. Lucia	1	2047	12.86%	0.3885	4.9957	South Africa	1	11,166	3.12%	0.3673	1.1467
Paraguay	2	1921	12.16%	0.4015	4.8827	Denmark	1	4016	3.10%	0.3691	1.1446
Greece	2	16,573	11.99%	0.3959	4.7457	Switzerland	1	5831	2.99%	0.3606	1.0781
Macedonia	2	2440	11.88%	0.3950	4.6941	New Zealand	1	3949	2.91%	0.3639	1.0572
Brazil	1	36,292	12.06%	0.3889	4.6909	Northern Ireland	1	1030	2.57%	0.3891	0.9992
Liberia	1	6037	11.93%	0.3902	4.6566	Sweden	1	6080	2.65%	0.3659	0.9714
Malaysia	2	7340	11.45%	0.3970	4.5466	Australia	1	11,444	2.55%	0.3747	0.9554
Montenegro	1	892	12.13%	0.3742	4.5382	Norway	1	3583	2.41%	0.3706	0.8931

N = Number of ACS observations used in the calculations; H = Headcount ratio; A = Average deprivation intensity; and MPI = $H \times A \times 100$

Table 9.8 Home country-specific frequency of non-deprived, vulnerable, moderately deprived, and severely deprived, by group, ranked by MPI

Home country	*Group*	*Not deprived (DS < 0.20)*	*Vulnerable (0.20 ≤ DS < 0.33)*	*MD poor (0.33 ≤ DS < 0.50)*	*Severe poverty (DS ≥ 0.50)*	*Home country*	*Group*	*Not deprived (DS < 0.20)*	*Vulnerable (0.20 ≤ DS < 0.33)*	*MD poor (0.33 ≤ DS < 0.50)*	*Severe poverty (DS ≥ 0.50)*
Guatemala	3	0.3280	0.2188	0.3301	0.1231	Korea	1	0.6974	0.1857	0.1053	0.0116
Bhutan	3	0.2901	0.2489	0.3635	0.0975	Sierra Leone	1	0.7335	0.1511	0.1020	0.0134
Honduras	3	0.3394	0.2399	0.3110	0.1096	Argentina	2	0.7326	0.1569	0.0943	0.0163
Mexico	3	0.3516	0.2605	0.2971	0.0908	Russia	1	0.7365	0.1511	0.1024	0.0100
Somalia	3	0.3769	0.2444	0.2921	0.0866	Cameroon	2	0.7110	0.1784	0.0979	0.0126
El Salvador	3	0.3902	0.2590	0.2769	0.0739	Bahamas	2	0.7191	0.1703	0.0994	0.0111
Myanmar	3	0.4361	0.2318	0.2630	0.0691	Albania	1	0.6910	0.1967	0.1018	0.0105
Yemen	3	0.3580	0.3086	0.2713	0.0620	Turkey	1	0.7264	0.1623	0.1017	0.0095
Iraq	3	0.4657	0.2288	0.2419	0.0636	Italy	1	0.7049	0.1852	0.1014	0.0086
Congo, Rep. of	3	0.4910	0.2100	0.2357	0.0633	St. Vincent & The Grenadines	1	0.7167	0.1744	0.1024	0.0066
Micronesia	3	0.4547	0.2614	0.2246	0.0593	Chile	1	0.7351	0.1580	0.0978	0.0092
Ecuador	3	0.5059	0.2256	0.2185	0.0500	Saudi Arabia	1	0.6501	0.2406	0.1012	0.0080
Dominican Republic	3	0.4844	0.2460	0.2202	0.0494	Tunisia	1	0.6941	0.2018	0.0965	0.0075
Marshall Islands	3	0.4822	0.2516	0.2244	0.0417	Bosnia and Herzegovina	2	0.7674	0.1360	0.0802	0.0164
Afghanistan	2	0.5188	0.2376	0.2077	0.0359	Kazakhstan	1	0.7468	0.1524	0.0899	0.0108
Syria	2	0.5704	0.1936	0.1867	0.0493	Poland	1	0.7319	0.1675	0.0931	0.0075
Cuba	2	0.5318	0.2293	0.1972	0.0417	Guyana	1	0.7320	0.1686	0.0932	0.0062
Guinea	2	0.5417	0.2257	0.1830	0.0497	United Arab Emirates	2	0.7523	0.1551	0.0892	0.0034
Sudan	2	0.5272	0.2432	0.1940	0.0357	Jamaica	1	0.7426	0.1627	0.0874	0.0073
Eritrea	2	0.5533	0.2236	0.1831	0.0400	Romania	2	0.7691	0.1406	0.0784	0.0120
Nicaragua	2	0.5582	0.2233	0.1795	0.0390	Kuwait	2	0.7328	0.1778	0.0781	0.0113
Dem. Rep. Of Congo	2	0.5417	0.2358	0.1833	0.0391	Hungary	1	0.7604	0.1507	0.0824	0.0065

(*continued*)

Table 9.8 (continued)

Haiti	2	0.5741	0.2167	0.1693	0.0398	Antigua & Barbuda	1	0.7626	0.1476	0.0810	0.0088
Uzbekistan	2	0.5743	0.2195	0.1788	0.0274	Grenada	1	0.7386	0.1721	0.0817	0.0076
Cambodia	2	0.5681	0.2325	0.1653	0.0340	Kosovo	2	0.6980	0.2181	0.0682	0.0157
Armenia	1	0.5859	0.2062	0.1888	0.0191	Kenya	1	0.7621	0.1500	0.0823	0.0056
Azerbaijan	2	0.6150	0.1855	0.1735	0.0260	Trinidad & Tobago	1	0.7623	0.1513	0.0810	0.0054
Bangladesh	2	0.5574	0.2441	0.1665	0.0320	Lithuania	1	0.7584	0.1578	0.0745	0.0093
Senegal	1	0.6083	0.1881	0.1879	0.0157	St. Kitts-Nevis	1	0.7694	0.1460	0.0806	0.0039
Laos	2	0.5938	0.2156	0.1563	0.0343	Fiji	1	0.7524	0.1645	0.0766	0.0065
Uruguay	2	0.6124	0.2070	0.1493	0.0314	Uganda	1	0.7839	0.1327	0.0780	0.0053
Dominica	2	0.6367	0.1827	0.1445	0.0362	Panama	1	0.7947	0.1255	0.0728	0.0069
Rwanda	2	0.5484	0.2635	0.1556	0.0326	Sri Lanka	1	0.7901	0.1313	0.0696	0.0090
Vietnam	2	0.5950	0.2215	0.1561	0.0275	Ghana	1	0.7591	0.1621	0.0722	0.0065
Jordan	2	0.6108	0.2052	0.1625	0.0215	Indonesia	1	0.7761	0.1449	0.0724	0.0066
China	2	0.6146	0.2032	0.1546	0.0276	Slovakia	1	0.7679	0.1568	0.0664	0.0090
Nepal	1	0.6064	0.2064	0.1650	0.0222	Croatia	2	0.7803	0.1447	0.0667	0.0083
Gambia	2	0.6814	0.1500	0.1399	0.0287	Barbados	1	0.7883	0.1335	0.0758	0.0024
Cape Verde	2	0.6142	0.2155	0.1429	0.0275	Nigeria	1	0.7822	0.1413	0.0713	0.0051
Mongolia	2	0.6919	0.1435	0.1394	0.0252	Hong Kong	1	0.7942	0.1313	0.0674	0.0070
Togo	2	0.6502	0.1924	0.1342	0.0233	Latvia	1	0.7950	0.1281	0.0718	0.0051
Costa Rica	2	0.6511	0.1887	0.1375	0.0227	Israel	1	0.7820	0.1447	0.0667	0.0065
Georgia	2	0.6295	0.2078	0.1476	0.0151	Taiwan	1	0.8037	0.1233	0.0676	0.0054
Kyrgyzstan	2	0.6932	0.1498	0.1485	0.0085	Spain	1	0.8007	0.1286	0.0637	0.0070
Azores Islands	2	0.6321	0.2121	0.1347	0.0212	Bermuda	1	0.8163	0.1156	0.0660	0.0022
Tonga	2	0.6183	0.2271	0.1301	0.0245	Serbia	1	0.7992	0.1395	0.0585	0.0028
Moldova	2	0.6486	0.1979	0.1301	0.0235	Cyprus	1	0.8292	0.1132	0.0570	0.0006
Morocco	2	0.6658	0.1803	0.1362	0.0176	Bulgaria	1	0.8099	0.1341	0.0531	0.0029
Iran	2	0.6927	0.1565	0.1297	0.0210	India	1	0.8474	0.1010	0.0460	0.0057
Ukraine	2	0.6621	0.1868	0.1333	0.0178	Estonia	1	0.7554	0.1873	0.0553	0.0020
Thailand	2	0.6602	0.1892	0.1333	0.0173	Czech Republic	1	0.8168	0.1292	0.0519	0.0021
Colombia	2	0.6623	0.1890	0.1286	0.0201	Philippines	1	0.8267	0.1225	0.0472	0.0036

Libya	2	0.6451	0.2088	0.1333	0.0128	Japan	1	0.8325	0.1181	0.0467	0.0026
Venezuela	2	0.6818	0.1734	0.1264	0.0183	Germany	1	0.8535	0.1021	0.0417	0.0026
Egypt	2	0.6757	0.1823	0.1264	0.0156	Finland	1	0.8615	0.0960	0.0383	0.0042
Belarus	2	0.7062	0.1546	0.1194	0.0199	France	1	0.8646	0.0946	0.0386	0.0022
Ethiopia	2	0.6660	0.1933	0.1231	0.0176	Iceland	1	0.8658	0.0958	0.0360	0.0024
Portugal	2	0.6479	0.2131	0.1227	0.0163	Austria	1	0.8410	0.1201	0.0372	0.0016
Lebanon	2	0.7056	0.1584	0.1153	0.0207	Canada	1	0.8643	0.0983	0.0350	0.0024
Algeria	1	0.6793	0.1788	0.1246	0.0173	Belgium	1	0.8567	0.1053	0.0363	0.0017
Peru	2	0.6670	0.1938	0.1230	0.0162	England	1	0.8722	0.0919	0.0343	0.0016
Pakistan	2	0.6688	0.1955	0.1187	0.0170	Singapore	1	0.8776	0.0871	0.0339	0.0014
Belize	1	0.6888	0.1785	0.1215	0.0112	Scotland	1	0.8695	0.0956	0.0327	0.0022
Ivory Coast	2	0.6535	0.2172	0.1107	0.0186	Netherlands	1	0.8784	0.0871	0.0333	0.0012
Bolivia	2	0.6925	0.1771	0.1140	0.0164	Zimbabwe	1	0.8656	0.1029	0.0299	0.0015
Tanzania	1	0.7042	0.1672	0.1167	0.0119	Zambia	1	0.8878	0.0787	0.0329	0.0007
Samoa	1	0.6743	0.1983	0.1101	0.0173	Ireland	1	0.8578	0.1099	0.0311	0.0012
St. Lucia	1	0.6870	0.1844	0.1188	0.0098	South Africa	1	0.8897	0.0791	0.0297	0.0015
Paraguay	2	0.7144	0.1640	0.1068	0.0148	Denmark	1	0.8728	0.0962	0.0292	0.0018
Greece	2	0.6965	0.1836	0.1058	0.0141	Switzerland	1	0.8817	0.0884	0.0287	0.0012
Macedonia	2	0.7185	0.1627	0.1044	0.0145	New Zealand	1	0.8949	0.0761	0.0282	0.0008
Brazil	1	0.6952	0.1842	0.1095	0.0111	Northern Ireland	1	0.8780	0.0963	0.0228	0.0029
Liberia	1	0.7120	0.1687	0.1077	0.0116	Sweden	1	0.8865	0.0869	0.0255	0.0011
Malaysia	2	0.7327	0.1527	0.0994	0.0151	Australia	1	0.8981	0.0764	0.0242	0.0013
Montenegro	1	0.6750	0.2037	0.1136	0.0077	Norway	1	0.8672	0.1087	0.0233	0.0008

References

Alkire, Sabine, and James Foster. 2009. Counting and Multidimensional Poverty Measurement. *OPHI Working Paper No. 32*. Oxford Poverty & Human Development Initiative (OPHI), December. http://www.ophi.org.uk/wp-content/uploads/OPHI-wp32.pdf

Brucker, Debra L., Sophie Mitra, Navena Chaitoo, and Joseph Mauro. 2015. More Likely to Be Poor Whatever the Measure: Working-Age Persons with Disabilities in the United States. *Social Science Quarterly* 96 (1): 273–296.

Dhongde, Shatakshee, and Robert Haveman. 2015. Multi-Dimensional Poverty Index: An Application to the United States. *Institute for Research on Poverty Discussion Paper No. 1427-15*, March.

Mitra, Sophie, and Debra Brucker. 2014. Income Poverty and Multiple Deprivations in a High-Income Country: The Case of the United States. *Fordham Economics Discussion Paper Series No. dp2014-05*, May.

U.S. Bureau of the Census/American Factfinder (U.S. Census). 2019. American Community Survey (Annual Data, 2008–2018). U.S. Census Bureau's American Community Survey Office. http://factfinder.census.gov

White, Roger, and Stacy Yamasaki. 2017. Multidimensional Poverty among the Native- and Foreign-born in the United States: Evidence from the 2010–2014 American Community Surveys. In *Measuring Multidimensional Poverty and Deprivation: Incidence and Determinants in Developed Countries*, ed. Roger White. New York, NY: Palgrave Macmillan.

CHAPTER 10

Multidimensional Poverty over the Life Cycle

Because the Multidimensional Poverty Index (MPI) is a comprehensive measure of deprivation, it addresses the deficiencies of traditional, income-based poverty measures while also serving as a useful complement to indirect poverty measures. For example, in Chap. 4 it is noted that the 2018 U.S. MPI value was equal to 2.34, with 6.0 percent of the population identified as being multidimensionally poor and the average deprivation intensity value (i.e., censored deprivation score) equal to 0.3877. By contrast, the official income-based U.S. poverty rate in 2018 was 11.8 percent (Semega et al. 2020). The MPI also can be used to identify deprivation for different cohorts of the population. Looking again to values for 2018, we find that the MPI value for individuals aged 18 to 64 was equal to 2.73. This value is higher than the 2018 aggregate MPI value. Similarly, the MPI value for those less than 18 years of age was equal to 1.27, which was markedly below the overall MPI value. Further, we can look to the head-count ratio values for the age cohorts to see that the frequency of multidimensional poverty among the working age population was equal to 7 percent which was more than twice the level overserved for the under-18 years of age cohort (i.e., 3.45 percent).

This chapter is the third of our examples of multidimensional poverty analysis. Having documented differences in multidimensional poverty incidence and intensity across broad age cohorts in Chap. 6 (i.e., 0–17 years of age, 18–64 years of age, and 65 years of age and older), we now explore differences over the life cycle in terms of the underlying dimensions and

R. White, *Multidimensional Poverty in America*,
https://doi.org/10.1007/978-3-030-45916-1_10

indicators. This includes examination of variation in indicator and dimension series values across age-specific cohorts (i.e., age 0 through age 95 and above) as a means to better understand variation in the headcount ratio series and in the MPI series. The decomposition of the MPI into its four component dimensions and the nine associated indicators allows for an even more detailed depiction of deprivation. For example, more than one in five members of the U.S. population (21.4 percent) experienced a form of health-related deprivation in 2018. More specifically, in that year, 13 percent of the population lacked health insurance while 9.1 percent were disabled.[1] The information regarding Health dimension-related deprivations, coupled with similar information for the Economic Security, Education, and Housing dimensions, permits individuals to be classified according to the extent of their multidimensional deprivation. This, in turn, allows measurement of the incidence and intensity of multidimensional poverty at the national level.

The ability to identify and target the specific forms of deprivation that contribute to poverty is of immense value for the formulation of related public policies. To further illustrate this point and to demonstrate the usefulness and applicability of the Multidimensional Poverty Index (MPI) to policy formulation, we present an empirical example of multidimensional poverty in the U.S. over the life cycle (i.e., for each age cohort (i.e., ages 0 through 95 years and above)).[2] Using annual, individual-level data from the American Community Survey (ACS) Public Use Microdata Sample (PUMS) for our 2008–2018 reference period (U.S. Census 2019), we identify the incidence of deprivation across each of the nine indicators for each observation (i.e., for each individual) in our data set. We then weight and aggregate the resulting indicator values to produce corresponding deprivation incidence values for each of the four dimensions. These dimension values are then used to quantify the incidence of multidimensional poverty (i.e., the headcount ratio), and average censored deprivation scores are calculated to identify the intensity of deprivation. Once the incidence and the intensity of multidimensional poverty were known, the calculation of MPI values is straightforward.

[1] Since an individual may experience multiple forms of deprivation, the sum of the listed population shares (i.e., 22.1 percent) is greater than the share of the population that experienced health-related deprivation (i.e., 21.4 percent).

[2] Due to relatively small numbers of observations for each age beyond 94 years (as compared to younger ages), we aggregate all ages greater than 94 years to form a "95 years and above" cohort.

In the next section, we document variation in the MPI and the headcount ratio series over the life cycle (i.e., by age, from 0 years of age through 95 years of age and older). We follow with examinations of dimension-specific deprivation incidence values and the timing of variation in indicator series as a means to explain observed variation in the MPI and headcount series. We close with a brief summary and a discussion of the relevance for public policy formulation.

10.1 Observed Variation in Deprivation over the Life Cycle

Over the life cycle, there is significant variation in the MPI series. Figure 10.1 presents the MPI, headcount ratio, and average deprivation intensity values for each age cohort. We see that the MPI generally increases in value until we reach the age 9 cohort—reaching a high value of 3.29 at age 6—after which we see a consistent decrease in the MPI series to a level of 1.56 for the age 15 cohort.[3] Over the age 16 through 35 cohorts, the series generally increases in value, peaking at an MPI value of 5.4 for the age 30 cohort.[4] Starting with the age 36 cohort, we observe a considerably prolonged period marked by rather steadily decreasing values. During this period, the MPI series decreases in value by more than one-half, reaching 2.3 for the age 67 cohort.[5] From this point onward—

[3] For all observations identified as less than 16 years of age, the indicator that identifies unemployment is set equal to zero. The reason for this is simply that individuals who are younger than 16 years of age are not included as part of the labor force and the official definition of unemployment in the United States excludes any individuals who are not in the labor force. Similarly, the indicator that identifies individuals as having an educational attainment level of less than a high school diploma or equivalent are set equal to zero for all observations who are below six years of age and for those who are at least six years of age and who report being currently enrolled in school and who have not reported having earned a high school diploma or equivalent degree.

[4] We do witness decreases between ages 22 and 23 (ΔMPI = -0.02), between ages 23 and 24 (ΔMPI = -0.05), between ages 30 and 31 (ΔMPI = -0.33), and from age 32 and age 33 (ΔMPI = -0.10); however, the decreases are minor and are not persistent (e.g., the age 32 value is 5.32 and the age 35 value is 5.31, both of which are quite near in value to the age 30 MPI value of 5.4). Thus, we treat the decreases as aberrations from the general, observed trend.

[5] During this period, we do observe periodic increases in MPI values. In total, across the 32 age cohorts in this span of the life cycle, we see eight increases in MPI values; however, the general trend is downward, in no instance do we observe successive increases across age cohorts, and the increases range in value from 0.01 to 0.18 with an average value of 0.0675.

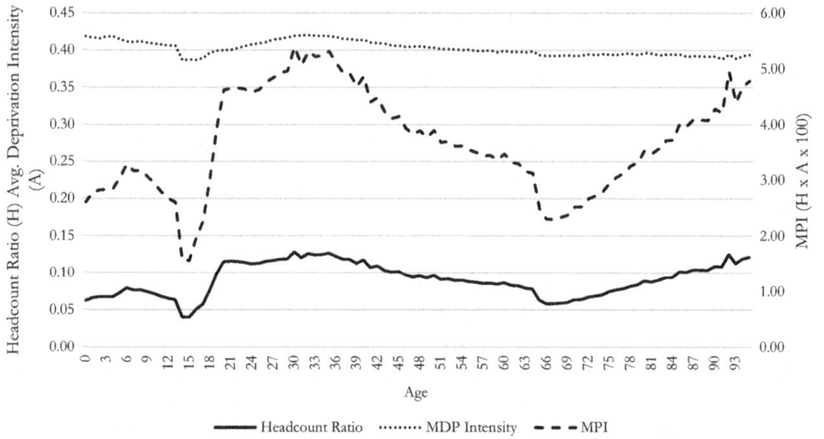

Fig. 10.1 Multidimensional Poverty Index (MPI), frequency, and intensity by age, 2008–2018

that is, the age 68 cohort through the age 95 and above age cohort—the MPI series increases in value, reaching a value of 4.95 for the age 92 cohort.[6]

The undulating path of the MPI series leads to the question of what explains the observed variation in the series across the age cohorts. Because the MPI is calculated as the scaled product of the headcount ratio and average deprivation intensity series, we can attempt to answer this question, or to otherwise provide guidance that may help to understand the observed variation, by looking to the paths of the component dimensions. Both the headcount ratio and the average deprivation series are included in Fig. 10.1. A cursory look at the figure reveals much less variation in the average deprivation intensity series across the age cohorts as compared to what we observe for the headcount ratio series. In fact, the average deprivation intensity series is so consistent over some portions of the life cycle that, to some degree, it is essentially a constant in the MPI calculation.

[6] Over this span of 28 age cohorts, we observe six decreases, of which only two occur across successive age categories. Aside from one very large decrease from ages 92 to 93 (ΔMPI = -0.55), the decreases range in value from -0.01 to -0.08 and have an average value of -0.046. Thus, all but one is quite minor and the decreases do not persist. The large decrease from ages 92 to 93 is followed by considerable increases such that the MPI value for the age 95 and above cohort is equal to 4.79 and quite similar to the age 92 value.

More specifically, the mean value for the average deprivation intensity series is equal to 0.4029 and the series ranges quite minimally from a low of 0.3869 for the age 14 cohort to a maximum value of 0.4207 for the age 32 cohort. By contrast, the headcount ratio series exhibits considerably more variation over the life cycle, and the variation in the series generally corresponds to the variation that is observed for the MPI series. This similar path is evident from the correlation coefficient value for the MPI and headcount ratio series (ρ = 0.9956), which is much higher than the correlation value for the MPI and the average deprivation intensity series (ρ = 0.4736).

While we can state with certainty that the observed variation in the MPI series over the life cycle is more closely linked to changes in the value of the headcount ratio series than to the path of the average deprivation intensity series, this leads us to a second question: What accounts for the observed variation in the headcount ratio over the life cycle? In the following section, we address this question by comparing rolling three-year average values for the headcount ratio, primarily, and for the MPI series to the deprivation frequency values of the four dimensions of deprivation that are utilized when calculating the MPI series.

10.2 Explaining Variation in Dimension Series Values over the Life Cycle

Figure 10.2 illustrates the paths of the deprivation frequency series across the age cohorts for each of our four dimensions. Interesting first impressions include that we see greater variation in series values over the range that spans the age 0 through age 22 cohorts relative to the variation that is observed for the range that begins with the age 23 cohort and continues through the age 64 cohort. Additionally, there is considerable similarity in terms of relative series values from the early-20s cohorts through the early-60s cohorts. There also are significant upticks in the Education and the Health dimension series that begin with the mid-60s cohorts. A closer examination of the figure reveals additional insights, which are discussed in greater detail below.

Beginning with the path of the Economic Security dimension, we see that it slowly decreases in value through the age 15 cohort. At this point, there is a sharp increase in the path through the age 22 cohort which is then followed by a steady, persistent decrease in the series through the age

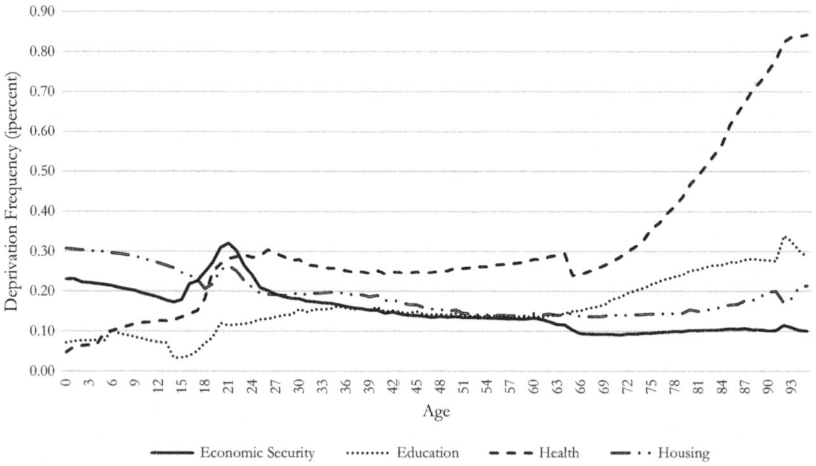

Fig. 10.2 Deprivation frequencies by dimension and age, 2008–2018

71 cohort.[7] Beginning with the age 72 cohort, another period of increasing values is observed. This continues until the age 88 cohort when we see four consecutive decreases that are followed by increases until we reach the age 95 and above cohort. The Health dimension steadily increases in value through the age 18 cohort, sharply increases in value through the age 22 cohort, and then continues to increase, although at a slower pace, until the age 28 cohort when it reaches a value of 29.7 percent. From this point through the age 64 cohort, the series dips gently, reaching a minimum value over this range of 24.7 percent for the age 43 cohort, before returning to a value of 29.1 with the age 64 cohort. Note that this value is nearly equal to that which is observed for the age 28 cohort (i.e., 29.7 percent). Following a brief three-year period of decreasing values, the series begins to increase and continues to do so through age 95 and above cohort. The Housing dimension, with few exceptions, follows a decreasing path through the age 60 cohort at which point the series begins to increase and, again with some exceptions, follows such a path through the

[7]There are only two increases in the series value over this five-decade span of age cohorts; from age 49 to age 50, the MPI value rises from 13.61 percent to 13.68 percent before decreasing to 13.59 percent for the age 51 cohort, and from ages 59 to 60, the MPI value increases from 13.11 percent to 13.17 percent before declining to 13.14 percent for the age 61 cohort.

95 and above age cohort.[8] Finally, perhaps more than any other dimension, the Education dimension mirrors the path of the headcount ratio series. The series generally increases through the age 8 cohort, decreases through the age 16 cohort, and then increases again—in this case, quite rapidly—through the age 22 cohort before entering a period of continued smaller increases that persists until the age 36 cohort. The series then decreases until the age 63 cohort when it again begins to increase—this time, at a generally decreasing rate—through the age 95 and above cohort.

Comparing the paths of the dimension series to that of the headcount ratio series, we see that the Education dimension closely follows the path of the headcount ratio while the paths of the three other dimensions are less aligned with the headcount ratio series. For example, consistent with the headcount ratio series, the paths of all four dimensions are seen to increase over the age cohorts that range from age 67 through 95 years and above. Similarly, over the range from the age 35 cohort to the age 67 cohort, all paths other than that of the Health dimension mirror the increasing pattern observed for the headcount ratio. For cohorts under age 35, deviation from the path of the headcount ratio series becomes more commonplace across all dimensions other than Education. The result is that, while we observe similarities between dimension-specific paths and the path of the headcount ratio series, we cannot point to any uniform or near-uniform pattern among dimensions that define the headcount ratio path and, thus, the path of the MPI series.

10.3 Explaining Variation in Indicator Series Values over the Life Cycle

Because each dimension is comprised of two or three indicators, we can rather easily examine the paths of the indicator series for changes that correspond with the inflection points identified in the headcount ratio path. The four panels in Fig. 10.3 present the paths for the indicator series, grouped by the corresponding dimensions.

Beginning with the indicators for the Education dimension and looking to the frequency of individuals living in limited English-speaking households, we see that the series begins to decrease in value after the age

[8] Seven increases are observed through the age 60 cohort (i.e., for the age 20–22, 30–32, and 35 cohorts), and an additional seven decreases occur over the range from the age 60 through age 95 and above cohorts (i.e., for the age 63, 66–68, 73, 92–93 cohorts).

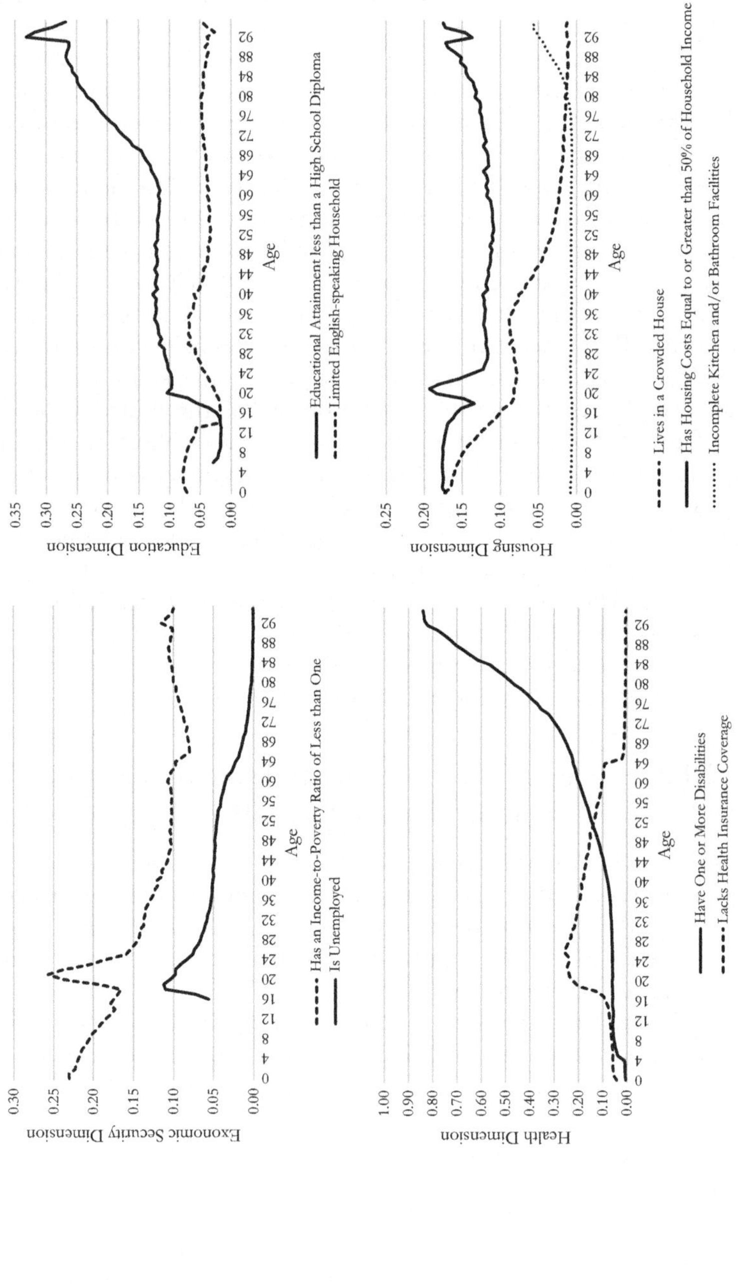

Fig. 10.3 Deprivation frequencies by indicator across age cohorts, 2008–2018

5 cohort with significant decreases observed beginning with the age 14 cohort. In almost all likelihood, this is an artifact of how the indicator is constructed. The corresponding variable in the ACS data identifies a household as being limited in terms of English-speaking abilities if no one 14 years of age or older only speaks English at home or, if another language is spoken at home, there is no one age 14 or older who can speak English "very well". Since children younger than 14 years of age may speak English quite well but are not captured by the variable, the higher series values for cohorts below 14 years of age likely overestimate the extent to which English abilities are limited. The increases in the series values that begin with the age 18 cohort are consistent with children who have English-speaking abilities leaving their limited English-speaking parents' homes. That the series peaks with the age 35 cohort, at a value quite similar to those observed at ages below 14 years, before generally declining until the early-50s cohorts and then increasing slightly, but remaining largely constant, is consistent with this notion.

We note that the series that identifies the frequency at which individuals lack a high school diploma remains at a very low level until the age 16 cohort when it increases sharply until the age 21 cohort.[9] It then rises slightly through the mid-30s before remaining stable until after the age 61 cohort when it again rises significantly. Educational attainment is not something that comes and goes. Once an individual earns a high school diploma that achievement remains with them. Thus, the higher values for this series after the age 60 cohort reflect not a change in educational attainment over the life cycle but instead a lower high school (or General Equivalency Diploma (GED)) completion rate during the period prior to about 1980 as compared to more recent years. Returning to the Education dimension series in Fig. 10.2, we can now see that the decline observed in the early teen years seems principally due to English-speaking abilities properly being accounted for. The subsequent increase in the series appears attributable to the occurrence of high school dropouts while the further rise that begins after the age 60 cohort is most likely representative of lower high school completion rates several decades prior.

Turning attention to the frequencies of the indicators that comprise the Health dimension, we see very different paths. Until the age 26 cohort, the health insurance series follows a path that is quite similar to that of the

[9] Observations/individuals below six years of age and those that indicate being enrolled in school are not categorized as lacking a high school diploma (or equivalent credential).

overall Health dimension. We also see similar sharp decreases in the Health dimension series and the health insurance series at the age 64 cohort. This decrease coincides with the general ages at which individuals enroll in Medicare. The disability series generally increases in value beginning with the mid- to late-30s age cohorts. Because the two indicator series are equally weighted in the Health dimension series, it appears that the observed stability of the Health dimension series during the period from the age 27 cohort to the age 64 cohort is largely attributable to the regular and consistent decline in the health insurance coverage indicator being offset by equally steady increases in the disability indicator series. Beginning with the age 65 cohort, the Health dimension series increases due to individuals being more likely to suffer one or more disabilities coupled with the health insurance indicator series having decreased to almost zero and, thus, being unable to offset further increases in the disability indicator series.

Simultaneously considering the frequency values of the indicators that are most-directly related to individual income, we see three commonalities. First, between the age 18 through age 21 cohorts, there are stark increases in the frequencies of individuals facing housing costs in excess of one-half of their monthly incomes and in the frequencies of individuals who experience income poverty. Likewise, we see sharp increases in the frequency of unemployment beginning with the age 16 cohort and persisting through the age 19 cohort. In all three instances, the series decrease sharply after only a few years. The path for the unemployment indicator series largely continues to decrease from the age 20 cohort through the age 95 and above cohort.[10] The income poverty series decreases until the age 48 cohort and remains fairly constant until the early-60s cohort before a more pronounced decrease is seen, followed by rising values from the age 67 cohort through the age 95 and above cohort. This is somewhat similar to the housing costs series which remains largely constant from the age 25 cohort through the age 60 cohort before slowly increasing thereafter.

Lastly, rounding out the Housing dimension, the crowded house indicator series decreases through the age 25 cohort, increases marginally

[10] Observations/individuals under 16 years of age are not included in the labor force and, thus, are not identified as unemployed. The increase in unemployment observed between the ages of 16 and 19 years likely results from increased labor force participation among teens as they age.

through the age 35 cohort, and then consistently declines through the age 88 cohort before remaining generally constant through the age 95 and above cohort. By contrast, the kitchen and bath amenities indicator series remains low in value and near-constant until the age 80 cohort when it begins to increase and continues to do so through the age 95 and above cohort.

We can now figuratively overlay the paths of the indicator series onto the paths of the MPI and headcount ratio series. These latter two series are presented in Fig. 10.4, and we have identified four periods (i.e., age cohort ranges) that indicate trend changes in these two paths. For each period, we now discuss the respective changes in the paths of the indicator series values. Doing so works toward the goal of identifying the sources of the observed variation in the MPI series, the headcount ratio series, and the dimension-specific deprivation incidence series.

In Fig. 10.4, Period I is identified as spanning the age 0 through age 16 cohorts. During this period, we see increases in the disabled and health insurance indicator series. The effects of both indicators, which combine to form the Health dimension, appears to be tempered by decreases in the values of the income poverty, English language, and crowded house indicators. Additionally, the housing cost indicator series increases during the initial portion of this period before decreasing in value through the latter

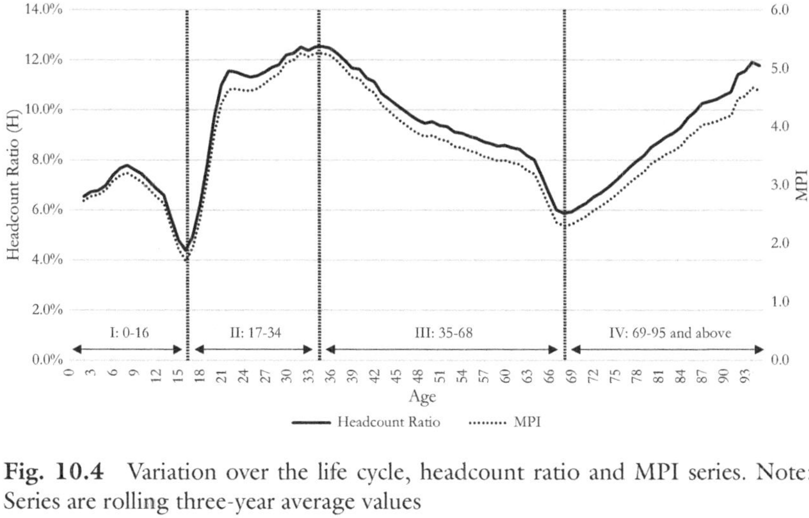

Fig. 10.4 Variation over the life cycle, headcount ratio and MPI series. Note: Series are rolling three-year average values

half of the period. Changes in relative magnitudes contribute to the observed changes in MPI and headcount ratio series from increasing to decreasing following the age eight cohort.

During Period II (i.e., the age 17 through age 34 cohorts), we see more uniformity in the paths of indicator series. Throughout the period, we see both the MPI series and the headcount ratio series increasing in value. Over the age 17 through age 22 cohorts, all indicator series increase with the exception of the kitchen and bath amenities and crowded house indicator series, both of which remain largely constant, and the housing costs series, which increases sharply at the beginning of this period before sharply decreasing. Beginning with the age 23 cohort and continuing to the end of the period, the high school diploma and English language indicators (i.e., the Education dimension), the crowded house indicator, and the disability indicators all consistently increase in value. The health insurance indicator initially increases before decreasing. The income poverty and unemployment indicators, which comprise the Economic Security series, decrease throughout the period, and the housing costs indictor initially decreases in value before levelling and remaining largely constant. Thinking in terms of the indicator values generally, we can say that the increases observed beginning with the age 17 cohort and continuing to the age 22 cohort persists even with the decreasing values for the Economic Security series and the housing costs indicator.

The final two periods span the age 35 through age 68 cohorts (i.e., period III) and the age 69 cohort through the age 95 and above cohort (i.e., period IV). In the former period, the MPI and headcount ratio series decrease in value. The corresponding changes in indicator series includes decreases in all indicators with the exceptions of the disability indicator series and the high school diploma indicator series, both of which increase throughout the period, and the housing costs series that initially declines before a sustained period of increasing values. During period IV, we see that the MPI and the headcount ratio series both increase in value. This is driven by increases in the income poverty, high school diploma, disability, housing costs, and amenities series. The increase appears to be offset to some degree by decreases in the crowded house and unemployment series. Both the English language and the health insurance indicator series are largely constant throughout the period.

10.4 Summary and Policy Implications

The observed variation in the MPI series and in the headcount ratio series is due to a confluence of changes in the values of the dimension and indicator series. While the path of the Education dimension across age cohorts most closely resembles that which is seen for the MPI series and for the headcount ratio series, changes in the Education dimension coincide with changes in several other series. As a result, it is neither prudent nor entirely possible to point to a given dimension(s) or indicator(s) as the base influence on the path of the MPI and headcount ratio series. Instead, we see that some changes may be attributable to changes in particular groups of dimensions and/or indicators while other changes may be the result of variations in a wholly different set of dimensions and/or indicators. While this result may seem less than ideal—since it certainly would be helpful for policy makers to identify a single dimension or small set of indicators, for example, that account for all multidimensional poverty—it is a quite useful finding if we think of potential public policy formulation aimed toward reductions in or the elimination of deprivation.

In the following chapter, we build on the information provided in this chapter and in the two chapters immediately prior by considering several counterfactual scenarios that correspond with broad policy changes. For example, relative to the situation that is observed for 2018, we consider the effects of increased K-12 school funding and/or free or highly subsidized college tuition and ancillary expenses on multidimensional poverty. The counterfactual exercise assumes the policy change applies universally over the life cycle. That is, all individuals who do not have a high school diploma would immediately cease to be deprived in that particular indicator. While the exercise is informative, the assumption of a universal benefit will certainly be more appropriate for some policy changes (e.g., universal health insurance or universal basic income) than for others. If the overarching policy goal is to engineer improvements in social welfare via reductions in specific deprivations then understanding the timing of such deprivations may allow for more targeted and, thus, more efficient public policy interventions.

References

Semega, Jessica L., Melissa A. Kollar, John Creamer, and Abinash Mohanty. 2020. Income and Poverty in the United States: 2018. U.S. Census Bureau, Current Population Reports, P60-266(RV). Washington, DC: U.S. Government Printing Office.

U.S. Bureau of the Census/American Factfinder (U.S. Census). 2019. American Community Survey (Annual Data, 2008–2018). U.S. Census Bureau's American Community Survey Office. http://factfinder.census.gov

PART IV

Towards the Elimination of Multidimensional Poverty in America

CHAPTER 11

Reducing Multidimensional Poverty: A Series of Counterfactual Analyses

In the preceding chapters, we introduced our topic, surveyed the related literature, detailed the measurement of multidimensional poverty, provided an accounting of America's multidimensionally poor, examined the determinants of multidimensional poverty, and presented three related empirical studies. We hope that the information that is contained in these earlier chapters fosters a more complete understanding of poverty and deprivation in the U.S. We now conclude our examination of multidimensional poverty in America by presenting a number of counterfactual exercises. This serves to further expand our understanding of our topic and as an appropriate cap to the information conveyed in earlier chapters.

We consider a series of counterfactual scenarios, each of which identifies the potential impacts of one or more discrete public policy interventions on the incidence and intensity of multidimensional poverty in America. More specifically, examining data from the 2018 American Community Survey (ACS) Public Use Microdata Sample (PUMS) (U.S. Census 2019), we calculate the Multidimensional Poverty Index (MPI), the corresponding headcount ratio (i.e., our measure of incidence) and average deprivation intensity values, and the number of multidimensionally poor individuals. We focus on 2018 as it is the most recent year in our data sample. These values serve as the baseline to which the results of our counterfactual exercises are compared.

Each counterfactual exercise that we consider represents the enactment of one or more assumed public policy change(s). These scenarios include:

R. White, *Multidimensional Poverty in America*,
https://doi.org/10.1007/978-3-030-45916-1_11

(1) the implementation of universal health insurance; (2) the adoption of a universal basic income that is equal to at least 130 percent of the federal poverty threshold; (3) the provision of free/discounted college to facilitate universal completion of high school; and (4) the expansion of English as a Second Language programs to avoid and/or eliminate linguistic isolation. Each scenario corresponds with one or more of the deprivation indicators that comprise the MPI.

Universal health insurance would provide all U.S. residents with health insurance coverage. This would result in no U.S. resident being deprived in terms of the health insurance indicator. Universal basic income would guarantee all U.S. residents a household income that is at least equal to 130 percent of the federal poverty level given the size and composition of their household (i.e., the threshold for receipt of benefits from the Supplemental Nutrition Assistance Program (i.e., SNAP benefits)). This would have a primary effect of eliminating income poverty, while for some it would have a secondary effect of reducing deprivation in the indicator that identifies housing costs being equal to or greater than 50 percent of income. A free/discounted college program would provide all graduates of U.S. high schools with free undergraduate education, heavily discounted college tuition and fees, student stipends, and/or a student loan forgiveness program. Of course, different or additional incentives could also be used. Regardless of which incentive(s) is chosen, the goal would be to incentivize completion of high school by significantly lowering the cost of higher education. We assume the cost reduction to be sufficiently high as to facilitate universal high school completion. This would result in no U.S. resident being deprived in terms of the educational attainment indicator. Expansion of English as a Second Language (ESL) programs would provide all U.S. residents with free access to ESL courses with the goal of achieving universal English language fluency. This would entail an increase in the availability and capacity of ESL courses/programs with the goal being to meet a threshold of at least one individual per household who is at least 14 years of age and who speaks English very well. Accomplishing this goal would alleviate deprivation in the English language indicator. Notice that each assumed scenario corresponds with the elimination of one of our indicators of deprivation and, thus, all else held constant, will result in a reduction of multidimensional poverty.

Before considering any of the counterfactual scenarios, we first generate the observed 2018 values for the MPI, the headcount ratio, the average deprivation intensity value, and the number of multidimensionally poor U.S. residents. These values serve as our baseline levels. We then assume each of our four antecedents in turn, documenting the resulting levels of the MPI and related measures. These are the values that we assume would have been observed had the respective antecedent(s) been realized. We can then compare the observed/baseline values to those obtained from each of our counterfactual exercises.

Performing these counterfactual exercises permits us to address several related questions:

1. We ask the obvious question of what is the estimated effect of each scenario on the MPI, headcount ratio, and average deprivation intensity values?
2. As part of each counterfactual exercise, we ask what are the effects at the national, region, division, and state levels of detail? Are some geographic areas more/less affected by a given counterfactual as compared to others and, if so, does this inform policy actions in terms of how best to target deprivation?
3. Under each counterfactual scenario, how many U.S. residents are estimated to be multidimensionally poor and how do these values compare to the observed numbers for 2018?
4. Do we find variation across socio-demographic cohorts in terms of reductions in multidimensional poverty?
5. What counterfactual scenario(s) decreases the number of multidimensionally poor U.S. residents by the largest amount?

Note that in each exercise we assume complete success. For example, the third counterfactual exercise listed above involves incentivizing completion of high school. We assume that the incentive structure employed will achieve a 100-percent high school completion rate. Of course, achievement of a lower success rate—or a range of potential success rates (e.g., 80 percent, 90 percent, and 100 percent)—could also be evaluated. We also assume that the counterfactual occurs in isolation. That is, we assume that all else would remain as observed. Clearly, this is not an ideal assumption. Incentives that influence human behavior can certainly have indirect effects. Unfortunately, as we cannot foresee with any requisite degree of accuracy the specific indirect effects or their influences, we proceed as best we can. Lastly, while some counterfactual scenarios would yield reductions in multidimensional poverty in the immediate- or the very short-run, others may require the passage of years or even decades before the full effects are realized. Returning to the example of incentivizing the completion of high school, while this may certainly be welcome among the current youth population it likely would not hold great appeal to older adults and, as a result, would likely not affect their educational attainment. In other words, even with generous incentives in place, it could be decades before universal high school completion is achieved. To the contrary, the implementation of universal health care or the adoption of a universal basic income could affect the entire population with the effects being realized over a very short time horizon. With these assumptions stated explicitly, we now can begin our counterfactual exercises.

11.1 Four Counterfactual Exercises

Beginning with the baseline levels that represent the starting points for each of our exercises, we estimate that in 2018 a total of 19,710,056 U.S. residents were multidimensionally poor. This number equaled 6.02 percent of the country's population. We also calculate that the average deprivation intensity value (i.e., the average deprivation score among those categorized as being multidimensionally poor) was 0.3877. Thus, the U.S. MPI value for 2018 was equal to 2.34. This is the lowest MPI value during our 2008–2018 reference period. Similarly, the 2018 headcount ratio and the average deprivation intensity values were also the lowest among their series during the reference period. It is fortuitous that the baseline to which the results of our counterfactual exercises are compared includes relatively conservative values; thus, it can be argued that the differences between the results of our exercises and the corresponding baseline values are restrained.

Results from each of our counterfactual exercises, when conducted at the national level, are provided in Table 11.1. Our first counterfactual scenario assumes that, in 2018, no U.S. resident lacked health insurance. The effect of universal health care on the frequency of multidimensional poverty is considerable—a 27.9 percent decrease in the value from the 6.02 percent baseline to a headcount ratio of 4.34 percent. The corresponding change in the intensity of multidimensional poverty, however, is a rather small decrease from the baseline average deprivation intensity value of 0.3877 to 0.3753 (i.e., a decline of only 3.2 percent). The resulting effect of the introduction of universal health insurance on the MPI is a 29.8 percent decrease from the baseline value of 2.34 to 1.63. Stated in different terms, had a universal health care program been in place in the U.S., an estimated 5.52 million U.S. residents would not have suffered

Table 11.1 Four counterfactuals, national level

Scenario/ Counterfactual (CF)	*Headcount ratio (%)*	*Average intensity*	*MPI*	*Multidimensionally poor population*		
				N	$\Delta N \mid CF$	$\%\Delta N \mid CF$
Observed	6.02	0.3877	2.3356	19,710,056	.	.
Universal health insurance	4.34	0.3753	1.6277	14,188,025	-5,522,031	-28.02
Universal basic income	2.36	0.3699	0.8720	7,712,527	-11,997,529	-60.87
Free/discounted college	4.07	0.3672	1.4931	13,304,778	-6,405,278	-32.50
Expanded ESL	4.84	0.3772	1.8247	15,828,080	-3,881,976	-19.70

N = 3,214,539

multidimensional poverty during 2018. This represents a 28 percent reduction in number of individuals who were multidimensionally poor, from 19.7 million U.S. residents to fewer than 14.2 million. While this is a substantial reduction in the number of multidimensionally poor individuals, the implementation of a universal health care program in America yields only the third largest impact, in terms of reducing multidimensional poverty, among the four counterfactual exercises that we consider.

Our second counterfactual exercise involves the adoption of a universal basic income. Specifically, in this scenario, we assume that all U.S. residents are guaranteed a minimum income that is equal to 130 percent of the federal poverty level (i.e., the Official Poverty Measure) given the size and composition of their household. Such a policy change, all else held constant, would produce a primary, or direct, effect in that a universal basic income at this level would effectively eliminate income poverty and, for some, a secondary, indirect effect of an increase in income relative to housing costs. This secondary effect would lead to a decrease in the deprivation frequency value for the indicator that identifies individuals who face housing costs that are equal to or greater than 50 percent of their income. When performing our counterfactual, we have accounted for the effects of the increases in income both on the income poverty indicator and the housing costs indicator.

The effects of adopting a universal basic income are quite large. In Table 11.1 we see an estimated decrease in the headcount ratio of more than one-half from the baseline value of 6.02 percent to 2.4 percent.

Additionally, the average deprivation intensity value falls from 0.3877 to 0.3699. The MPI value declines considerably to a value of 0.8720. This is a decrease of more than 62 percent. Looked at in terms of affected individuals, in 2018, had the assumed universal basic income been in place, nearly 12 million fewer U.S. residents would have been multidimensionally poor. This is a 60.9 percent decrease in the number of multidimensionally poor. To an extent, a large impact is to be expected. The income poverty rate for the U.S. in 2018 was 11.8 percent (U.S. Census 2020). Alleviating this form of deprivation has potentially wide-ranging implications, since doing so affects almost one in every eight U.S. residents.

Adding to the impact of a universal basic income on multidimensional poverty is that, while the primary effect operates through the income poverty indicator, there is the additional, secondary effect that is related to the housing costs indicator. To identify the separate primary and secondary effects, we conduct a separate counterfactual exercise in which the adoption of a universal basic income is assumed to affect the income poverty indicator but has no influence on the housing costs indicator. In such an instance, the headcount ratio is estimated to decrease to only 2.9 percent and the average deprivation intensity value declines to 0.3711. The corresponding MPI value is equal to 1.0773. Considering these values in conjunction with the values presented in Table 11.1, we see that an estimated 85.2 percent of the total decrease in the headcount ratio is attributable to the primary effect. An even larger proportion of the decrease in the average deprivation intensity value (93.2 percent) is due to the primary effect. As a result, we estimate that the primary effect accounts for 85.1 percent of the observed decline in the MPI value. Lastly, we estimate that the primary effect reduces the number of multidimensionally poor individuals by slightly more than 10.2 million individuals, while the secondary effect reduces the number of multidimensionally poor by almost 1.8 million individuals.

Compared to our first two counterfactual exercises, our third scenario is somewhat indistinct in that, while there is a corresponding policy goal, the potential paths to achieving the goal are less than clear. Specifically, we consider the effects of a loosely defined set of incentives that are assumed to produce the desired result of universal high school completion. The overarching goal would be a reduction in, or the elimination altogether of, the direct costs associated with attending college as an encouragement for students to complete high school. If we set aside the specifics of the incentive(s), allow the details to be managed by policy makers, and simply assume that the incentive(s) achieve their goal of universal high school completion, then the related effects on multidimensional poverty can be seen in Table 11.1. Under such a scenario, we estimate a decrease of nearly two percentage points in the headcount ratio from 6.02 percent, our baseline value, to 4.07 percent. Similarly, we observed a corresponding reduction in the average deprivation intensity value from 0.3877 to 0.3672. These effects are estimated to combine for a decrease in the MPI value from the baseline of 2.34 to a more modest 1.49. Lastly, the number of U.S. residents who suffer multidimensional poverty under this counterfactual scenario is 32.5 percent lower (i.e., 13.3 million individuals) than the baseline estimate of 19.7 million residents.

Our fourth counterfactual exercise produces the smallest decrease in multidimensional poverty. Even so, had an expansion of ESL programs occurred prior to 2018 and had achieved the desired/assumed results, an estimated 3.9 million fewer U.S. residents would have suffered multidimensional poverty during 2018. This is a significant reduction of nearly 20 percent. Further, the corresponding values that are presented in Table 11.1 indicate an estimated decrease in the headcount ratio of almost 20 percent from the baseline value of 6.02 percent to 4.84 percent. The average deprivation intensity value decreases marginally from 0.3877 to 0.3772. Thus, the MPI value is estimated to decrease by 21.9 percent.

Having detailed the results that were obtained when performing our counterfactual exercises at the national level, we now undertake each of the four exercises to determine the respective impacts at the region, division, and state levels of detail. By repeating our exercises at varying levels of geographic specificity, we mirror our accounting of multidimensional poverty incidence and intensity at the sub-national level that is presented in Chap. 5. We also gain useful information of the respective impacts of the policy changes that correspond with the four counterfactual exercises. Results for regions and divisions are presented in Table 11.2, while state-specific findings are provided in Table 11.5 which we relegate to the chapter appendix.

Continuing our pattern of working from the broadest to the most-specific geographic unit, we begin our discussion at the region level of detail. Relative to the observed levels for 2018, we estimate that had a universal basic income been in place, the number of multidimensionally poor individuals in that year would have 54.1 percent lower in the West region and 70.4 percent lower for the Midwest Region. For all regions, the adoption of a universal basic income is estimated to have the largest

Table 11.2 Counterfactual results, region and division levels

Scenario/Counterfactual (CF)	*Headcount ratio (%)*	*Average intensity*	*MPI*	*Multidimensionally poor population*		
				N	Δ*N*|*CF*	%Δ*N*|*CF*
Northeast region						
Observed	5.62	0.3865	2.1716	3,152,782	.	.
Universal health insurance	4.60	0.3787	1.7418	2,580,578	-572,204	-18.15
Universal basic income	2.22	0.3691	0.8206	1,247,615	-1,905,167	-60.43
Free/discounted college	3.80	0.3663	1.3924	2,133,138	-1,019,644	-32.34
Expanded ESL	4.19	0.3729	1.5613	2,349,158	-803,624	-25.49
New England division						
Observed	4.43	0.3835	1.6988	657,883	.	.
Universal health insurance	3.79	0.3770	1.4293	563,189	-94,694	-14.39
Universal basic income	1.64	0.3694	0.6061	243,702	-414,181	-62.96
Free/discounted college	3.03	0.3630	1.0991	449,718	-208,165	-31.64
Expanded ESL	3.33	0.3703	1.2338	494,931	-162,952	-24.77
Middle Atlantic division						
Observed	6.05	0.3873	2.3418	2,494,899	.	.
Universal health insurance	4.89	0.3792	1.8543	2,017,389	-477,510	-19.14
Universal basic income	2.43	0.3690	0.8978	1,003,913	-1,490,986	-59.76
Free/discounted college	4.08	0.3671	1.4980	1,683,420	-811,479	-32.53
Expanded ESL	4.49	0.3736	1.6792	1,854,227	-640,672	-25.68
Midwest region						
Observed	4.55	0.3812	1.7333	3,105,792	.	.
Universal health insurance	3.41	0.3705	1.2624	2,327,303	-778,489	-25.07
Universal basic income	1.35	0.3679	0.4957	920,522	-2,185,270	-70.36
Free/discounted college	3.15	0.3613	1.1375	2,150,734	-955,058	-30.75
Expanded ESL	3.99	0.3753	1.4970	2,724,516	-381,276	-12.28

East North Central division						
Observed	4.65	0.3802	1.7667	2,180,602	.	.
Universal health insurance	3.55	0.3704	1.3157	1,666,957	-513,645	-23.56
Universal basic income	1.38	0.3659	0.5049	647,640	-1,532,962	-70.30
Free/discounted college	3.16	0.3600	1.1373	1,482,798	-697,804	-32.00
Expanded ESL	4.08	0.3740	1.5261	1,914,981	-265,621	-12.18
West North Central division						
Observed	4.33	0.3835	1.6599	925,190	.	.
Universal health insurance	3.09	0.3708	1.1453	660,346	-264,844	-28.63
Universal basic income	1.28	0.3725	0.4755	272,882	-652,308	-70.51
Free/discounted college	3.12	0.3642	1.1380	667,936	-257,254	-27.81
Expanded ESL	3.79	0.3785	1.4332	809,535	-115,655	-12.50
South region						
Observed	6.80	0.3900	2.6526	8,486,094	.	.
Universal health insurance	4.43	0.3733	1.6544	5,528,421	-2,957,673	-34.85
Universal basic income	2.62	0.3712	0.9710	3,263,004	-5,223,090	-61.55
Free/discounted college	4.68	0.3688	1.7247	5,833,615	-2,652,479	-31.26
Expanded ESL	5.62	0.3801	2.1379	7,017,160	-1,468,934	-17.31
South Atlantic division						
Observed	6.05	0.3862	2.3378	3,953,937	.	.
Universal health insurance	3.99	0.3709	1.4789	2,604,264	-1,349,673	-34.13
Universal basic income	2.25	0.3703	0.8343	1,471,877	-2,482,060	-62.77
Free/discounted college	4.17	0.3660	1.5250	2,722,111	-1,231,826	-31.15
Expanded ESL	5.02	0.3778	1.8952	3,276,923	-677,014	-17.12

(*continued*)

Table 11.2 (continued)

Scenario/Counterfactual (CF)	*Headcount ratio (%)*	*Average intensity*	*MPI*	*Multidimensionally poor population*		
				N	Δ*N*|*CF*	%Δ*N*|*CF*
East South Central division						
Observed	6.36	0.3862	2.4567	1,215,834	.	.
Universal health insurance	4.46	0.3711	1.6563	853,114	-362,720	-29.83
Universal basic income	1.69	0.3694	0.6256	323,656	-892,178	-73.38
Free/discounted college	4.33	0.3647	1.5799	828,020	-387,814	-31.90
Expanded ESL	5.92	0.3816	2.2607	1,132,221	-83,613	-6.88
West South Central division						
Observed	8.23	0.3958	3.2557	3,316,323	.	.
Universal health insurance	5.14	0.3773	1.9379	2,071,043	-1,245,280	-37.55
Universal basic income	3.64	0.3726	1.3563	1,467,471	-1,848,852	-55.75
Free/discounted college	5.66	0.3738	2.1170	2,283,484	-1,032,839	-31.14
Expanded ESL	6.47	0.3823	2.4730	2,608,016	-708,307	-21.36
West region						
Observed	6.37	0.3886	2.4739	4,965,388	.	.
Universal health insurance	4.81	0.3790	1.8231	3,751,723	-1,213,665	-24.44
Universal basic income	2.93	0.3692	1.0800	2,281,386	-2,684,002	-54.05
Free/discounted college	4.09	0.3686	1.5065	3,187,291	-1,778,097	-35.81
Expanded ESL	4.79	0.3757	1.8001	3,737,246	-1,228,142	-24.73
Mountain division						
Observed	5.22	0.3854	2.0107	1,280,938	.	.
Universal health insurance	3.64	0.3735	1.3583	892,911	-388,027	-30.29
Universal basic income	1.98	0.3697	0.7335	487,110	-793,828	-61.97
Free/discounted college	3.51	0.3648	1.2822	862,888	-418,050	-32.64
Expanded ESL	4.35	0.3753	1.6309	1,066,897	-214,041	-16.71

Pacific division						
Observed	6.89	0.3897	2.6867	3,684,450	.	.
Universal health insurance	5.35	0.3807	2.0366	2,858,812	-825,638	-22.41
Universal basic income	3.36	0.3691	1.2392	1,794,276	-1,890,174	-51.30
Free/discounted college	4.35	0.3700	1.6095	2,324,403	-1,360,047	-36.91
Expanded ESL	5.00	0.3758	1.8778	2,670,349	-1,014,101	-27.52

impact on multidimensional poverty. For the Northeast, Midwest, and West regions, the second most impactful counterfactual scenario is that of free/discounted college. For the South region, universal health care is the second most impactful scenario with an estimated reduction in multidimensional poverty of 34.9 percent; however, free/discounted college is estimated to produce only a slightly smaller reduction (31.3 percent) in the number of multidimensionally poor.

When comparing the estimated effects of our counterfactual exercises that vary in magnitude across regions, less variation is found when we order the impacts of the different scenarios. Specifically, as noted, adoption of a universal basic income is the most impactful counterfactual scenario regardless of region, and free/discounted college is the second most impactful scenario for three regions. Similarly, for all regions, the expansion of ESL programs is estimated to have only the third or fourth highest impact in terms of reducing the number of multidimensionally poor. For three regions, the scenario in which universal health insurance is implemented is also estimated to have either the third or fourth highest impact. While we find some uniformity in the orderings of estimated impacts, we also find considerable variation in the magnitudes of estimated effects.

When looking at the nine divisions which comprise the four regions, we again find the adoption of a universal basic income is estimated to provide the largest decreases in the number of multidimensionally poor. The estimated reductions in the number of multidimensionally poor, again relative to observed 2018 values, range from 51.3 percent for the Pacific division, which is part of the West region, to 73.4 percent for the East South Central division, which is located in the South region. The reductions that are estimated for the East North Central and West North Central divisions—that is, the two divisions that comprise the Midwest region—are also quite high, being equal to 70.5 percent and 70.3 percent, respectively. While the largest proportional decreases in multidimensional poverty are estimated to involve the East South Central, East North Central, and West North Central divisions, it is the South Atlantic division that is estimated to have the largest number of residents who would be lifted out of multidimensional poverty (i.e., 2.48 million individuals) by the adoption of a universal basic income.

Free/discounted college is the second most impactful counterfactual scenario for six of the nine divisions; however, implementation of universal health coverage has the second highest impact on multidimensional poverty in the South Atlantic, East North Central, and West North Central divisions. Similarly, expansion of ESL programs is estimated to be the least impactful scenario in six of the nine divisions with implementation of universal health insurance being the least-effective scenario for the New England, Middle Atlantic, and Pacific divisions. Of all scenarios, it is the effect of the implementation of universal health insurance that varies the most across divisions.

Continuing our discussion to the state level of detail, as we see at the region and division levels of detail, the adoption of a universal basic income is the most impactful counterfactual scenario for all 50 states and the District of Columbia. The estimated decreases in the number of individuals who live in multidimensional poverty range from a low value of 49.1 percent for California to a high of 82.6 percent for West Virginia. We see that, in response to the adoption of a universal basic income, slightly more than half of the states (i.e., 27 of the 51) are estimated to realize proportional decreases in multidimensional poverty of at least two-thirds and all states except California would see at least a 51.5 percent reduction in the number of multidimensionally poor residents. As noted, California would be the least-affected state in terms of the proportional decrease in multidimensional poverty. Texas is estimated to be the second least-affected state; however, due to their large populations, these two states are estimated to have the two largest absolute decreases in the number of multidimensionally poor residents (i.e., a decrease of 1.49 million individuals in California and a decline of 1.34 million individuals in Texas).

Consistent with the orderings observed at the region and the division levels, free/discounted college is the second most impactful counterfactual scenario for a majority of states (i.e., 30 of 51). The implementation of universal health care is estimated to be the second most impactful scenario for 20 states, and by the slimmest of margins the expansion of ESL programs would be the second-most impactful scenario for a single state (i.e., Connecticut). No counterfactual is ranked as the third-most impactful scenario for a majority of states. Instead, the implementation of universal health care is third-ranked for a plurality of states, leaving the expansion of ESL programs as, again, the least-impactful scenario the majority (i.e., 43 of 51 states).

11.2 Counterfactuals and Socio-Demographic Cohorts

Extending beyond the estimated effects of our counterfactual scenarios on various geographic locales, we perform these exercises for each of the socio-demographic cohorts for which multidimensional poverty incidence and intensity is detailed in Chap. 4. As is the case with the performance of counterfactual exercises for individual regions, divisions, and states, consideration of individual cohorts provides useful information about the respective impacts of the policy changes that are associated with our exercises. Table 11.3 presents the estimated changes in the values of the MPI, the related measures, and the numbers of individuals who are estimated to suffer multidimensional poverty.

When we consider socio-demographic cohorts, we generally see the adoption of a universal basic income as the most impactful scenario; however, unlike our findings for the various sub-national geographic units, we observe three cohorts for which the adoption of a universal basic income is not the most-impactful scenario. Specifically, individuals who lack a high school diploma and those who are foreign-born are estimated to benefit most from free/discounted college. Similarly, we estimate that individuals who are employed benefit most from the implementation of universal health insurance.

As may be expected, there appears to be more variation across socio-demographic cohorts than across geographic units in terms of ordering scenarios from most- to least-impactful. Specifically, in addition to the lack of uniformity that is observed across cohorts in the most-impactful scenario, we see a broad mix of scenarios ranked as the second-, third-, and least-impactful scenarios. For example, while a slight majority of cohorts (i.e., 15 of 29) identify free/discounted college as the second-most impactful scenario, the remaining 14 cohorts are divided across the other three scenarios with nine indicating they would be better-served by the implementation of universal health insurance, three identifying the universal basic income scenario, and two gaining most from an expansion of ESL programs. The three scenarios of free/discounted college, universal health insurance, and the expansion of ESL programs collectively account for all of the third-ranked and least-ranked scenarios among the 29 cohorts.

Table 11.3 Counterfactual results, socio-demographic cohorts

Cohort	*Category*	*Scenario/ Counterfactual (CF)*	*Headcount ratio (%)*	*Average intensity*	*MPI*	*Multidimensionally poor population*		
						N	*ΔN|CF*	*%ΔN|CF*
Gender	Female							
		Observed	6.19	0.3874	2.3999	10,288,571	.	.
		Universal health insurance	4.68	0.3759	1.7595	7,775,373	-2,513,198	-24.43
		Universal basic income	2.18	0.3682	0.8018	3,616,794	-6,671,777	-64.85
		Free/discounted college	4.27	0.3665	1.5635	7,084,699	-3,203,872	-31.14
		Expanded ESL	5.05	0.3762	1.8998	8,388,121	-1,900,450	-18.47
	Male							
		Observed	5.85	0.3880	2.2693	9,421,485	.	.
		Universal health insurance	3.98	0.3747	1.4919	6,412,652	-3,008,833	-31.94
		Universal basic income	2.54	0.3714	0.9443	4,095,733	-5,325,752	-56.53
		Free/discounted college	3.86	0.3679	1.4205	6,220,079	-3,201,406	-33.98
		Expanded ESL	4.62	0.3783	1.7472	7,439,959	-1,981,526	-21.03
Age	0–17 years of age							
		Observed	3.45	0.3683	1.2701	2,527,086	.	.
		Universal health insurance	2.66	0.3609	0.9591	1,947,458	-579,628	-22.94
		Universal basic income	0.49	0.3515	0.1717	357,902	-2,169,184	-85.84
		Free/discounted college	3.18	0.3654	1.1604	2,327,242	-199,844	-7.91

(*continued*)

Table 11.3 (continued)

Cohort	*Category*	*Scenario/ Counterfactual (CF)*	*Headcount ratio (%)*	*Average intensity*	*MPI*	*Multidimensionally poor population*		
						N	*ΔN|CF*	*%ΔN|CF*
		Expanded ESL	1.88	0.3588	0.6734	1,374,966	-1,152,120	-45.59
	18–64 years of age							
		Observed	6.96	0.3920	2.7267	14,013,678	.	.
		Universal health insurance	4.56	0.3765	1.7160	9,183,404	-4,830,274	-34.47
		Universal basic income	2.36	0.3699	0.8720	7,712,527	-6,301,151	-44.96
		Free/discounted college	4.59	0.3695	1.6959	9,248,470	-4,765,208	-34.00
		Expanded ESL	5.92	0.3813	2.2584	11,933,102	-2,080,576	-14.85
	65 years of age and above							
		Observed	6.05	0.3839	2.3215	3,169,292	.	.
		Universal health insurance	5.83	0.3811	2.2233	3,057,163	-112,129	-3.54
		Universal basic income	2.54	0.3646	0.9264	1,331,547	-1,837,745	-57.99
		Free/discounted college	3.30	0.3572	1.1786	1,729,066	-1,440,226	-45.44
		Expanded ESL	4.81	0.3674	1.7668	2,520,012	-649,280	-20.49
Race	American Indian and Alaskan Native							
		Observed	11.06	0.3925	4.3428	312,708	.	.
		Universal health insurance	7.48	0.3797	2.8382	211,290	-101,418	-32.43
		Universal basic income	4.38	0.3724	1.6293	123,653	-189,055	-60.46
		Free/discounted college	7.40	0.3725	2.7563	209,153	-103,555	-33.12
		Expanded ESL	9.93	0.3852	3.8247	280,645	-32,063	-10.25

Asian							
	Observed	6.62	0.3873	2.5625	1,220,847	.	.
	Universal health insurance	5.29	0.3810	2.0146	975,627	-245,220	-20.09
	Universal basic income	3.25	0.3676	1.1945	599,480	-621,367	-50.90
	Free/discounted college	4.46	0.3692	1.6485	823,709	-397,138	-32.53
	Expanded ESL	3.50	0.3702	1.2955	645,554	-575,293	-47.12
Black							
	Observed	7.88	0.3789	2.9868	3,286,121	.	.
	Universal health insurance	5.84	0.3700	2.1596	2,433,022	-853,099	-25.96
	Universal basic income	1.90	0.3619	0.6888	793,253	-2,492,868	-75.86
	Free/discounted college	5.52	0.3597	1.9861	2,301,636	-984,485	-29.96
	Expanded ESL	7.44	0.3767	2.8044	3,102,959	-183,162	-5.57
Native Hawaiian and Pacific Islander							
	Observed	7.73	0.3903	3.0191	46,950	.	.
	Universal health insurance	5.60	0.3787	2.1197	33,973	-12,977	-27.64
	Universal basic income	3.36	0.3705	1.2454	20,401	-26,549	-56.55
	Free/discounted college	4.94	0.3811	1.8816	29,970	-16,980	-36.17

(*continued*)

Table 11.3 (continued)

Cohort	*Category*	*Scenario/ Counterfactual (CF)*	*Headcount ratio (%)*	*Average intensity*	*MPI*	*Multidimensionally poor population*		
						N	Δ*N*|*CF*	%Δ*N*|*CF*
		Expanded ESL	6.27	0.3777	2.3680	38,058	-8892	-18.94
	White							
		Observed	4.90	0.3870	1.8981	11,579,361	.	.
		Universal health insurance	3.51	0.3741	1.3120	8,280,643	-3,298,718	-28.49
		Universal basic income	1.88	0.3692	0.6948	4,442,517	-7,136,844	-61.63
		Free/discounted college	3.32	0.3667	1.2178	7,841,905	-3,737,456	-32.28
		Expanded ESL	4.03	0.3768	1.5173	9,508,561	-2,070,800	-17.88
	Multiple races							
		Observed	5.28	0.3811	2.0130	592,930	.	.
		Universal health insurance	3.93	0.3730	1.4643	440,625	-152,305	-25.69
		Universal basic income	1.78	0.3665	0.6537	200,228	-392,702	-66.23
		Free/discounted college	3.82	0.3642	1.3910	428,660	-164,270	-27.70
		Expanded ESL	4.50	0.3732	1.6782	504,705	-88,225	-14.88
	Other race							
		Observed	16.41	0.4024	6.6052	2,671,139	.	.
		Universal health insurance	11.14	0.3852	4.2916	1,812,845	-858,294	-32.13
		Universal basic income	9.42	0.3770	3.5517	1,532,995	-1,138,144	-42.61
		Free/discounted college	10.26	0.3786	3.8846	1,669,745	-1,001,394	-37.49
		Expanded ESL	10.74	0.3825	4.1077	1,747,598	-923,541	-34.57

Ethnicity	Hispanic							
		Observed	13.62	0.4012	5.4640	8,135,901	.	.
		Universal health insurance	9.24	0.3845	3.5516	5,517,638	-2,618,263	-32.18
		Universal basic income	7.44	0.3749	2.7902	4,446,306	-3,689,595	-45.35
		Free/discounted college	8.70	0.3778	3.2864	5,196,319	-2,939,582	-36.13
		Expanded ESL	9.09	0.3828	3.4783	5,427,597	-2,708,304	-33.29
	Non-Hispanic							
		Observed	4.33	0.3782	1.6367	11,574,155	.	.
		Universal health insurance	3.24	0.3695	1.1980	8,670,387	-2,903,768	-25.09
		Universal basic income	1.22	0.3631	0.4435	3,266,221	-8,307,934	-71.78
		Free/discounted college	3.03	0.3603	1.0925	8,108,459	-3,465,696	-29.94
		Expanded ESL	3.89	0.3742	1.4553	10,400,483	-1,173,672	-10.14
Nativity	Foreign-born							
		Observed	16.22	0.4070	6.6010	7,259,769	.	.
		Universal health insurance	10.94	0.3895	4.2616	4,897,142	-2,362,627	-32.54
		Universal basic income	10.32	0.3759	3.8793	4,619,530	-2,640,239	-36.37
		Free/discounted college	9.87	0.3819	3.7677	4,415,644	-2,844,125	-39.18
		Expanded ESL	10.33	0.3833	3.9608	4,625,343	-2,634,426	-36.29
	Native-born							
		Observed	4.41	0.3764	1.6595	12,450,287	.	.
		Universal health insurance	3.29	0.3679	1.2103	9,290,883	-3,159,404	-25.38
		Universal basic income	1.10	0.3609	0.3953	3,092,997	-9,357,290	-75.16

(continued)

Table 11.3 (continued)

Cohort	*Category*	*Scenario/ Counterfactual (CF)*	*Headcount ratio (%)*	*Average intensity*	*MPI*	*Multidimensionally poor population*		
						N	*ΔN|CF*	*%ΔN|CF*
		Free/discounted college	3.15	0.3598	1.1326	8,889,134	-3,561,153	-28.60
		Expanded ESL	3.97	0.3746	1.4861	11,202,737	-1,247,550	-10.02
Educational attainment	Less than a high school diploma							
		Observed	12.11	0.4019	4.8656	12,437,014	.	.
		Universal health insurance	9.30	0.3871	3.6008	9,556,124	-2,880,890	-23.16
		Universal basic income	6.16	0.3743	2.3067	6,330,023	-6,106,991	-49.10
		Free/discounted college	5.87	0.3717	2.1824	6,031,736	-6,405,278	-51.50
		Expanded ESL	9.41	0.3898	3.6694	9,669,339	-2,767,675	-22.25
	High school graduate							
		Observed	5.09	0.3650	1.8590	3,574,392	.	.
		Universal health insurance	3.15	0.3517	1.1087	2,211,935	-1,362,457	-38.12
		Universal basic income	1.00	0.3494	0.3500	702,932	-2,871,460	-80.33
		Free/discounted college	5.09	0.3650	1.8590	3,574,392	0	0.00
		Expanded ESL	4.28	0.3582	1.5313	2,999,929	-574,463	-16.07
	Some college							
		Observed	3.34	0.3610	1.2049	2,598,682	.	.
		Universal health insurance	2.16	0.3499	0.7569	1,684,597	-914,085	-35.17

Universal basic income	0.56	0.3497	0.1945	432,940	-2,165,742	-83.34
Free/discounted college	3.34	0.3610	1.2049	2,598,682	0	0.00
Expanded ESL	2.97	0.3566	1.0591	2,312,310	-286,372	-11.02
Bachelor's degree						
Observed	1.65	0.3648	0.6038	792,143	.	.
Universal health insurance	1.07	0.3527	0.3785	513,751	-278,392	-35.14
Universal basic income	0.38	0.3504	0.1328	181,461	-610,682	-77.09
Free/discounted college	1.65	0.3648	0.6038	792,143	0	0.00
Expanded ESL	1.28	0.3559	0.4562	613,576	-178,567	-22.54
Master's degree						
Observed	1.06	0.3598	0.3825	216,563	.	.
Universal health insurance	0.77	0.3503	0.2699	156,954	-59,609	-27.53
Universal basic income	0.22	0.3446	0.0762	45,060	-171,503	-79.19
Free/discounted college	1.06	0.3598	0.3825	216,563	0	0.00
Expanded ESL	0.81	0.3541	0.2882	165,847	-50,716	-23.42
Professional degree						
Observed	1.15	0.3669	0.4228	56,495	.	.

(*continued*)

Table 11.3 (continued)

Cohort	*Category*	*Scenario/ Counterfactual (CF)*	*Headcount ratio (%)*	*Average intensity*	*MPI*	*Multidimensionally poor population*		
						N	*ΔN|CF*	*%ΔN|CF*
		Universal health insurance	0.81	0.3531	0.2860	39,718	-16,777	-29.70
		Universal basic income	0.23	0.3494	0.0815	11,431	-45,064	-79.77
		Free/discounted college	1.15	0.3669	0.4228	56,495	0	0.00
		Expanded ESL	0.85	0.3582	0.3056	41,832	-14,663	-25.95
	Doctorate							
		Observed	1.07	0.3625	0.3862	34,767	.	.
		Universal health insurance	0.76	0.3549	0.2713	24,946	-9821	-28.25
		Universal basic income	0.27	0.3575	0.0951	8680	-26,087	-75.03
		Free/discounted college	1.07	0.3625	0.3862	34,767	0	0.00
		Expanded ESL	0.77	0.3571	0.2763	25,247	-9520	-27.38
Marital Status	Married							
		Observed	4.46	0.3947	1.7612	5,679,996	.	.
		Universal health insurance	3.09	0.3799	1.1721	3,926,757	-1,753,239	-30.87
		Universal basic income	2.47	0.3709	0.9154	3,141,841	-2,538,155	-44.69
		Free/discounted college	2.60	0.3719	0.9674	3,310,787	-2,369,209	-41.71
		Expanded ESL	3.40	0.3790	1.2889	4,328,517	-1,351,479	-23.79
	Single							
		Observed	6.06	0.3840	2.3265	9,128,576	.	.

		Universal health insurance	4.17	0.3714	1.5482	6,281,490	-2,847,086	-31.19
		Universal basic income	1.90	0.3702	0.7025	2,859,492	-6,269,084	-68.68
		Free/discounted college	4.52	0.3670	1.6594	6,812,066	-2,316,510	-25.38
		Expanded ESL	4.78	0.3765	1.7980	7,195,977	-1,932,599	-21.17
	Divorced, separated, or widowed							
		Observed	9.96	0.3864	3.8491	4,901,484	.	.
		Universal health insurance	8.09	0.3771	3.0497	3,979,778	-921,706	-18.80
		Universal basic income	3.48	0.3677	1.2784	1,711,194	-3,190,290	-65.09
		Free/discounted college	6.47	0.3625	2.3436	3,181,925	-1,719,559	-35.08
		Expanded ESL	8.75	0.3765	3.2924	4,303,586	-597,898	-12.20
Labor market status	Employed							
		Observed	3.37	0.3859	1.3015	5,327,000	.	.
		Universal health insurance	1.75	0.3678	0.6429	2,761,031	-2,565,969	-48.17
		Universal basic income	1.85	0.3705	0.6847	2,919,230	-2,407,770	-45.20
		Free/discounted college	1.92	0.3639	0.6998	3,037,797	-2,289,203	-42.97
		Expanded ESL	2.45	0.3699	0.9078	3,876,671	-1,450,329	-27.23

(continued)

Table 11.3 (continued)

Cohort	*Category*	*Scenario/ Counterfactual (CF)*	*Headcount ratio (%)*	*Average intensity*	*MPI*	*Multidimensionally poor population*		
						N	*ΔN|CF*	*%ΔN|CF*
	Unemployed							
		Observed	33.47	0.4117	13.7807	2,710,899	.	.
		Universal health insurance	25.75	0.3897	10.0326	2,085,269	-625,630	-23.08
		Universal basic income	16.25	0.3838	6.2361	1,316,046	-1,394,853	-51.45
		Free/discounted college	28.77	0.3916	11.2660	2,329,910	-380,989	-14.05
		Expanded ESL	32.45	0.4053	13.1510	2,628,321	-82,578	-3.05
	Not in the labor force							
		Observed	7.25	0.3829	2.7740	11,672,157	.	.
		Universal health insurance	5.80	0.3744	2.1709	9,341,725	-2,330,432	-19.97
		Universal basic income	2.16	0.3641	0.7859	3,477,251	-8,194,906	-70.21
		Free/discounted college	4.93	0.3612	1.7796	7,937,071	-3,735,086	-32.00
		Expanded ESL	5.79	0.3723	2.1543	9,323,088	-2,349,069	-20.13

11.3 Additional Counterfactual Exercises

Given the relative influence that is estimated for the adoption of a universal basic income, it would not be unreasonable to think that the eradication of income poverty is key to the elimination of multidimensional deprivation. It certainly would seem to be a major step toward that end. We see that for all regions, divisions, and states, as compared to the other counterfactual scenarios that we have considered, a universal basic income is estimated to result in the largest reductions in the number of U.S. residents who experience multidimensional poverty. Likewise, when performing our counterfactual exercises while focused on various socio-demographic cohorts, we find that with the exceptions of those individuals who are foreign-born, did not complete high school, and/or who are employed, the elimination of income poverty and the related reduction in deprivation that is associated with high housing costs relative to income are estimated, relative to our other counterfactual scenarios, to produce the largest decreases in the number of U.S. residents who were multidimensionally poor.[1] Even so, the adoption of a universal basic income would not eliminate multidimensional deprivation in its entirety as several forms of deprivation that are unrelated to income would persist.

Our initial counterfactual scenarios, performed at the national level, provide numerous insights; however, with the ideal of eliminating, rather than reducing, multidimensional poverty in mind, we now consider several additional counterfactual exercises in which we assume the simultaneous realization of pairs, trios, and even all four of our antecedents. Exhausting all possible combinations of multiple antecedents results in 11 additional counterfactual scenarios. The corresponding results are presented in Table 11.4.

For purposes of comparison, the first row of the table presents the baseline results from Table 11.1. The first set of counterfactual results presented correspond to the six possible pairings of antecedents. For example, when we assume the simultaneous implementation of universal health insurance and the expansion of ESL programs, the headcount ratio is estimated to decrease considerably from our baseline value of 6.02 percent to

[1] For each of the three excepted socio-demographic cohorts, adoption of a universal basic income is estimated to have the second largest impact on the number of individuals who suffer multidimensional poverty.

Table 11.4 11 additional counterfactual scenarios, national level

Scenario/Counterfactual (CF)				*Headcount ratio (%)*	*Average intensity*	*MPI*	*N*	*ΔN | CF*	*%ΔN | CF*
				Multidimensionally poor population					
Observed				6.02	0.3877	2.3356	19,710,056	.	.
Universal health insurance	Universal basic income	Free/ discounted college	Expanded ESL						
✓	✓			1.15	0.3546	0.4078	3,762,879	-15,947,177	-80.91
✓		✓		2.67	0.3549	0.9491	8,748,260	-10,961,796	-55.62
✓			✓	3.28	0.3664	1.2016	10,730,666	-8,979,390	-45.56
	✓	✓		0.82	0.3486	0.2872	2,695,158	-17,014,898	-86.33
	✓		✓	1.44	0.3546	0.5119	4,723,002	-14,987,054	-76.04
		✓	✓	3.04	0.3578	1.0859	9,929,524	-9,780,532	-49.62
✓	✓	✓		0.21	0.3398	0.0711	684,112	-19,025,944	-96.53
✓	✓		✓	0.54	0.3434	0.1844	1,756,748	-17,953,308	-91.09
✓		✓	✓	1.78	0.3466	0.6158	5,813,353	-13,896,703	-70.51
	✓	✓	✓	0.32	0.3479	0.1105	1,039,474	-18,670,582	-94.73
✓	✓	✓	✓	0.06	0.3372	0.0195	188,723	-19,521,333	-99.04

$N = 3{,}214{,}539$

3.28 percent. The average deprivation intensity also declines, although somewhat marginally (i.e., by 5.5 percent), and the MPI value is nearly halved from the baseline value of 2.34 to 1.20. Under such a scenario, the number of multidimensionally poor U.S. residents is estimated to decline from 19.7 million individuals to 10.7 million individuals, a decrease of 45.6 percent. While this is a substantial reduction in multidimensional poverty, among the six possible antecedent pairs, this combination produces the smallest decrease in multidimensional poverty. Looking to the most effective pairing, if we assume the simultaneous adoption of a universal basic income and implementation of incentives (e.g., free/discounted college) to encourage universal completion of high school, the headcount ratio falls, again from the baseline value of 6.02 percent, to 0.82 percent. The average deprivation intensity decreases by 10.1 percent, and the MPI value falls to 0.2872. This represents an 87.7 percent decline in the MPI value. If this pair of antecedents were to be realized, the number of U.S. residents who live in multidimensional poverty is estimated to decrease from the baseline value of 19.7 million individuals to slightly fewer than 2.7 million individuals. This is an 86.3 percent reduction in the number of multidimensionally poor U.S. residents.

In Table 11.4, immediately below the results obtained when conducting our paired counterfactual exercises, we present the results from the four possible scenarios in which three of our four antecedents are simultaneously realized. Illustrative of the strong influence of a universal basic income, the only scenario among the four that does not result in at least a 91.1 percent reduction in multidimensional poverty is that which excludes the adoption of a universal basic income. In this single instance, the antecedents that are assumed to be realized are the implementation of universal health insurance, provision of free/discounted college as an incentive to high school completion, and an expansion of ESL programs to eliminate linguistic isolation. The realization of this set of antecedents results, relative to the observed 2018 values, in an estimated 70.5 percent reduction of the headcount ratio, a 10.6 percent decrease in the average deprivation intensity value, and a 73.6 percent drop in the MPI value.

While a decrease of nearly three-quarters in the MPI value is substantial, each of the remaining counterfactual scenarios among this set is estimated to produce significantly larger decreases in multidimensional poverty. The scenario that produces the largest decrease in the number of multidimensionally poor U.S. residents is that which assumes simultaneous implementation of universal health insurance, adoption of a universal basic income, and free/discounted college. Under these conditions, the headcount ratio is estimated to decrease to only 0.21 percent, the average deprivation intensity value falls to 0.3398, and the MPI declines to 0.0711. The corresponding change in the number of multidimensionally poor U.S. residents is a nearly 97 percent reduction from the baseline of 19.7 million persons to only 684,112 individuals.

Finally, we consider the scenario in which all four of our antecedents are simultaneously realized. We assume the implementation of universal health care, the adoption of a universal basic income, a program of free/discounted college, and the expansion of ESL programs. Obviously, as we increase the number of antecedents we eliminate potential forms of deprivation and, thus, observe larger and larger decreases in multidimensional poverty. Even so, with these four antecedents realized there remains five indicators of deprivation and, assuming one is deprived in all indicators, the five indicators carry a maximum deprivation score value of 0.5. This means that, while we should anticipate a large reduction in multidimensional poverty, we should not expect the elimination of all deprivations and, thus, we should not expect the elimination of multidimensional deprivation.

The results from this counterfactual exercise are presented in the final row of the Table 11.4. While the remediation of the four identified forms of deprivation does not eliminate multidimensional poverty, it does come very close to that outcome. In this scenario, the headcount ratio falls to only 0.06 percent. This frequency is equivalent to about one in every 1700 individuals suffering multidimensional poverty, which is vastly lower than the baseline frequency of 1 in every 16.6 individuals being multidimensionally poor. The average deprivation intensity value decreases to 0.3372 which is significant since, as the average censored deprivation score, the minimum value that can be observed for this series is our threshold for classification as multidimensionally poor: 0.3333. The MPI value decreases to 0.0195, and only an estimated 188,723 U.S. residents would remain multidimensionally poor. In proportional terms, under this scenario, we would observe a decrease of more than 99 percent in the number of U.S. residents who are multidimensionally poor.

11.4 Concluding Thoughts

It may be tempting to take the perspective that multidimensional poverty would be all but eradicated if the four forms of deprivation included in these counterfactual scenarios were simultaneously eliminated. Unfortunately, this is not the case. While the elimination of these deprivations would certainly improve collective human well-being, other forms of deprivation which are not included in the construction of the MPI would continue to exist and additional/new deprivations would likely arise. For example, the ACS data we consider does not measure deprivations such as a lack of access to affordable child care and/or elder care, limited (or no) access to the Internet, social inequities, inequality of opportunity, social isolation, biases based on gender, race, ethnicity, sexual identity, etc., and the lack or absence of various freedoms (e.g., economic or political). To the extent that these deprivations can be quantified, improvements can be made to the formulation of the MPI. This would allow the MPI to evolve over time so that it best represents the forms of deprivation that society wishes to address and reduce or, ideally, eliminate. In this sense, differences in the construction of the MPI over time correlate with differences in a society's levels of human, social, and economic development. This is akin to variation in MPI construction, at a given point in time, across societies that are characterized by differences in their respective levels of human, social, and economic development.

At the outset, we identified five questions that we sought to address. We have detailed the estimated effects of each counterfactual on the MPI, its related measures, and the number of multidimensionally poor. Our counterfactual exercises were performed at the national level, for individual regions, divisions, and states, and for a large number of sociodemographic cohorts. While we observe that the adoption of a universal basic income equal to 130 percent of the federal poverty level consistently produces the largest decreases in multidimensional poverty, we also observe variation in both the magnitudes to which multidimensional poverty is reduced and in the relative impacts of our antecedents. Further, while the counterfactual scenarios vary in terms of the extent to which decreases are realized in the number of multidimensionally poor, nearly all such decreases are substantial. The variation that is observed and reported here can facilitate targeted public policy actions to most efficiently and completely counter multidimensional poverty. We consider this possibility as part of our closing chapter.

Appendix

Table 11.5 Counterfactual results, state level

State and scenario/Counterfactual (CF)		Headcount ratio (%)	Average intensity	MPI	Multidimensionally poor population		
					N	Δ*N*|*CF*	%Δ*N*|*CF*
Alabama							
	Observed	6.56	0.3865	2.5341	320,513	.	.
	Universal health insurance	4.18	0.3711	1.5507	204,222	-116,291	-36.28
	Universal basic income	1.80	0.3697	0.6657	88,002	-232,511	-72.54
	Free/discounted college	4.44	0.3635	1.6140	217,042	-103,471	-32.28
	Expanded ESL	6.18	0.3826	2.3650	302,155	-18,358	-5.73
Alaska							
	Observed	4.49	0.3888	1.7465	33,124	.	.
	Universal health insurance	3.04	0.3799	1.1565	22,450	-10,674	-32.22
	Universal basic income	1.49	0.3825	0.5714	11,015	-22,109	-66.75
	Free/discounted college	3.20	0.3823	1.2218	23,570	-9554	-28.84
	Expanded ESL	4.39	0.3895	1.7087	32,355	-769	-2.32
Arizona							
	Observed	6.28	0.3839	2.4089	450,045	.	.
	Universal health insurance	4.36	0.3746	1.6322	312,493	-137,552	-30.56
	Universal basic income	2.35	0.3659	0.8604	168,635	-281,410	-62.53
	Free/discounted college	4.07	0.3649	1.4836	291,613	-158,432	-35.20
	Expanded ESL	5.14	0.3748	1.9283	368,945	-81,100	-18.02
Arkansas							
	Observed	5.80	0.3770	2.1866	174,823	.	.
	Universal health insurance	4.19	0.3660	1.5341	126,337	-48,486	-27.73
	Universal basic income	1.47	0.3656	0.5377	44,322	-130,501	-74.65
	Free/discounted college	4.04	0.3543	1.4325	121,872	-52,951	-30.29

	Expanded ESL	5.35	0.3729	1.9947	161,224	-13,599	-7.78
California							
	Observed	7.65	0.3911	2.9917	3,025,573	.	.
	Universal health insurance	5.99	0.3824	2.2903	2,369,101	-656,472	-21.70
	Universal basic income	3.89	0.3686	1.4340	1,538,995	-1,486,578	-49.13
	Free/discounted college	4.74	0.3714	1.7608	1,875,614	-1,149,959	-38.01
	Expanded ESL	5.43	0.3762	2.0413	2,146,277	-879,296	-29.06
Colorado							
	Observed	3.98	0.3811	1.5169	226,667	.	.
	Universal health insurance	2.76	0.3694	1.0182	156,969	-69,698	-30.75
	Universal basic income	1.56	0.3713	0.5784	88,732	-137,935	-60.85
	Free/discounted college	2.72	0.3590	0.9759	154,838	-71,829	-31.69
	Expanded ESL	3.34	0.3715	1.2420	190,424	-36,243	-15.99
Connecticut							
	Observed	5.05	0.3904	1.9733	180,565	.	.
	Universal health insurance	4.07	0.3804	1.5466	145,236	-35,329	-19.57
	Universal basic income	2.01	0.3783	0.7621	71,972	-108,593	-60.14
	Free/discounted college	3.65	0.3704	1.3509	130,299	-50,266	-27.84
	Expanded ESL	3.65	0.3739	1.3634	130,276	-50,289	-27.85
Delaware							
	Observed	4.27	0.3808	1.6275	41,335	.	.
	Universal health insurance	3.12	0.3700	1.1540	30,169	-11,166	-27.01
	Universal basic income	1.59	0.3637	0.5798	15,420	-25,915	-62.70
	Free/discounted college	2.71	0.3711	1.0054	26,200	-15,135	-36.62
	Expanded ESL	3.71	0.3677	1.3634	35,866	-5469	-13.23
District of Columbia							
	Observed	6.03	0.3839	2.3133	42,330	.	.
	Universal health insurance	5.48	0.3772	2.0671	38,491	-3839	-9.07
	Universal basic income	1.88	0.3668	0.6888	13,191	-29,139	-68.84

(*continued*)

Table 11.5 (continued)

	Free/discounted college	4.11	0.3591	1.4768	28,886	-13,444	-31.76
	Expanded ESL	5.29	0.3772	1.9950	37,149	-5181	-12.24
Florida							
	Observed	7.14	0.3882	2.7720	1,520,944	.	.
	Universal health insurance	4.81	0.3725	1.7917	1,024,589	-496,355	-32.63
	Universal basic income	2.94	0.3703	1.0875	625,606	-895,338	-58.87
	Free/discounted college	5.10	0.3680	1.8786	1,087,168	-433,776	-28.52
	Expanded ESL	5.52	0.3764	2.0794	1,176,690	-344,254	-22.63
Georgia							
	Observed	6.64	0.3859	2.5635	698,846	.	.
	Universal health insurance	3.86	0.3688	1.4229	405,850	-292,996	-41.93
	Universal basic income	2.38	0.3694	0.8783	250,074	-448,772	-64.22
	Free/discounted college	4.56	0.3647	1.6619	479,412	-219,434	-31.40
	Expanded ESL	5.68	0.3798	2.1564	597,228	-101,618	-14.54
Hawaii							
	Observed	3.84	0.3777	1.4521	54,611	.	.
	Universal health insurance	3.02	0.3729	1.1261	42,896	-11,715	-21.45
	Universal basic income	1.75	0.3606	0.6318	24,889	-29,722	-54.42
	Free/discounted college	2.43	0.3672	0.8930	34,546	-20,065	-36.74
	Expanded ESL	2.95	0.3659	1.0776	41,833	-12,778	-23.40
Idaho							
	Observed	4.36	0.3896	1.6965	76,397	.	.
	Universal health insurance	2.93	0.3745	1.0962	51,355	-25,042	-32.78
	Universal basic income	1.51	0.3769	0.5673	26,406	-49,991	-65.44
	Free/discounted college	3.06	0.3657	1.1190	53,676	-22,721	-29.74
	Expanded ESL	3.85	0.3796	1.4622	67,564	-8833	-11.56
Illinois							
	Observed	5.11	0.3820	1.9518	650,972	.	.

	Universal health insurance	3.81	0.3722	1.4184	485,569	-165,403	-25.41
	Universal basic income	1.85	0.3667	0.6775	235,414	-415,558	-63.84
	Free/discounted college	3.46	0.3623	1.2546	441,174	-209,798	-32.23
	Expanded ESL	4.11	0.3739	1.5352	523,158	-127,814	-19.63
Indiana							
	Observed	4.81	0.3805	1.8316	322,119	.	.
	Universal health insurance	3.51	0.3688	1.2936	234,760	-87,359	-27.12
	Universal basic income	1.43	0.3657	0.5217	95,455	-226,664	-70.37
	Free/discounted college	3.27	0.3572	1.1681	218,830	-103,289	-32.07
	Expanded ESL	4.34	0.3766	1.6332	290,204	-31,915	-9.91
Iowa							
	Observed	3.77	0.3824	1.4400	118,854	.	.
	Universal health insurance	2.88	0.3727	1.0743	90,973	-27,881	-23.46
	Universal basic income	1.01	0.3741	0.3796	32,024	-86,830	-73.06
	Free/discounted college	2.71	0.3635	0.9864	85,639	-33,215	-27.95
	Expanded ESL	3.28	0.3742	1.2264	103,428	-15,426	-12.98
Kansas							
	Observed	5.36	0.3931	2.1060	155,991	.	.
	Universal health insurance	3.56	0.3783	1.3462	103,609	-52,382	-33.58
	Universal basic income	2.02	0.3793	0.7651	58,732	-97,259	-62.35
	Free/discounted college	3.96	0.3734	1.4784	115,292	-40,699	-26.09
	Expanded ESL	4.26	0.3858	1.6437	124,050	-31,941	-20.48
Kentucky							
	Observed	5.46	0.3814	2.0832	244,030	.	.
	Universal health insurance	4.57	0.3717	1.6982	204,156	-39,874	-16.34
	Universal basic income	1.31	0.3668	0.4794	58,399	-185,631	-76.07
	Free/discounted college	3.48	0.3582	1.2464	155,470	-88,560	-36.29
	Expanded ESL	5.03	0.3761	1.8923	224,811	-19,219	-7.88

(*continued*)

Table 11.5 (continued)

Louisiana							
	Observed	6.21	0.3826	2.3756	289,382	.	.
	Universal health insurance	4.80	0.3727	1.7875	223,519	-65,863	-22.76
	Universal basic income	1.65	0.3646	0.6007	76,783	-212,599	-73.47
	Free/discounted college	3.98	0.3602	1.4323	185,279	-104,103	-35.97
	Expanded ESL	5.70	0.3784	2.1582	265,771	-23,611	-8.16
Maine							
	Observed	4.10	0.3780	1.5503	54,886	.	.
	Universal health insurance	3.27	0.3642	1.1914	43,780	-11,106	-20.23
	Universal basic income	1.09	0.3599	0.3917	14,566	-40,320	-73.46
	Free/discounted college	2.96	0.3594	1.0642	39,626	-15,260	-27.80
	Expanded ESL	3.82	0.3792	1.4483	51,115	-3771	-6.87
Maryland							
	Observed	4.21	0.3814	1.6050	254,312	.	.
	Universal health insurance	3.00	0.3690	1.1053	181,013	-73,299	-28.82
	Universal basic income	1.77	0.3723	0.6603	107,181	-147,131	-57.85
	Free/discounted college	2.78	0.3620	1.0078	168,237	-86,075	-33.85
	Expanded ESL	3.29	0.3733	1.2277	198,723	-55,589	-21.86
Massachusetts							
	Observed	4.41	0.3817	1.6842	304,554	.	.
	Universal health insurance	3.98	0.3780	1.5033	274,515	-30,039	-9.86
	Universal basic income	1.69	0.3668	0.6196	116,597	-187,957	-61.72
	Free/discounted college	2.89	0.3602	1.0399	199,249	-105,305	-34.58
	Expanded ESL	3.11	0.3674	1.1427	214,661	-89,893	-29.52
Michigan							
	Observed	4.41	0.3770	1.6618	440,643	.	.
	Universal health insurance	3.62	0.3696	1.3379	361,839	-78,804	-17.88

	Universal basic income	1.00	0.3666	0.3670	100,068	-340,575	-77.29
	Free/discounted college	3.03	0.3563	1.0786	302,583	-138,060	-31.33
	Expanded ESL	4.04	0.3725	1.5035	403,486	-37,157	-8.43
Minnesota							
	Observed	3.48	0.3789	1.3203	195,515	.	.
	Universal health insurance	2.75	0.3716	1.0220	154,330	-41,185	-21.06
	Universal basic income	1.06	0.3671	0.3896	59,542	-135,973	-69.55
	Free/discounted college	2.49	0.3594	0.8956	139,833	-55,682	-28.48
	Expanded ESL	2.88	0.3713	1.0686	161,511	-34,004	-17.39
Mississippi							
	Observed	7.55	0.3883	2.9327	225,548	.	.
	Universal health insurance	5.01	0.3692	1.8495	149,616	-75,932	-33.67
	Universal basic income	1.92	0.3734	0.7152	57,208	-168,340	-74.64
	Free/discounted college	5.27	0.3685	1.9414	157,340	-68,208	-30.24
	Expanded ESL	7.21	0.3860	2.7835	215,369	-10,179	-4.51
Missouri							
	Observed	5.08	0.3845	1.9543	311,391	.	.
	Universal health insurance	3.57	0.3683	1.3134	218,467	-92,924	-29.84
	Universal basic income	1.41	0.3720	0.5251	86,461	-224,930	-72.23
	Free/discounted college	3.61	0.3647	1.3167	221,200	-90,191	-28.96
	Expanded ESL	4.76	0.3824	1.8212	291,741	-19,650	-6.31
Montana							
	Observed	3.58	0.3709	1.3277	38,028	.	.
	Universal health insurance	2.68	0.3633	0.9744	28,489	-9539	-25.08
	Universal basic income	0.72	0.3647	0.2610	7602	-30,426	-80.01
	Free/discounted college	2.76	0.3569	0.9861	29,354	-8674	-22.81
	Expanded ESL	3.58	0.3703	1.3257	38,028	0	0.00

(continued)

Table 11.5 (continued)

Nebraska							
	Observed	4.22	0.3834	1.6189	81,455	.	.
	Universal health insurance	2.86	0.3659	1.0454	55,122	-26,333	-32.33
	Universal basic income	1.05	0.3728	0.3926	20,314	-61,141	-75.06
	Free/discounted college	3.23	0.3625	1.1692	62,218	-19,237	-23.62
	Expanded ESL	3.73	0.3785	1.4116	71,951	-9504	-11.67
Nevada							
	Observed	6.41	0.3915	2.5109	194,605	.	.
	Universal health insurance	4.52	0.3749	1.6948	137,174	-57,431	-29.51
	Universal basic income	2.75	0.3697	1.0182	83,559	-111,046	-57.06
	Free/discounted college	4.40	0.3714	1.6325	133,361	-61,244	-31.47
	Expanded ESL	5.08	0.3797	1.9309	154,297	-40,308	-20.71
New Hampshire							
	Observed	2.87	0.3731	1.0694	38,877	.	.
	Universal health insurance	2.28	0.3712	0.8480	30,988	-7889	-20.29
	Universal basic income	1.04	0.3676	0.3827	14,122	-24,755	-63.68
	Free/discounted college	1.93	0.3488	0.6717	26,116	-12,761	-32.82
	Expanded ESL	2.66	0.3637	0.9674	36,080	-2,797	-7.19
New Jersey							
	Observed	5.66	0.3908	2.2116	504,102	.	.
	Universal health insurance	4.10	0.3796	1.5576	365,572	-138,530	-27.48
	Universal basic income	2.67	0.3709	0.9904	237,888	-266,214	-52.81
	Free/discounted college	3.99	0.3706	1.4802	355,790	-148,312	-29.42
	Expanded ESL	4.02	0.3762	1.5120	358,048	-146,054	-28.97
New Mexico							
	Observed	7.75	0.3935	3.0484	162,316	.	.
	Universal health insurance	6.13	0.3821	2.3432	128,518	-33,798	-20.82

	Universal basic income	2.99	0.3756	1.1218	62,584	-99,732	-61.44
	Free/discounted college	4.91	0.3695	1.8145	102,905	-59,411	-36.60
	Expanded ESL	6.48	0.3756	2.4324	135,682	-26,634	-16.41
New York							
	Observed	7.16	0.3896	2.7898	1,399,463	.	.
	Universal health insurance	6.06	0.3824	2.3166	1,183,710	-215,753	-15.42
	Universal basic income	3.04	0.3691	1.1212	593,641	-805,822	-57.58
	Free/discounted college	4.69	0.3691	1.7299	916,034	-483,429	-34.54
	Expanded ESL	5.05	0.3740	1.8881	986,485	-412,978	-29.51
North Carolina							
	Observed	5.96	0.3873	2.3082	618,857	.	.
	Universal health insurance	3.89	0.3719	1.4482	404,324	-214,533	-34.67
	Universal basic income	1.96	0.3719	0.7289	203,519	-415,338	-67.11
	Free/discounted college	4.02	0.3667	1.4743	417,416	-201,441	-32.55
	Expanded ESL	5.21	0.3803	1.9801	540,613	-78,244	-12.64
North Dakota							
	Observed	3.23	0.3638	1.1748	24,544	.	.
	Universal health insurance	2.05	0.3630	0.7455	15,608	-8936	-36.41
	Universal basic income	0.83	0.3603	0.2986	6299	-18,245	-74.34
	Free/discounted college	2.27	0.3444	0.7827	17,275	-7269	-29.62
	Expanded ESL	2.76	0.3661	1.0090	20,947	-3597	-14.66
Ohio							
	Observed	4.75	0.3823	1.8159	555,226	.	.
	Universal health insurance	3.64	0.3718	1.3552	426,054	-129,172	-23.26
	Universal basic income	1.32	0.3668	0.4843	154,333	-400,893	-72.20
	Free/discounted college	3.24	0.3622	1.1742	378,963	-176,263	-31.75
	Expanded ESL	4.35	0.3755	1.6328	508,281	-46,945	-8.46

(continued)

Table 11.5 (continued)

Oklahoma							
	Observed	6.22	0.3876	2.4126	245,453	.	.
	Universal health insurance	3.90	0.3672	1.4321	153,795	-91,658	-37.34
	Universal basic income	2.06	0.3677	0.7565	81,126	-164,327	-66.95
	Free/discounted college	4.40	0.3687	1.6216	173,438	-72,015	-29.34
	Expanded ESL	5.60	0.3825	2.1414	220,740	-24,713	-10.07
Oregon							
	Observed	5.27	0.3838	2.0219	220,769	.	.
	Universal health insurance	3.92	0.3726	1.4614	164,371	-56,398	-25.55
	Universal basic income	1.94	0.3726	0.7242	81,445	-139,324	-63.11
	Free/discounted college	3.60	0.3660	1.3183	150,939	-69,830	-31.63
	Expanded ESL	4.40	0.3740	1.6452	184,325	-36,444	-16.51
Pennsylvania							
	Observed	4.62	0.3787	1.7487	591,334	.	.
	Universal health insurance	3.66	0.3708	1.3552	468,107	-123,227	-20.84
	Universal basic income	1.35	0.3658	0.4924	172,384	-418,950	-70.85
	Free/discounted college	3.21	0.3598	1.1564	411,596	-179,738	-30.40
	Expanded ESL	3.98	0.3710	1.4766	509,694	-81,640	-13.81
Rhode Island							
	Observed	5.62	0.3876	2.1779	59,413	.	.
	Universal health insurance	5.04	0.3801	1.9171	53,326	-6087	-10.25
	Universal basic income	1.89	0.3632	0.6857	19,962	-39,451	-66.40
	Free/discounted college	3.89	0.3667	1.4280	41,179	-18,234	-30.69
	Expanded ESL	4.32	0.3690	1.5950	45,703	-13,710	-23.08
South Carolina							
	Observed	5.71	0.3864	2.2071	290,402	.	.
	Universal health insurance	3.89	0.3680	1.4300	197,548	-92,854	-31.97

	Universal basic income	1.72	0.3749	0.6450	87,454	-202,948	-69.89
	Free/discounted college	3.93	0.3632	1.4263	199,652	-90,750	-31.25
	Expanded ESL	5.26	0.3819	2.0071	267,171	-23,231	-8.00
South Dakota							
	Observed	4.24	0.3766	1.5981	37,440	.	.
	Universal health insurance	2.52	0.3634	0.9160	22,237	-15,203	-40.61
	Universal basic income	1.08	0.3699	0.3987	9510	-27,930	-74.60
	Free/discounted college	3.00	0.3652	1.0961	26,479	-10,961	-29.28
	Expanded ESL	4.07	0.3725	1.5161	35,907	-1533	-4.09
Tennessee							
	Observed	6.29	0.3876	2.4373	425,743	.	.
	Universal health insurance	4.36	0.3715	1.6196	295,120	-130,623	-30.68
	Universal basic income	1.77	0.3686	0.6536	120,047	-305,696	-71.80
	Free/discounted college	4.40	0.3669	1.6158	298,168	-127,575	-29.97
	Expanded ESL	5.76	0.3817	2.1980	389,886	-35,857	-8.42
Texas							
	Observed	9.08	0.3993	3.6266	2,606,665	.	.
	Universal health insurance	5.46	0.3798	2.0742	1,567,392	-1,039,273	-39.87
	Universal basic income	4.41	0.3737	1.6473	1,265,240	-1,341,425	-51.46
	Free/discounted college	6.28	0.3770	2.3681	1,802,895	-803,770	-30.84
	Expanded ESL	6.83	0.3836	2.6199	1,960,281	-646,384	-24.80
Utah							
	Observed	3.54	0.3801	1.3438	111,755	.	.
	Universal health insurance	2.08	0.3637	0.7551	65,636	-46,119	-41.27
	Universal basic income	1.38	0.3665	0.5051	43,573	-68,182	-61.01
	Free/discounted college	2.57	0.3618	0.9285	81,132	-30,623	-27.40
	Expanded ESL	2.91	0.3752	1.0932	92,098	-19,657	-17.59

(*continued*)

Table 11.5 (continued)

Vermont							
	Observed	3.13	0.3726	1.1654	19,588	.	.
	Universal health insurance	2.45	0.3626	0.8883	15,344	-4244	-21.67
	Universal basic income	1.04	0.3637	0.3765	6483	-13,105	-66.90
	Free/discounted college	2.12	0.3592	0.7600	13,249	-6339	-32.36
	Expanded ESL	2.73	0.3695	1.0085	17,096	-2492	-12.72
Virginia							
	Observed	4.61	0.3837	1.7704	393,003	.	.
	Universal health insurance	2.93	0.3694	1.0811	249,274	-143,729	-36.57
	Universal basic income	1.80	0.3673	0.6601	153,105	-239,898	-61.04
	Free/discounted college	3.02	0.3657	1.1053	257,407	-135,596	-34.50
	Expanded ESL	3.89	0.3760	1.4623	331,271	-61,732	-15.71
Washington							
	Observed	4.65	0.3829	1.7803	350,373	.	.
	Universal health insurance	3.45	0.3716	1.2823	259,994	-90,379	-25.80
	Universal basic income	1.83	0.3732	0.6831	137,932	-212,441	-60.63
	Free/discounted college	3.18	0.3615	1.1500	239,734	-110,639	-31.58
	Expanded ESL	3.52	0.3736	1.3164	265,559	-84,814	-24.21
West Virginia							
	Observed	5.20	0.3763	1.9566	93,908	.	.
	Universal health insurance	4.04	0.3714	1.5015	73,006	-20,902	-22.26
	Universal basic income	0.90	0.3605	0.3259	16,327	-77,581	-82.61
	Free/discounted college	3.20	0.3549	1.1345	57,733	-36,175	-38.52
	Expanded ESL	5.11	0.3760	1.9197	92,212	-1696	-1.81
Wisconsin							
	Observed	3.64	0.3756	1.3675	211,642	.	.
	Universal health insurance	2.73	0.3657	0.9984	158,735	-52,907	-25.00

	Universal basic income	1.07	0.3600	0.3862	62,370	-149,272	-70.53
	Free/discounted college	2.43	0.3586	0.8713	141,248	-70,394	-33.26
	Expanded ESL	3.27	0.3695	1.2068	189,852	-21,790	-10.30
Wyoming							
	Observed	3.66	0.3836	1.4028	21,125	.	.
	Universal health insurance	2.13	0.3652	0.7760	12,277	-8848	-41.88
	Universal basic income	1.04	0.3914	0.4078	6019	-15,106	-71.51
	Free/discounted college	2.77	0.3634	1.0069	16,009	-5116	-24.22
	Expanded ESL	3.44	0.3795	1.3047	19,859[1]	-1266	-5.99

References

U.S. Bureau of the Census/American Factfinder (U.S. Census). 2019. American Community Survey (Annual Data, 2008–2018). U.S. Census Bureau's American Community Survey Office. http://factfinder.census.gov

U.S. Bureau of the Census, Current Population Survey, Annual Social and Economic Supplements (US Census). 2020. Table 2. Poverty Status of People by Family Relationship, Race, and Hispanic Origin. https://www2.census.gov/programs-surveys/cps/tables/time-series/historical-poverty-people/hstpov2.xls

CHAPTER 12

A Summary and Some Implications for Public Policy

The preceding 11 chapters provide ample coverage of multidimensional poverty in the U.S. From discussing the limitations of income-based poverty measures to detailing multidimensional poverty measurement, documenting the extent of multidimensional poverty in America, offering examples of multidimensional analysis, and, finally, presenting the results of a series of counterfactual exercises, a considerable amount of territory has been covered. Rather than presenting a summary that largely repeats what appears in the earlier chapters, here we wish to give a more general synopsis. This will provide an overview of the material that has been presented; however, we will forgo discussing many of the details that are found in earlier chapters and instead aim to provide a broad overview that serves as motivation for the discussion of the related public policy implications that follows.

When discussing poverty and deprivation as related concepts, we stressed the narrowness of income-based measures of poverty such as the Official Poverty Measure (OPM) and the Supplemental Poverty Measure (SPM). Given the purpose of these two measures is to identify the proportion of the population that is income poor, they are ill-suited to measure non-monetary forms of deprivation and, accordingly, are of limited use in measuring multiple deprivations. Certainly, if income poverty were the only form of deprivation that an individual may face, then the OPM and SPM would work quite well. This, however, is not the case. Poverty and deprivation are not restricted to a lack of income. As we have discussed, well-being can be hindered in myriad ways, including insufficient access to

R. White, *Multidimensional Poverty in America*,
https://doi.org/10.1007/978-3-030-45916-1_12

health care, limited education, inadequate and/or unaffordable housing and so on. The Multidimensional Poverty Index (MPI) and its related measures of deprivation incidence and intensity offer a broader, more encompassing and, thus, more accurate depiction of deprivation as compared to the traditional, income-based measures of poverty.

Following our initial discussion of poverty and deprivation and the resulting introduction of the MPI, we provided a survey of the related literature. Considering the voluminous literature on our topic, a complete review of the literature is simply not possible, especially if intended to fit within a single chapter. As an alternative, we structured our literature review to consist of two, related parts. The first part samples the related literature that involves countries other than the U.S. with the goal of demonstrating the depth and the breadth of earlier works and the wide-ranging application of multidimensional poverty analysis. This is followed by a more detailed discussion of the limited number of studies that examine multidimensional poverty in the U.S. Structuring the survey in this way allowed for the presentation of foundational knowledge on which subsequent chapters could build. It also provided a bridge from our initial discussions of poverty, deprivation, and income-based measures of poverty to our more detailed illustration of multidimensional poverty measurement.

As part of our discussion of multidimensional poverty measurement, we described the Alkire-Foster (AF) method and noted that it has largely become the standard methodology among studies of multidimensional deprivation. In a few words, the AF method involves the selection of dimensions and corresponding indicators that represent deprivation, determination of the criteria for the classification of an individual as deprived in terms of each indicator, assignment of appropriate weights to the dimensions and indicators, identification of the threshold deprivation score that determines classification as multidimensionally poor, calculation of deprivation scores, and generation of the headcount ratio, average deprivation intensity, and MPI values. We note these specifics here as they featured heavily throughout the book. To provide an example of the AF method in practice and to illustrate the flexibility of the MPI as a tool to measure deprivation, we discussed the 2019 Global MPI. Finally, to reinforce the process of multidimensional poverty measurement, we presented a detailed numerical example for a fictitious society.

The second part of the book includes three chapters that, collectively, provide a portrait of America's multidimensionally poor. The fourth chapter presents an analysis of the determinants of multidimensional poverty. Our accounting of the multidimensionally poor begins by documenting multidimensional poverty incidence and intensity, along with corresponding MPI values, at the national level of detail. We examine the full 2008–2018 reference period and each year during the period to consider trends in deprivation across time. We then consider variation in multidimensional poverty across several geographic units (i.e., regions, divisions, states, and Public Use Microdata Areas). This is followed with the estimation of MPI values and related measures for several socio-demographic cohorts. Specifically, we consider variation in multidimensional poverty by race, gender, levels of educational attainment, ethnicity, age categories, nativity, etc. Documenting variation across geographic locales and socio-demographic cohorts provides motivation for the topic-specific analyses that are presented in Chaps 8 through 10. We close the second part of the book with our presentation of the determinants of individual deprivation scores and of multidimensional poverty incidence.

In the third part of the book, we present three examples of multidimensional poverty analysis. The first example considers whether expansion of Medicaid benefits under the Affordable Care Act (ACA) led to reductions of the incidence and/or intensity of multidimensional poverty. Utilizing logistic regression techniques and the difference-in-difference methodology to isolate the effects of the Medicaid expansion, we conclude that the ACA led to small but statistically significant decreases in deprivation as represented by the health care indicator, the deprivation frequency of the Health dimension, and in the incidence of multidimensional poverty. Our second example explores variation in multidimensional poverty incidence across the native- and foreign-born populations of the U.S. Again relying on econometric techniques, we identify statistically significant differences in the determinants of multidimensional poverty across native- and foreign-born individuals and we find that, even when controlling for other determinants of multidimensional poverty, foreign-born residents of the U.S. face an estimated probability of being multidimensionally poor that is higher than that estimated for their native-born counterparts. Our final example considers variation in deprivation over the life cycle. This involves documenting multidimensional poverty incidence, intensity, and MPI values for each age (i.e., 0 years of age through 95 years or more) and then examining the paths of deprivation frequency values at the dimension and indicator levels of detail. We identify the specific dimensions and indicators that primarily contribute to multidimensional poverty over different portions of the life cycle. In all three instances, in addition to being relevant for public policy formulation, the findings add to the portrait of multidimensional poverty that is presented in earlier chapters.

We close our analysis of multidimensional poverty by presenting the results of a series of counterfactual exercises. We use data for 2018, the most recent year in our reference period, to produce a series of baseline values. The scenarios we consider include (1) the implementation of a universal health care system; (2) the adoption of a universal basic income, (3) the provision of free or highly discounted undergraduate education to encourage high school completion; and (4) the expansion of ESL programs to eliminate linguistic isolation. Assuming that each of these are realized, individually and in combinations, we estimate corresponding values for multidimensional poverty incidence, intensity, and MPI values. Comparison of the resulting values to the baseline series provides an estimate of the impact each scenario would have had on multidimensional poverty in the U.S. during 2018. We find that, while the realization of each antecedent produces a significant reduction in multidimensional poverty, the adoption of a universal basic income is estimated to provide the greatest reduction in the size of the multidimensionally poor population. Considering the simultaneous fulfillment of multiple antecedents produces additional interesting results. For example, in the extreme scenario when all four antecedents are simultaneously realized, the number of multidimensionally poor individuals is estimated to decrease by slightly more than 99 percent.

12.1 Some Implications for Public Policy and Concluding Thoughts

Much of the information we have provided has implications for public policy. We have documented multidimensional poverty at the national level, at a variety of sub-national levels, and across a large number of socio-demographic cohorts. This includes measurement of the incidence and the intensity of multidimensional deprivation and the identification of specific forms of deprivation. An accurate accounting of deprivations is beneficial for the formulation of related public policies. Further, beyond the documentation of multidimensional poverty, we provide guidance in the form of examples of multidimensional analysis that can be used to better understand deprivation and, thus, contribute to more efficient and more effective policies. Finally, we offer additional information that may inform public policy by presenting the results of a series of counterfactual exercises that include estimated reductions in multidimensional poverty that follow from the assumed realization of several antecedents.

Based on the observed variation in multidimensional poverty incidence and intensity, whether viewed over time, across geographic units, or between socio-demographic cohorts, it seems reasonable that a variety of targeted policies may be more efficient and more effective in terms of the reduction or elimination of deprivation than would broad, overarching policy efforts. Supporting this view is that we identify variation in the forms of deprivation suffered in different locales, at different points in time, by different cohorts, and over different portions of the life cycle. This strongly suggests that a "one size fits all" solution is likely, at best, an inefficient outcome and, at worst, is both inefficient and largely ineffective. It may be more efficient if policies are crafted, implemented, and evaluated at the state or local level. Similarly, government/policy makers working directly with private sector organizations—non-profits, for example—may prove the most effective path.

Another related piece of information that may be helpful to policy makers is that macroeconomic policies that seek to produce economic growth do little in the way of engineering large-scale reductions in multidimensional poverty. Unfortunately, improved conditions at the macro level do not necessarily result in a wide realization of beneficial change. As we have noted, an estimated 25,328,644 U.S. residents lived in multidimensional poverty during the typical year in our 2008–2018 reference period. In 2018, the U.S. economy was in its tenth consecutive year of uninterrupted growth following the end of the Great Recession. The national unemployment rate was 3.9 percent, the lowest value observed since 1969, and the levels of both total economic output and average income were higher than at any previous point in U.S. history.[1] At a time characterized by maximum output, a record high level of average income, and minimum unemployment, an estimated 19,710,056 U.S. residents were multidimensionally poor. The high headcount ratio and MPI values observed during the 2008–2010 period indicate that a period of strong macroeconomic performance is preferable to weak or middling performances. Even so, a strong macro economy simply does not translate to large-scale reductions in multidimensional poverty, just as the massive economic growth witnessed over the past half-century has not resulted in large reductions in the income poverty rate. Rather than assuming (or hoping) that improved

[1] In 2018, real Gross Domestic Product (i.e., total output) and real Gross Domestic Product per capita (i.e., a measure of average income), both expressed in 2010 U.S. dollars, were equal to $17.8 trillion and $54,659, respectively (World Bank 2020).

economic conditions will be "the rising tide that lifts all boats", to produce sizeable reductions in multidimensional poverty, policy makers should purposefully pursue deliberate and targeted efforts that seek to address specific deprivations.

Perhaps the most obvious policy implication that we can point to is the most direct: If policy makers wish to enhance the general well-being of society, one way to do so is to reduce or eliminate the deprivations we have identified as being experienced by large numbers of U.S. residents. Some examples include reducing the number of income poor individuals, increasing the number of U.S. residents who have access to free/affordable health care, encouraging the completion of high school, or undertaking any other actions that address one or more of the nine deprivations we have targeted in our measure of multidimensional poverty. Of course, public policy efforts need not be limited to the forms of deprivation we have considered. Other actions that policy makers can pursue to reduce deprivation include improving access to affordable child care, providing support for elder care, eliminating discrimination and other forms of bias, pursuing systemic reforms to ensure economic and social justice and so on.

Of course, one may argue that generating a wish list for policy makers to act upon is a very limited contribution. Similarly, identifying forms of deprivation to be addressed without offering a plan(s) to address the deprivations may not be viewed as terribly helpful. Others may argue that a policy wish list and the identification of forms of deprivation provide reasonable value since it is likely policy makers who are best-able, given a policy target, to devise an efficient and effective plan. Another way to view the message in the preceding paragraph is that the means necessary to reduce deprivation already exist and if deprivation is reduced or eliminated there will be a corresponding increase in social welfare. It may be best to close by noting that the preface to this book asserts that, when the necessary resources are in hand, the elimination of deprivation requires that three conditions are met. First, forms of deprivation that are to be countered must be identified. Second, accurate measurement of these deprivations must be possible. And third, the public and policy makers must acknowledge that deprivations exist and that the elimination of deprivations is an important policy goal. Our hope is that the information presented here, even if only to the extent of further the conversation, contributes to the fulfillment of the first and second conditions. We also hope that the information we have provided encourages the fulfillment of the third condition.

Index[1]

[1] Note: Page numbers followed by 'n' refer to notes.

R. White, *Multidimensional Poverty in America*,
https://doi.org/10.1007/978-3-030-45916-1

The manufacturer's authorised representative in the EU is Springer Nature Customer Service Centre GmbH, Europaplatz 3, 69115 Heidelberg, Germany. If you have any concerns regarding our products, please contact ProductSafety@springernature.com

Printed and bound by CPI Group (UK) Ltd, Croydon, CR0 4YY

30/09/2026

02225461-0017